GURDJIEFF

By the same author

GURDJIEFF AND MANSFIELD

JAMES MOORE

GURDJIEFF

THE ANATOMY OF A MYTH

A BIOGRAPHY

ELEMENT

Shaftesbury, Dorset • Rockport, Massachusetts

Published in Great Britain in 1991 by
Element Books Limited
Longmead, Shaftesbury, Dorset

Published in the USA in 1991 by
Element Inc
42 Broadway, Rockport, MA 01966

Text designed by Roger Lightfoot
Typeset by Footnote Graphics, Warminster
Printed and bound in Great Britain by
Billings Ltd, Hylton Road, Worcester

British Library Cataloguing in Publication Data
Moore, James
Gurdjieff : the anatomy of a myth.
I. Title
133

Library of Congress data available

ISBN 1–85230–114–7

In homage to
Henriette Lannes

Contents

——— ✣ ———

Acknowledgements

———— ❖ ————

I have been fortified by a sense of the general goodwill of Maurice Desselle, Michel de Salzmann, and Henri Tracol (although they are not at all implicated in my specific presentation). To Michel I am especially indebted: not only did he give me personal encouragement to pursue a project bound to impinge dangerously on sensibilities near to him, but volunteered data unavailable elsewhere.

In my sketch of Gurdjieff's final years I have sought fidelity to the sense of his presence generously shared with me over a long period by the following of his pupils: Elizabeth Bennett, Dr Bernard Courtenay-Mayers, Michael Currer-Briggs, Tim Dahlberg, Helen Entwhistle, Hylda Field, Dr Joanna Haggarty, Rina Hands, Lucette Heuseux, Dr John Lester, Cathleen Murphy, Adam Nott, Dorothy Philpotts, George Philpotts, Basil Tilley, Pamela Travers and Dr Kenneth Walker.

My access to written material has been assisted by staff of the British Library, the Public Record Office, the Foreign Office Library, the Royal Asiatic Society, the Royal Geographical Society, the Gurdjieff Society, the Gurdjieff Foundation in New York, the Gurdjieff Foundation of California, the Warburg Institute, the Society for Cultural Relations with the USSR, the Armenian Society for Friendship and Cultural Relations with Foreign Countries, and His Excellency the late Soviet Ambassador, Leonid Zamyatin.

Various byways have been kindly researched for me by Rose Brookhouse, John Hunter, and Dr Christopher Solomon; my further thanks to John Hunter and Christine Lambert for translations. I am indebted to Thomas C. Daly and Robin Waterfield for recourse in manuscript form to the definitive edition of *Our Life with Mr Gurdjieff* by Thomas and Olga de Hartmann, forthcoming from Penguin Books in 1992. No response to my enquiries touched me more than that by Samvel Mkrtchian of Merkurov Memorial House, Leninakan — posted to me just days after the devastating Armenian earthquake of 1988. Professor Jacob Needleman has always been quick with helpful advice.

I express my sincere gratitude to Michel de Salzmann and the Institut Gurdjieff in Paris for permission to publish the preponderant majority of portraits of Gurdjieff and his immediate circle; to Thomas C. Daly for permission to reproduce photographs of Thomas and Olga de Hartmann; to William Segal for the photograph of his daughter Margaret with Gurdjieff; and to Sona Harutunian for the photograph of Gurdjieff's eminent cousin Sergei Dmitrievich Mercourov. My special thanks to Jeremy Finlay for the photograph of Gurdjieff as motorist; to The Hon. Mrs Daphne Mackneile-Dickson for the photograph of Lady Rothermere; and to Mrs Anne Orage for the photos of A. R. Orage and Jessie Orage. My general search for photographs has been aided by Rose Brookhouse, Marian Imhasly and, pre-eminently, by Peter Irvine; Paddy Maffett made a useful intervention on my behalf. For kind permission to reproduce certain locale pictures I am indebted to Professor David Marshall Lang and to my old friend Professor Tilo Ulbricht.

The enthusiasm and personal support of Michael Mann, Chairman of Element Books, afforded me indispensable encouragement at all stages in a challenging project which has occupied four years. My copy editor was Rosemary Pettit.

Finally, my old and trusted friend Jeffrey Somers FRAS, archivist of the Gurdjieff Society, has helped so much with encouragement, critique, and suggestion that he must be looked on as a fellow-begetter of this book.

Copyright Acknowledgements

The provenance of quotations is acknowledged in the References section. In instances not amply covered by fair usage, every effort has been made to obtain permissions from holders of copyright material. If, however – either through inadvertence or through circumstances beyond our control – any copyright owner has been omitted, the author and publisher extend their apologies and undertake to rectify the situation at the next edition.

The author and publisher are grateful to the following for explicit permission to quote excerpts from copyright material:

For permission to quote from the works of G. I. Gurdjieff: Triangle Editions Inc. and Penguin Books Ltd. For permission to quote from *Our Life with Mr Gurdjieff* by Thomas de Hartmann (1983 edition, revised and enlarged from memoirs of Olga de Hartmann): Thomas C. Daly. For permission to quote from *In Search of the Miraculous* by P. D. Ouspensky (copyright 1949 by Harcourt Brace Jovanovich Inc. and renewed 1977 by Tatiana Nagro): Harcourt Brace Jovanovich Inc. and Penguin Books Ltd. For permission to quote from the works of Fritz Peters: A. M. Heath & Co. Ltd, and Russell & Volkening Inc. For permission to quote from *Gurdjieff: Making a New World* by J. G. Bennett and *Idiots in Paris* by J. G. and Elizabeth Bennett: Mrs Elizabeth Bennett. For permission to quote from *Witness* by J. G. Bennett: Mrs Elizabeth Bennett and Thorsons Publishing Group Ltd (HarperCollins Publishers). For permission to quote from *God is My Adventure* by Rom Landau: Unwin Hyman Ltd (Harper-Collins Publishers). For permission to quote from the works of C. S. Nott: Adam and James Nott, and Penguin Books Ltd. For permission to quote from *Undiscovered Country* by Kathryn Hulme: Little, Brown & Co., and Brandt & Brandt Literary Agency. For permission to quote from *The Unknowable Gurdjieff* by Margaret Anderson: Penguin Books Ltd. For permission to quote from *The Fiery Fountains* by Margaret Anderson: Hutchinson & Co. Ltd (Random Century Group). For permission to quote from *The Harmonious Circle* by James Webb: Thames and Hudson Ltd. For permission to quote from *Katherine Mansfield's Letters to John Middleton Murry 1913–1922*: The Society of Authors as literary representative of the Estate of Katherine Mansfield. For permission to quote from *The Unending Quest* by Sir Paul Dukes: Macmillan Publishing Co. Inc. For permission to quote from *Who are You, Monsieur Gurdjieff?* by René Zuber: Jenny Koralek and Penguin Books Ltd.

In conclusion, the author and publisher express their sincere gratitude to all quoted authors for recourse to their material however brief.

Introduction

———— ✣ ————

George Ivanovitch Gurdjieff had an extraordinarily rich and vivid life, though the jury is out on its significance. Two extreme views may serve as points of reference: that he was a charlatan, and conversely that he was 'the most immediate, the most valid and the most totally representative figure of our times.' This latter accolade (awarded by Peter Brook) raises fascinating issues, Gurdjieff being arguably *unrepresentative* to the nth degree: the advocate and agent of tradition in a hectically 'progressive' epoch; an unrepentant patriarch in an age of post-feminist sensibilities; a champion of quality in an era seduced by quantity; a hero in an anti-heroic cultural frame; and above all an *avatar* of consciousness in a world surrendered to trance.

The journalistic cliché 'charlatan' however leaves me even less happy, in fact it leaves me aghast! Without presuming to censor the censorious, one can only wonder about their familiarity with the historical Gurdjieff and the etymology of epithets. The Italian root *ciarlare* means to prattle, yet Gurdjieff economized with speech and was distinguished by the quality of his silences; for thousands of sensitive and intelligent people, who had the wit to see beneath his occasional mask of fraudulence, he came to represent the breathing embodiment of authenticity.

There are fashions in biography and the contemporary urge is evidently to dissect primary establishment figures. Does Gurdjieff rank as such? Perhaps not yet in Britain – though the world of cultural *bon ton* (which incidentally he disdained) seems slowly, almost tremblingly, drawing him to its bosom. He dominates at least fifty memoirs and studies; he is cited in the Encyclopaedia Britannica; in 1979 his autobiographical book *Meetings with Remarkable Men* was rendered into a major film; and in March 1987 I gave the first seminar on his ideas at Oxford University. In any case his posterity is all to play for, since only in the most mechanistic sense can this man's œuvre be defined as four books, one ballet, 300 piano pieces, and some 100 Sacred Dances or 'Movements'. Gurdjieff was the decisive and vivifying factor in countless lives and his true legacy may yet be

discerned as a subterranean current of influence which is far indeed
from having spent itself.

To offer the reader an entertaining and informative introduction to
my subject's life; to tackle the basic question 'And what happened
next?' – these have been my aims in preparing this first standard
biography. *Gurdjieff: The Anatomy of a Myth* is a title chosen
advisedly, but it imposes on me a duty to explain. The word 'myth'
has never been pejorative for me, and in the present context it is
dignified by the immense significance which Gurdjieff himself attached
to tradition. It is thus in the most positive sense that Gurdjieff is a
creature of myth – reiterating in modern dress the urgent quest of
literature's first hero Gilgamesh, King of Uruk. But every stick has
two ends. If Gurdjieff is not to become the amorphous plaything of
extravagant imaginations, his myth requires the skeleton of an
articulated chronology and the musculature of a robust historicity. It
is precisely towards the calibration of myth and history that I have
worked.

Readers who misconstrued my title as promising some species of
character assassination will unfortunately be disappointed. Nor can
they altogether be blamed. Modern biography is wearisomely icono-
clastic, and tends to pivot on the sexual exposé. The defenceless
subject is presented horizontally – his or her sexual proclivities,
performance, and perversions graphically detailed in service to contemporary candour and to book sales. Doubtless there are men
principally illuminable through their relationships with women:
Antonys scarcely thinkable except in their polarity with Cleopatras
. . . Well and good if Gurdjieff had been such a man. But he was not.
It is perfectly true, as T. S. Matthews says, that 'His women followers
obviously adored him, and some who had found favor in his sight
had visible mementoes; swarthy and liquid-eyed children.' Yet if
Gurdjieff's casual couplings ever turned his head, seriously engaged
his heart, or deflected his course of action by a hair's breadth – the
evidence is peculiarly lacking. Episodes so brief, and clearly tangen-
tial to the trajectory of my subject's life, I have judged extrinsic.
Gurdjieff's poignant marriage to Julia Ostrowska (who died from
cancer in 1926) is another matter entirely, and that finds ample place
here.

Like Caesar's Gaul, my biography is divided into three parts. Part
1 tackles the first half of Gurdjieff's life, when he was a fervent seeker
and pupil. I have called it Auto-Mythology, not wishing to disguise my
chastening (though not exclusive) reliance here on autobiographical

elements in my subject's own four works. In my short Part 2, The
Revelation in Question, I offer a sketch of Gurdjieff's principal ideas.
This nettle must be grasped. We are not dealing here merely with a
man who aspired to bring a major critique suited to the modern
temper, but one whose life and thought were profoundly integrated.
Finally Part 3 sets out in full panoply the second half of Gurdjieff's
life, when with daemonic energy he pursued his destiny as an esoteric
teacher. It is a period abundantly if confusingly documented in the
emphatic memoirs of his followers and detractors, and I have called
it (with apologies to Hermann Hesse), The Archives of the League.

So much for structure and content. What of idiom? First be
forewarned that Gurdjieff himself seems to speak with a bewildering
variety of voices. Reportage offers his direct speech in two strongly
contrasted modes: couth and uncouth. Albeit a polyglot in Asiatic
languages, Gurdjieff seldom attempted more than a rudimentary
English (nouns without articles, verbs without adverbs) which lends
an entire genre of English and American memoirs their picaresque
quality. By contrast, in the masterly translations by P. D. Ouspensky,
a pupil he taught in Russian, Gurdjieff is seen to command a clear,
grammatical, and even sophisticated prose. Similarly in Gurdjieff's
own writings, the stylistic simplicity of Meetings with Remarkable
Men is sharply at variance with the intentional opacity of Beelzebub's
Tales to His Grandson, which in places verges on the baroque.

Only one technical expression cries out for preliminary explanation, namely, 'The Work'. The term emerged modestly in Petrograd
in 1916 simply as Gurdjieff's convenient contraction of 'the group's
work'. Gradually however it became a portmanteau expression,
pressed into service as a noun and an adjective to denote virtually
anything specifically 'Gurdjieffian'. The intelligent reader will quickly
and easily pick up the sense of discrete meanings bestowed by
context.

Here a rider might be added about my own biographic idiom. In
the 'Gurdjieffian' thesaurus the word 'idiot' does not mean dullard
but simply (from the ancient Greek root) 'I make my own'. The
'idiocy' of this book is inescapably mine. Although at the outset I
sought primary help from those rare sources qualified to give it, no
individual and no organization – absolutely no one – is implicated in
my viewpoint, my mistakes of fact or tone. Throughout his life
Gurdjieff provoked intense antipathies and allegiancies, which in
their clash again and again refreshed the questions posed by his
work. Little or nothing has changed. Today's biographer – contrive

as he may – will find one or another camp genuinely nettled by his tone of voice: some will accuse him of *lèse-majesté*, others of fawning sycophancy... I must speak as I myself have found. For me to have trimmed my style and viewpoint to accommodate the strong pre-dilections of others whomsoever would have been a betrayal both of my craft and of Gurdjieff himself. Then – if there is a deep existential urgency in Gurdjieff's message (and there undoubtedly is) – it warrants gravitas; yet if his sense of humour was developed to surreal heights (and it undoubtedly was), it legitimizes here and there some contrapuntal levity. It is precisely Gurdjieff's intriguing duality which cries out for an 'appropriate hagiography'.

Gurdjieffian literature being so piquantly encumbered with pseudepigrapha, partisan critiques, and inventive self-advertise-ments, a personal footnote may help towards assessing my quotient of authenticity. I was nineteen when Gurdjieff died in 1949 and I never met him. Of his pupils from the classic Russian period, I am grateful to have met Mme Olga de Hartmann and Mme Jeanne de Salzmann, two of the five founder members of his Institute for the Harmonious Development of Man. Of those whose attachment began later in London, Paris, and New York in the early 1920s, I have met Jane Heap, Jessmin Howarth, Rowland Kenney, Louise March, Rose Mary Nott, Stanley Nott, and Jessie Orage; and of subsequent pupils – often very striking – too many to nominate. I have visited certain places where Gurdjieff was. I have immersed myself in his music. I have needless to say read assiduously in Gurdjieffian literature published and unpublished, and (not least in my judgement) have continuously since 1956 made honest trial of his methodology... The degree to which these 'qualifications' are ade-quate in practice must be for the reader to judge but they do at least stand on a bedrock of commonsensical and verifiable experience reaching back to within seven years of my subject's death.

I am painfully aware of having dedicated my book to someone who might have frowned on it. The standard which Mme Henriette Lannes set for herself and for others was exacting indeed. To those of my generation able to approach her, she was far more than the voice of Gurdjieff's teaching in England for nearly thirty years: she became the living proof of its transmissability and potency. I am obliged to bear witness to her astonishing richness of being, which it would be an impertinence to praise.

No anniversary lends mechanical advantage to this book's publica-tion yet it could hardly appear in the world at a moment of more painful importance to 'Gurdjieffians' of every stripe. The death of his most senior pupil Jeanne de Salzmann on 25 May 1990 at the age of 101, closed so-to-say the 'Age of Silver'. On other shoulders now are descending the great responsibilities which she bore so magnificently into extreme old age. May good fortune attend them.

James Moore
London, July 1991

PART I

❖

Auto-Mythology

1

❖

THE AROUSING OF THOUGHT

(1866–1886)

In 1925 the Parisian habitués of the Grand Hôtel-Café de la Paix were augmented by a figure who aroused some curiosity. He appeared to be a writer of sorts in his late fifties. His recourse to a pencil and cheap ruled exercise book hinted at his poverty, though this assessment left unexplained his fine lambswool karakul hat and gold-topped walking stick. Sometimes he would lingeringly coax the juice of a lemon into his modest cup of black coffee; sometimes, however, he would prefer a double Armagnac and tip the waiter with a liberal scattering of chocolates, marzipan, caramels or pepper-mints. Seated oriental fashion on the green velour banquette, with one leg tucked discrepantly beneath him, he seemed strangely inde-pendent of his surroundings. Occasionally – fiercely licking his pencil – he muttered in an unknown language, casting about for the perfect phrase; more commonly, he remained inordinately still, a centre of containment in the café's Babel of chattering voices.

Night and day, hour after hour, the writer bent to his composition; weeks blended into months; months into years. What could it be which so engaged him? What thought was he mobilizing within his imposing shaven cranium? What unknown spirit was he evoking on the little round, marble-topped table? And when would publication come, permitting that emancipated – and perhaps insurrectionist – spirit to leap from its strict circle into the unsuspecting world? Who could tell? At best the writer remained a perplexing and equivocal figure. The waiters liked him and celebrated him as 'Monsieur Bon-bon', but whispering detractors rumoured he was 'the man who killed Katherine Mansfield'.

Today one thing at least is clearer: if there were customers who

suspected the writer of plotting some piffling social annoyance –
some vexing change to the Code Napoléon for example – they did him
a grave injustice. The enterprise he had in prospect was altogether
larger. His dedication was to create a new and more wholesome
world – and in the process to crush our old world like a louse.

This singular man was Mr Gurdjieff and his epic took as its hero
the fallen angel Beelzebub.

For any understanding of the author's position, it must first
be grasped that he had begun life's journey far from the gilded
Corinthian pilasters of the Grand Café de la Paix and the effete
androgynous cherubs which floated across its frescoed ceilings.
Moreover he had come there by a route so hard, so circuitous, and so
extraordinary as to be utterly unique.

George Ivanovitch Gurdjieff was born in his parents' house in the
Greek quarter of Alexandropol, in Russian Armenia. No one can
give a precise birthday – our best informed guess is 1866.[1] The
brash new garrison town defended Russia's border with Turkey, and
its heaped-up walls, bastions, and gun-emplacements conveyed a
sense of immemorial disputes, wars and forced migrations; a prudent
man did not register a birth; a prudent man registered nothing. Nevertheless, there was calm and even sweet reassurance in the first sounds
heard by the infant Gurdjieff:[2] his mother's Armenian lullabies, the
bells of the nearby Greek Chapel of St George, and the lowing of
numerous cattle which his father's herdsmen drove to their summer
pastures along the banks of the western Arpa Chai or Barley River.

Giorgios Giorgiades, the father, was about thirty-two. He had
inherited with his herds the rough tasks and *seigneurial* obligations
which filled his long hard day. A grazier only by force of circumstances, he was by choice an *ashokh* or bardic poet; as he worked
with his cattle on the inhospitable plain, he rehearsed through chap-
ped lips his phenomenal repertoire of folklore, myth and legend. He
had little free time to see his first-born son but sometimes, late in the
evenings, he would tell him stories of Mullah Nassr Eddin,[10] or of
the *One Thousand and One Nights*, and especially of 'Mustapha the
Lame Carpenter', an embodiment of resourcefulness who could
make anything including a flying armchair.

The Giorgiades' house was a goodish one, far better than most in
the Greek enclave; it had a little rose garden and it boasted windows
sealed with glass, not the customary greased paper; and it was warm
in the fierce six-month winter when the brawling wind ran in across
the Shiraki Steppe. Soon – by the time Gurdjieff was three or

thereabouts – it sheltered his paternal grandmother and his newly born brother, Dmitri; his favourite uncle Giorgi Mercourov paid frequent visits. If the atmosphere round the ample family hearth was one of geniality, order, simplicity and calm, it was also one of patriarchal hierarchy where everyone kept their place. 'If you are first,' Giorgiades would say, 'your wife is second; if your wife is first, you had better be zero: only then will your hens be safe.'

Though Gurdjieff received in early childhood all that was satisfying and really necessary, he was certainly not indulged. Hardly could he walk and talk, than his father began to impose on him a spartan regime. In winter the boy was mercilessly compelled to rise around dawn, go to the fountain, strip, wash, and run about naked – experiencing in his very bones the sharpest transition between sleep and waking. In summer he was compelled to handle non-poisonous snakes. Even in bed he was not safe for he might find, between the blankets, a worm, a frog or a mouse, put there occasionally by Giorgiades to 'immunize' his son against fear and squeamishness.

The aim was not to raise up some monstrous Nietzschean superman but a normal human being able to surmount fear and sloth. Life in Transcaucasia was hard and called for hardihood – earthquake, drought, war, pestilence, and flood had savagely punctuated the story of its peoples. Giorgiades acted remorselessly towards his eldest son but with underlying and far-seeing love. The process which would select Gurdjieff, not merely from his brother and sisters but from thousands and tens of thousands of children, had already begun in Alexandropol – that little raft of commonplace and pretentious buildings in the ocean of grass.

When Gurdjieff was seven years old he saw his father put to the test: in 1873 a virulent strain of rinderpest or cattle plague swept in from Asia and, in two harrowing summer months, exterminated the now vast herds of Giorgiades and those of neighbours who ran their stock with his. The *ashokh* met this calamity with exemplary interior calm but could never quite adjust to a new livelihood. His generous spirit, reflective nature, and sense of honour (which required him to compensate his petty graziers) were crippling handicaps in a commercial world dominated by shrewd Armenians. Nevertheless he sold the household furniture, put together a small parcel of money, and opened a lumber-yard where wood carted from the forests of Soghanlu Dagh in the Pashalik of Kars could be converted to Alexandropol's expanding needs.

Gurdjieff, young though he was, took this calamity in the spirit of

Mustapha the lame carpenter, and began to contribute a little to family income by satisfying a growing clientele of childhood friends with 'firearms', ingeniously contrived from bits and pieces like empty cartridge shells. His character was gradually taking shape: he was robust, resourceful, energetic; he might perhaps appear angelic in the candlelit, incense-filled choir of the Greek Chapel, but in fighting, in escapades with his friend Fatimov, in blasting sparrows and snaring pigeons with horsehair, he had more than the devilment normal for his age.

His first and most significant prompting towards unorthodoxy came, surprisingly, from his revered grandmother on her deathbed:

> Eldest of my grandsons! Listen and always remember my strict injunction to you: In life never do as others do. Either do nothing – just go to school – or do something nobody else does.

The boy followed the advice immediately and literally, skipping round her grave at the requiem service and singing an irreverent ditty; before long however, her words became a deeper principle, not condoning cheap eccentricity but leading towards strenuous experiment and revolutionary thinking. The sense of being essentially different – the sense of being unique – came very early to Gurdjieff and was tinged with a precocious mysticism. There was, for example, the peculiar incident of his tooth, knocked out in an altercation:

> This strange tooth had seven shoots and at the end of each of them there stood out in relief a drop of blood, and through each separate drop there shone clearly and definitely one of the seven aspects of the manifestation of the white ray.

For most of its inhabitants, Alexandropol stifled all questions with its dull provincialism. It smelled of horse-dung. It had no tradition. It offered nothing on which the imagination could feed. But beyond the town, where Gurdjieff ranged in the whispering trembling grass, lay fragments of statuettes and sculptural reliefs, which told of antiquity piled on antiquity; of forgotten languages; of the fated processional of dynasties; of a universe of feelings and passionate convictions, fallen away into oblivion and subsumed in dust.

At home conditions grew steadily harder and stranger. As the skies darkened round Giorgios Giorgiades, as his affairs foundered, as he was tricked and exploited on all sides by Armenians, as parental responsibilities grew on him by the addition of three charming daughters – he seemed if anything more serene, more withdrawn into the world of poetic values, which transcended his material problems without resolving them. His lumber-yard business finally collapsed and he was reduced to providing his family a marginal subsistence by making small wooden objects in his workshop. At this point fate intervened.

On 24 April 1877 Tsar Alexander II went to war against Sultan Abdul the Damned and launched his army westward across the river from Alexandropol. Gurdjieff's mother and all Christian Armenia fervently approved; not only did long-remembered Turkish cruelties cry out for revenge, but the Russian force was commanded, with eloquent justice, by an Armenian – the redoubtable Count Mikhail Tarielovich Loris-Melikov. Gurdjieff and round-eyed Dmitri watched the white-bearded Metropolitan blessing the banners; thousands of Armenians streamed out from Alexandropol, yoked themselves to wagons, seized hold of gun-carriages, thrust at wheels, hauled on ropes, and with wild shouts helped the army up the far bank. At sunset the last faint bugles died away, the Russian troopers disappeared into the sea of grass and the Armenians back into their houses.

For six months Alexandropol was swept with uneasy rumour. Then on Sunday 18 November 1877 Gurdjieff heard all the bells – Gregorian and Catholic, Armenian, Greek and Russian Orthodox – ringing jubilantly across the thick snow. During the night the Church Militant had won a famous victory: Loris Melikov and the Tsar's brother, Grand Duke Michael Niklayevich, had routed the Turkish forces at the town of Kars. Although in humanitarian terms the question, 'And what good came of it at last?', remains devastating, in Gurdjieff's life this event had undeniable importance. Giorgios Giorgiades, having by now little or nothing to lose in Alexandropol, was persuaded by relatives that he had something to gain in Kars; within months both family and workshop had moved and were modestly re-established in the conquered town.

Gurdjieff now shared in that long-forgotten spring of 1878 when hopes briefly rose and Kars bustled importantly under its new Russian administration. And yet as he explored, clambering here and there, he could hardly have failed to register the town's sullen, even sinister, air. The geography of history dictates that invaders from the East are funnelled through the Kars gap – but not without enormous difficulty. For where the boiling black waters of the river Kars Chai pierce the easternmost spur of the Soghanlu range they enter a gorge, swirl right, and form a near-encircling moat about a dead volcanic stump; high on the summit of this natural strongpoint looms the squat black citadel of Kars. It is a stark place, engrimed in history. Time and time again it has seen cruel sieges, wicked betrayals, desperate assaults and horrible bloody capitulations: the Seljuks, the Mongols, Tamerlane the Great – all have come riding here. The Greek quarter of 1878 lay below in its dark shadow on the western side and Gurdjieff knew its constant presence.

The family must soon have wondered if they had made the right decision. The climate of Alexandropol had been severe enough but Kars, at an altitude of 5750 feet, had a climate which was brutal: first snow, then mud, then dust, then rain; extremities of temperature; flood and drought; the river alternatively in spate and then parched and cracked. The great citadel lay at the mercy of the winds. The narrow streets were medieval in their squalor, and the chief employment of the women was the fabrication of *tezek* or dried cow-dung fuel, cakes of which plastered the outer wall of every house. Not that Giorgiades even had a house in the usual sense, for in the Greek quarter (and in the desolate suburbs of Bayram Pasha, Orta Kapi and Timur Pasha) most dwellings were mere burrows in the uneven hillside, overlaid with earth and entered through a door in the roof. As formerly in Alexandropol, local timber was scarce and cartage dear. With seven mouths to feed, Giorgiades remained grindingly poor.

If many humble people had shared Giorgiades' dubious impulse to begin again in Kars, thousands more were simply lifted up by the cyclone of history and dumped there. As the Turks melted away, a singular conglomoration of in-coming tribes and factions (resettled forcibly, or fleeing persecution, or driven by passionate hope of religious freedom) converged on the vacant lands. To the creak of wagons, the neighing of gaunt horses, the shuffle of weary feet, a mêlée of desperate people embroiled Kars. The mosques were commandeered for the cavalry of the Kuban regiment; the minarets were silent; and had the outraged muezzin returned and looked downward into the mean, familiar streets, he would have missed the red flowerpot fezes of the faithful. Astrakhans and shakos, forage caps and helmets, the hieratic headgear of Orthodox ecclesiastics, and enormous turbans of twisted yellow, black, green and white kerchiefs – these were everywhere to be seen. The Ottomon Empire had recoiled, and Kars was full of Aisors, Tartars, Kurds, Karapapaks, Daghestanis, heterodox Dukhobors, blond Caucasian Molokans, Lutherans from far-off Estonia, and Yezidi 'Devil Worshippers'.

Gurdjieff, now eleven, was exhilarated by this kaleidoscope of races. He was soundly beaten for running off for five days with a tribe of semi-nomadic gypsies from the Carpathian mountains who could predict the future and read the past. 'Such people *see*, can *see*.' Already he could manage several languages: from his strong illiterate mother he had learned Armenian (used in the household and all Alexandropol); his father had passed on to him a Cappodocian dialect and the rudiments of Turko-Tartar, the lingua franca in which the *ashokhs* shared their songs; a refugee priest had been hired to teach him a modern Greek; bored soldiers had conveyed their uncouth Russian; and now in Kars the boy quickly picked up the Turkish of the eastern provinces. His intellect was strong. He could read, write and calculate – but his remarkable formal education was only about to begin.

The Christian schools in Kars were strongly nationalistic but commonly unsatisfactory: the Greek one small and politicized; the Russian one offering a second-rate curriculum; and the Armenian dealing only with the psalms, the Gospels, the Acts, and *The Lamentations* of Gregory of Narek. Giorgiades, who groped as best he could in these matters, quickly withdrew his son from Greek influence and placed him in the Russian municipal school. Here – in the loud monotonous recitation of largely erroneous information – the boy's curiosity and entire intellectual development might too easily have been stifled. But the misapplied young voice had also been trained in the choir of Alexandropol; within weeks Gurdjieff had successfully auditioned as a chorister at Kars military cathedral, and there – to his everlasting gratitude – he fell under the attention of Dean Borsh.

No one stood higher in the Russian Orthodox Church than Father Dean Borsh – not only in Kars but throughout its environs annexed by Russia. In his tall thin frame and fine sensitive face was concentrated a spiritual authority so unchallengeable that many other churchmen must have been tempted to translate it into temporal power. But the Father Dean was an enigma: he gave most of his stipend to the poor, dispensed with a platoon of servants, refused to avail himself of sumptuous officers' quarters, and made his residence in a single room in the cathedral guardhouse. Here, in quiet solitude, he played the violin and composed sacred canticles: 'Glory to Thee', 'O Thou Almighty God', and 'Calm Light'. He did not mix in garrison society, and to any serious inquirer confessed his preferred interest in astronomy, chemistry and the ancient Assyrians.

Something about the young Gurdjieff quickly intrigued Dean Borsh. Perhaps it was less his voice – though that proved excellent –

than his eyes; and when, in late 1878, those eyes were threatened
with trachoma, the Dean arrived unannounced at the Giorgiades
home bringing two military physicians who successfully treated their
patient with copper sulphate cauterization and golden ointment.
Happily, Giorgiades and Dean Borsh liked each other from the outset
and arranged to meet regularly. Thus on evenings when ecclesiastical
duties did not detain him, the frail figure of the Dean would be noted
to emerge from the cathedral guardhouse, make his way to the Greek
quarter, climb delicately in through a roof door and disappear below.
And had the curious bystander been able to penetrate that grassy
roof, he would have discovered the supreme spiritual authority of
Kars relaxed on a big pile of woodshavings, and exchanging thoughts
with a jobbing carpenter on such unexpected themes as the lost
world of Atlantis, the benefits of arranged marriages, the Epic of
Gilgamesh, the Flood before the Flood, the paramount importance of
deferring until maturity the satisfaction of sexual desire, and the
present whereabouts of God. And he would also have observed a
silent, attentive boy who drank in every word.

Early in 1879 the family took council together on the subject of
Gurdjieff's long-term future. Giorgiades and his wife wished their
son to become a priest; Dean Borsh readily acceded but wished him
also to be a physician; Gurdjieff himself – excited by the new Western
technology gradually filtering south – dreamed of some sort of
engineering specialization. One thing was common ground: if this
evidently unusual child were to realize his potential, he must be
removed from his dead-end school and coached privately. Henceforward the Dean himself taught his 'little garlic-head' mathematics,
chemistry, and astronomy. Various other subjects were delegated to
a gaggle of military deacons – all graduates of the theological Seminary, all seeking elevation to the priesthood, and all soberingly
reliant on the Dean's goodwill. Though singled out in this way,
Gurdjieff retained close contact with his friends. Each evening they
met at their 'club' – an octagonal wooden structure high up in the
bell-tower of the fortress cathedral; here they smoked, ate halva,
cracked jokes, and even prepared lessons.

Gurdjieff's education strengthened his legs as well as his mind: he
would be off four miles to the military hospital at Fort Chanak to
study anatomy and physiology; then back pell-mell to town for his
history and geography lessons in lodgings overlooking the miserable
little public garden (ironically named the Paradise of Kars); then up
to the cathedral guardhouse to make tea for Dean Borsh. He began to

study hard. Reading fluently in Greek, Armenian and Russian, he
devoured the libraries of his teachers. A passion for knowledge
overwhelmed him; he puzzled, he correlated, he questioned, until the
military deacons could only shake their heads.

Of all these candidates for the priesthood, one alone shared
Gurdjieff's sense of deep inquiry; this was Deacon Bogachevsky –
himself very young – who became especially attached to his pupil. At
his lodgings near the military fire brigade Bogachevsky set up a small
discussion circle, where bored young garrison officers – drinking
their vodka, smoking their cigars, and scarcely noticing Gurdjieff in
the corner – debated abstract questions late into the night. But there
were also private moments, fuller moments, when Bogachevsky
heard Gurdjieff's confession, and insistently presented to him the
idea of two contrasting moralities: firstly 'objective morality' –
absolute, constant, established by God, confirmed by life, and deeply
implanted in everyman's conscience; secondly 'subjective morality' –
relative, changeable as a chameleon, culturally dependent, pernicious
in its silly unexamined compulsions and prohibitions. And Gurdjieff
agreed. How could he not? For objective morality he already sensed
in his father and Dean Borsh; and subjective morality he met daily in
Kars' strident clash of cultures.

Gurdjieff energetically supported himself during these years, but
like most boys in Kars he also stole: cigarettes disappeared from
cigarette cases; quantities of lead and copper from the army firing-
range. Gurdjieff's unique link with the town's adult intelligentsia,
and his aspiration one day to find a place in the Archdeacon's choir
in Tiflis, made him embarrassed to cut the figure of a poor boy
scratching a living with his hands. But he did not lack resource or
courage; in any weeks which were free he jolted by mail-coach forty
miles to Alexandropol, where, staying in the house of his uncle
Giorgi Mercourov, he set feverishly to work mending locks, repairing
watches, shaping stone, and even embroidering cushions.

About the age of fifteen Gurdjieff was confronted by death, and led
into that twilight zone where some 'occult' sense of death's meaning
glimmers, beckons and retires. First his eldest sister died. She had
always been especially close to him, and when one evening
Bogachevsky's circle experimented with an impromptu seance, he felt
a wild hope of recontact. Some inexplicable table-turning did indeed
transpire and, though it brought no message from beyond, it seemed
proof positive of an utterly mysterious force. Soon afterwards he
himself narrowly escaped death in a shooting accident on Lake

Alageuz – only to discover that the mishap had been predicted by the half-demented fortune-teller Eoung-Ashokh Mardiross. On another occasion in Alexandropol, Gurdjieff's uncle Mercourov and other respected witnesses described to him a strange event which had occurred only the day before: an 'evil spirit' had reportedly entered and reanimated the corpse of a young Tartar policeman. Gurdjieff was neither morbid nor credulous ('there was not a single book on neuropathology and psychology in the library of Kars military hospital that I had not read, and read very attentively'); on the contrary he emerged from these encounters with a renewed appetite to live, to search, and at all costs someday to understand.

As season followed season, it almost began to seem to Gurdjieff that he inhabited two distinct worlds: in one the canons of science, the sober domesticated laws of cause and effect, sufficiently explained everything; in the other they explained nothing. Admittedly, this second world revealed itself only briefly and problematically, but when it did . . . Ah then, the witness of one blazing moment dismayed the pedestrian evidence of a month of Sundays. Even here the boy did not clutch naively at miraculous explanations. The instantaneous cure of a paralytic, which he saw on a pilgrimage to Mount Djadjur, might conceivably be explained in psychosomatic terms; so too, at a pinch, could the overnight recovery of a Tartar woman dying of galloping consumption (it could certainly not be attributed to Reznik the town doctor, who had given her up for dead; the invalid herself credited a prescription of milk and rosehips, confided in a vision by the Virgin Mary). More baffling was the case of the sobbing, struggling Yezidi boy, trapped in nothing more substantial than a circle drawn around him on the ground; here Gurdjieff innocently appealed for explanation to the Russian intelligentsia of Alexandropol, and was shocked to find their comments puerile, frivolous or tautological. 'I already well understood,' he observes caustically, 'that hysteria is hysteria, but I wished to know something more.' Perhaps most perplexing of all – and surely outstripping pyschological explanation – was the instance when a torrential downpour coincided with an archimandrite's fervent prayers for rain. How extraordinary it all was!

In this climate of perplexity, Gurdjieff was suddenly deprived of both his guides: Bogachevsky left Kars for good on appointment as a chaplain in the Transcaspian region; and Dean Borsh went away on sick leave. Gurdjieff began to drink a little (evidently initiated by the choirmaster), and coincidently fell dangerously in love with the thirteen-year-old daughter of Riaouzov the vodka manufacturer. He would play the guitar to her, make intricate designs for her to embroider, and generally compete for her favours with a fellow student Piotr Karpenko.

A cordial hatred predictably seized the adolescent rivals, as intense – indeed, rather more intense – than their calf-love for the Riaouzov girl. There were battles of will on the cathedral steps; deadly glances which led to blows; and a disgraceful fight which provoked a formal duel. The choice of weapons was a peculiar one: not owning pistols, Gurdjieff and Karpenko madly resolved to lie out on the artillery range during target practice until one of them was killed. There, crouched for hours in an old shell-hole between the bucking earth and the howling shot, Gurdjieff was overwhelmed by new inner experiences; an unprecedented feeling of self-awareness, 'a whole sensation of myself', blended with 'an unconquerable living terror' of annihilation.

Viewed biographically, there is an inscrutable fate in the trajectory and velocity of a bit of shrapnel: not one but countless lives and consequences ride on the shrieking, twisting metal; the nicest calibration counts for everything. As it transpired, Gurdjieff emerged from this folly unscathed but with his valuation of living transformed. He was flooded with remorse and pity when the lightly wounded Karpenko recovered consciousness and smiled at him, and he spent every night at his bedside until he was well again.

With his two mentors gone, his family contemplating a return to Alexandropol, and General Fadeef the fortress commandant apoplectic over the duel episode, Gurdjieff found Kars no longer worth the candle. Tiflis called him and in 1883 to Tiflis he went. But there in the bustling Georgian capital, the centre of the Russian Caucasian viceroyalty, events did not turn out as expected. His father had hoped he would commit himself to the famous Georgian Theological Seminary on Pushkin Street, but its arid formalism found no response in him. He himself had dreamt of entering the Archdeacon's choir, but its doors were mysteriously closed against him. The only gates which he found conveniently open in his early Tiflis days were those of the railway yard. He must have been the strangest stoker in the entire Transcaucasian Railway Company. He was seventeen and his ordeal on the firing range had lent an intense existential urgency to his questions on the paranormal; he despaired now of finding explanations in science and turned avidly to religion. A judicious friendship with the railway engineer Yaroslev allowed him to come and go as a casual labourer: he took three months off to study under

Father Yevlampios in the monastery of Sanaine; he made pilgrimage on foot to Echmiadzin, the holy city of the Armenians. But nothing he found, nothing he heard, spoke to his condition.

At this impasse Gurdjieff made a vital connection with two contemporaries who shared his capacity for question – Sarkis Pogossian and Abram Yelov. Pogossian was an Armenian and Yelov an Aisor. Pogossian, having studied in the Theological Seminary of Erivan and graduated from the Theological Seminary of Echmiadzin, had only to marry to obtain a parish, but felt that his inner state did not correspond to this. Yelov was a bookseller. Pogossian seemed frail, and his right eye – burning with inner fire – was slightly crossed; he wore a shy ecclesiastical moustache. Yelov was more or less covered with virulent black hair, his shaggy eyebrows merging into a beard which laid siege to his nose. Yelov was thickset and a slave to his habit of hitching his trousers up. Pogossian's idiosyncracy was to experiment consciously with physical movement – clapping rhythmically, marking time, exploring gesture. Yelov made comparable demands on his intellect, wrestling with figures and practising more than twenty languages.

The close-knit young trio was exceptional in ability, intensity, and purpose, but the Tiflis to which they adapted was not a moral academy. Through a murky underworld of practised carpet dealers and sly entrepreneurs; through the vicious *kinto* freemasonry of delinquent street poets; through the labyrinthine bazaar on the Maidan and the dubious sulphur baths of Prince Orbeliani; through the cruel and desperate pack of guttersnipes and parasites and triple-entry book-keepers – they glided like sharks. 'Boil down nine Jews and you get one Armenian; boil down nine Armenians and you get one Aisor.' In Pogossian the wish to be a priest was curiously replaced by a wish to be a locksmith; in Yelov a prodigious bibliographic and philological scholarship was deployed with extreme commercial cunning. Gurdjieff, if anything, outdid them both. Nothing surpasses his coup as overseer and interpreter on the survey party for the Tiflis–Kars line, when, knowing in advance those towns and villages the railway would serve, he prevailed on local dignitaries to pay him a small fortune to 'arrange it'. If Giorgios Giorgiades could have seen his son, or Borsh and Bogachevsky their pupil – they would surely have frowned. But Tiflis was like that. What differentiated these three youths was not their veniality but the chivalry which they maintained among themselves, and even extended to rustic people who were defenceless.

The moral ambiguity of the Tiflis apprenticeship was arguably part
of a larger pattern. Had not Gurdjieff's entire childhood and adoles-
cence been fraught with contradiction? Christendom was opposed
by Islam; Western 'progress' by oriental tradition; materialism by
religion; sexual impulses by societal prohibitions; the unitary Godhead of Jews, Christians and Muslims by the dualism of Aisors and
Yezidis; liberal dreams by reactionary secret police; commonsense by
paranormal incident; sharp human necessities by a merciless geographical environment; and men's essential brotherhood by war –
the vile process of reciprocal destruction. This marked him. It created
in him a definite pyschic tension: he was moved by the suffering of
others, but ruthless in his own determination to survive; he aspired to
be guided by the 'Calm Light' of Dean Borsh's canticle, yet was swept
by fits of rage and passion. He had in embryo a real existential
question. Measured against this question, physical discomfort was as
nothing, and conventional morality beat its wings in vain. Vistas now
opened where his personal happiness was an absurd irrelevance –
and all mankind, past, present and future, no more than a speck of
dust on a vast plain.

What then was Gurdjieff's question? To say he had been bitten by
the 'paranormal' and yearned to investigate strange incidents and
powers is the truth – but nothing like the whole truth. His outlook
was a singular one. Three factors at least – his paranormal sightings;
society's tragi-comic anomalies; and the soaring conjectures of his
father, Dean Borsh, and Bogachevsky – had so aroused his thought
that he simply found it impossible to take anything for granted, least
of all the phenomenon of life itself. He felt (and communicated to
Pogossian and Yelov):

> an 'irrepressible striving' to understand clearly the precise significance, in
> general, of the life process on earth of all the outward forms of breathing
> creatures and, in particular, of the aim of human life in the light of this
> interpretation.

But why this deep speculation upon life? Gurdjieff after all was a
grazier's son, and had learnt to shoot a wolf or squash a louse
without the least philosophizing. Perhaps, in one special sense, the
stars in their courses had drawn him to his transcendent question.
Giorgios Giorgiades was a lifelong stargazer, and Gurdjieff –
borrowing from his father's perspective – found life on earth an
enigma which staggered the imagination.

A vast, cohesive, organic sphere enveloped our modest planet;

breathing creatures flew in the gas, swam in the liquid, swarmed on the earth's crust. Where was this phenomenon paralleled in the whole universe? Even on earth life was a novelty – though on a man's timescale it was inconceivably old. Somewhere, sometime, perhaps a thousand million years ago, there had appeared the protobiont, precursor of all living beings. How, in God's name? By supernatural intervention; by some convenient spontaneous combustion of inert elements; by some emanation from the sun; by some seeding from meteorite or comet, or by spores from outer space? Who could tell? What common insight, if any, could ever reconcile science, religion, and the conflicting creation myths recited by the *ashokhs*? What was the meaning of the Hindu invocation: 'O Life, older than the stars themselves'?

Then again (beyond any technical explanation of creation), what of meaning? What planetary function had this vast and variegated envelope of living tissue? What was the specific purpose of this immense filter, interposed between earth's inorganic strata and cosmic radiations of every type and wavelength? And for what goal had simple life afterwards become a vehicle for consciousness? For what end had man, with his unique complexity and powers, arisen from a one-cell infusorium? Did it not follow that man had some correspondingly unique – yet unsuspected – role? And if indeed any function and purpose whatever existed, who had ordained them?

Here, in this complex of agonized questions, is the mainspring which set Gurdjieff's feet marching through deserts and mountains to remote monasteries and encampments; which steeled him to bear privation, danger, condemnation, and exile; made him the emphatic turning point in countless lives; and established him, years after his death, on a world stage. But already difficulties loomed. The library of Kars military hospital and the monastery of Sanaine had proved equally dumb on life's functional significance. The question itself, let alone the answer, was hardly given hospitality. Western science – happily surrendered to Darwin's mechanistic theory of evolution – side-stepped any notion of purpose. Institutional religion was more willing to handle the issue but only in self-serving and redemptionist terms.

With youth's impatience, Gurdjieff thrust aside his hope of finding answers from accessible modern sources and refocused all attention on the past. Surely some former men had shared his question; surely some had searched; surely some had found; surely some had left traces. In Tiflis, in the cluttered bookshops of the Soldiers' Bazaar and the streets along the west side of the Alexander Gardens, the three young men rummaged and searched for some written memorial of truth. A babble of voices, of insistent and largely incompatible certainties, reached them from long ago and far away: from the Classical, Byzantine, Medieval and Renaissance worlds; from the vast and diffuse Christian heritage; from Kabbalist sources; from Hindu and Buddhist classics.

It was during this period that Gurdjieff's thinking about sources underwent a further critical development. The ultimate meaning of organic life on earth was either a preposterous study – and that he could not accept – or it was very special. It was the Holy Grail, the Golden Fleece, the Philosopher's Stone; it was a knowledge which so far surpassed all mundane knowledge as to be inaccessible to ordinary people. And if those who spoke about it did not know, then perhaps those who knew about it did not speak. The undeniable existence of closed orders of monks and dervishes; the natural human propensity to conceal treasures; and the *ashokh*'s vast poetic tradition – all licensed the hypothesis of an oral and initiatic transmission of hidden knowledge. An extravagant concept? Indeed it was. Yet much in religion, myth, heroic legend and fairy-tale tended towards it. History too brought specific instances – the mysteries of Delphi, Eleusis and Philae, the architecture of the cathedral at Chartres, the labours of the alchemists. Perceived on a timescale of millennia, the very birth and rebirth of cultures hinted at an alternative history (not the popular history of slaughter and regicide and crime), recording how spiritual schools, and brotherhoods of seekers and learned beings, navigated their ark of significance from epoch to epoch across the recurrent floods of barbarism. A romantic concept? He knew it was; and that did not necessarily make it wrong. The whole thesis had to be tested, preferably by direct contact. But where were they now, those mysterious groups of initiates he had read of? Where were the 'Pythagoreans', the 'Essenes', the 'Sarmoung Brotherhood'?

Around 1886, when Gurdjieff was twenty, he stumbled on his first decisive clue. A bulky and promising collection of old Armenian books had proved too abstruse to assimilate in the hurly-burly of Tiflis; taking only Pogossian, Gurdjieff had carted them off, for leisurely study, to the silent and abandoned city of Ani, former capital of the Bagratid Kings of Armenia. Here fate intervened. Digging irresponsibly and haphazardly in the ruins, the young men made a series of dramatic finds: an underground passage, a crumbling monastic cell, a wall niche, a pile of ancient Armenian parchments – and in one of these parchments an obscure but exhilarating reference to the 'Sarmoung Brotherhood'. Textual analysis suggested that the Brotherhood has been an Aisorian school, situated 'between Urmia and Kurdistan' in the sixth or seventh century AD. Gurdjieff's response was immediate: he 'decided to go there and try at any cost to find where the school was situated and then enter it.'

In all the material shedding light on Gurdjieff's enigmatic character there can hardly be a more extraordinary passage. Consider. The area he sought was vast and preposterously vague; the existence of the 'Sarmoung' was at best problematical, and their trail obscured by the historical debris of twelve centuries. How can all this be decoded? Perhaps here is simply the seeker's youth and inexperience, his stormy and overbrimming energy, his precipitate hope. Perhaps. Yet Gurdjieff was never naive. He may even have 'believed' in the 'Sarmoung' *because* it was absurd and, more empirically, because its absurdity imparted to his general quest that potent enabling energy granted only to visionaries – that dangerous current which prevails wherever white-knuckled faith exults over reasonable hesitation, and logical propriety is cuckolded by psychological passion. It may have been so. In any case to 'find the Sarmoung' was not utterly beyond the bounds of possibility. Perhaps the sheer mass of his aim would bend reality itself from its dull commonsensical course!

2

❖

THE LONG SEARCH

(1887–1911)

Of Gurdjieff's history for the next twenty years or more we know everything and nothing. And we know it thanks to him. We know nothing because we possess not one shred of independent evidence to confirm his own extraordinary account – nor indeed to invalidate it; and though we 'know everything', we do so only by virtue of an intuition which senses in the myth of his peculiarly composed life a self-sufficient authenticity.

In his autobiography *Meetings with Remarkable Men*, Gurdjieff confides an impressionistic version of his early manhood, unrolling the lands of Transcaucasia and Central Asia before us, even while he hints at a parallel geography of man's pysche and the route he followed to penetrate it. Well and good on the level of essential meaning. Yet judged by more straight-laced historical criteria the book is unhelpful. The disciplined biographic mind stands aghast at its contradictions and omissions: dates quiver and dance in the heat; the hero's footprints are lost in the shifting sand, and frequently enough the entire narrative disappears over the rim of some telling allegory. It is all the more exasperating because of the centrality of this epoch in Gurdjieff's life: he begins it aged twenty-one and ends it at forty-two; he begins it as a youth with a burning question and ends it a mature man endowed with quite extraordinary powers and capacities.

What can we say for certain? Gurdjieff travelled – that much at least is confirmed by his brother's family. One speaks here not of saunters but of epic journeys which returned him intermittently to Dmitri's door in Tiflis, exhausted, penniless, and racked with intractable and unpronounceable diseases; he complained of Bokharian malaria, Beluchistan dysentery, Kurdistan scurvy, Ashkhabadian *bedinka*, and Tibetan hydropsy; he revealed the scars of three successive bullet wounds. Clearly he had been somewhere out of the ordinary.

It was Gurdjieff's world-view and self-imposed task which made him a nomad, and forbad him the complacent gratifications of family life. His 'Sarmoung Brotherhood' was a shining needle buried somewhere in the prodigious haystack of the Euro-Asian land mass; the significance of organic life on earth was a lost truth whose scattered fragments – like the dismembered body of the Egyptian God Osiris – lay embedded in 100 obscure cultures. To search, to gather, and to reunify – such was Gurdjieff's perceived role. The task was urgent. Already a cocksure European technology had begun to infiltrate east along precarious railway tracks. In 100 years, in fifty years, the beliefs, customs, and ritual of millennia would be swept away forever by a blank tidal wave of modernism. Gurdjieff read the signs of the times with rare and painful prescience. The fakirs, yogis, *staretz* and shamans would be displaced; monasteries, ashrams, and dervish *tekkhes* would fall into ruin or survive only as curiosities; the remote theocratic societies of Tibet and Abyssinia would be overtaken. The entire continent of traditional knowledge which summoned Gurdjieff in 1887, lay in sunset's lurid glow, and dark shadows lengthened from the West.

In *Meetings with Remarkable Men* we journey to the interior in company with Gurdjieff's friends – priests, engineers, doctors, princes – men remarkable not from their surface appearance but from their resourcefulness, self-restraint, and compassion. We see them as though face to face; their words are lodged in us as though spoken directly in a moment of intimate quietness.

> I was not alone. There were all kinds of specialists among us. Everyone studied on the lines of his particular subject. Afterwards, when we foregathered, we put together everything we had found.

Gurdjieff was the moving spirit in this shadowy grouping; it coalesced around him in Alexandropol in 1889 and was formally constituted in 1895 as the Seekers of Truth – to study people, customs, literature, and monuments; to make experiments, observations and comparisons; and to give unstinting mutual help while serving a common aim. In his more jocular moments Gurdjieff referred to it as the seekers of pearls in manure.

Pogossian and Yelov were naturally involved from the start. More surprisingly Piotr Karpenko soon joined. Next to muster were relative strangers – yet essentially in harmony with Gurdjieff, sharing his critical temper and almost painful sense of question; and persuasible of sharing his ambitious hope. At length there had banded together some fifteen men and one woman, Vitvitskaia, numbering among them experts in archaeology, astronomy, engineering, mining, music and philology. Most were young and brought youth's qualities. They were raw, they had misconceptions. But no one following today the now faint imprint of their footsteps can fail to sense their rare willingness to pay in advance, by dint of effort, for the real knowledge they sought together. Any tendency towards giddy adventurism was soon grounded and sobered by 100 privations and exigencies. And if indeed they got understanding it was – arguably – less by sudden consummation in some Shambhala or Shangri-La, than in the long abrasive process of the search itself.

Gurdjieff was utterly possessed by his aim; every atom of stoicism inculcated in him by Giorgios Giorgiades was mobilized. His itinerary is impossible to confirm or even to discern with perfect clarity, but he certainly tramped through deserts and rocky wastes and made 'journeys to inaccessible places'. In so far as he contributed any speciality to the common aim – he concentrated on a certain 'something' which in the physical sciences is construable as vibration; in music as pitch and tonality; and in man as attention, energy and psychic state. Seen from his new viewpoint, everything was vibration. If only this subject could be mastered, its unifying rationale might tender in one breathtaking synthesis, an equal explanation of the paranormal and of organic life. It was for the sake of intimately knowing this 'something', that Gurdjieff plunged into the study of art, music, gesture and posture; that he immersed himself in traditional religious and secular dancing; and, above all, that he struggled to observe his inner and outer life.

The fact that a rolling stone gathers no moss raises here a basic question: where did Gurdjieff's money come from all this while? Not – as he ironically points out – from the Bolsheviks, from a black-magic organization, or from the legendary Georgian Prince Mukransky. Nor was he occupied as a priest as his father had hoped, or a doctor as Dean Borsh had wished; indeed there is more of Tiflis than of Kars in Gurdjieff's amazing self-portrait. We are shown a free-booting entrepreneur, materially reliant only on an astute wit and titanic bursts of energy. Nothing is too large and nothing too small to engage his attention; he deals shrewdly in antiques, oriental carpets and Chinese cloisonné; he services sewing machines and typewriters; trades in oil-wells and pickled herrings; cures drug addicts and psychosomatic patients by hypnotism; opens restaurants, works them up, and sells them; remodels corsets; poses as a sword-swallower; and even paints sparrows, off-loading them as 'American canaries'. It is summed up in Gurdjieff's masterly understatement – 'I also am businessman.'

He was indeed; and if any one could survive like this, he could. Yet twenty years is a long time to keep body and soul together, and the figure of the opportunist and jack-of-all-trades acquires more plausibility when framed within another more sombre legend. It is obstinately rumoured among intelligence circles, Russian émigré circles, and even among family and followers, that Gurdjieff conducted his long search while casually employed as a political agent. Official files and dossiers are lacking. Perhaps they no longer exist; perhaps, on some forgotten shelf in Moscow, Paris or New Delhi, they lie surrendered to the spider and the scuttering mouse. They would show – if circumstantial evidence means anything – an intriguing gallery of Gurdjieffs: in 1887 a courier for the Armenian protectionist society the Armenakans; from 1890 an associate of the Armenian secret society the Dashnakzutiun; by 1896 a combatant for the Hellenic Spartacist society the Ethnike Hetairia; and throughout the decade from 1898 to 1908 a Tsarist political agent.

Admittedly Gurdjieff's memoirs are not explicit here. He alludes disapprovingly but vaguely to 'all sorts of terrors flowing from ... violent events'; he grudgingly recalls 'conversations with various revolutionaries ... first in Italy and then in Switzerland'; he instances 'journeys undertaken on behalf of some government or other for a certain political aim'. Perhaps he comes closest to full candour in his declaration:

> I had, in accordance with the peculiar conditions of my life, the possibility of gaining access to the so-called 'holy-of-holies' of nearly all hermetic organisations such as religious, philosophical, occult, political and mystic societies, congregations, parties, unions, etc, which were inaccessible to the ordinary man.

What are such conditions and facilities if not those of a member of the secret service? And thirty years later, when Gurdjieff arrived in Constantinople in 1920, he was – however mistakenly – placed under surveillance by British Intelligence as a dangerous political agent.

Granted Gurdjieff's link with these disparate political movements, what was the degree of his emotional engagement? No personal embroilment whatsoever, reply most apologists. The fretful and exquisite complications of nineteenth-century Greek and Armenian nationalism, and the operatic death-throes of Tsarist and Ottoman imperialism, held no conceivable interest for a man addressing the meaning of organic life on earth. Once Gurdjieff had glimpsed his goal, his circumstantial alliances were governed solely by a ruthless pragmatism: 'It was all the same to me how I got there, whether on the devil's back or even arm-in-arm with the priest Vlakov.'

Au fond – so continues the apologia – he was wholly a-political. He was internationalist. He was in the world but not of it. And Gurdjieff himself boldly endorses this line:

> Even my propensity during this period for always travelling and trying to place myself wherever in the process of the mutual existence of people there proceeded sharp energetic events, such as civil war, revolutions, etc, had sprung also from this my ... [spiritual] aim.

What is the strength of this?

There existed, doubtless, even in the youthful Gurdjieff, the seed of that extraordinary impartiality, which in later years elevated him high above the arena, rendering him less an historical than a transhistorical figure. But at twenty-eight? Was it the case then? What could Gurdjieff's feelings have been when in 1894 Abdul the Damned – the evil genius of the Armenians – launched his Turkish footsoldiers, and incited savage Kurdish cavalry, in the first of those genocidal attacks which would decimate and scatter the Armenian nation? When twenty-four villages, with all their inhabitants, simply disappeared in the space of a few hours? When the streets of Erzurum ran with the blood of 80,000 slaughtered Armenians? And above all when the crescent drifted east to threaten his mother and her family in Alexandropol? To deny Gurdjieff a strong reaction here is to deny his fundamental humanity; and to deny those feelings translation into action is to miss the very essence of the man.

Once Gurdjieff was assured of his parents' safety, he took passage for Crete under the stress of a quite different impulse. He remembered a legend recited by his father: how ages ago, 7000 years before the Noachian flood, a great civilization had existed on 'the island of Haninn ... approximately where Greece is now situated'; and how all its complex and long redundant affairs had been guided by the 'Imastun Brotherhood', a caste of wise men occupied with astrology and telepathy. If the poem could survive, passing from mouth to mouth, from generation to generation, until it reached his father in remote Armenia – might not the oral tradition burn more brightly nearer its source? Might it not illuminate his own question? As usual commonsense rebuked hope, but something in the poem was infinitely stronger than commonsense.

Though Gurdjieff came to Crete essentially as a seeker, he came circumstantially as a revolutionary. The mountainous island – populated by Greeks but dominated by Turkey – seethed with a discontent which the Ethnike Hetairia, gliding at will among the people, fomented and shaped. For the ferocious, bearded, hook-nosed Cretan *palikares* of the Sfakia region, revolution was something between a profession and a religious vocation. In February 1896, the Greeks rose up again: in spasms of long-rehearsed violence, a ferocious affirmation of liberty was ferociously denied. Gurdjieff was shot. (And not, as he protests, by a 'stray bullet' but by one which found in the 'Black Greek' a legitimate target.)

How the wounded Gurdjieff found his way back to Alexandropol, by way of Jerusalem and Cairo, is obscure. . . . Egypt at least was familiar and evocative ground: it was here that the very first expedition with Pogossian had foundered, and here long ago in 1887, while scratching a living as a tourist guide to the Sphinx and the Pyramid of Cheops, that Gurdjieff had first encountered his 'elder comrade and closest friend', the Russian Prince Yuri Lubovedsky. The two men's lifelong bond had arisen instantaneously from their shared fascination in discovering a map of pre-sand Egypt. 'My God! What I experienced in that moment! I shall never forget it.'

What conceivably is meant by this 'pre-sand Egypt'? Some historico-geographical Egypt? A green Edenic pasture hunted over by paleolithic or neolithic man, before the encroachment of the sands? Not impossibly. Yet here as elsewhere a dull uncomplemented literalism merely invites ridicule. Gurdjieff connected Egypt with Atlantis, Atlantis with the subconscious mind, and the subconscious with man's most precious possession, his buried conscience.

Lubovedsky's intense preoccupation with such themes had begun years earlier in Moscow, with the unbearable death of his young wife; thenceforward he had dedicated all his energies to travel, chiefly in Africa, India, Afghanistan, Ceylon and Persia:

> The prince was a very rich man, but he spent all his wealth on 'searches' and on organising special expeditions to the places where he thought he might find an answer to his questions. He lived for a long time in certain monasteries and met many persons with interests similar to his own.

As the type and icon of an aristocratic Russian savant, Lubovedsky holds his place; but as the exemplar and dearest companion of George Ivanovitch Gurdjieff he disappoints. He does not seem altogether real: his aura is pure white; his idealism is unspotted; his goodness, love and patience veil him in a smokescreen of sanctity. Even his fox terrier Jack is dog *sans reproche*. There exists in Gurdjieffian literature one powerful cameo which seems to distil Lubovedsky's purest essence, but intriguingly enough it is a passage written decades later describing Gurdjieff himself. Perhaps there is some clue here?

Implanted in Gurdjieff's chapter on Prince Lubovedsky – like a sour black pip in an over-bland fruit – is a separate chapter on a certain 'Soloviev'. Where Lubovedsky is all sweetness and light, Soloviev is gallows-bait; where Lubovedsky verges on being an abstraction, one can almost smell Soloviev's sweat. Driven by circumstance from pillar to post, he has become a liar, a cheat, a thief, and a counterfeiter, and is now a pathetic slave to drink. Although his chance contact with Gurdjieff in Bokhara in 1898 has its intrinsic drama, more intriguing by far is a curious parallelism. Gurdjieff too, at that particular moment, was unusually full of self-reproach – perceiving himself as 'spoiled and depraved to the core'; preoccupied with food, sex, and revenge; and surrendered to 'self-love, vanity, pride, jealousy and other passions'. He too felt enslaved – not by drink but by his reliance on quite formidable powers of hypnotism and telepathy which he had developed along the way:

> We finally brought them into such a state of hypnosis that one could stick a large pin into their chests, sew up their mouths and, placing them between two chairs ... put enormous weights on their stomachs.

There is indeed something horrifyingly exploitative in Gurdjieff's tone of voice at this time.

Independently both men now swear abstinence. 'Help me, O Lord,' cries Soloviev, 'to be able never again to drink this poison which has brought me to such a life.' And Gurdjieff affirms, 'I take an oath to remember never to satisfy this inherency of mine and thereby to deprive myself from satisfying most of my vices.' The essential pattern of sin, repentance, and redemption veers so near to perfect congruence, that it might almost refer to one man.

By 1895 Gurdjieff was widely travelled: he had already been to Mecca and Medina in disguise; to Thebes with Lubovedsky; and to Abyssinia, the Sudan, and Babylon with a certain Professor Skridlov.

It is nevertheless, the years 1896–1900 which are tendered as the period of his heroic journeys. We glimpse the now formidable figure of the 'Tiger of Turkestan' struggling ever onward, bowed against the wind, on the horizon of probability. Sometimes he is in company with Lubovedsky and the Seekers; sometimes starkly alone.

We may stumblingly follow him to Tabriz, Turkestan, Orenburg, Sverdlovsk, Siberia, Bokhara, Merv, Kafiristan, the Gobi desert, Chardzou, the Pamirs, and northern India. 'In one place symbol, in another technique and in another dance.' His secret path does not cross with those of the great geographers of this epoch: with Sven Hedin, Sir Aurel Stein, Albert von Le Coq, Paul Pelliot or Count Kozui Otani. He does not plunder rich artefacts as they do, but unlike them he professedly finds his way to a source of primordial knowledge and values.

Gurdjieff's provocative claim to have found and entered 'the chief Sarmoung Monastery' is in effect a litmus test, differentiating literal minds from those preferring allegory. The strength – and also the weakness – of the literalists' case is that the monastery's where-abouts remains so plausibly unspecifiable: Gurdjieff was obliged to make the journey blindfolded; contemporary maps were defective; and above all he was sworn to eternal secrecy. Basically what Gurdjieff tells us is that sometime in 1898 or 1899 he and Soloviev started out from Bokhara with horses, asses, and four Kara-Kirghiz guides. After crossing rivers and mountains, they reached their goal at sunset on the twelfth day. Bokhara is – needless to say – an ancient city on the Silk Road, to the north of Afghanistan, which had fallen under Russian suzerainty in 1873. Given its grim environs, the Sarmoung magic circle can hardly be more than 500 miles in diameter; and of this we can provisionally discount the northern and western segments, which verge respectively on the Kizil Kum and Kara Kum deserts. Indeed Gurdjieff's tantalizing references to the valleys of the rivers Zarovshan and Pyandzh (or Ab-i-Pandj), point us directly eastward along 'the golden road to Sarmakand'. Some-where in the vicious tangle of mountains just to the south ... somewhere ... somewhere.

Here, at this critical point, the geographers' brave exegesis peters out, like a river lost in the sands. The allegorists, perhaps more adroitly, construe Gurdjieff's entire monastery story symbolically, beginning with a wayside episode involving a dangerous rope bridge over a deep gorge. The hero on the 'perilous bridge' is noted as the very stuff of myth and folklore: in the West we have Lancelot's sword-bridge, and Bifrost the Scandinavian rainbow bridge; in the East there is Sirat, the Muslims' bridge over hell, and the awesome Chinvat bridge of the Zoroastrian last judgement. As to the remote and secret spiritual centre ringed by mountains, it is a glyph which, as 'Shambala', pervades Tibetan and Mongolian culture; and in the West has touched minds as diverse as Helena Blavatsky, René Daumal, Alexandra David-Neel, Mircea Eliade, René Guénon, James Hilton, Ferdinand Ossendowski, Nicholas Roerich, Guiseppe Tucci and Emanuel Swedenborg. Note too observe the symbolists, warming to their task, that Gurdjieff's monastery has three main courtyards – surely these are the exoteric, mesoteric, and esoteric circles of humanity. It follows that within the courtyard every detail – even the inlay on certain equipment – is heavy with coded significance: 'Since ebony was brought from Africa and mother-of-pearl from India, this suggests the apparatus represents a synthesis of Semitic and Aryan teachings.' All in all, the symbolists' 'Sarmoung Monastery' is such stuff as dreams are made of – though of course the better class of prophetic dreams, which have their place in any spiritual topography.

The Sarmoung issue cannot simply be smiled away: as the purported source of Gurdjieff's profoundest insights, Sacred Dances and enneagram symbol[8] it is central to his story. Of our many attendant problems by far the trickiest is the want of an agreed historical basis for the name itself. Already a dozen lax and incompatible theories have been sucked in to fill this notable vacuum. Sarmoung and Sarmakand are close phonetically and geographically – perhaps there is some link? Then again, it was under the Samanid dynasty that Bokhara, in the tenth century, attained its brief and glittering zenith as a centre of civilization, art, and learning, producing amongst others Avicenna author of the Canon of Medicine. Alternatively, the word *Sarman* in ancient Persian may be interpreted – by those so predisposed – to suggest the essence of Zoroastrian tradition and enlightenment. The obvious difficulty here is that the bearers of all these traditions – certainly in the Emirate of Bokhara – ended up on the skull piles of Genghiz Khan's Golden Horde in AD 1219. The incoming Mongol religion was the powerful, unstructured, nature sorcery of the 'shamans' – a name itself sometimes chronicled with spellings close to Sarmoung. At this point, all the historian is left with is Gurdjieff's infuriatingly unfulfilled promise: 'The details of everything in this monastery, what it represented, what was done there and how, I shall perhaps recount at some time in a special book.' If we end completely baffled, it is presumably because he wanted it so.

As the twentieth century began, one of Gurdjieff's great goals was still unattained – the mountain citadel of Tibet. How could a temperament like his neglect the challenge of its sealed borders? How could he possibly resist its potent blend of Tantric, Mantric and Mudra practices, its 'priestly mixture of Sivaite mysticism, magic and ... demonolatry'? How could he not feel magnetized by the very existence of the forbidden city of Lhasa and the monasteries of Drepung, Sera, and Ganden? – those vast holy ant-heaps where the prayer-wheels turned and the gongs strained, and, in an atmosphere of unbelievable spiritual incandescence and material filth, so many ancient secrets were cached away.

He could not. Nor, fortunately, did he need to, since his personal aim now chimed in so perfectly with his political utility. Gurdjieff has left us a scathing memoir of his formal presentation to His Imperial Majesty Nicholas II, among 'beings who appeared there in all the blaze of various what are called "orders" and "regimentals"'. His vignette has the unmistakable ring of authenticity. We may conclude that over the years Gurdjieff had become a Tsarist pawn in that 'Great Game' tirelessly played out between Pan-Russian imperialists and the British Raj, for superior influence in Afghanistan, Chitral and Kashmir. Any white pawn now advanced to the Tibetan square was guaranteed the necessary roubles and porters and doctored papers.

Given his linguistic range and Greco-Armenian cast of features, Gurdjieff's best hope of penetration was from the north-west, disguised as a Transcaspian Buddhist, a Kalmuck from Astrakhan; the speculative biographer may thus, with reasonable propriety set him climbing the Mustagh pass in the spring of 1901. For a year or more he lingered in Upper Tibet, preoccupied with the 'Red Hat' lamas. He studied the Tibetan language, ritual, dance, medicine, and above all psychic techniques. Long years afterwards he would fan the rumour that he took a wife in Tibet and fathered two children there. Whatever the validity of this family idyll, it was shattered in 1902, when, during some obscure affray between mountain clans, Gurdjieff 'was punctured by a second stray bullet' and brought again to the brink of annihilation.

Loyal friends – rendered anonymous by time – somehow got him back down the Mustagh pass to Yangi Hissar, an oasis huddled on the western rim of the dreadful Taklamakan desert. Here he hovered between life and death. At length – because his body was 'steel-cast', and because he received the loving attention of three European and two Tibetan doctors – he recovered. Perhaps his physical weakness and the utter strangeness of his situation contributed to his ensuing mystical experience, when the dry doctrine of correspondences – 'As above: so below' – suddenly blossomed for him with intimations of awesome potential and awesome responsibility:

> He is God and I am God! Whatever possibilities He has in relation to the presences of the universe, such possibilities and impossibilities I should also have in relation to the world subordinate to me. He is God of all the world and also of my outer world. I am God also, although only of my inner world.

This exhilarating insight was to permeate all his future thinking, to illuminate his question about organic life, and to intensify his long hard struggle for self-mastery.

The urgency of Gurdjieff's re-ascent to Tibet reflected its worsening political predicament. 'After three or four months of unconscious life, for me there flowed still another year of constant physical tenseness and unusual psychic contrivance.' External events were gathering speed: Sir Francis Edward Younghusband crossed the Tibetan–Sikkim frontier with his peppery little army on 5 July 1903, impelled by patriotic feeling, a deep mystical love of desolate places, and a personal fancy to 'smash those selfish filthy lecherous Lamas'. The party in Tibet which forlornly opposed him, is so dimly lit by history that only its extraordinary leader, the Tsanit Khanpo, Agwhan Dordjieff, can now be seen with much clearness. But somewhere in profoundest shadow Gurdjieff must be suspected. The rape of Lhasa in 1904 moved him not to anger but to sorrow. He is silent concerning the 700 ill-led Tibetan soldiers mown down at Guru in one ninety-second burst from Younghusband's Maxim guns; they and their ancestral broadswords and their pathetic matchlock guns, so prettily embossed with turquoise and coral, belong to the irredeemable history of crime. When Gurdjieff does bitterly protest it is about the shooting of a single man (an illuminated lama whose untimely death severed irretrievably a unique initiatic line begun in the eighth century by Padma Sambhava, the father of Tibetan Tantrism); this seemingly slight event he presents as the root cause of disproportionate calamities.

Although this focus would seem sheer elitism, the Gurdjieff of 1904 had in fact been deeply stirred by the anguish in Armenia and Tibet; he perceived man as deeply asleep, blindly and aimlessly suffering, torn by war and passion, fouling everything around him; and yet, through a strange flaw in his nature, clinging ingeniously to the very instruments which wound, the patterns which betray. All this he sensed as the 'Terror of the Situation'. He longed to comprehend – and even to challenge – the dreadful process of war, and the hysteria underlying it: 'I must discover, at all costs, some manner or means for destroying in people the predilection for suggestibility which causes them to fall easily under the influence of "mass hypnosis".'

Experiencing, as never before, 'the being-impulse called "love-of-kind"', Gurdjieff accordingly broadens his aim: a ruthless compassion is henceforward to complement wisdom; the heart is to soften the eye; benign intervention is to ensue from understanding. With ironic self-deprecation he mocks his new 'two-headed worm of inquisitiveness', but more than inquisitiveness is entailed – he is aspiring towards his strange ideal, the 'good egotist'.

The hydropsy which Gurdjieff developed in 1904 obliged him to leave the high altitudes of Tibet, and he struggled home. His parents had long since abandoned Kars and moved back to their old house in Alexandropol; his father, serene and vigorous, was now in his seventies; his mother was undaunted and his sisters thriving; only the handsome Dmitri was away breaking hearts in Tiflis. Gurdjieff must have seemed a strange son and a strange brother: enigmatic, impressive, driven, vulnerable; unestablished in life, and, as far as anyone knew, unmarried. Having been fêted and fretted over like the prodigal returned, he rested and diverted himself with small things. Imagination may grant him some autumnal sunshine in the little rose garden, and even set him practising 'The Peaks of Manchuria' and 'Valse Ozhidanie' on the mouth-organ given him by one of his sisters.

He could not remain inactive for long; his search had residual momentum. Although he had vowed with genuine passion to abandon hypnotism, he was re-routed to this very study by his aim to liberate men from their suggestibility. In Alexandropol he commenced interesting experiments with the 'exteriorization of sensitivity'; he dreamt of entering a Sufi monastery in Central Asia where dervishes studied mehkeness or the 'taking-away-of-responsibility'. At last, in the dead of winter 1904, Gurdjieff embraced his parents and set out again, but – either with poetic justice or preposterous ill-luck – fell an immediate victim to the revolutionary psychosis simmering in the Caucasian viceroyalty, as elsewhere in the Tsar's vast empire. Near the Chiatura railway tunnel 'this third bullet . . . was plunked into me, of course unconsciously, by some "charmer" from among . . .

the so-called Russian army, chiefly Cossacks, and the so-called
Gourians.'

Yet again Gurdjieff marginally escaped death; and one companion
(ostensibly 'very weak' but actually displaying exemplary resource
and loyalty), brought him to safety. Though Tiflis and Dmitri lay
a mere eighty-five miles away, uncontrollable events now swept
the wounded Gurdjieff eastward, first to Ashkabad, then to his
beloved Yangi Hissar where he completed his recovery, and finally to
Tashkent.

Even in 1905 Tashkent was no mean city; for forty years this
expropriated stronghold of the Uzbeks had been developed as the
seat of the Governor-General of Russian Turkestan. Gurdjieff the
political agent and Gurdjieff the student of mass suggestibility must
have found convergent interest in the fierce anti-government strikes
and demonstrations which agitated the railway workers between 1905
and 1907. Doubtless too he had some selective interest in the Alisher
Navoi Library and the rare library of the Mufti of Central Asia. But
the true fascination of Tashkent was as Gurdjieff's proving ground.

The year 1908 is an incisive watershed. Until then Gurdjieff had
been overwhelmingly intent on learning; now at last he began to
think of attracting pupils. He had acquired and crystallized, over a
period of twenty years, a formidable repertoire of powers, techniques,
and ideas. He had made a unique study of Sacred Dance; his entire
being had evolved; and, not least, he felt that he finally understood –
as far as that is granted to man – the unsuspected significance of
organic and human life. Meanwhile however, the fellowship of the
Seekers had been scattered: Pogossian and Yelov were about their
own business; Soloviev had died in the Gobi desert; so had Piotr
Karpenko in Central Russia; and Prince Yuri Lubovedsky had gone
to his conscious death in the Olman Monastery. Gurdjieff alone
remained; and – now in his early forties – felt on his shoulders the
stupendous responsibility for conveying all this accumulated knowledge into the future, and for awakening mankind to the 'Terror of
the Situation'.

He began very strangely indeed, offering fragments of truth in the
form of a lie. His apprentice advertisements set a precedent in intentional bad taste: they are pervaded by a spirit of blatant self-parody
and provocative boasting – as if positively courting that epithet
'charlatan', which was fated to pursue him to the grave and beyond.
He gave himself out as a professional hypnotist; a curer of alcoholism, drug addiction, and sexual disorders; a 'professor-instructor' in

supernatural sciences; and a 'maestro' in evoking 'phenomena-of-the-beyond'. His venue certainly was appropriate. In Old Tashkent the effects of opium and hashish were harrowingly evident, and in New Tashkent vodka was a curse; the market place was actually called the 'Drunken Bazaar' and most of the intelligentsia were intoxicated by ideas. As elsewhere in pre-revolutionary Russia, interest in occultism, theosophy, and spiritualism was rampant; among the bored colonial society of New Tashkent groups flourished everywhere and fashionable seances were held in the palace of Grand-Prince Nikolai Konstantinovich.

Gurdjieff by no means viewed these gatherings through rose-coloured spectacles, regarding them on the contrary as 'workshops-for-the-perfection-of-psychopathism'. They were merely expedient in providing him with a social entrée and a ready-made platform. His attitude was characterized by the strangest blend of compassion and dispassion; although he earned the gratitude of many physical and spiritual derelicts by invariably 'rendering conscientious aid to sufferers', his personal and secret aim remained the investigation of human types and psychology: 'I began to observe and study various manifestations in the waking state of the psyche of these trained and freely moving "Guinea-Pigs", allotted to me by Destiny for my experiments.' It is outrageously expressed but true nonetheless: if Gurdjieff were to teach successfully in the West, the mentality, idiom and typology of Europeanized Russian 'guinea-pigs' was very much to the point. After decades among Asiatics, it was imperative he refresh his perceptions and modulate his tone of voice.

From this singular time we have our earliest authenticated photo of Gurdjieff. *Ecce Homo!* There he stands. It is the man's eyes which make the first and strongest impression; they pierce and assess, as if referring back to us our indiscreet questions. What dangerous voltage of thought is insulated by that neutral brow? Why the improbable formalism of the European dress coat, winged collar, and Napoleonic stance? How does the compact figure impart its quality of gathered power – arguably even of majesty, of the royal afflatus 'termed by Great Solomon, King of Judah, *tzvarnoharno*'?

An old photograph, a daguerreotype – never speaking, never moving – provokes a curiosity it cruelly fails to satisfy. Here surely is the very Gurdjieff who was curing vices and fluttering the spiritualist dovecots of Tashkent; and who, to finance his impending teaching mission, was frenziedly opening stores, restaurants and cinemas, trading in oil-wells and fisheries, arranging cattle drives from Kashgar, and investing in rare carpets and Chinese cloisonné. Ironically enough, a speaking photograph might only confound confusion. Certainly Gurdjieff's claim that he established his first three groups in successive cities in Turkestan, sidling crabwise towards Russia, has no ring of conviction, and his half-intimation that he obtained a teaching mandate from some Brotherhood in Central Asia (conceivably the Sarmoung), and even referred many pupils to the monastery, invites a decent scepticism. Doubtless these last days of Gurdjieff's Asiatic calendar were lived as intensely and richly as ever, but he presents them in wild bombastic terms, as though mocking the historian's growing impatience for exactitude: who, for example, can guess where he was and how he was circumstanced on 13 September 1911?

Was our man finally in Moscow, suitcase in hand? Or was this conceivably his forty-fifth birthday? Or the occasion he truly began to teach? Such hypotheses are tempting because 13 September 1911 was undoubtedly a red-letter day (or perhaps better say a black-letter day) when Gurdjieff took a second oath, binding himself for twenty-one years to lead a high-principled but 'absolutely unnatural life, absolutely irreconcilable, too, in every way with the traits that had entrenched themselves in my individuality'. There is more here than a renewed abjuration of hypnotism; there is a steely determination not to allow his charisma or *tzvarnoharno* to poison his life's work; not to create a fashionable cult, a mass following of spiritual jellyfish; not to enjoy brilliant short-term success at the cost of long-term oblivion. Instead he resolves to disguise himself, regality and all, by conscious acting; and (under the maxim 'Outwardly play a role: inwardly never identify') to become in effect invisible. His chosen theatricality will, more often than not, positively invite blame – masking Lubovedsky with Soloviev, and acting out the mountebank with ferocious relish.

A strange passenger indeed to arrive at Moscow railway station! A modern *Boddhisattva* entering the city with bliss-bestowing hands; a moustachioed prophet carrying in his portmanteau an urgent, radical and overwhelming message; an ideological carpet dealer, who has cunningly woven together all those precious heterogeneous strands of knowledge gathered with his friends. Now myth at last evaporates, like the engine's steam, and history reveals George Ivanovitch Gurdjieff 'moving like a being apart from other men, bearing in his presence the weight of his function and obligation and unfelt by the crowd which, unknowing, left a little space around him'.

PART II

✤

The Revelation in Question

---❖---

THE REVELATION IN QUESTION

From the moment Gurdjieff set foot in Moscow until his last poignant days in Paris, his life moved directly under his compulsion to teach. If circumstance provides the bare bones of life, his ideas are its very marrow. Even the most enthusiastic narrative biographer (or literary critic) must therefore pause to grapple with the revelation in question.

What then precisely is Gurdjieff's teaching? This natural line of inquiry seems to promise clarification, but is spoilt by its own rigour. Time deadens authorized versions like hemlock, and Gurdjieff (though he came close) never actually issued one; the vivifying power of his ideas entails the moment, the conditions, the pupil's type, state, receptivity and potential. One solitary constant emerges: Gurdjieff's ideas and methods, in all their breathtaking scope, are constellated around the idea of conscious evolution.

Many interesting people found in Gurdjieff a spring which answered to their special thirst; their need, shorn of its accidental elements, was simple, and his response simple. Then no one need fear to meet in Gurdjieff intellectual virtuosity for its own sake; he considered most of the intelligentsia as titillators or intellectual masturbators. Despite this essential simplicity, Gurdjieff did not come West in order to market some sherbet-flavoured vagary, or offer impractical advice that everyone should be good and kind. His ideas had virility, form, and content; one simply cannot approach them without attention and dogged staying power. J. B. Priestley understates in warning, 'In order to study this movement, nobody will have to do any intellectual slumming.'

The rare elements which overtopped Gurdjieff's ideological crucible had cost twenty years to gather. Firing and melting and recasting
them, he produced a semantic critique, an epistemology, cosmology,
cosmogony, psychology, human typology, phenomenology of consciousness, and practical *Existenzphilosophie* – an astonishing set of
ideas and techniques which stirred Philip Mairet to proclaim: 'No
system of gnostic soteriological philosophy that has been published
to the modern world is comparable to it in power and intellectual
articulation.'

Such a compliment from a complete stranger might have surprised
Gurdjieff, for even on his own lips he never completely trusted
ordinary language to convey the spectrum of his work. At the
infra-red end so-to-speak words were superfluous. 'I teach', he said
tartly, 'that when it rains the pavements get wet.' At the ultra-violet
end, words were impotent: by definition there existed no words
adequate to describe a metaphysical essence which lay beyond them,
in a vibrating and active silence. As to the communication spectrum's
middle band, it was unfortunately occupied by a Tower of Babel, a
'confusion of tongues', where any feasible meaning was tragically
warped by each man's linguistic and cultural subjectivity.

Gurdjieff accordingly wrestled with the problem of transmitting
his teaching, like Jacob with the angel; and was similarly obliged to
vary his approach and grip. In early days he favoured an idiom so
precise it had almost the quality of gunmetal; in later years one of
unbelievable complication and opacity. Simultaneously he cultivated
his gift for non-verbal transmission: he taught through diagrams and
symbols; he taught through money, through alochol and through the
preparation, cooking and eating of food; he taught through music –
building his neo-Platonic ideas into the very structure of his compositions. He taught through his Sacred Dances[13] (and at least a handful
of dedicated pupils appeared transformed by bodily deciphering his
'universal language' of posture, gesture and movement). Perhaps most
remarkable of all were those moments when – abandoning all external procedures – Gurdjieff projected a special doctrine of attention
through his sheer being and 'the exacting benevolence of his gaze'.

By now it is clear that no potted version of Gurdjieff's teaching can
remotely do it justice, still less have the transforming power which is
its distinctive hallmark. Nor should we be surprised. After all, if
Richard Rees' breathless assertion can be credited, 'It is scarcely an
exaggeration to say that Gurdjieff undertook to teach his pupils how
to secrete God-stuff.'

Gurdjieff believed in God. He had, of course (like Schweitzer, Jung, Simone Weil, Teilhard de Chardin, Buber and Jaspers), somehow to accommodate his conviction to a cultural establishment which still today sets its voguish heel on the numinous as a topic for polite conversation. As Gurdjieff grew older, he grew bolder. In an early teaching period – intent not to provoke the 'edgy resistance of today's "a-religious" man' – he alluded bleakly to 'the Absolute'; but a decade later, confessing his deeper reverence, he extolled 'Our Almighty Omni-Loving Common Father Uni-Being Creator Endlessness'. Even this personification fell prudently short of our conventional stereotype, at which Gurdjieff gently laughed: ('They picture this famous "God" of theirs exactly as an "Old Jew".'): in his own conception, however patriarchal, there remained ample scope for a theology of subtle refinement.

The sublime myths of creation and man's fall have come down to us from the infancy of humanity; that infancy which, in its innocence and wonder, centred naked man in the context of a universal question and dignified him as an icon of great meaning. Difficult to guess how literally Gurdjieff believed the modern myth of his own devising; it suffices perhaps that at the symbolic or bardic level it projects his deepest insights. He is silent (as confident science[9] falls silent) before the primal enigma, the grandfather of all insoluble riddles – namely the miraculous existence of 'something' rather than nothing. He blithely assumes his First Cause and his cosmic stage properties. But once he is granted his premise of a dramatic universe, Gurdjieff develops a mystery play of rare persuasion and heroic proportions. Whether it amounts to a new revelation must be left to the sober judgement of history; certainly it will light here and there a candle of spirituality in a darkness currently profound.

Gurdjieff's 'Common Father Endlessness' is not located in Heaven. (Both 'Heaven' and 'Hell' he regarded as malign inventions of Babylonian dualism). Nor does his God belong to some ethereal or psychic plane, some wispy parallel world, peculiarly accessible through drugs or ouija boards or wafers. He is centred here in our vast but ultimately apprehensible material universe, on the 'Most Most Holy Sun Absolute'.

In the beginning only the Sun Absolute was physically concentrated in endless space, which was already charged with the primordial cosmic substance *Etherokrilno*. Because this nebulous

Etherokrilno was in static equilibrium, the super-sun existed and was maintained by our Common Father, quite independently of outside stimulus, through the internal action of his laws and under the dispensation termed *Autoegocrat* ('I keep everything under my control'). There and thus Our Father might have existed forever, delightfully choired by his Cherubim and Seraphim ... might have, but for the Merciless Heropass.

The Heropass is Gurdjieff's name for time – God's shadow or alter ego, the inescapable concomitant of existence: just and pitiless, blending subjectively with all composite forms, and, in its blending, destroying them forever. Here we revisit Locke's familiar idea, 'Time is a perpetual perishing', and Kipling's, 'Time like an ever-rolling stream bears all its sons away' – but with the significant Gurdjieffian addendum that time is a holy entity, coeval with God.

Immediately our Common Father perceived time's remorseless entropic effect – the infinitely slow but irreversible diminution in volume of his dwelling-place the Sun Absolute – he urgently sought a remedy. Bending all his divine will, he issued from himself the 'Word-God' *Theomertmalogos*, which, in one stupendous dialectical coup (strangely redolent of contemporary astronomy's 'Big Bang'), reacted everywhere with the *Etherokrilno* to create our *Megalocosmos* or great universe. Henceforward this sacred and living creation was nourished by an open system of symbiosis or reciprocal maintenance, termed by Gurdjieff *Trogoautoegocrat* ('Eating myself, I am maintained'): throughout a vast holistic eco-system, each order of beings now produced the very energies or substances which guaranteed the survival of other groups. Such was God's amended scheme of things and time itself would not prevail against it.

So God had won ... and lost. He had won by ensuring, for himself and the Holy Sun Absolute, perpetual immunity from entropy; he had lost by creating a universe with which – especially at its involutionary frontiers – he could enjoy only the most attenuated contact. From the first syllable of recorded time, the latent omnipotence of God's unmanifested being had been subtly contradicted; but now – world by descending world – his potency suffered progressive degradation. He was like the Emperor in Kafka's haunting allegory, 'The Great Wall of China', who immured in the innermost palace of the Forbidden City, was fatally unable to project his imperial will into remote provinces; he was like a deviser of games, who, once having settled the rules, could not himself beat the Ace of trumps with the two of hearts; he was like the deists' 'absentee landlord'.

Henceforward all God's inferior creation was necessarily maintained in its new and dynamic equilibrium not by him directly, but through the mechanical action of two primary sacred laws: *Triamazikamno* the Law of Three, and *Heptaparparashinokh* the Law of Seven –the former governing the causality of each isolated phenomenon; the latter governing the trajectory of every process or series of phenomena.

Gurdjieff's Law of Three, unsurprisingly, lays down that each phenomenon, from the cosmic to the sub-atomic, springs from the interaction of no less and no more than three forces: the first, or Holy Affirming, being active; the second, or Holy Denying, passive; and the third, or Holy Reconciling, neutralizing. His formulation, 'The higher blends with the lower in order to actualise the middle', is clear and easy to example: the sperm merges with the ovum to create the embryo (or alternatively the sexual drive is inhibited, giving rise to 'sublimation' or 'complex'); a teacher relates with a pupil ensuring transmission; *Theomertmalogos* animates *Etherokrilno* to actualize the *Megalocosmos* – and so on.

But although this 'sacred dialectic' is straightforward, the Law of Three in its totality should not be written off as simplistic. Gurdjieff would not have been Gurdjieff had he not also countenanced another and pretty incompatible version – here the third force was not itself the resultant, but the arbiter, agency, or catalyst yielding the resultant. This slightly more complex model breeds its distinctive family of examples: flour and water become bread only when bonded by fire; plaintiff and defendant have their case resolved only through a judge; nucleus and electrons constitute an atom only within an electromagnetic field. In this variant, the third or reconciling force is to Gurdjieff what the Holy Ghost is to the Christians, time to Darwinians, and history used to be to Marxists: with it all things are possible.

In any case time and reciprocal maintenance ensure that no phenomenon can stand in splendid isolation: 'The higher blends with the lower in order to actualise the middle *and thus becomes either higher for the preceding lower, or lower for the succeeding higher.*' Thus each event is quickly braided into a process which is itself subject to new constraint – the Law of Seven.

The Law of Seven is undoubtedly difficult to grasp or précis, and Gurdjieff himself left no tidy formula. Seemingly it comes to this:

THE REVELATION IN QUESTION 45

Every completing process must without exception have seven discrete phases: construing these as an ascending or descending series of seven notes or pitches, the frequency of vibrations must develop *irregularly*, with two predictable deviations (just where semi-tones are missing between Mi-Fa and Si-Do in the untempered modern major scale EDCBAGFE.)

The absence of straight lines in nature; the customary slackening of human effort; the diversion of enterprises from their original objective; the obscene transition from the Sermon on the Mount to the Spanish Inquisition – all such phenomena arise from the two inescapable deflections inherent in the Law of Seven. Exceptionally, adds Gurdjieff, a process or octave can indeed perfectly maintain its original line – but only when (by accident or design) extraneous and exactly appropriate 'shocks' plug the intervals Mi-Fa and Si-Do.

Gurdjieff's most stupendous and contentious example of the Law of Seven is his 'Ray of Creation'. In this primordial descending octave, Do is God or the Absolute, Si is the universe, La is our own constellation, Sol our sun, Fa the sun's planets, Mi the earth and Re the moon. Gurdjieff's apparent decoding of a cosmological solfeggio (*DOminus* the Lord, *SIdera* the stars, *LActea* the Milky Way, the *SOlar* system – right down to *REgina Coelis*, the moon or Queen of Heaven) is a fascinating historical distraction. The Ray of Creation is far more rewardingly dwelt on as a philosophical model of the universe, which comes as near as is humanly possible to reconciling the irreconcilable: involution and evolution, determinism and freewill, entropy and negative entropy, suffering and God's benignity.

But how does the Ray cope with the discontinuity of vibrations? – here unsuspectingly we have arrived at an existential question for mankind!

The break between Do and Si (the *Megalocosmos*) is magisterially bridged by *Fiat!*, the will of the Absolute, and the octave descends unimpeded to Fa our planetary system. At this remove however, God's potency has become so attenuated that his direct aid in reaching note Mi is out of the question: 'In order to fill the "interval" at this point ... a special apparatus is created for receiving and transmitting the influences coming from the planets. This apparatus is *organic life on earth*.'

With this extraordinary concept of a global organic transformer or filter of cosmic rays, Gurdjieff presents the hard-won solution to his burning question concerning the 'precise significance, in general, of the life process on earth of all outward forms of living creatures.' Very few geo-chemists today would trouble to challenge a 'bio-sphere' proposition of sorts, but Gurdjieff's emphatic version in his epoch was strikingly original. Like some sudden and terrible climatic reverse, his vision withers all our humanistic dreams. The proud and beautiful apparatus of organic life has never existed in its own right or for its own sake, but entirely for the unsuspected and alien advantage of the planetary system.

And if humanism is rebuffed in Gurdjieff's scheme of things, so too is terrestrial parochialism. Our particular Ray of Creation is only one of an infinite number of creative radii. Extrapolating from Nicholas of Cusa and Giordano Bruno, Gurdjieff renews assault on our obstinate emotional 'truth' that somehow, despite all, we and our little earth are central and especially important. Though in practice he loved and respected our planet, he did not mince words in describing it as 'a source of "offensive-shame" for that poor [solar] system'; a petty, paltry, peculiar 'lopsided monstrosity', situated in the Siberia of the universe, 'almost beyond the reach of the immediate emanations of the Omni Most Holy Sun Absolute.'

With the notion that the earth is 'lopsided', we have finally arrived at the myth of man's fall. A thousand antique legends commemorate some terrible tragedy which overwhelmed our earliest parents; Gurdjieff's amazing and bitter-sweet version has exposed him to more ridicule than any other facet of his teaching. For him it evidently embodied a truth – literal or symbolic – which was pivotal, and in service to which he could welcome even the most spiteful critical dismissal.

Once upon a time (due, as he wryly puts it, to 'the erroneous calculations of a certain Sacred Individual'), a vast wandering comet named Kondoor violently struck the as yet uninhabited earth, creating an 'asphyxiating stink' and precipitating into elliptical geo-centric orbit two detached earthly fragments – the moon and Anulios. This unnatural and untimely Caesarean birth of the moon threatened such serious consequences and scandals to the whole solar system that the Most Great Archangel Sakaki was urgently despatched by our Common Father to pacify the situation.

Sakaki concluded that the moon and Anulios could be stabilized and enabled to evolve normally, only if they were steadily supplied with 'the sacred vibration "Askokin"'. Since this precious vibration or substance Askokin was liberated principally on the death of living organisms, Sakaki caused mortal beings, of various shapes and sizes, to be seeded on earth by emanations from the sun. Here on the surface of the planet these little creatures breathed and fed and excreted and procreated; at death their physical remains were digested by the planet, but their Askokin passed by a sort of umbilical cord to feed the moon.

Aeons passed. At length there arose among species a true *Tetartocosmos*: a being triply possessed of thought, sensation, and feeling; a being in whom the Law of Three had intrinsic play ... the first man. Not only did this new breed promise a surpassing contribution to the Askokin-economy, but it possessed a potential for the attainment of 'Objective Reason'. As generation succeeded generation, men and women did indeed draw closer to an objective understanding of their true situation, 'of their slavery to circumstances utterly foreign to them'. But wait! – if ever these underlings comprehended the futile irrelevance of all their personal struggles and suffering, might they not be tempted towards mass suicide? Sakaki feared so. And if they did that, would it not grossly and dangerously distort the flow of Askokin to the moon? Sakaki feared so ... and, from his sombre analysis and contingency planning, ensued that terrifying scourge, 'the organ Kundabuffer'.

This 'maleficent Kundabuffer', intentionally implanted at the base of the spine, obliged mankind to perceive reality upside-down and to experience indiscriminate gratification from every repetition of stimuli. Man's progression towards objective understanding was instantly arrested: he was as if subdued by opium; he walked in hypnotic sleep through a waking dream; his suggestibility became total; his energies were fatally surrendered to egoism, self-love, vanity and pride. Just as Sakaki intended, man now served the moon blindly – ironically doomed to imagine himself the monarch of all he surveyed.

Not an atom of spite or malevolence was entailed – either in the general creation of the Askokin factory-farm or in man's special corruption. On the scale of the moon's imperious need to 'grow in consciousness' and to fulfil the note Re of the Ray of Creation, organic life, man included, was simply expendable. 'That pale traitress the moon, the cause of all our woes' (the words are Powys's) was a cosmological innocent, sucking the vitality out of organic life from pure infantile necessity. Sakaki himself meant no harm; indeed, as soon as the moon's crisis abated and the organ Kundabuffer became redundant, it was promptly removed from man.

Precisely here Gurdjieff drives home the dreadful irony of man's present situation. The organic compulsion to see reality upside-down had gone forever. The gift of man's extraordinary potentiality had been restored; he was a 'simulchritude of the whole' – a being who through 'conscious labour and intentional suffering' might slowly perfect himself to the level of Objective Reason and attain immortality by reintegrating with his source, the divine sun. Alas! Though the compulsion to lunacy had gone, the propensity had become crystallized. Delusion, suggestibility, malpractice, and every kind of rotten feeling so permeated human life; so festered in customs, language, social institutions and the family circle; had gained such stormy momentum – that to all intents and purposes man was still in Kundabuffer's thrall. Such was, and still is, the 'Terror of the Situation'.

Our ill-fated tribe and its ensuing story is accorded great significance in Gurdjieff's prodigious and unclassifiable masterpiece *Beelzebub's Tales to His Grandson*. 'Everything in *Beelzebub* historical', claims its author outrageously: an academic provocation easier to forgive when we recall the *Mahabharata*, St Augustine's *Civitas Dei*, Dante's *Divina Commedia*, and Milton's *Paradise Lost* and *Paradise Regained* – those towering historico-metaphysical precedents, where the temporal drama is also monitored solely for its bearing on man's spiritual evolution.

Gurdjieff presents his 'theatre of history' in dualistic terms, as an intense struggle between the personified forces of darkness and light; between 'the consequences of the properties of the organ Kundabuffer' and conscious influences incarnated in Moses, Buddha, Christ, Muhammad, and other messengers from our Common Father. It first appears that Gurdjieff, by the sheer humanity of his tale, and by his turbulent cast of exemplary and malign characters, is light years away from Comte's anaemic *histoire sans noms*. Familiar matinée idols (Pythagoras, Alexander the Great, Leonardo da Vinci, Franz Mesmer, Trotsky, Lenin) mingle here with personages completely unknown. Whether the latter are merely the author's creatures or mystery figures who await time's unmasking, who can say? In either case, Gurdjieff is no historian in the formal sense; he is a latterday *ashokh* whose narrative emerges very reluctantly from the domain of primordial myth and of incredibly sophisticated allegory.

To give an example of the allegorical strand: although Gurdjieff is clearly a geological 'catastrophist' in the mould of Cuvier, his daring corollary is that the psychic history of mankind, and even of each individual, recapitulates point-by-point the successive insults suffered by mother earth. (Freud incidentally comes intriguingly close to this in *Phylogenetic Fantasy*, his twelfth tract on metapsychology.) Thus in simple psychological terms the madcap comet Kondoor may represent puberty, the first organic buffet sustained by every life; the moon, the unconscious in its lunatic mode; Anulios the tiny countervailing prompting to sanity; and Atlantis the voice of conscience, tragically engulfed beneath subjective conventional morality.

In 'historical' terms, Gurdjieff presents Atlantis as the one glorious exception to man's general debasement, affording in its brief Golden Age a model response to the Terror of the Situation. The Atlantean savant Belcultassi is the protagonist of all group work and self-observation; his successor Makary Kronbernkzion studies the Law of Three and a special technique of liberating Askokin before physical death, through 'conscious labour and intentional suffering'. Great benefits ensue – alike to these innovators and their pupils, to mankind at large, and to the moon – yet all is suddenly plunged again into chaos, when the earth's lopsidedness is abruptly accommodated by a horrendous shift in its centre of gravity – and Atlantis disappears beneath the estranging sea.

Gurdjieff is an arch-disturber. Having ushered us soothingly from this apocalyptic scene to more familiar and reassuring tableaux, he sternly insists that we revalue our values, challenge and even invert our historical preconceptions. The classical Greek philosophers are reduced to 'poor bored fishermen pouring-from-the-empty-into-the-void'. Alexander the Great is indicted as an 'arch-vainglorious' psychopath; the equivocal hypnotist Mesmer becomes 'an honest and humble Austro-Hungarian learned being who was very meticulously pecked to death'; King John is the best English monarch; and Judas Iscariot is canonized as a practical and self-sacrificing saint – 'the devoted and favourite Apostle initiated by Jesus Christ himself.'

Nor is there the slightest consolation in the strange causal perspective, the sinister rehabilitation of Comte's *histoire sans noms*, which troubles the mind immediately Gurdjieff's Askokin hypothesis is seriously entertained; for example that the carnage of the trenches in the First World War ensued from the cessation of worldwide animal sacrifice centuries earlier; or that the moon was very hungry – and will be hungry again!

Happily Gurdjieff's world-view and historical account does not forbid hope; on the contrary, just when the clouds are darkest, our Common Father sends us his emissaries of light. Their message sounds with the resuscitating power of trumpets – Kundabuffer as such is gone forever. Although man is still inescapably fated to serve the moon, he alone among earthly creatures may also serve the sun and realize his potential for immortality.

Of all these incarnations provided from above, the most luminous in Gurdjieffian mythology is Ashiata Shiemash. Whom then does he represent? Zoroaster? Gurdjieff himself? Some impending messiah? Or is he (as portrayed), an unjustly forgotten historical figure born near Babylon *c*.1210 BC? He it was, insists Gurdjieff, who saw most deeply, felt most keenly, faced most squarely, the poisonous legacy of Kundabuffer: the decay of love into egoism, hope into procrastination, faith into credulity. He it was who divined the redemptory potentiality of conscience, that precious emanation of the sorrow of God – still unsullied, still unatrophied, because embedded deep in man's subconscious. He it was who translated his insights into a spiritual action which, for one blessed decade, eradicated nationalism and castes and war itself, throughout the length and breadth of Asia. An astonishing figure, beloved of God himself . . . and yet none of his teachings passed in any form even to the third generation.

The blame is heaped on a certain Lentrohamsanin, a late contemporary of Ashiata Shiemash. Lentrohamsanin is an only child, the 'Papa's and Mama's darling' of a rich merchant and his abortionist wife – spoilt, conscienceless, stuffed with unmerited and undigested knowledge, full of swagger, desperate for fame. Obsessed with the Kingdom of this World, he is a utopian rationalist who reeks symbolically of the Russian (and French) revolutions: Len for Lenin, Tro for Trotsky. He is the archetypal subversive – incensed against tradition; incensed against spiritual meritocracy; incensed fundamentally against his contingent human state. He demands unconditional freedom, leisure, happiness, liberty, equality, fraternity. He demands it now; he demands it with bravura on 'a parchment of 100 buffalo hides'. . . And in the current of mass psychosis and civil strife which he instigates and foments, the precious work of Ashiata is swept away.

Scrutinizing societies across continents and down the ages, Gurdjieff identified three independent formative impulses in ceaseless interplay. Of these, infinitely the most rare, elevated, and potent was what he called 'C' influence. Perhaps he adopted this neutral designation to minimize sceptical reaction? Certainly he is conveying here something extraordinary and contentious: the quintessence of truly conscious minds, of messengers from our Common Father, of initiatory schools – influences transmitted by an enlightened master directly to his disciples. Contradicting and superficially overwhelming these was ordinary 'A' influence: big mechanistic societal forces, centred on such perennial obsessions as 'digestion, mother-in-law, John Thomas, and cash'. And finally, uneasily accommodated between the two, was 'B' influence – conscious in its origin but fallen into the vortex of life, and mediated more or less mechanically through religion, science, philosophy and the arts.

To label Gurdjieff 'traditionalist', 'pacifist', 'internationalist', 'patriarchal', a 'proto-ecologist' and so forth, is defensible as a rough and ready truth; and to note that his ideas were often in advance of his times is fair comment – but to leave matters there is to miss the most interesting point. For although Gurdjieff spoke as he found, although he drew his observations directly from a life of Rabelaisian engagement – his critique's full dimensionality entails not merely his breadth of personal experience but the vertical axis of transcendent laws.

The indignation, pity, and benevolence which he unquestionably felt as a human being, could not possibly moderate his grim analysis arrived at *sub specie aeternitatis*: the hypnotized masses, led by equally hypnotized leaders under the banner of preposterous slogans, must fall again and again into the ditch; leech-like 'power-possessors', under one convenient rubric or another, would suck the blood of subservient millions; the 'burning question of the day' would change again and again, but not the instability of human reason or the accents of 'infuriated offensive abuse'. Reform, on its own level, was futile: 'There is no progress whatever ... The outward form changes. The essence does not change ... Modern civilisation is based on violence and slavery and fine words.' In effect, the consequences of Kundabuffer would be eradicated by a spiritual action – or not at all.

There are photographs of Gurdjieff in old age which convey, particularly about the eyes, a measure of sorrow. It cannot have helped that he was a pacifist who perceived the virtual inevitability of war. This 'reciprocal destruction' was for him the abomination of abominations, 'the most terrible of all horrors which can possibly exist in the whole universe.' But, failing a radical spiritual regeneration, nothing could be done. All utopias, Leagues of Nations, peace pledges, disarmament conferences, treaties, alliances and balances of power – all political 'solutions' on the horizontal level – were nothing but ironic embellishments on the moon's implacable need for Askokin.

This cosmic standpoint made Gurdjieff and his followers radically a-political. They would try their utmost to render unto Caesar what was Caesar's and unto God what was God's. And in their studied compliance with a society full of glaring and painful absurdities, they would cultivate a sense of humour and an inner detachment. They would help their neighbour; they would help each other; they would live quietly and astutely. And if and when sheer survival dictated that they howl with the wolves on the nightwind of the prevailing mass psychosis, they would simultaneously struggle for a secret dispassion: 'It does not refer to us. War or no war it is all the same to us. We always make a profit.' The sense of an independent evolutionary orientation is absolute.

One final glance confirms the singularity of Gurdjieff's social viewpoint. He, perhaps more than anyone, qualifies as the philosophical father of our contemporary ecological and holistic movements.[7] (At the very least he ranks in the pantheon with Haeckel, J. C. Smuts and Albert Schweitzer.) But Gurdjieff is different. He is not so much advocating a policy of sensitivity to other life-forms on moral, aesthetic, religious, or even utilitarian grounds, as proclaiming – whether we like it or lump it – a universal and inescapable principle of reciprocal maintenance. The nub of the question for Gurdjieff is each human being's unique option within the grand ecology. If a man lives passively and reactively, only his death and final obliteration will furnish Askokin to the moon; but if he works persistently for consciousness (along productive lines), he can create and liberate Askokin even during his lifetime, together with two complementary substances *which may elaborate in him a soul that can survive death*. The choice is stark indeed: eat or be eaten.

So much for Gurdjieff's world-vision: one full of objective hope for the cosmos at large, but undeniably sombre on the parochial scale of mankind. Turning now to Gurdjieff's 'Everyman', his model of the individual human being, we encounter the same poignant ambivalence, the same sense of potentiality betrayed.

The infant is born in hope and in 'essence'. Essence is what is essential. It is the self: not the little body in the cradle, but what the being innately and really is; his true, inexpungeable, and fate-attracting *particularity*. It is mysteriously predetermined, perhaps by the stars and planets while he is in embryo or at his birth; thenceforward it is meant to grow and mature, fed by real experiences.

Alas! Essence is quickly overtaken and arrested by personality; it is enveloped and suffocated as Laocoon was by writhing serpents. 'Personality' is what we pick up; it is the mask (Latin *persona*) or societal veneer. It is the crystallization in us of those 'A' and 'B' influences which happen to prevail wherever and whenever we were 'educated'. We unconsciously copy 'our' personality from our parents and from various little tin gods – and later randomly reimpose it on our children. Personality is indispensable, and at its best incorporates a valuable portion of man's linguistic and cultural heritage. At its worst it is a hodge-podge of prejudices, dreams, tones of voice, body-usage, manipulative stratagems and pitiable neuroses, *quite arbitrarily aligned to essence*. Personality is other people's stuff made flesh in us.

Worse is to come. For although essence is single, personality is legion. The idea of hysterical multiple personality was popularized only recently in Thipgen and Cleckley's well-attested case history, *The Three Faces of Eve*. Gurdjieff's version, put forward in 1916, entails marginally less disassociation among personalities, but escalates the condition from a clinical oddity to a universal malaise. All men and women, he warns, play host to scores if not hundreds of different parasitic identities, each with its blinkered repertoire of behaviour. A snub, a flattering letter, a no-smoking sign, a slow queue, a come-hither look – and we are strangely altered. We have one personality with subordinates, another with superiors, one with our mother, another with the tax man – each is Caliph for an hour. One scatters promissory notes which others must redeem: 'Certainly. See you in the morning. Only too delighted.' One despairing humourless personality may even take an overdose or jump off a cliff – crazily destroying the habitat of all the others. To sum up, our professed citadel of individuality is common as a barber's chair. Very few men are strong enough to confront this impression emotionally and to work within the compass of its appalling implications.

Confounding confusion, all these personalities share behavioural 'norms' which Gurdjieff (in an indictment that ranks with Hieronymus Bosch's 'Seven Deadly Sins') reveals as tragically abnormal.

He speaks more in sorrow than in anger; one may almost feel the
weight of his suffering as he concludes that his bleak picture is 'a
photographically exact snapshot from life'.

Chiefly to blame, in Gurdjieff's eyes, is man's irresponsibility
towards his godlike faculty of attention:[5] he does not reverence it, he
does not mobilize it, he does not govern it; and what little he finds
access to, he casts to the dogs. Unsurprisingly man's enfeebled
attention has no autonomy but is always attached, glued, surrendered
to this or that 'identification': here for example it hardens into
sharp configurations of self-pity, irritability, anxiety, resentment,
envy, vanity, hatred and every sort of 'negative emotion'; there it
softens into treacherous interior fantasies, 'imagination', daydreams
and delusional systems; here it supports a complacent judgement on
other poor devils, and here, paradoxically, a squirming fear of their
verdict on us; here it embellishes ignorance to seem like knowledge
. . . and invariably it provides voltage for our inner and outer chattering, for the despotic associations which flitter ceaselessly through our
weary brain.

All this pantomime, all this posturing, cannot (in Gurdjieff's eyes)
disguise the fact that man is essentially an impersonal *machine*: a
wonderfully complex stimulus-response mechanism which 'eats impressions and excretes behaviour'; an apparatus characteristically
devoid of self-cognisance and independent initiative; simply a cosmic
transformer used by 'Great Nature' to separate the fine from the
gross and translate each to its proper sphere.

In the detailed exactitude of Gurdjieff's blueprint, there is something at once astounding and frightening. His human 'machine'
simultaneously burns three fuels of ascending refinement: food, air,
and sensory impressions. These fuels blend to power five *independent*
brains or 'centres', which govern five functions: the intellectual
centre controls our thinking; the emotional centre our feeling; the
moving centre all learned external movement of the body in space;
the instinctive centre all the organism's unlearned interior functioning (respiratory, digestive, cardio-vascular, etc.); and the sex centre
all authentic sexual manifestation.

The general design of this human machine or 'food factory' is
admirable, but in practice nothing works properly. The five centres
– unsupervised and uncalibrated – relate inefficiently, jarring and
grating on each other. Some subordinate parts have rusted, some

are overheating, and others are inexplicably kept in mothballs. Breakdowns are frequent and component spares difficult or impossible to obtain. Such a ramshackle contraption is neither efficient nor cost-effective; after a short time it will certainly be demolished, and any valuable constituents recycled in the continuing process of mass production.

Is the situation hopeless then? A closed Yezidi circle? An inescapable prison of mechanicity? Sadly but inevitably Yes, for the great lumpen mass of people who perversely imagine themselves already free. But not for everyone fortunately; not for the statistically insignificant minority whose frank and unbelievably painful confrontation of their interior slavery presages a long realistic struggle for emancipation. Psychologists take note: in the final analysis Gurdjieff is not propounding the iron-clad determinism of Pavlov and Watson, but a neo-behaviorism which generously provides for the re-entry of consciousness and freewill. In Gurdjieff's scheme of things, man is a very special machine which, uniquely on earth, can fully come to know and sense itself alive. The breathing proof of this we may dimly intuit in such as Buddha, Pythagoras, Christ, Leonardo da Vinci . . . and perhaps some moderns?

We start as unconscious machines then . . . but just as bulldozers, theatre organs and computers are machines of different sorts, so are men creatures of different and classifiable temperaments. Gurdjieff's clearcut idea is that in any given individual, one or another of his three main centres so dominates that in effect it constitutes his type: in 'Man Number One' this is the moving centre; in 'Man Number Two' the emotional centre; and in 'Man Number Three' the intellectual centre. Personality may mask but can never totally suppress these three categories' respective and lifelong inclination towards the hand, the heart, and the head. Here are Shakespeare's Falstaff, Othello, Hamlet; Dostoevsky's Dmitri, Alyosha, and Ivan. All human culture, all artistic forms, all religions and philosophical systems, may be classified and illuminated from this triadic standpoint.

Such (in a claustrophobic nutshell) is Gurdjieff's basic typology — one which intriguingly enough seems echoed by several empirical psychologists (Kretschmer in 1925, Sheldon in 1940, and more recently and debatably by Eysenck). But beware! The resemblance is superficial. To begin with Gurdjieff is not propounding what the psychologists grandly style a 'constitutional somatotypology'; in

plain English he does not, as they do, match the body's shape and size
with character. But the philosophical distinction is even more important. The many 'constitutional' typologies assign men their type
forever and a day but *Gurdjieff affirms that type can evolve*; all
secular psychologists dump us in a cul de sac but Gurdjieff plants our
feet on an arduous spiritual way.

Here, as elsewhere, Gurdjieff adopts a stance which is profoundly
traditional. The hope of perfecting oneself, of escaping from the
painful morass of mundane life, of accomplishing some pilgrim's
progress towards immortality – this has always relied on the ideal, if
not the guidance, of unmistakably higher types. Though Gurdjieff
elaborates this pantheon with clarity and verve ('Man Number Four'
or balanced man, 'Man Number Five' unified man, 'Man Number
Six' conscious man, and 'Man Number Seven' perfected man) he
allows us only Hobson's choice as to our modest starting point.

The long evolutionary search has from time immemorial engaged
small minorities of every temperament; but three distinctive religious
'ways' have opened to meet the respective needs of Man Number
One, Two and Three:

1. the way of the fakir
2. the way of the monk
3. the way of the yogi.

The 'fakir' attains will by subduing his body; the 'monk' refines and
dedicates his feelings; the 'yogi' cultivates his intellectual powers.
(Note incidentally that Gurdjieff goes strictly by these procedural
criteria, not by cultural labelling; thus, however paradoxically, a
Bhakti yogi pursues 'the way of the monk' and a Zen monk 'the way
of the yogi'.)

All three classical religious ways would indeed be empty dreams –
as influence 'A' cruelly and raucously asserts – were it not for a
double blessing: compassionate guidance from those already at higher
stations on the evolutionary path; and two mysterious 'reservoirs of
grace' already present in every man ('Higher Emotional Centre' and
'Higher Intellectual Centre' as Gurdjieff awkwardly calls them).
In consequence the three hallowed institutional ways remain valid
and precious avenues of aspiration. Each however demands its
exhorbitant downpayment – behavioural constraints, celibacy, the
wholesale renunciation of normal life – and offers in return a
development which, however powerful, is inherently lopsided. In this
connection Gurdjieff sounds a cautionary note: to attain Man

Number Five without having first attained Four is in effect to crystallize in an unbalanced form.

Gurdjieff situates his own teaching within the shadowy tradition of a Fourth Way (or 'way of the sly man'), which demands no 'dying to the world', and studiously avoids lopsidedness by the *simultaneous and harmonious* development of body, emotion and intellect. The man of the Fourth Way picks no quarrel with 'the daily round, the common task'; he accepts his ordinary circumstances, good or bad, and his attitude to money and sex, as temporary indices of his 'being' and a field of struggle. On his long evolutionary journey, life becomes not only the terrain but the guide. Peter Brook puts it excitingly:

> Is the saint the man who withdraws furthest from the squalor and the action of the market place, who artificially lops off the undesirable aspects of human experience to make more room for the holy ones?. . . All of Gurdjieff's life and teaching make an opposite statement. . . In his own spiritual search he was constantly moving, and bringing others with him, through the most rich and intense participation in life.

It must be admitted here that the authentic Fourth Way – setting aside its thousand contemptible modern parodies – has proved 'in the depths too deep and in the shallows too swift' to be netted and anatomized by historians of religion. Its lineage remains obscure. The various archetypal groupings specified by Gurdjieff – the societies Akhaldan, Heechtvori, Olbogmek etc. – mean nothing to history. And yet the ancients were men like us. That some would feel drawn to a balanced way, 'in the world but not of it'; would receive and validate and pass on its characteristic initiations – this is hardly an extravagant idea. Amateur historians who have gone altogether further, and pronounced for the existence of wandering Fourth Way colonies among the builders of Mont St Michel, among the Cluniacs, the Templars, the Alchemists, the early Quakers, the Russian Freemasons, and certain obscure schools of acting, music, craftsmanship and painting – must bear responsibility for their intuitions. But certainly a Fourth Way influence may be decently suspected wherever a special quality of attention and questioning had a power upon the hour.

Though Gurdjieff shaped his own life with self-imposed vows, he exacted none from his pupils. Their commitment – albeit serious – was to remain, at each successive step on 'the road to Philadelphia', voluntary, provisional, and experimental. He insisted they cultivate a critical mind; he forbad blind faith – commending in its place 'understanding'. The word commend is really not strong enough here. Understanding was for Gurdjieff vitally important; it was an indispensable inner validation, subsuming mere knowledge; and, far from encouraging any intellectual self-congratulation, often brought an awed sense of 'standing under' an entity infinitely greater than oneself.

Today's 'Gurdjieffian', through all the trials of his inner and outer life, strives at the very least to understand; like the youthful Prince Siddhartha (emerging from his golden palace only to meet painful impressions of sickness, decrepitude, and death) he longs almost passionately to penetrate his own nature and the mystery offered him. How absurd to take everything for granted! How much begs to be understood: the great laws of world creation and world mainte- nance; the enigma of time; geology and pre-history in their deep but forgotten significance; the processional of civilizations; the subtle intimations of fairy-tales, myths and legends; and the overt and disguised currents of influence at play in our contemporary world . . . The challenge is profound. After all the aim is not to convert oneself into a hot-air pie – a bloated personage belching hearsay learning; rather it is to become a 'learned being'. And for this, one's own type, one's chief feature, one's place in the scheme of things, must be worked into the fabric of understanding.

'Being' – what does this word, evidently so crucial for Gurdjieff, actually signify? Here again we need our best intuition: it means something like the 'quality of beingness'; it is a man's grain, his whole mass, his atomic weight: what he really *is*. And, as Gurdjieff devastatingly insisted, 'the being of two people can differ from one another more than the being of a mineral and an animal'. Compared with essence, being is more amenable, more dynamic, more the function of conscious effort; it is a man's quotient of unity and gathered presence, his degree of 'being there'. With the idea of gathered presence and of 'being there', we are finally groping our way towards Gurdjieff's model of consciousness and the practical existential core of his teaching.

That consciousness is the taproot of our experience, the bedrock of all knowledge, and the ground of self-cognition – are truisms we owe to philosophy, strangely without feeling much indebtedness. There is probably more human interest in the peculiar ingenuousness of most Western commentary. Mournfully one traces from Leucippus to Clifford, Huxley, and Hodson, the stubborn materialist heresy that consciousness is merely an 'epiphenomenon', a flickering and accidental by-product of the brain's neural activity. As to degrees of consciousness, Ladd typifies the intelligentsia in owlishy denying them: 'Whatever we are when we are awake, as contrasted with what we are when we sink into a profound and dreamless sleep, that is to be conscious.' Bravo! Between this binary naivety and the Gobi desert of Husserl's phenomenology it would be difficult to choose.

Gurdjieff's model of consciousness, or Zoostat as he calls it, comprises six levels, arranged in two tiers. The unconscious mind (more or less synonymous with instinctive centre) exercises its miraculous stewardship over the body's big autonomic systems – cardio-vascular, respiratory, endocrinological, digestive, nervous etc. Superimposed, and completing the lower tier, is the mysterious subconscious – a whole theme in itself – which Gurdjieff repeatedly extols as the citadel of Objective-Conscience. The Zoostat's upper tier comprises four ascending levels:

1. objective consciousness
2. self consciousness
3. waking consciousness
4. sleep

We need not – for converse reasons – dwell here on the lowest and highest categories: sleep needs no elaborate definition, and 'objective consciousness' outreaches any definition (though we may hazard that it relates somehow to 'C' influence).

Now let us pay attention! For the qualitative distinction between the two intermediate categories, (2) and (3), provides the key to Gurdjieff's whole evolutionary psychology. Let us begin with category (2): Gurdjieff's impartial critique of our purported 'waking consciousness' finds our attention so scattered or entrapped, our suggestibility so high, our reactions so mechanical, our sense of 'I am' so marginal – that the state is better scientifically classified as one of mild hypnotic coma. *We are all asleep.* This is not a metaphor but a fact. It is also a social perception more subversive and revolutionary than anything remotely conceived by all the Trotskys and Kropotkins of history; an idea which, like death and the sun, cannot be looked at steadily – a world in trance!

How to emerge from this trance? That is indeed the question. But

Gurdjieff at least makes clear the immediate goal, namely the third level of consciousness (which he actually preferred to call 'self-remembering'). Until this state more or less prevails in a man's life, even his sincerest evolutionary aspiration remains tinged with subjective fantasy and neurosis. Fortunately, to no one is this experience a complete stranger. Rare spontaneous episodes of self-remembering have visited all of us in situations of danger, real novelty, intense emotion, quandary, or acute stress – bringing their unmistakable and inimitable impression of '*I here now!*' and depositing their special sediment of memory. *Suddenly we are awake!* It is Gurdjieff's demand that we acclimatize ourselves, by slow degrees, to living at this altitude. 'A man may be born, but in order to be born he must first die, and in order to die he must first awake.'

At outset the psycho-physical process of awakening seems entirely cohesive: the scattered limbs of Osiris are re-membered; for the sake of a higher unity, a man's three lower centres – intellectual, emotional, and moving – briefly sacrifice their terrible chaotic autonomy. In the enigmatic promise of Christ: 'Where two or three are gathered together in my name, there am "I" in the midst of them.' Cohesion then. Yet paradoxically, in the very act of self-remembering, a separation (*Djartklom* as Gurdjieff terms it) is implicit. The fragilely unified or individuated self splits off sharply from its habitual dreams and identifications. A double-bladed arrow of attention points outward to the functional life and inward to the unknown master of those functions.

Well . . . do we not share for a moment Gurdjieff's despair of words?

If there are any tablets from Gurdjieff's particular Mount Sinai, they are surely graven with the five 'being-obligolnian-strivings' – commandments inescapable for all men who wish to evolve:

> *The first striving:* to have in their ordinary being-existence everything satisfying and really necessary for their planetary body.
> *The second striving:* to have a constant and unflagging instinctive need for self-perfection in the sense of being.
> *The third:* the conscious striving to know ever more and more concerning the laws of World-creation and World-maintenance.
> *The fourth:* the striving from the beginning of their existence to pay for their arising and their individuality as quickly as possible, in order afterwards to be free to lighten as much as possible the Sorrow of our COMMON FATHER.

And the fifth: the striving always to assist the most rapid perfecting of other beings, both those similar to oneself and those of other forms, up to the degree of the sacred 'Martfotai' that is up to the degree of self-individuality.

Under their aegis, a man's redemption entails his whole-hearted and lifelong struggle against 'the consequences of the properties of the organ Kundabuffer': against egoism, habit, lying, chattering, fantasy, negative emotions, and hypnotic sleep. And a complementary struggle for attention, presence, unity, being, and understanding.

One may acknowledge without a breath of sarcasm that these are fine resolutions. And yet the orientation of spiritual ascent, the mere plan to move 'upwards not Northwards', guarantees nothing. All too easily it can transpose into an imaginary levitation or a comfortable romantic despair. Kundabuffer is tenacious, and at the very heart of any programme for self-development there lurks an insidious paradox. One example must suffice. Understanding and being – both absolutely vital – contend for precedence like the chicken and the egg: a man's being entirely governs his capacity to understand; and yet, conversely, 'Only understanding can lead to being, whereas knowledge is but a passing presence in it.' How to proceed?

It is this cruel psychological impasse – and a dozen others exactly like it – which make a teacher indispensable. Without the benign shock of his intervention, the pupil's evolutionary octave cannot develop; again and again the Law of Three must be invoked and the master's indefinable 'higher' blend with the disciple's 'lower' to actualize the middle. There is of course no salvation by proxy. The path remains long and hard. 'Blessed is he who has a soul,' said Gurdjieff, 'and blessed is he who has none, but woe and grief to him that has it in embryo.' Only the pupil can work his inner transformation but only the teacher can create and sustain becoming conditions. As Gurdjieff wryly added, 'I have very good leather to sell to those who want to make themselves shoes.'

So Gurdjieff's ideas blend imperceptibly into method; theory into *pratique.* Among the 'becoming conditions' he initiated – virtually his hallmark – was the 'group':

One man can do nothing, can attain nothing. A group with a real leader can do more . . . You do not realise your own situation. You are in prison. All you can wish for if you are a sensible man, is to escape. But how escape? It is necessary to tunnel under a wall. One man can do nothing. But let us suppose there are ten or twenty men – if they work in turn and if one covers another they can complete the tunnel and escape.

Concepts of being, unity, presence, awakening – remain glib and treacherous idealizations, until tested and proved by direct experience. The group with its manifold transactions and inner exercises provided a climate in which narcissism withered and real work blossomed. No less significant, the Movements or dances linked a pupil's quest for self-knowledge with his sense of service to the sacred. Who could manifest a lie, or be a lie, in front of that Teacher of Dancing?

We have come full circle. If this man cannot be understood without his teaching, neither can the teaching be understood without the man. Gurdjieff and his revelation are not to be separated by a hair's breadth:

> Gurdjieff was a master ... According to traditional conceptions, the function of a master is not limited to the teaching of doctrines, but implies an actual incarnation of knowledge, thanks to which he can awaken other men and help them in their search simply by his presence.

So there looms our quarry: the grandfatherly provoker of fierce and irreconcilable pronunciamentos; a learned being; a mock charlatan; a poet of situations; a saint with balls.

PART III

❖

The Archives of the League

1

❖

PRINCE OZAY

(1911–November 1914)

A few weeks before Gurdjieff died, he declared of his life's work, 'Remember what I now say. Begin in Russia, finish in Russia.' What he meant by 'finish in Russia' is dangerously problematical, perhaps especially today. But why he chose to begin there in the first place also tests our understanding.

This whole epoch in Gurdjieff's life is set so long ago and far away, that viewing it now we register a cultural alienation more or less inevitable. And yet our sense of shock is not due solely to distance. In Russia's self-contradictions and queer juxtapositions; in the unique dialectical clash between neo-medievalism and a frantic modernity; in the all-pervasive temper of dream, lunacy, hypnosis, and foreboding – we feel 'the normal' powerfully subverted by a torrent of surrealism. The angular St Petersburg street-grid is a net of European rationality, restraining – but only just restraining – the steppe-wolf of the Russian unconscious.

No Western society was more stiff with social inhibitions. Notwithstanding the abortive revolution of 1905 and the bogus constitution grudgingly conceded, the laity remained stratified in three estates – nobility, townspeople, and peasants; the double-headed Romanov eagle was parasitically infested by 2000 hereditary princes and two million lesser nobles; and throughout the ramshackle ennui-ridden administration, precedence was still fixed by Peter the Great's Table of Ranks, which even stipulated the number of buttons on one's jacket.

Yet in fact Gurdjieff arrived in Russia just when an irrevocable change was gathering momentum. More and more the pluperfect social order was threatened by anarchic forces from below, and made irrelevant by a brilliant cultural establishment which transcended it:

Diaghilev, Nijinsky, Stanislavsky, Stravinsky, Blok; Artzibashev the sensualist; Mamankov, the Maecenas of the opera; *prima ballerina assoluta* Mathilde Kschessinska, the Tsar's former mistress and Madame du Barry of the coming cataclysm. Despite the lingering whiff of feudalism, the country was now incongruously driven by a raw and buoyant capitalism (in its own terms a huge success). Under superb stucco ceilings, the millionaire owners of horrible new cotton mills and rubber factories compared profit margins; below in the streets there were trams and electric lights. The nobility in their marble palaces went on cracking their pedigrees and chattering in French about diabolo and American jigsaw puzzles; but only a day's train journey from Moscow were millions of peasants or 'Dark People' who lived in thatched hovels and ate a bread made from the bark of a tree.

At the apex of St Petersburg's courtly pyramid, Tsar Nicholas II, Autocrat of all the Russias, felt the giddiness of his elevation. His unpopular German wife Alexandra Feodorovna and his own suicidal belief in the divine right of kings kept him in place, but with diminishing satisfaction. Born on 18 May 1868, the Feast of Job, Nicholas had always been unlucky; even the joyful celebrations of May 1886 to mark his accession to the throne had been dampened by the death of 1200 people in a stampede to acquire coronation cups. His empire comprised a sixth of the earth's land mass, stretching from the Arctic to the Himalayas, and from the Baltic to Alaska. He had always wanted to extend it. Long ago in Livadia Gurdjieff had been formally presented, in the context of His Majesty's mystical fantasies of annexing Manchuria, Mongolia, and Tibet; of subjugating China; of expelling the British from India; and of making Moscow the Third Rome – but this over-ambitious programme had been quietly shelved even before the débâcle of the Russo-Japanese War. Affairs of state were now in the capable hands of His Excellency Piotr Arkadievitch Stolypin, the gifted President of the Council of Ministers. But poor Stolypin was never free from imperial interference. The Tsar was under the Tsarina's influence, and by July 1907 the Tsarina was wholly under Rasputin's; for nearly a decade the son of a Siberian horse-dealer kept the grand-daughter of Queen Victoria in a state of permanent exaltation, in which she apparently sought the guidance of providence.

The Gurdjieff of the earliest Russian years (beyond any explanation afforded by the prevailing surrealism) seems a man mysteriously in hiding and in volatile disguise. Evidently his vow of 13 September 1911 to adopt an artificial life, impelled him to assume various roles – this being an unfailing stimulus to self-awareness:

If I am acting, I have to direct at every moment. It is impossible to leave it to momentum. And I can direct only if there is someone present who is able to direct... A man who has 'I' and who knows what is required in every respect can act... In order to be a real actor, one must be a real man.

By day, in seedy backstreet cafés frequented by prostitutes and betting agents, history can just discern him sipping tea, wearing a bowler hat and a dirty celluloid collar. In this particular role we may almost identify some city equivalent of Dmitri Merezhkovsky's unforgettable religious character, Tifon the Sordid. But once Gurdjieff had come home, bidden a quiet good evening to the *dvornik*, and closed his own door behind him ... Ah then, he would wash, comb his short bushy black beard, select a patterned silk dressing-gown, wind on a cream-coloured turban, and become 'Prince Ozay' or even 'the nephew of Prince Mukransky'.[26] Strange unaccountable people visited him late at night and went away on errands which are not extant.

By now he had successively acquired and furnished three properties: a modest Moscow flat on the Bolshaia Dmitrovka; a second in the capital St Petersburg at the junction of Nevsky Prospekt and Pushkin Street, conveniently near to the Nikolaevski Station; and a large two-storied *dacha* in a country resort near Moscow. Among these he moved 'in accordance with a rhythm known only to himself'. He had originally brought with him from Tashkent two valuable collections: one of rare carpets and the other of porcelain and Chinese cloisonné. He possessed in addition a vast miscellaneous store of carved pipes, *narghiles*, ornamental daggers, *yataghans*, icons, ebony tables, tasselled cushions, every species of oriental musical instrument, ivory figurines of Christ, Buddha, Moses, Muhammad, and Padma Sambhava... altogether sufficient artefacts to set up a minor ethnographic museum. Experimenting, he now lovingly created his required ambience: floor and walls vibrating with his best carpets; the ceiling subtly understated in Chinese and Benares silks; the lighting mathematically exact; and subordinate objects guilefully juxtaposed ... the whole *mise en scène* a work of objective art which 'astonished ... by its special atmosphere.'

Gurdjieff was no longer alone. Soon after arriving in Moscow and visiting St Petersburg, he had married Julia Osipovna Ostrowska, daughter of Osip Ostrowska and Marie Fédérowska Misich. It was an uneven match. How could it not have been? To say nothing of deeper aspects, he was forty-five, she twenty-two; he

Greco-Armenian, she Polish; he rich, she poor. But Gurdjieff would cherish the young Julia as his 'uniquely and sincerely beloved wife'; he would make her his chief dancer; she would follow him, step for step, through war, revolution, and exile, with all the fidelity of Ruth.

Discounting for argument's sake the conjectural Tibetan interlude, Gurdjieff had hitherto led a life of lonely wandering, doubtless punctuated 100 times by hectic casual alliances. His individuality – by any standards remarkable – imparts to his ultimate choice an aura of mystery and special significance. Despite his proverbial self-command and his biting contempt for the literary genre which describes 'how some John Jones and Mary Smith attain the satisfaction of their "love"', Gurdjieff is surprised here in his ordinary humanity. Was he indifferent? Was he not stirred? When he describes (in his fictional character Gafar) jaded disillusion . . . and the miraculous resurgence of hope – surely he draws on confrontative experience:

> All that he has seen has utterly disenchanted him. He has never known a woman for whom he could feel the trust and esteem which, according to his views, should belong to his wife. He has become accustomed to look on all the fine words about love and the sympathy of souls as the mere fantasy of poets, and gradually women have become more or less alike to him, differing only in their type of beauty and in their varying manifestations of passion . . . And now, suddenly there has arisen within him this strange curiosity towards this incomprehensible woman. Can it be possible that she is in truth so utterly different from all the others?

The question lingers: what inward quality – beyond the chemistry of polarity – had singled out Julia Ostrowska?

Gurdjieff once let slip that his young wife was an 'old soul' who had lived many lives. A certain kind of beauty which she possessed evidently came from an interior core. It lent her silence, authority, economy and plasticity of movement: 'She never hurried but at the same time she worked at an incredible speed . . . she seemed surrounded by an aura of gentle firmness.'

Gurdjieff made Julia the central figure in his great dance, The Initiation of the Priestess; in his narrative writings she seems the heroine's archetype, the pattern both of Vitvitskaia and Zeinab. Altogether his regard for her qualities seems beyond the shadow of a question.

Historically speaking, whom had he chosen? The earliest years of Julia Ostrowska are plunged in mystery: in one breath we are assured she was a countess, a lady-in-waiting to the Tsarina; in the next it is hinted she was 'a woman who had stood on the verge of moral ruin'.

Several independent observers noted in her eyes (as in the nocturnes of Chopin which she most preferred) an intimation of obscure regret. All intuition whispers that, in one sense or another, Gurdjieff 'rescued' Julia. But on how many levels? His so-to-say strict distinction between geese and ganders (marvellously offensive to today's intellectual *sauciers*) and between real men and 'men in quotation marks' – implied, without gratuitous condescension, a sort of spiritual rescue:

> Nature of woman is very different from that of man. Woman is from ground and only hope for her to arise to another stage of development – to go the Heaven as you say – is *with* man. Woman already know everything, but such knowledge is of no use to her, in fact can almost be like poison to her, unless have man with her... If woman can find real man, then woman become real woman without necessity work.

Critics may violently dissent... Why not? But Julia herself did not dissent. Grateful to number herself among her husband's pupils, she even declined to assume his name. In Gurdjieffian annals she stands for all time merely as Mme Ostrowska; rather it was he who insisted that her place was unique and who composed in her honour his touchingly feminine piano piece, 'The Wife of Mr Gurdjieff'.

If Julia Ostrowska was indeed a lady-in-waiting to Alexandra Feodorovna, with access to that peculiar centrum of power the Empress's mauve boudoir in the palace at Tsarskoye Selo, the biographer may perhaps be forgiven one picaresque extrapolation. Here is Colin Wilson: 'It seems likely that if it had been Gurdjieff and not Rasputin, who was introduced to the Tsar in 1905, Gurdjieff might easily have become the most powerful and hated man in Russia.'

The mystical stream in Russian Orthodoxy, which had so curiously impinged on the Tsarina, had pure and impure forms. Indeterminate holy men, or *staretzy*, wandered the vast land, pilgrims traversed it, and those graced with insomnia of the heart bore from place to place the perpetual interior prayer, 'Lord Jesus Christ have mercy on me.' Gregory Efimovitch Rasputin's was an unique case: he loved God; he loved the intensity of prayer; he loved Madeira wine; and he loved women to the point of satyriasis. He had evidently walked (imagine it!) from Siberia to Jerusalem and back; then, differently advised, he had walked to St Petersburg – and into history.

We cannot so easily shake the kaleidoscope to install Gurdjieff in Rasputin's place, and, despite the royal couple's suggestibility, any dream of the court's Constantinian conversion to Gurdjieff's system of ideas is sheer fantasy. The two men's co-existence in St Petersburg nevertheless intrigues. In an era of nihilism and even of suicide clubs, both were 'Yea-sayers' with a superb, leonine confidence in life. Both possessed in abundance what Gurdjieff calls *hanbledzoin* or animal magnetism. Gurdjieff, restrained by his oath, used his chiefly for his pupils' benefit and for posterity: Rasputin – not altogether ignobly – cast his *hanbledzoin* into the scales of profane history and was destroyed by it.

On 13 September 1911 a vague biographical parallelism evident throughout early years, converged into sharp synchronicity. This was the day not only when Gurdjieff began his 'artificial' life, but when Rasputin, by foretelling Stolypin's doom ('Death is after him! Death is driving behind him!'), effectively pronounced the downfall of the *ancien régime*. Next evening the 14 September at the gala performance of Rimsky-Korsakov's *The Legend of Tsar Saltan*, extraordinary precautions were taken to protect the Imperial family, particularly since Dmitri Bogrov, a solemn bespectacled young Jewish agent of the Okhrana or secret police, had got wind of an assassination plot. Despite draconian security arrangements, His Majesty was disturbed during the second interval by two untoward sounds. 'I thought', Nicholas later confessed, 'an opera glass might have been dropped on someone's head.' But the case was more serious: in the stalls directly below the Imperial box Piotr Stolypin – the blood welling from his chest – painfully struggled to his feet, turned his face upwards to the Tsar, made the sign of the cross, and fell. Bogrov had shot him.

Gurdjieff – practised as he was in politics and dialectic – must instantly have understood that, with the death of Stolypin, the moderate centre had fallen away. On the right, a fine brew of paleo-fascist impulses now simmered unrestrainedly: the Tsar's airless supremacism; the Tsarina's neurosis; the hauteur of old blood and the rapacity of the nouveau riche; the Okhrana's licence; the Jew-baiting sadism of Monarchist gangs like the Black Hundreds; and the psychopathic exhibitionism of deputy Purishkevich, who mounted the parliamentary rostrum wearing a red carnation in his flies. On the left the liberals and drawing-room nihilists were industriously chipping at the branch they sat on. 'One cannot shed blood,' protested the poetess Zenaida Hipius, 'it's impossible. But in order that this impossibility should become real, one must!' Through the haze of such 'progressive' logic, the Russian intellectual had glimpsed, with a delightful shudder of anticipation, the dénouement to which all things now tended: the annihilation of his own class. 'And distant yet,' wrote Maxim Gorky in October 1911, 'already foams the crest

of that wave which will sweep us away'. 'In our hearts,' echoed
Alexander Blok, 'the seismograph's arm has already moved.' If they
all saw the time's inherency, Gurdjieff saw it: it promised him not
permanency for his small groups but – sooner or later – 'sharp
energetic events' and the seeding effect of a diaspora.

Perhaps the sinister perspectives of 1911 had some initial braking
effect on Gurdjieff's plan? For who can seriously doubt that he
commanded enough charisma, or *baraka*, or *hanbledzoin* (call it
what we will) to have 'magnetized' hordes of disciples, and to have
excited a powerful current far sooner than he did? Eyewitness reports
from this early epoch are unanimous: 'He was extraordinary! You
cannot possibly imagine how extraordinary Gurdjieff was.' Nor was
there any lack around him of people avid for ideas. Youth was in
ferment. Artistic and speculative groups of every stripe flourished:
Futurists, Symbolists, Acmeists, Ego-Futurists, Cubists, Cubo-
Futurists; the Jack of Diamonds coterie, the Ass's Tail gang, the
Errant Dog set. These various schools of aesthetes, philosophers, and
subscribers to the 'Romantic Agony', had almost all some curricular
interest in spiritual or psychological evolution. Arguably only one .
per cent were embarked on a real search, and the rest were simply
'pouring from the empty into the void', but even this one per cent
was a huge and deserving constituency, which Gurdjieff left largely
to its own devices.

The hypothesis is tempting that Gurdjieff was inhibited by some
obscure necessity or contract (such as surely track political and
religious agents from sphere to sphere) – even that he stood in special
danger. Undoubtedly the police (and not without good reason)
subscribed to Charles Péguy's dictum, *'la mystique conduit à la
politique'*; no one with a distinctive viewpoint knew when to expect
disaster or from what angle it might strike. The *Ossybyi Korpuss
Gendarmov*, the Special Corps of Gendarmes, kept their suspicious
unmollifiable eye on commoners holding meetings of any sort. These
gendarmes were at least identifiable, in neat gentian-blue uniforms
synonymous with injustice and splintered bones. By contrast the
Okhrana, the secret police or Pharaohs, were largely invisible – their
vast empire of spies, interrogators, and agents provocateurs extending
from unspeakable camps and mines in Siberia to the appalling
Trubyetskoy Bastion in the Fortress of Peter and Paul (locations
where, as Gurdjieff put it, '"French champagne" could not be taken').

All such speculation, albeit only human, is chastened by the solid
pragmatism of the Gurdjieffian fathers:

At first I was ... much intrigued by the identity of 'Prince Ozay' ... who was he? Why this secrecy? ... but whether he was Turk, Tartar, Teuton, or Tibetan; whether his profession was tinker, tailor, soldier, sailor, or tramp; whether his reclusion was voluntary, forced, or prompted by political, social, commercial or religious motives – what did any of these matter as long as I could glean from him something I needed and that he was willing to impart?

In later decades most of Gurdjieff's disciples would necessarily adopt precisely this position (and a 'noble a-historicism' is even today very much in vogue).

It must be admitted that the epic cadences of Gurdjieffian pre-history (The Long Search of 1887 to 1910) transpose with notorious awkwardness into the starchy prose of evidential biography; to calibrate the images of the 'Tiger of Turkestan' and 'G. I. Gurdjieff' will always present problems. If any subordinate figure straddles and authenticates both worlds, it is surely Lev Lvovitch, Gurdjieff's earliest associate in St Petersburg.

To dismiss Lvovitch the 'Lion' as a character escaped from a John Buchan novel is dangerously tempting; he had died, so he claimed, on an expedition to Central Asia. He had died, but fortunately he had been 'brought back' by a shaman. His physique and wardrobe are entirely of the genre: his poker back, shining boots, and crisp riding breeches proclaim him a military man; blue eyes beneath shaggy eyebrows speak of command; he has an infectious laugh. Piddling little Buchanesque clues and enigmas complicate his appearance – why no shoulder-straps or insignia or regimental buttons? And yet ... and yet. In St Petersburg's strange menagerie of faith-healers and medicine men, Lvovitch the 'Lion' had no less historicity than Badmaieff the 'Owl' (Tsar Alexander III's Buryat godson). Lvovitch lived. He is not a literary construct, not a sympathetic reworking of the type of the Seekers of the Truth. Sober and independent witnesses heard Lvovitch talking with Gurdjieff in 'a language of the rocky wastes and inaccessible hills'; grateful patients emotionally attested to his benign command of hypnotism. The historical hinterland stretches away vast and mysterious. Where and when did Lev Lvovitch first impinge on the Gurdjieffian scene? We cannot guess. He remains an unclassifiable nonconformist who in his capacity for action and his profound deference to Gurdjieff, seems established as one of the sorcerer's most virile apprentices.

In Moscow the first of Gurdjieff's young pupils was Vladimir Pohl a talented composer, formerly a Director of the Russian Musical

Society, and now at just thirty-one Rachmaninov's successor as
Director of the Empress Maria Musical Institute. It was through Pohl
that Gurdjieff chose to approach his own cousin the sculptor Sergei
Dmitrievitch Mercourov,[16] who evinced a dilettante interest in
occultism and Hindu philosophy. Born in Alexandropol next door to
the Giorgiades family, Sergei had lived a life of some panache. His
first commissions had been from the concubines of the Khan of
Nakhichevan; he had sat next to Rodin in Paris when 'the Thinker'
was unveiled; and in 1910 he had taken the death mask of Leo
Tolstoy. Gurdjieff was deeply patriarchal; this long-postponed contact with his extended family undoubtedly meant something to him,
and a certain tenderness, falling short of indulgence, may be suspected in the relationship. Gurdjieff was forty-five and Sergei thirty,
but the actual disparity in experience was prodigious, and they met
for a while on the basis of teacher and pupil. (Significantly enough,
older and younger male kinsmen frequently feature in Gurdjieff's
writing as wisdom-figure and neophyte – Beelzebub and his grandson
Hassein constituting the prime example.)

The butcher, the baker, the candlestick-maker could expect
Gurdjieff's casual help if they genuinely asked it, but his selection and
treatment of intimate disciples conveys the shadowy impression of a
vast plan – not infallibly realized but staggering in its ambition.
Perversely enough, many of the instruments he first chose turned in
his hand: Lev Lvovitch (like so many others) would simply disappear, 'leaving no trace, at the time of the great agitation of minds
in Russia'; Pohl would escape to Paris and dissipate his talent in
minor ballets and incidental music; Mercourov – strangest of all –
would remain to sculpt heroic monumental statues of Lenin and
Stalin, become director of the Pushkin Museum of Fine Arts in
Moscow, and receive the Order of Lenin. If in these discrepant tales
there is some pattern of intentionality, it is too well hidden. But the
grand design is arguably a little clearer in the case of Gurdjieff's most
famous pupil, the author Piotr Demianovich Ouspensky.

In principle Gurdjieff put books second. And he put contemporary spiritual books by Western philosophers a distinctly poor second:

> 'Read, by all means,' he once said to me, 'if only to see what nonsense
> people can sometimes write, but there is only one book to study – this
> one' – and he gave me a whack on the chest to indicate that he meant the
> Book of You. In other words, 'Know thyself'.

Imagine then his uncharacteristic interest when in 1912 he noticed

Ouspensky's new publication *Tertium Organum* (a work of un-
steady and precocious genius challenging the constraints on human
consciousness implicit in Aristotle's *Organon* and Bacon's *Novum
Organum*). The subject matter was startlingly familiar. Gurdjieff is
here an Odysseus of the spirit who, returning to Ithaca disguised as a
beggar, is immediately welcomed with a bound copy of the *Odyssey*
got out by Telemachus – and what is more, the geography proves
almost accurate! Not of course completely accurate:

> A map, as my friend Yelov used to say, is called in a certain language by
> the word *khormanoupka*, which means 'wisdom', and 'wisdom' in that
> language is characterised as follows: 'Mental proof that twice two makes
> seven and a half, minus three and a little bit of something.'

But Ouspensky's small inexactitudes and brazen guesswork could be
forgiven him for the shimmer of his writing and his crashing final
chord: 'The meaning of life is in eternal search. *And only in that
search* can we find something truly new.' If the being of the author of
Tertium Organum could be raised to the level of his knowledge; if his
cascading insights into time, dimensions, and consciousness could
actually change his character – what a disciple, what an evangelist,
that might be! Gurdjieff waited. He knew how to wait. For a year or
so 'Ouspensky-Fourth-Dimension' was contentedly preoccupied –
doted on by his attractive and talented mistress Anna Ilinishna
Butkovsky, and lionized in St Petersburg's café society. Then in
autumn 1913, Moscow newspapers reported his departure on a
journalistic assignment to the East.

Immediately Ouspensky's stiff silhouette appears over Gurdjieff's
horizon, history trembles in the balance with myth. History's mechanistic conception, deadly fairness, and fastidious chronology restrict
the biographer to a single defensible banality: that in 1912, or shortly
afterwards, Gurdjieff marginally noted P. D. Ouspensky (perhaps
among several others) as a potential pupil. The mythic perception is
altogether richer and more precarious. Its vision up-ends causality: it
does not construe the present and the future in terms of the past; but
the past and present in terms of the future. The mythic future is
foreknown. The totemic figure of Ouspensky, although still on the
horizon's rim (and now apparently travelling in the wrong direction),
is essentially moving with the assurance of a sleepwalker towards his
singular destiny as the supreme apologist of Gurdjieff's ideas – not
exactly St Peter (he will deny his master once too often for that) but
St Paul the Apostle. Gurdjieff, fortunate in his supra-mundane

sensitivity to the rhythm of fate, pretty well knows the plot already —
that proposition, queer as it sounds, is actually part of the plot! The
mythic re-enactment is mysteriously bound up with man's memory
of the future.

To come back to earth, Gurdjieff had by now a handful of Russian
followers, and one in prospect: a modest enough beginning for
someone planning the spread of his ideas throughout the West. Then
in the winter of 1913 he acquired his first foreign pupil — significantly
enough an Englishman. Paul Dukes was a music student aged just
twenty-four: his piano teacher at the Conservatoire in St Petersburg
was the arch-formidable Annette Essipov, who combined a technique of 'cat-like strength and subtlety' with an interest in theosophy.
Dukes had read Helena Blavatsky's *The Secret Doctrine* and *The Veil
of Isis*; had dabbled in spiritualism with no less a person than Sidney
Gibbes, English tutor to the Royal family; had practised hypnotism
on unsuspecting peasants at Tula — and yet Gurdjieff accepted him.
The 'yet' is essential because twenty years' research in the field of
traditional knowledge had left Gurdjieff with a profound contempt
for dreamy theosophical speculation about 'thought-forms', and for
'intellectual dabblers in the occult who were so enamoured of their
"subtle" bodies that they let this one rot.' Dukes was thus received
not for his mish-mash of preconceptions, but for his sensitivity,
intelligence, and audacity (qualities which, as Secret Agent ST 25,
would earn him a knighthood by the age of thirty).

The young man's induction was almost masonic in its initiatory
contrivance. Lev Lvovitch swore him to secrecy and brought him to
'Prince Ozay' late at night — but not directly. Led by his sponsor,
Dukes entered a drab back-street tenement near the Nikolaevski
Station, negotiated a dark passage to a door improbably set in the
flat's partition wall — and emerged with revelatory shock into a
setting from the Arabian Nights. A turbaned Gurdjieff sat playing
chess with a man of high cheekbones, slanting eyes, and a little goatee
beard (in all probability the formidable Shamzaran Badmieff).

Having mated his opponent, Gurdjieff offered Dukes a game,
motioning him to sit cross-legged beside him on a low divan. Dukes
politely removed his shoes and discovered with acute embarrass-
ment a hole in his socks. 'You believe in ventilation!' said Prince
Ozay. 'Good thing — nothing like fresh air!' After beating Dukes,
Gurdjieff diverted the conversation to the theme of the Lord's Prayer,
which was, he strikingly demonstrated, originally intended as a devotional breathing exercise chanted on single even breath. 'A low,

rich musical bass note about G2 below middle C, began to sound in the room, pure and dry amid the muffled hangings.' Gurdjieff's entire torso was vibrating, inducing in Dukes something 'like a mild electric current'.

An unexpected psycho-somatic unity was implied: 'soul' and body, aspiration and respiration, were complementary; prayer was connected with digestion and even with the quality and circulation of the blood. The attention (always the fulcrum of Gurdjieff's methodology) must be totally mobilized and equally divided among three elements: the words, the sound, and the breathing. Christ himself had taught his disciples to pray like this – secretly 'in a desert place' – and individually because the practice was 'closely concerned with how a man breathes and no two persons breathe exactly alike.' Prayer's truest aim was not to petition or extol but to attune with the Logos: 'What you might call the World's tonic note.' And because 'every octave is a replica at a different level of every other octave', a man could develop his individual being through resonating this primordial note.

For two or even three years Dukes went sporadically to the mysterious flat on the corner of Pushkin Street. Through long strange nights only the melancholy hooting of trains as they approached the Nikolaevski Station, protested faintly and unconvincingly the existence of the mundane world. 'Prince Ozay' – radiating force, sugaring his profundities with blue jokes, strong coffee, oriental songs, and outrageous drinks ('Try my own concoction ... much better than whisky') – concentrated his willing young protégé's attention on vibrations of a subtle order. Fragments of a mantric doctrine ascribed to the ancient Egyptians, Chaldeans, and Brahmins were transmitted. Dukes was encouraged to compose and chant his own prayers to the Supreme Being; he was encouraged to observe another of Gurdjieff's pupils, a young priest at the nearby Alexander Nevsky Lavra. Here is his technical memoir:

> He begins on a note about an octave below middle C, rising one semitone with each phrase, at the same time swelling the volume. Already at the dominant his voice resounds in mighty waves among the vaults and arches. When finally, at the octave, he reaches the climax of the 'reading' the note is like a last trump – triumphant, exultant, majestic, overpowering ...

Dukes in fact passed the endurance threshold when the pitch reached E-flat – sensing something analagous to the piercing eye pain provoked by moving abruptly from gloom into strong light.

Although in his rich later life Sir Paul Dukes concentrated on yoga, he generously acknowledged his fundamental debt to Prince Ozay's 'esoteric Christianity':

> The gospel became intensely personal, free of any kind of dogma whatsoever, a living message, with the Lord's Prayer its emblem, the parables its illustrations. 'Seek and ye shall find' sounded like a clarion call out of the deep...

Add to this tribute the fact that when the young priest chanted, the whole congregation of the second largest monastery in Russia was on its knees and in tears – and the biographer must flirt with a broader question: was Gurdjieff ever tempted to present his teaching explicitly in Christian terms?

It is undeniable that Gurdjieff reverenced Christ, and all his life strove to braid together diverse strands of Christian pietism. As a youth his precocious visits to Echmiadzin and the monastery of Sanaine had presaged longer journeys: seeking in Cappodocia the origin of Christian liturgy; in Mount Athos the legacy of Hesychasm; in Jerusalem the link with the Essenes; and in Coptic Abyssinia the roots of Christian Gnosis. The esoteric synthesis he achieved was full of animation, and might if disseminated in Russia have had tonic effect. The established Church there – threatened on the one side by atheism and on the other by exuberant schism – lacked precisely the vision and balance which Gurdjieff could have imparted. The Orthodox were divided from 20 million Old Believers or Raskolniki by dangerously gratifying procedural anomalies: the Orthodox crossed themselves with three fingers – the Raskolniki with two; the Orthodox wrote the word *Iisus* (Jesus) with two i's – the Raskolniki with one. A popular reaction of forgivable impatience had favoured the Stranniki or priestless sect; an ecstatic messianism diverted the Khylysty flagellants; and a spirit of unusual recklessness characterized the Skoptsy or self-castrators. In 1913 Christendom in Russia – for all its rich texture and exhilarating power – was mentally distracted.

But 1913 was also the year of Husserl's *Phenomenology* and Freud's *Totem and Taboo*. In such an era Gurdjieff must summon spirits – like Ouspensky's – which were sensitized to truth in emphatically a-religious forms, not least in psychology. Gurdjieff's next convert in St Petersburg was in fact the eminent 'alienist' Dr Leonid Stjoernval.

Aged thirty-eight, the doctor was a thoroughly decent, serious, and dependable man: scientific in outlook, phlegmatic in temperament, and guarded in self-revelation. He liked to drink and smoke but not to excess; no one could call him fat but he was a little 'inclined to stoutness'. An application of odourless wax compounded the twirled ends of his moustache into fashionable spikes; his fine eyes were deeply set; and his spade-like beard showed those little touches of silver which actually enhance a consultant's professional authority and natural gravitas. To meet Dr Stjoernval in his Petersburg consulting room, or at his club, or at his large electro-massage institute in Finland, was to meet moderation pushed to extremes; his proverbial equilibrium was such that only Gurdjieff could disturb it. The ensuing outbursts, however, revealed the psychologist in an entirely new light – almost impossible to explain:

> Wearing a trance-like expression and making nervous, excitable gestures as if he were suddenly waking out of a reverie, he burst out in a voice that was hoarse, like subdued thunder, and quite unlike his usual tones: 'Yes I believe that Georgi Ivanovitch is not less than *Christ himself*!

On hearing this, Gurdjieff vigorously cut the doctor short.

Leonid Stjoernval, perhaps of all Gurdjieff's major pupils, was a creature of the *belle époque*: a man who would forgivably have wished to accommodate his arcane studies within the familiar verities and uxorious amenities of bourgeois life – a man who never dreamt of anything else. And yet it was not towards a feather-bedded superannuation that providence was slyly beckoning Dr Stjoernval or his wife Elizabeta Grigorievna, but across cruel mountains and bitter seas into perpetual and indigent exile. He had met Gurdjieff and he simply would not let go.

Even now great events were precipitating. At 7 pm on Saturday 1 August 1914, Count Friedrich von Pourtales, the German Ambassador, racked with profound emotion, entered the office of His Excellency Serge Sazanov the Russian Foreign Minister to deliver the intention of Kaiser Wilhelm II: 'His Majesty the Emperor, my august sovereign, accepts the challenge in the name of the Empire and considers himself at war with Russia.'

From the early hours of the following day, ant-like columns of marching men began processing through St Petersburg; they seemed exalted, holding up portraits of the Tsar and the banner of the double-headed eagle. In front of the Winter Palace – its façade the colour of clotted blood – the crowd massed ... waiting ... waiting. Just after 4 pm, high on the balcony overlooking the vast square, Nicholas II materialized, and with a look of ardent concentration

pronounced the simple formula with which Alexander I had repelled
Napoleon: 'Solemnly I swear that I shall not conclude peace so long
as a single enemy remains on the soil of the fatherland.'

The people sank to their knees. Their upturned faces were resolved. With a gaze of deep atavistic piety they contemplated their
sovereign and the miraculous icon of the virgin of Kazan, which had
been hastily brought from the national sanctuary on the Nevski
Prospekt. They sang 'God Save the Tsar' and then – as if vaguely
divining what the future really held – they sang 'Lord, Save the
People and Bless Thine Inheritance'. A long living silence claimed
the languorous August afternoon ... and gave way to tumultuous
cheering. As the Tsar remarked privately to the Tsarina, 'I felt that
everything was finished between Wilhelm and myself.'

Where Gurdjieff was that day we have no idea – but we know his
utter disengagement and his unconventional analysis:

> What is war? *It is the result of planetary influence.* Somewhere up there
> two or three planets have approached too near each other: tension results
> ... here, on the earth, people begin to slaughter one another ... They fail
> to realise to what extent they are pawns in the game ... it must be
> understood that neither Emperor Wilhelm, nor generals, nor ministers,
> nor parliaments, signify anything or can do anything.

His own plans already accommodated the near-certainty of a cata-
clysmic national revolution; now he must cope with the actuality of a
world war. Gurdjieff's first personal concern was for the safety of his
aged parents in Alexandropol. Once, when he was a little boy, his
father had hypothesized that God was 'in Sari Kamish' nearby to
Kars, making pinewood ladders there so that the nations might
ascend to happiness: now Enver Pasha the Turkish War Minister was
in Sari Kamish, making plans for the genocide of the Armenian
people. Not only Gurdjieff but Mercourov watched the situation
with growing unease.

All Europe mobilized. The great powers, roped together by deeply
considered precautionary treaties, dragged each other one by one
into the abyss. The Tsar's first personal contribution to the national
effort was to rename St Petersburg 'Petrograd', to ban the sale of
vodka, and to order from Fabergé a jewelled Easter egg mounted on
shrapnel. Hardly less surreal in the prevailing circumstances was
Gurdjieff's decision to occupy himself in devising an occult ballet
entitled *The Struggle of the Magicians*. Already he had in mind
its chief characters: the hero Gafar – handsome, well-built, and

wealthy; Zeinab the beautiful heroine – flame to Gafar's moth; Roussoula – Gafar's fat cunning major domo; the White Magician – spiritual master of Zeinab; and his evil rival the Black Magician, whose aid Gafar solicits. With these simple Arabian Nights stereotypes, Gurdjieff planned a dialectical extravaganza, but more importantly a living teaching experience for his participating pupils.

The autumn equinox passed and the nights gradually closed in. On the population of Moscow and Petrograd the remotely distant process of 'reciprocal destruction' conferred its paradoxical grace: a sharpened sense of living. The emotions which filled the air, conversation, and newspapers were immensely powerful and swept most people away; but a telegram or a name on a casualty list could deliver at one stroke the deathblow to all exhilaration. The vast majority of the bereaved and perplexed construed their suffering within the prevailing socio-political orthodoxies: but here and there some reflective temperaments found themselves querying the very significance and aim of human life. Some – like the testy lawyer A. Y. Rachmilievitch and the young bullock Alexander Nikorovitch Petrov – we vaguely glimpse. To others we can ascribe no faces. Time, the Merciless Heropass, has obliterated them with all their frowning problems. Slowly and surely (always preferring those whose inner or outer situation was unbearable), Gurdjieff consolidated round Mercourov and Pohl his smallish Moscow group.

Three months after the outbreak of war, Piotr Ouspensky returned to Russia full of romantic images of the Indian sub-continent: he had met the yogi philosopher Aurobindo; he had seen the Taj Mahal by moonlight; he had conferred with Annie Besant at Adyar while seated on a white llama skin. On Friday 13 November 1914, as he leafed through the pages of his newspaper *The Voice of Moscow*, his eyes chanced on the anonymous column 'Round about the Theatre': it referred to the scenario of a new ballet, *The Struggle of the Magicians*, supposedly set in India and the property of a certain Hindu. Ouspensky took up a pair of scissors and cut the notice out.

With this prosaic but symbolically momentous action, the curtain slowly rises on the heroic epoch in the transmission of Gurdjieff's ideas.

2

❖

Holy Affirming

(November 1914–March 1917)

King Solomon's metaphor of 'casting bread upon the waters', which so peculiarly hyphenates a feckless liberality and the shrewdest calculation of long-term advantage, might almost have been coined to describe the pre-revolutionary Gurdjieff – with the proviso that he committed to the ideological stream the produce of a complete bakery.

Glimpses of Truth, the first literary production of the vast Gurdjieffian œuvre, is a singular document. Written by an anonymous pupil at Gurdjieff's instigation in December 1914, it floridly describes how a certain individual cuts from *The Voice of Moscow* the notice of *The Struggle of the Magicians*; how he is subsequently introduced to Gurdjieff; and is profoundly impressed by the man and his teaching. The neophyte might so easily be Piotr Ouspensky: a browser in newspapers; an intellectual seeker drawn to occultism and philosophy; a disappointed wanderer in India and Egypt – such nudging hints abound. Yet strangely enough in 1914 Ouspensky had made no contact with Gurdjieff whatsoever.

Certainly *Glimpses of Truth* was not written under normal or easy conditions. The winter of 1914–15 was a peculiarly bitter one: far away at the front Russia's peasant soldiers, blessed with holy water, were thrown en masse against the German machine-guns and artillery, sometimes armed with no more than a bayonet tied to a stick; four million died in the first five months. Gurdjieff's pupils on their way to group negotiated their way through dark streets, infested with muggers and deserters. The venal Minister of War, General Vladimir Sukhomlinov, who had not read a military manual for twenty-five years, was terrified of Zeppelins and had placed

Moscow and Petrograd under blackout. Only the very rich could keep warm. Even the Diplomatic Corps complained that their allotment of coal had been taken by Mathilde Kschessinska the *prima ballerina assoluta* – evidently requisitioned while she was in bed with Grand Duke Andrei Vladimirovitch.

In April, as the ice was melting, Ouspensky finally did arrive in Moscow. He had come on a wave of success to repeat his theosophical lectures, 'In Search of the Miraculous' and 'The Problem of Death', which had recently packed the vast Alexandrovsky Hall in Petrograd. Gurdjieff acted quickly. Vladimir Pohl and Dmitri Mercourov were tasked to make the essential first link, to confide Gurdjieff's identity as the true begetter of *The Struggle of the Magicians*, and to draw Ouspensky into a direct encounter.

In Gurdjieff's life there are many important convergences, and if we try impartially to rank them, we risk making complete fools of ourselves. What may perhaps be asserted is that within the Gurdjieffian myth the conjunction with Ouspensky enjoys a place which is unique: it is by analogy the coming together of Socrates and Plato; Shems-eddin and Djellaleddin Rumi. The contemporary boot seemed of course wholly on the other foot. Gurdjieff was an unfashionable provincial; Ouspensky a published author lionized in his own enlarging circle – an 'upwardly mobile' establishment figure who approached this episode with fastidious reserve, anticipating a mish-mash of superstition, self-suggestion, and silly thinking. 'My first meeting with him', Ouspensky later wrote of Gurdjieff, 'entirely changed my opinion of him and of what I might expect from him.'

Gurdjieff had no lack of money. If he had wished to dazzle Ouspensky with externals he could have appeared in the gaudy of 'Prince Ozay' or at least have booked a table in one of the grander Moscow restaurants, perhaps the Yar or Stryelna in Petrovsky Park. In fact he chose a rowdy little backstreet café patronized by petty traders and betting agents, and waited there wearing a bowler hat. Somehow, by deliberately presenting himself in the poorest light, by speaking his worst Russian in his coarsest Caucasian accent, Gurdjieff seized the initiative. Ouspensky's fine penetrative mind, so naturally attuned to a subcutaneous reality, in effect restored to Gurdjieff all the exoticism he had sacrificed; seeing 'this man with the face of an Indian raja or an Arab sheikh' Ouspensky mentally replaced the bowler hat with a gilded turban and a white burnoose.

The question of dominance was settled immediately the two men really looked at each other. Ouspensky felt that Gurdjieff had gently weighed him in the palm of his hand and put him back again. In memoir after memoir this figure of speech, this intimation of ordeal, recurs:

> To meet him was always a test. In his presence every attitude seemed artificial. Whether too deferential or, on the contrary, pretentious, from the first moment it was shattered; and nothing remained but a human creature stripped of his mask and revealed for an instant as he really was.

No one need suppose here that Ouspensky was particularly susceptible to authority figures or easily overawed. On the contrary he himself was formidable. With receding hair cropped short and a square Teutonic skull jam-packed into a powerful neckless torso, he might have been an understudy for Erich von Stroheim. Beneath militant black eyebrows, rimless pince-nez amplified a gaze which was almost alarming in its blue intensity; his chin and heavy jawline conveyed an obstinate determination; his lips were chiselled and the mouth permanently downturned in an expression of incorruptible professorial rectitude which bordered on disapproval. And yet for all this, he was a man it was impossible not to respect – 'simple, courteous, approachable, and intelligent'.

Gurdjieff handled the interview good-humouredly but without compromise. He categorized his work and groups as esoteric and journalistically 'off the record'; he stressed that pupils must pay him 1000 roubles annually ('Take neither purse nor scrip! And need not a railway ticket be taken either? The hotel paid? You see how much falsity and hypocrisy there is here'); and he superbly trumped Ouspensky's allusions to his own travels in the East:

> You know ... when you went to India they wrote about you in the papers. I gave my pupils the task of reading your books, of determining by them *what you were*, and of establishing on this basis what you would be able to find. So we knew what you would find while you were still on your way there.

Ouspensky's thirst for knowledge kept him in his chair and minute by minute Gurdjieff grew in his estimation. He liked his naturalness, inner simplicity, and sense of humour; his lack of affectation, or pretence to sanctity and miraculous powers. Nor did Gurdjieff disappoint Ouspensky's mind. 'In his explanations I felt the assurance of a specialist, a very fine analysis of facts, and a *system* which I could not grasp, but the presence of which I already felt.'

Emerging from the café, Gurdjieff hailed a carriage and took Ouspensky to an empty flat over a school near the Red Pond, where he introduced him to his pupils – three young men and two municipal schoolmistresses. Gurdjieff had boasted they were going to his luxurious apartment to meet a number of professors and artists. The average man would surely have reacted violently to such a transparent bluff – but Gurdjieff was not in search of average men. Ouspensky, who had felt from earliest childhood that so-called 'normal' life consisted of obvious absurdities, was evidently refreshed to meet someone dealing in contraries and enigmas. Arguably Ouspensky found Gurdjieff trustworthy *because* he appeared fraudulent (after all it was the *métier* of fraudulent people to look trustworthy). As Gurdjieff once said:

> Truth can only come to people *in the form of a lie* – only in this form are they able to accept it; only in this form are they able to digest and assimilate it. Truth undefiled would be, for them, indigestible food.

On Gurdjieff's instructions one of his pupils began to read outloud from *Glimpses of Truth*. One must feel for Ouspensky now, squatting there uncomfortably on a cushion among strangers, in a situation of such peculiar ambivalence.

> G. listened attentively the whole time. He sat on a sofa, with one leg tucked between him, drinking black coffee from a tumbler, smoking and sometimes glancing at me. I liked his movements which had a great deal of a kind of feline grace and assurance; even in his silence there was something which distinguished him from the others.

Before driving home to Okhotny Nad, Ouspensky urgently asked to see Gurdjieff again; so they met together in the same café at the same table the next day, and the next, and the next ... until finally Gurdjieff agreed to accept Ouspensky as his pupil. At the end of this momentous week, Ouspensky's work obliged him to return to Petrograd, where he rushed from the Nikolaevski station to his protégé Anna Ilinishna and burst out, 'I have found the Miracle.'

With this expression of enthusiasm, the Gurdjieff–Ouspensky relationship surprisingly loses impetus: not for another six months did the two men even meet. We know that Ouspensky was engrossed in the publication of his novellas, *Talks with a Devil* and *The Inventor* – both coloured by his outrage at the war. And the blessed pinch of commonsense which restores to the iconic Gurdjieff his ordinary humanity, convinces us that he too had concerns directly linked with the fighting.

On 2 November 1914 Russia had declared war on Turkey, resuming that perennial Caucasian brawl which nearly forty years before had brought the Giorgiades family to Kars. Other things being equal, Gurdjieff might well have shrugged away the spiteful little campaign which developed now between General Nicholas Yudenich and Enver Pasha. But other things were not equal. As the Russian columns, breaking out from the railhead at Sari Kamish, surprisingly fought their way into eastern Turkey in early 1915, the retreating Turks embarked on the genocide of their Armenian subjects. They felt it superfluous even to code the instructions; Talaat Pasha, the Interior Minister, explicitly telegraphed the Governor of Aleppo:

> The Government has decided to exterminate all the Armenians living in Turkey ... Without pity for women, children and invalids, however tragic the methods of extermination may be, without heeding any scruples of conscience, their existence must be terminated.

Sub specie aeternitatis Gurdjieff doubtless did perceive the World War as a planetary spasm, and this latest Caucasian butchery as a minor footnote to 'the history of crime': but on the human level he cared passionately that his Armenian mother and sisters in Alexandropol remain safely on the Russian side of a front line which could fluctuate east as well as west. In this sense he certainly had his war: his theatre of existential concern.

Gurdjieff woke on 9 June 1915 to find Moscow swept by riots: morale was abject, and slowly but surely society was beginning to totter. August and September brought a new series of shattering defeats, which variously led Grand Duke Nicholas Nikolaievich to sense the presence of Joan of Arc and General Samsonov to commit suicide. His Majesty the Tsar assumed direct command of the European front and installed himself in Military HQ at Mogilov, where he unaccountably devoted almost all his energies to playing dominoes. While the poor bloody infantry was shovelled into mass graves, and the factory workers of Moscow and Petrograd failed from malnutrition, a swarm of virile opportunists seized their golden moment:

> Everybody splashed about in the bloody mud – bankers, heads of the commissariat, industrialists, ballerinas of the Tsar and the grand dukes, Orthodox prelates, ladies-in-waiting, liberal deputies, generals in the front and rear, radical lawyers, illustrious mandarins of both sexes, innumerable nephews, and more particularly nieces.

These conditions were of no help to Gurdjieff. He was not implicated in the profiteering, and his fundamental work was hindered in a dozen niggling ways: several of his promising young men had been swept away in the first mobilization. Some were already dead; and Pohl and Mercourov were exercised to keep out of it all.

It was not ordained that either of Gurdjieff's small Moscow groups should thrive: the big flowering of his work was reserved for Petrograd. The seed from which it sprang was planted there by Gurdjieff in autumn 1915 and generously watered by Ouspensky. Immediately on arrival Gurdjieff phoned with positive news: he had decided to lecture and demonstrate, to attract people of quality, and to build a real esoteric group such as alone offered a context for development.

Immediately we seem to register the eager answering glint of Ouspensky's pince-nez, as of a man who has long prepared himself for this moment. The 'professors and artists' of his acquaintance were real enough; he knew authors, editors, politicians and policemen; he was receivable in theosophical, Tolstoyan, and symbolist circles; through dazed summer evenings at the Errant Dog he had drunk his way into the confidence of more articulate and intelligent people than he could conveniently remember. He knew the celebrated critic A. L. Volinsky, whose book *Leonardo da Vinci* had won him the honorary citizenship of Milan; he knew Nicholas Evreinoff, author of *The Theatralization of Life*; he knew the president of the Imperial Geographical Society.

Gurdjieff's address to this body concerning the Gobi and Taklamakan deserts alerted Ouspensky to a difficulty he had not fully anticipated:

> Gurdjieff discoursed long and authoritatively on the subject, and then towards the end he told of having discovered a small valley with precipitous sides which made the valley impossible of access. The floor glittered with diamonds which the natives gathered by a novel method. They threw down lumps of meat, and trained vultures to retrieve the diamond-studded morsels. Many suspicious glances were exchanged among the savants; many of them rose and left. The whole lecture ended in a fiasco.

This incident proved typical. Besides Gurdjieff's anarchic sense of humour, he was something of the Tarot juggler – the eternal 'situationalist' plucking advantages out of the air he himself had set quivering. And if this almost invariably cost him the disdain of people who judged by surface behaviour, well and good – he did not want them anyway.

Ouspensky soldiered on, doggedly accommodating his efforts to his master's incalculable response. Each time Gurdjieff arrived in Petrograd, Ouspensky handed him a meticulously written aide-mémoire of speaking engagements – either with some suitable society or with select audiences convened in private houses. Although Gurdjieff invented many difficulties, chopping and changing arrangements, there had emerged by early November a core of thirty or forty regular attenders, two of whom invariably sat in the front row: Dr Stjoernval who knew the pangs of an uninhibited personal attachment, and Ouspensky who considered he 'already had a grasp of some fundamental points of G.'s system'.

Such was the swell of interest, that after January 1916 Gurdjieff made the effort of coming to Petrograd every fortnight, sometimes inviting his senior Moscow pupils. A convenient walk from his flat on Pushkin Street were many agreeable cafés, notably Phillipoff's, where he sat all day holding dialogue with a stream of individual petitioners. For hours at a time Ouspensky hovered on the fringe, trying (not for him an easy task) to seem unobtrusive; drinking coffee *à la Varsovienne* until his cup rattled in its saucer; dutifully intent to anticipate Gurdjieff's needs and serve them. Slowly but surely the clock ticked towards the moment when Gurdjieff must catch the train back to Moscow. Then casually he would beckon Ouspensky: 'Why not have a meeting tonight? Ring up those who wanted to come and tell them we shall be at such and such a place.' Ouspensky's equanimity was admirable, his response innocent of exasperation or excitement. Holding his book of phone numbers inches from his nose, he studied them evenly over the top of his pince-nez and somehow coped.

Rather to Ouspensky's surprise, Gurdjieff of the Phillipoff's café period proved a keen entrepreneur. Finding that carpets commanded higher prices in Petrograd, he always brought from Moscow any discards from his own collection, plus moderate stuff picked up there at the Tolkutchka. But money was only one factor: the rugs themselves were intrinsically dear to Gurdjieff, both for their craftsmanship and their associations. A standing advertisement in the Petrograd newspapers brought to his door a medley of customers, so that in selling carpets he was buying piquant incident. To one avaricious society hostess, desperately bargaining for a dozen really fine items, Gurdjieff suddenly offered all the carpets in the room for a quarter of the contested price. For a moment she was stunned: then she recovered and started bargaining again. With a shrug, a spread of his hands, an evasive Levantine smile – Gurdjieff blurred the issue; next day he returned to Moscow and the woman got nothing.

What eludes mere reportage of Gurdjieff's role-playing, or his apparent 'perversity' in dealing with various inquirers, is its rationale

— its extraordinary substratum of psychic tension and contrivance. All his being was in fact strained towards finding serious pupils, yet paradoxically he could not afford to facilitate their approach. Why? Because to imagine that any step in the direction of conscious evolution could possibly be 'facile', was for him a contradiction in terms. Hence the difficulties. Hence his self-production as Tifon the Sordid, or the 'illiterate Caucasian carpet dealer', or the bogus geographer:

> Our feeling of this 'acting' in G. was exceptionally strong. Among ourselves we often said we never saw him and never would. In any other man so much 'acting' would have produced the impression of falsity. In him 'acting' produced an impression of strength ...

And the mystery of Gurdjieff's blatant acting was wrapped in an enigma, since it somehow or other accommodated the perception that he was always innocently natural and straightforward!

February 1916 is a month of some importance in the Gurdjieffian canon. The teaching in all its plenitude was about to be delivered to the Petrograd group. A nucleus of six receptive pupils had emerged: Ouspensky, Stjoernval, Andrei Andreivitch Zaharoff, Anna Butkovsky, Anthony Charkovsky, and Nicholas R.; respectively a writer, psychiatrist, mathematician, musician, engineer, and government official.

Although the riddle of their true identity prevails over many facile answers, there cannot be much pretence at biographic fair play. Only in Anna's meandering memoir, written at ninety, do we catch any glimpse of Anthony (who built bridges and had exceptional 'purity of heart') and Nicholas (an emotional old widower fidgeting 'like a bird with ruffled feathers'). Anna's own status, as the one woman among the six, lends her individuality a special interest; perhaps her self-portrait does her an injustice, perhaps she had hidden depths. Her long delicious dalliance with Ouspensky — fuelled on unlimited quantities of coffee, theosophy, and currant buns — had brought her with huge improbability to Gurdjieff, at the height of his powers and at the threshold of his most intense teaching period. 'It is you,' she said, 'that I have looked forward to meeting with such joy.' Patently Anna Butkovsky was no Vitvitskaia or Mme Ostrowska, and Gurdjieff accepted her for real but lesser virtues. Although she was cruelly destined to lose Ouspensky without really finding Gurdjieff, the young lady flutters cheerfully through the darkening air of the Gurdjieffian myth like an escapee from 'All Things Bright and Beautiful'. Stjoernval and Zaharoff make awkward yoke-fellows

– the decent, maddeningly reasonable, doctor, and the shy, lock-jawed young bachelor tormented with existential questions all the more eloquent for being absolutely inexpressible. As for Ouspensky, he stands in lofty solitude. 'You may marvel', writes Anna cryptically, 'how a group of such seemingly ordinary people came to gather together in such an abstract eternal quest.'

These six, and the larger Petrograd group which slowly crystallized round them, took the full impact of Gurdjieff's teaching between February and August 1916. In twenty-five weeks of concentrated activity he handed on ideas and schemata which had cost him and his companions twenty-five years to gather. Although this ratio remains utterly extraordinary, the historical context hints at an explanation. Not only was the European world, where Gurdjieff ultimately aimed to plant his influence, convulsed by a war of unprecedented scale, indescribable horror, and dubious outcome, but the fighting was now on Russian soil and revolution was more and more in the air. Consider in this perspective his lonely obligation to shepherd his doctrine into the future; what if he were silenced by some brutal contemporary accident, before he had transmitted the essence of his discoveries? And dare we glimpse also a self-perceived compunction to mobilize his efforts precisely in that epoch of dreadful mechanicity, as the advocate and agent of consciousness; to create at least some antibodies to the infection of mass psychosis; to re-affirm man's high potentiality in the very moment of his utter degradation and desolation?

By August 1916 Gurdjieff had richly earned a moment of remission. The great 'Do' of the octave of transmission had been sounded. The Petrograd group had grown to thirty, and, although green in practice, had assimilated virtually all the cosmological and psychological theory – the Law of Three, the Law of Seven, the Ray of Creation, the Table of Hydrogens, the Food Diagram, and material on Cosmoses. Ouspensky in fact (and so much the better) had secretly taken notes ... Meanwhile the Russian Siberian Division had made a brilliant forced march: Erzurum had fallen; and Mush and Bitlis and Trebizond. All was quiet on the Caucasian front and Gurdjieff's anxieties for his family were temporarily allayed.

Yet far from slackening the demand on himself and his pupils, Gurdjieff intensified it, aware that at any instant the guillotine of history could fall. 'You must understand that ordinary efforts do not count. *Only super-efforts count.*' Every evening he held group. Every day he led his pupils on unfathomable excursions; newcomers with a focused interest in Raymond Lull or the Holy Grail were surprised to find themselves grilling *shashlik* miles up the River Neva. From their follies, incompetence, and petty squabbles Gurdjieff carved living object lessons. The work had become more practical; group exchanges more demanding and intimate: 'Everyone must strip himself, everyone must show himself as he is.'

Either such work on essence abrased personality, or by-passed it dramatically as in the case of the anonymous pupil 'P'. Some high-flown desideratum or other – eluding definition – apparently underpinned P.'s dithering preoccupation with the war, with the destiny of Russia, and with the fate of civilization. But what precisely did he want? This question was posed him after Gurdjieff had temporarily 'put his personality to sleep':

> On a small table beside him there stood an unfinished glass of tea. He gazed at it for a long time as though considering something. He glanced around him twice, then again looked at the glass, and said in such a serious voice and with such serious intonations that we all looked at one another:
> *'I think I should like some raspberry jam.'*

Biographically it is a pity the experiment was performed on P. and not on someone more significant; one glimpse of Ouspensky reduced to essence, Ouspensky with his primal wish revealed, might have been very useful.

As the midwife of consciousness, Gurdjieff's benignity was utterly ruthless; throughout the late summer of 1916 he brought his closest pupils to moments of illuminating crisis. Sometimes the entire group seemed to peer down the barrel of a loaded blunderbuss ('Mystics indeed! The best thing for you all would be to be put in gaol ...'); sometimes a delicate rapier thrust punctured a particular ego. Dr Stjoernval suffered cruelly during the confessional phase – the self-eviscerating candour which the alienist required professionally, he himself found impossible to deliver. Ouspensky's case was peculiar in that, although he too received his fair share of provocations ('Whatever is this rubbish you're talking? ... God preserve us from such people'), he actually throve on crisis and intensity. One succession of self-imposed fasts, reckless breathing exercises, and prayerful vigils had an extraordinary dénouement.

The time was ten o'clock on a languid August evening. Ouspensky was sitting Turkish fashion on the wooden boards of Madame Maximovitch's country house in Finland. Gurdjieff was opposite him, smiling and enigmatic, and to his left and his right sat Zaharoff and Dr Stjoernval. Gurdjieff demonstrated certain postures and movements, spoke a little while, and then fell silent: 'And with this the miracle began.' In some mysterious locus near his heart, Ouspensky 'heard' the renewed vibration of Gurdjieff's voice; it posed a question which provoked a surge of emotion and Ouspensky responded aloud. 'Why did he say that?' Gurdjieff asked disingenuously. 'Did I ask him anything?' But Zaharoff and Stjoernval – to their everlasting credit – offered no violence to a situation as fragile as it was inexplicable. For a full half hour they held their attention as Gurdjieff sat smoking and Ouspensky intermittently 'answered' him with increasing intensity. Gurdjieff's secret theme was sufficiently disquieting: Ouspensky must either accept certain special conditions or leave the Work.

The message is almost more astonishing than the medium. Having identified in Piotr Ouspensky not only a pupil of the highest intellectual quality, but one attuned on a subtle telepathic level, Gurdjieff immediately broaches the question of his severance. There is a leonine self-confidence here; shrewd psychological calculation; and plasticity towards the myth which, sooner or later, requires Gurdjieff to persuade necessity. For Ouspensky the immediate experience was of course overwhelming: 'I went into the forest, I walked about a long time in the dark, wholly in the power of the most extraordinary thoughts and feelings.' But better was to come, as Ouspensky recalls: 'A strange excitement again began in me, my pulse began to beat forcibly, and I again heard G.'s voice in my chest. On this occasion I not only heard *but I replied mentally*.' Yet later, the faculty of vision was added – Ouspensky conversing with Gurdjieff while seeing him miles away on the train to Moscow.

How did Gurdjieff do it? (And how did he affect P.?) Ouspensky's insistence that he employed no external means whatever – no narcotics and no hypnotism – disarms rationalist critique, while moonstruck solutions involving one or another modality of 'black magic' are rudely pre-empted by Gurdjieff himself: 'There is neither red, green, nor yellow magic... "Doing" is magic and "doing" can only be of one kind ... in true work, that is, in true "doing", the producing of infatuation in people is not allowed.' We are left, as so often, with the dubious tautological 'explanation' of *hanbledzoin* or animal magnetism.

Early in September Gurdjieff returned yet again to Petrograd, bringing a fierce emphasis on the practice of presence and a new ultimatum:

In future I shall work only with those who can be useful to me in attaining my aim. And only those people can be useful to me who have firmly decided to struggle with themselves, that is, to struggle with mechanical-ness.

In a room on Liteiny Street he confronted his anxious pupils one by one, and virtually all thirty agreed to make fresh efforts. Their implicit alignment with their teacher's aim was – to put it mildly – uninformed, since the immediacy of current challenges left no one much scope to dwell on the 'long body' of the Work: its trajectory from the remote past into the remote future.

Least of all did anyone except Gurdjieff himself wish to confront the impending diaspora, although the tell-tale signs of a fundamental social collapse already stared them in the face. Conditions at the front were quite appalling; at home the portfolio of the Minister of the Interior had passed into the surprised hands of Alexander Protopopov, who was unfortunately suffering from general paralysis of the insane. In October, when the jaded forces of law and order marched out to quell the latest civil disturbance in Petrograd, the soldiers unprecedentedly sided with the workers and levelled their rifles at the police. Protopopov was urged to resign, but, as he said, 'How can I resign? All my life I've dreamed of being a vice-governor and here I am – a Minister!' The Cossacks were accordingly sent in and 150 mutineers court-martialled and shot. At this inauspicious moment Piotr Ouspensky was mobilized and commissioned in the Guards Sappers.

So for an instant a grim and terrible war reached out to claim Gurdjieff's most eminent disciple; reached out, and then apparently thought better of it. If Ouspensky had been killed, a crêpe-edged melancholy would have descended over an episode which funda-mentally offers itself in terms of comic relief. Whenever a subaltern in the Russian Army was praised by an officer of field rank, it was incumbent on him to spring to attention and respond 'Eager to serve, Excellency!' Whether Ouspensky even once had this falsehood on his lips is a moot point, but his overall contribution to the war effort was necessarily impaired by his philosophic bent, acute myopia, and Tolstoyan pacifism. In 1915 he had witnessed:

> two enormous lorries on the Liteiny loaded to the height of the first floor of the houses with new unpainted wooden *crutches*. . . In these mountains of crutches *for legs which were not yet torn off* there was a particularly cynical mockery of all the things with which people deceive themselves.

Ouspensky was not eager to serve: on the contrary, he was eager not to serve. Besides being totally dedicated to his studies with Gurdjieff, he had recently received into his comfortable new apartment on the Troitskaia, Mme Sophie Grigorievna Maximenko, a Junoesque matron with chestnut hair, imperious eyes, and a vehemence which sent ordinary subordinable men groping for the smelling salts. Ouspensky's moments of psychological crisis were, for the time being, amply provided by life itself; every morning he had to make a two-mile tram journey to regimental HQ in Petrograd. His eyesight was bad and it got worse; he had some difficulty in reading brigade orders, and particularly wished he could see his medical discharge papers.

Gurdjieff himself missed the Petrograd mutiny and Ouspensky's mobilization by about a week, having returned to Moscow and taken up life again with Mme Ostrowska, Mercourov, and the Moscow groups. But he still needed pupils who needed him – this remained basic and perennial; even in the sunset glow of his teaching period in metropolitan Russia, he sought new prospects who possessed a strong 'magnetic centre'. Ouspensky sponsored a particularly unfortunate candidate who never stopped talking, especially about the dessication of onions. 'He is called a clever man,' objected Gurdjieff. 'But he would not have noticed it even if I had taken his trousers off him.' Other entrants were more welcome. Under the name 'Mme Ouspensky' (a title adopted from convenience and ratified by usage) Sophie Grigorievna joined the group. She was a woman with a strong character and a rather baffling past; twice before she had been married, firstly to a student when only sixteen, and secondly to a mining engineer, an adventurer whose far-flung travels in Central Asia suggest – no doubt misleadingly – something of Piotr Karpenko of the Seekers of Truth.

It was the tongue-tied Zaharoff who brought to Gurdjieff by far the most important recruit of this period. Among his acquaintances at Tzarskoye Selo (the Russian Windsor fifteen miles south of Petrograd) was a junior reserve officer in the illustrious Imperial Rifles, a certain Thomas Alexandrovitch de Hartmann. Fate had favoured Thomas with good health, a distinguished aquiline face, a private income, a rare gift for music, and the attentions of Olga Arcadievna, his charming, accomplished, and high-born wife. Ironically in the present context all these advantages were bittersweet: the more de Hartmann considered his stultifying garrison duties and his imminent posting to the Kiev front, the more he suffered from a sense of being blown off course. Although a patriot and personally indebted to the Tsar, his true allegiance was to universals: art, music, and the latent spiritual forces in man. Memories of early triumphs (his ballet for example, *The Pink Flower*, premièred at the Imperial Opera of St Petersburg, with Fokine, Karsavina, Nijinsky, and Pavlova in the cast, and Nicholas II in the audience) visited him like ghosts whispering 'Never again!'.

Throughout his life as a musician Thomas de Hartmann had drawn inspiration from words which seemed to predicate his meeting with Gurdjieff: 'Go – not knowing where; bring – not knowing what; the path is long, the way unknown; the hero knows not how to arrive there by himself alone; he has to seek the guidance and help of Higher forces.' And yet, was it really conceivable that this proud and sensitive spirit – nurtured musically by Anton Arensky and Serge Tanieff, afforded a lofty theosophical orientation by Annette Essipov, schooled in art by no less a prodigy than Wassily Kandinsky, and applauded even by His Majesty the Tsar – was it conceivable that such a man would totally surrender himself to an unknown Caucasian, who, adjusting his soiled pair of detachable shirt cuffs, explained at their first meeting, 'There are usually more whores here'? Evidently it was.

Gurdjieff's well-practised Tifon-the-Sordid procedure was a spiritual litmus test which separated genuine seekers from mere voyeurs. Some inquirers (and who can blame them) recoiled in shock from that mask; others had the sense to study Gurdjieff's eyes and found there ample confirmation of a far different being. Certainly Thomas de Hartmann did: 'I realised that the eyes of Mr Gurdjieff were of unusual depth and penetration . . . I had never seen such eyes or felt such a look.' There is persuasive evidence of an instant emotional rapport between de Hartmann and Gurdjieff, between the young musician and the poet of situations. Secretly Gurdjieff must have been well pleased, for upon this particular rapport very largely depended the musical extrapolation of his work.

De Hartmann had become Gurdjieff's pupil in a sombre time. As 1916 shrank miserably towards the winter solstice, a general sense of doom oppressed Russia. No one believed in victory any more, or in words. In mid-December Grigori Rasputin (always against the war) was treacherously assassinated in an episode of unbelievable *grand guignol*. The princely class which contrived and celebrated Rasputin's death, least perceived its implications – least understood that 'The bullet which killed him reached the very heart of the ruling dynasty.' Through a haze of cigar smoke and Möet et Chandon *brut imperial*, the nobility saw the ship of state as needing some minor personnel changes on the bridge, but never dreamed it could founder forever in the dark sea of the masses. Gurdjieff did. He saw the coming deluge and the relevance of Noah's Ark – the epoch when his teaching could only be preserved *by living in it*.

Olga Arcadievna de Hartmann had just turned thirty yet was marvellously innocent in worldly experience. Gurdjieff's kindness, delicacy, and sheer wit in approaching her (initially as much for her husband's sake as for his own) is certainly appealing. Immediately her husband had mentioned his contact with Gurdjieff, Olga became desperately impatient to share that experience; her chance came in mid-February 1917, when Gurdjieff made his final visit to Petrograd. She was sitting tentatively in her first group in Ouspensky's apartment listening to Dr Stjoernval when 'Quite unexpectedly – like a black panther – a man of oriental appearance . . . came in.' Olga was head over heels in love with Thomas and trembled when Gurdjieff asserted that love was the main impediment to spiritual development. Then looking at her, he added:

> But what kind of love?. . . When it is self-love, egotistical love, or temporary attraction it hinders, because it ties a man down and he is not free. But if it is real love with each wishing to help the other, then it is different; and I am always glad if husband and wife are both interested in these ideas, because they can help each other.

Olga could hardly raise her eyes. Soon afterwards she sought out Gurdjieff and engagingly offered to push him and her husband up the ladder of development! Gurdjieff did not snub her but replied: 'Look, you can push us perhaps from the second step to the third, from the third to the fourth, but then you cannot reach us. So in order to push us higher, you also have to go up one or two steps.' At that moment she became Gurdjieff's pupil and began with all her force and understanding to follow his indications.

The best historical inference has Gurdjieff leave Petrograd on Thursday 23 February 1917 Old Style, which was cutting things pretty fine. Nicholas II had left the day before; on Friday grave disorders broke out; on Saturday the Cossacks cut off the head of the Captain of Police in Znamenskaia Square right next to Gurdjieff's apartment; by Monday the Admiralty was blazing and the Fortress of Peter and Paul emptied of prisoners; and by Thursday 2 March the Tsar of All the Russias had gratefully abdicated in a railway siding at Pskov.

Gurdjieff was of course neither for nor against the Romanov regime, but Petrograd did not suit him and he was well content to go. The capital's tyrannous abstraction – its melancholy sunsets, vast dogmatic skies, and frozen palaces hung along the Neva quay – contradicted his earthy humanity and humour. In Petrograd (and only in Petrograd) Gurdjieff's dispensation assumes a majestic formalism suspiciously redolent of the city itself. Although by any standards he had accomplished there a momentous ideological affirmation, the *Doppelgänger* of antithesis was waiting in the wings. Only two months separate Gurdjieff's departure at the Nikolaevski Station from Lenin's arrival at the Finland Station. Such ironic juxtapositions could not be helped. Never had Gurdjieff's particular neo-Manicheism guaranteed victory to the forces of light: on the contrary Ashiata Shiemash and Lentrohamsanin enact a struggle of the magicians in which the dark forces seemingly prevail.

Goodbye then to Petrograd. Goodbye to the *ancien régime*. The railway station would be renamed and the capital itself renamed: Protopopov would be shot and His Majesty the Emperor shot; Mathilde Kschessinska, the *prima ballerina assoluta*, would pirouette into obscurity with her trembling fox-terrier Djibi under her arm; the wonder-working icon of Our Lady of Kazan would be missing from its accustomed place in the Kazan cathedral; the Tsar's Fabergé Easter eggs and the Tsarina's favourite novels of Marie Corelli would embarrass new cabinets; and the white-faced Okhrana would be hunted to death through the unforgiving streets. Millions of individual lives were converging towards their interlocking dénouements; millions of blind mice were scampering to a general rendezvous at the carving knife.

By common testimony some mysterious transfiguration marked Gurdjieff's actual departure:

> He was different! In the window we saw another man, not the one who had gone into the train. He had changed during those few seconds ... on the platform he had been an ordinary man like anyone else, and from the carriage a man of a quite different order was looking at us, with a quite exceptional importance and dignity in every look and movement, as though he had suddenly become a ruling prince or a statesman of some unknown kingdom ...

In the upturned faces of his chief followers – Dr Stjoernval, Zaharoff, the de Hartmanns, and the now demobilized Ouspensky – Gurdjieff could personify an objective hope. But nevertheless a hope which the coming cataclysm would test to breaking point. The departure bell followed the warning bell almost immediately; with a churning of wheels the long train began to move and was soon gone forever leaving only its historicity behind.

3

❖

MIRAGES OF SAFETY

(March 1917–August 1918)

Gurdjieff did not linger in Moscow but set out immediately to visit his parents. The journey to Alexandropol was tedious, exhausting, and long enough to encapsulate a bit of history: when Gurdjieff and Mme Ostrowska boarded the train the Tsar still reigned, and when they got off he did not. Their original intention had been to return to Petrograd at Easter (and a postcard telling Ouspensky so lay for weeks at the sorting office). Even the bloody turmoil which epitomized the 'bloodless revolution' did not close Gurdjieff's mind to the possibility of going back; his telegram to Ouspensky a week after Easter merely postponed his arrival until May. By May however the Russian army was everywhere disintegrating. With His Imperial Majesty no longer at Military HQ (playing dominoes) the last vestige of motivation was apparently gone. Although the troopers of the Siberian Division, inexplicably entrenched between Armenia and the Turks, had not yet begun nailing their officers' epaulets to their shoulders, they were increasingly exposed to the dangers of independent and inebriate thought.

Gurdjieff was now fifty-one and had not seen his family for thirteen years. Here at last was Alexandropol; here the Greek quarter; here the very house where he was born. Age had dressed his mother in traditional black and lined her face with a profound resignation, but his father had only a few silver hairs in his beard. Hard manual work, the incessant recitation of poetry, and a big intake of Latakia tobacco, had helped translate the *ashokh*'s ideals into a remarkably happy old age. Giorgios Giorgiades was a pattern of stoicism, deeply fulfilled, 'ready to reconcile himself to anything, provided there were only bread and quiet during his established hours for meditation . . . in the evening when he would sit in the open looking at the stars.'

Also on hand to greet Gurdjieff were his two sisters: Anna Ivanovna Anastasieff and Sophie Ivanovna Kapanadze. Dmitri his brother was there with Anna Grigorievna, daughter of Archbishop Martinian of Tiflis – the bride to whom, in his late forties, he had finally surrendered a bachelordom full of interest and incident. The Mercourov family came, eager for the latest news of Sergei Dmitrievitch; there were cousins and second cousins to feast the wanderer's return, and a gaggle of nephews and nieces to sit on his knee.

For a precious month or two Gurdjieff plunged into family life. He helped his father in his little workshop and listened to him with great seriousness, 'occasionally laughing a little, but evidently never for a second losing the line . . . and the whole time sustaining the conversation with questions and comments'. How tonic after Petrograd and how magically evocative in memory's nostrils was that old sweet blend of glue and resin and Latakia: boyhood's incense, through which there glided (leaving no footprint in today's sawdust) the frail companionable shade of Dean Borsh. A powerful sense of indebtedness demanded expression:

> One Sunday . . . the priests and congregation of Kars Military Cathedral were much astonished and interested when a man quite unknown in the neighbourhood requested the full funeral service to be held over a lonely and forgotten grave, the only one within the grounds of the cathedral. And they saw how this stranger with difficulty held back his tears. . .

Early in June Gurdjieff telegraphed Ouspensky: 'If you want to rest come here to me.' Ouspensky needed no urging, since the revolution had led him to the agonized perception that the entire group must emigrate. After an anarchic five-day train journey from Petrograd, Ouspensky indeed deserved a rest. He had seen three executions as he waited blamelessly in the understocked buffet of Tiflis railway station: 'The first man had been shot for theft. The second was shot by mistake because he had been mistaken for the first; and the third was also shot by mistake because he had been mistaken for the second.' When finally Ouspensky dragged himself into Alexandropol, he found Gurdjieff setting up a dynamo for Dmitri.

Why did Gurdjieff summon Ouspensky? Why only Ouspensky? And why as late as June? Evidently not to confer, for Ouspensky records: 'I hardly saw G. alone and seldom succeeded in speaking to him.' Just occasionally, in a 'lazy' tone of voice, Gurdjieff trailed a hodgepodge of peculiar intentions discrepantly through the prim landscape of Ouspensky's logicality: he knew a mountain hideaway in Transcaucasia; 'it would be good to go to Persia'; he fancied returning to Petrograd 'to see the Nevsky with hawkers selling sunflower seeds'.

Behind this veil of options, Gurdjieff was urgently trying to clarify and reconcile his responsibilities to his groups and his family. Time would implacably deliver (but when would it deliver?) a Turkish blow against Alexandropol; already the prudence of resettling the Giorgiades family was obvious. Again and again Gurdjieff spoke with his father, and the old *ashokh* sucked thoughtfully on his pipe. At eighty-three Giorgios Giorgiades 'led an almost pedantically regular life' and more to the point he led it in Alexandropol. Heavy in the air lay the unspoken understanding that he would sooner die than leave.

Gurdjieff saw his childhood home for the very last time early in July 1917, as he set off 'for Petrograd' with Mme Ostrowska, two relatives, and Piotr Ouspensky; he brought his father's blessing and – who knows why? – a big box of skein silk. The railway line between Alexandropol and Rostov is crooked as a dog's hind leg, with joints at Tiflis and Baku (where first it confronts the Caucasus range, then doubles its south-eastern extremity). In Tiflis the party ran into General S., formerly of the Petrograd group, who gave them – as generals sometimes will if sufficiently pressed – his politico-strategic analysis. Next day from a siding on the Baku–Derbent track, Gurdjieff watched reflectively as trainload after trainload of raucous 'comrades' rolled home from the collapsing Armenian front: 'It was very hot, a quarter of a mile away the surface of the Caspian sea was glittering, and all around us was nothing but fine shining flint with the outline of two camels in the distance.'

Ouspensky remarked gloomily that events were now all against them and that it was impossible to do anything in the middle of such mass insanity. Gurdjieff's unexpected response mirrors his appreciation of 'sharp, energetic events', and his long-term vision of the diaspora:

It is only now that it is possible ... and events are not against us at all. They are merely moving too quickly. This is the whole trouble. But wait five years and you will see for yourself how what hinders today will prove useful to us.

With cruel slowness Gurdjieff's train laboured inland, but when it reached the dusty town of Mozdok, he suddenly announced that he and his three companions would remain indefinitely in the nearby spa district of Mineralni Vodi, and Ouspensky must go on alone: 'Tell them in Moscow and Petersburg that I am beginning new work here. Those who want to work with me can come. And I advise you not to stay there long.' Only one rider was added: Dr Stjoernval and his wife Elizabeta might hold on in Petrograd if they preferred, until the political situation clarified itself.

The town of Essentuki, where Gurdjieff chose to settle, lies in the foothills near to Mount Elbruz in a valley watered by two rivers: the Bugunty and the Essentik. In Panteleimon Street there stood a small country villa, which – if walls have ears or stones sensibility – must have registered in July 1917 a remarkable quickening of atmosphere. When Gurdjieff moved in with Mme Ostrowska (high summer and the crickets singing in the grass) they brought a mood of private tenderness granted its brief occasion. But after only a fortnight Ouspensky returned from Petrograd – the spirit of pale expectancy. The doorbell which rang for Andrei Zaharoff and Alexander Petrov and Nicholas R. sounded a note of frayed but passionate commitment. Each new arrival contributed his increment of drama; none was remotely in a 'normal' frame of mind as normality is torpidly celebrated in provincial villas; by mid-July when thirteen pupils had forgathered, the establishment in Panteleimon Street incubated an extravagant hope.

Building on this expectation, Gurdjieff now threw everyone pell-mell into a six-week trial of unparalleled fervour:

> It would be difficult even in six years to find room for everything that was connected with this time ... In general, during the short period of our stay at Essentuki, G. unfolded to us the plan of the whole work. We saw the beginnings of all the methods, the beginnings of all the ideas, their links, their connections and direction.

Even today the Essentuki 'intensive' defies our crude litmus test, somehow remaining both a straightforward feasibility study in communal and holistic living, and an impenetrable spiritual arcanum.

Life was certainly not all tribulation:

> G. superintended the kitchen and often prepared dinner himself. He proved to be a wonderful cook and knew hundreds of remarkable eastern dishes. Every day we had dinner in the style of some eastern country; we ate Tibetan, Persian and other dishes.

But the company also submitted itself to periods of rigorous fasting, when it knew a kind of futility of existence through days which never seemed to end. At night pupils had four hours' deep sleep,

or occasionally five. Sometimes the villa cooped them up entirely
but sometimes Gurdjieff led them out at a brisk pace, his silver-
headed ebony walking-stick tapping out the route to Kislovodsk,
Jeleznovodsk, Pyatigorsk, and Beshtau. He taught on local trains; he
taught in Essentuki Park with the band playing; the smallest incident
was used to make points or exemplify type: 'This is astrology. Do
you understand? You all saw me drop the stick. Why did one of you
pick it up? Let each of you speak for himself.'

What Petrograd was to theory, Essentuki was to practice. Here for
example Gurdjieff first gave his formidable 'Stop!' exercise – suddenly freezing all pupils within earshot into complete voluntary
immobility, and ruthlessly conferring a moment of psycho-somatic
registration. Here was first offered the spartan 'arms sideways' experience. Here too, by traditional techniques, Gurdjieff prepared his
pupils for the grace of a moment which transcends all technique –
gently coaxing the 'blood' of a pure attention along arteries and
capillaries not featured in *Gray's Anatomy*, until a new 'body' was
sensed, blocked with presence and light.

According to Gurdjieff's memoir (vaguely corroborated by
Ouspensky), another presence hovered on the fringe of the Essentuki
experiment: that of Skridlov, Professor of Archeology and senior
member of the Seekers of Truth. Granted Skridlov was indeed in
Pyatigorsk in August 1917 to visit his elder daughter; granted he
encountered Gurdjieff; granted they climbed together the southern
slope of Mount Beshtau (the Five Hills) – both men must have felt it
a meeting charged with extraordinary poignancy and significance.
Gurdjieff was fifty-two and Skridlov in his seventies, and they were
never to meet again. Who would follow in their footsteps? Who
would reach upwards, as strenuously as they had, for the summit
itself?

> Far to the south arose the majestic snow-capped peak of Elbrus . . . Below
> us, as in miniature, could be seen the entire region of the Mineral
> Waters . . . Silence reigned all around. No-one was on the mountain, and
> no one was likely to come . . .

This analogy – if rightly construed – is sombre.

Meanwhile in Panteleimon Street the singular struggles of
Gurdjieff's contemporary pupils were running their course. It was
inevitable – and to an extent even desirable – that among participants
would eventually arise a friction verging on downright antipathy. Yet
late in August Gurdjieff seized on this pretext to end his successful

field study, suddenly announcing he was dispersing the group and going to the Black Sea coast with Zaharoff. This was a Stop exercise with a vengeance! What might we detect if we too could halt the film and study this important frame? Certainly Ouspensky's lips tightening from a generalized hauteur into the cast of a specific grievance:

> I have to confess that my confidence in G. began to waver ... what particularly provoked me is difficult to define ... But the fact is that from this moment there began to take place in me a separation between G. himself and his ideas.

Here, in deep obscurity, commences the seven-year cycle which will carry Ouspensky, through a series of exquisite vacillations, to the wholesale repudiation of Gurdjieff and the wholesale appropriation of his ideas.

It was the fate of Thomas and Olga de Hartmann to arrive in Essentuki precisely now, when work had been broken off. They brought with them two carriages full of luggage, their chambermaid Marfousha, an abundance of goodwill, and an evident misunderstanding about Gurdjieff's regime. On ringing the gate bell, they were admitted by a very rough fellow: 'a man dressed simply in a Russian belted shirt and a worn coat, unshaven and smelling of sweat, like a labourer. It was difficult to recognize the invariably smart and elegant Zaharoff.'

As the de Hartmanns sipped their tea by the oil-lamp's glimmering light, they needed all their breeding to mask their incredulity: in February on the Nikolaevski Station, they had parted from a transfigured Gurdjieff who seemed 'a ruling prince or statesman of some unknown kingdom to which he was travelling'; now with huge difficulty they had got to his 'kingdom' – and it suggested to Olga a scene from Gorki's *Lower Depths*. Gurdjieff watched them watching him. He evidently saw two young people of immense promise, trapped in a 'Yezidi Circle' of dainty behavioural constraint which sooner or later he must expunge with ruthless compassion.

The 'intensive' was over, and the grand rhythm of the Work permitted almost all the exhausted alumni of Panteleimon Street a quiet recuperative interval – but typically not Gurdjieff himself. The spiritual hunger of the latest arrivals evoked the question: 'Is it not better to continue?' Thus when Gurdjieff left Essentuki on 30 August 1917 and entrained for Tuapse on the Black Sea coast, he took with him not only Mme Ostrowska and Zaharoff but Thomas and Olga de Hartmann. Ouspensky at first followed them but, making no headway, stoically returned to Petrograd to salvage his affairs. Despite an extraordinary 'investment' in Ouspensky, Gurdjieff did not raise a finger to detain him – quite the contrary, he facilitated his pupil's withdrawal by promising to look after his adult step-daughter, Lenotchka Savitsky.

Hardly had the little party in Tuapse settled comfortably into an hotel, than Gurdjieff, to the de Hartmanns' consternation, calmly announced he would be leaving for Persia:

> I will make a contract to break stones on the road ... It is a most disgusting job. It is not possible for you, because after a day's work the women must wash the workers' feet, and Zaharoff's feet, for instance, will smell awfully bad. Lenotchka – well she can wash feet, but your wife cannot.

From Tuapse to Persia is 600 miles as the crow flies – and navvies lack wings. If the de Hartmanns had relied on mundane criteria rather than spiritual, they would have missed their opportunity. They had after all every excuse for hanging back: Thomas was still an officer on active service, and Olga a cosseted aristocrat who did not yet appreciate her own strength. But with heartening loyalty and a refreshing lack of proportion, they obtained respectively two weeks' leave and a sufficiency of soap.

The following Sunday a strangely discrepant trio kept rendezvous with Gurdjieff and Zaharoff at a flea-bitten inn in the foothills high above Tuapse: Mme Ostrowska in free-flowing peasant's clothes, Olga in a fashionable costume and high heels, and Thomas in the field uniform of the Imperial Rifles. They had climbed steeply for ten sun-blistered hours, and, although Mme Ostrowska was fresh, the de Hartmanns were already dog-tired and dying to sleep. 'The night is so wonderful,' countered Gurdjieff cheerfully, 'the moon is shining. Is it not better to continue?'

Is it not better to continue? Here was the master-question of a seven-day initiation, bitter-sweet with suffering and consolation. When Thomas's legs were rubbed raw by his military trousers; when he was required to push the cart with Zaharoff while sustaining for a whole day a complex counting exercise – was it not better to continue? And when Olga's feet had swollen; when she struggled on in cardboard sandals; and when these fell to pieces and she hobbled barefoot – was it not better to continue?

> What a beautiful night it was! Dark as it can be only in the south, the stars were brighter than ever. The Caucasus, wolves, jackals howling, knowing

nothing of what tomorrow would bring – we were nevertheless happy in a way we had not known before.

So from milestone to milestone, the expedition described a semi-circle in the hills, back in fact to the Black Sea coast, where in the little village of Uch Dere (or Three Gorges), it finally arrived . . . in 'Persia'.

The rigours of the trip had fallen short of actual stone-breaking and Thomas de Hartmann returned refreshed: it was paradoxically in Uch Dere – with its paradisal roses, ancient cypresses, and green mosses – that he contracted typhoid. The young composer burned with fever, raged in delirium, and failed by inches to murder Olga with a wine bottle. Only Gurdjieff could pacify him: 'Now he sleeps . . . but we have to take him to hospital as we have absolutely nothing here not even a thermometer. Later you will see this is important for other reasons also.'

So Gurdjieff carried his pupil to a cart, laid him on a straw mattress, tied him down with a clothesline, and drove him twenty-two miles south to Sochi; devout passers-by threw flowers onto the corpse-like body with its livid blue lips. Was he dead? Could he live? In a small country hospital for contagious diseases Olga sat with these cruel questions for thirteen successive days and nights. A last-minute injection of camphor revived her husband's failing pulse; a placebo of medicinal sugar (prescribed by Gurdjieff) briefly calmed his mind. Marfousha the chambermaid came, and in an inspired gesture collected in her apron the red musical notes which were running through the room and driving Thomas mad. Gurdjieff came and placed his hand tenderly on Thomas's forehead . . . and at last the crisis eased.

Once he was confident that Thomas would mend, Gurdjieff returned to his wife and his talismanic box of silk in Uch Dere. His entourage there now totalled seven; they chopped up trees for winter firewood; they collected wild pears; and they coped with the animosity of some neighbouring Letts. Despite this rustic isolation, Gurdjieff evidently remained sensitized to the national situation: his peremptory telegram to Dr Stjoernval – 'Realise everything you can and come at once!' – went out just a fortnight before the Bolshevik coup. When Lenin did seize power on 26 October 1917, the bridge to the past fell away behind Gurdjieff; for him there was no going back; the precious phonograph recordings of his father's songs were irretrievable now from the apartment on the Bolshaia Dmitrovka;

carpets, cloisonné, papers, books – all were subsumed in the Great Socialist Revolution. Soon the whole arc of the Black Sea coast from the Taman Peninsula to Batoum would be ravaged, as White and Red armies and assorted nationalist irregulars clashed bloodily and confusedly among the laurels and rhododendrons and cork-oaks.

The little company in Uch Dere was already far from safe and far from united: the newly arrived Stjoernvals were forgivably disorientated and ill at ease; Zaharoff had obscurely lost his footing in his relationship with Gurdjieff and soon left to winter in Petrograd; Ouspensky had just returned from there, but with the slow fuse of his personal revolution against his teacher steadily burning. To add to Gurdjieff's troubles, he disovered at the end of October a distinct danger of being cut off at Uch Dere and left without provisions. Dividing his forces, he directed four of his people (including the de Hartmanns) inland to Essentuki, while he and his nucleus edged warily north along the coast.

By the time Soviet power was established in Tuapse on 3 November 1917, Gurdjieff had found sanctuary in the village of Olghniki. The villa he rented there was a mile from the nearest habitation and overlooked the sea; but, with a cruel north-easterly wind delivering a succession of sleety skies as sombre as basalt, it was desolation itself. Gurdjieff was reduced to five companions now (the Stjoernvals, the Ouspenskys and Mme Ostrowska) each heavily preoccupied: Piotr Ouspensky for example was vexed about a supposed inconsistency in the 'table of hydrogens', while Mme Stjoernval wondered expressively how she had been manœuvred into her present social situation. Gurdjieff, whose pressing obligation was to guarantee food for the company and fodder for the horses, felt Ouspensky's line of inquiry ill-timed:

> You ought to know that ... it was spoken of in the lectures in St Petersburg : .. Well, if you now heard that someone was giving the same lecture at Tuapse, would you go there on foot? ... Think – twenty-five miles, darkness, snow, rain, wind.

'What is there to think about?' responded Ouspensky. 'Of course I would go without a word.' (Strangely prophetic: Ouspensky would pay generously to be with 'someone' – anyone – who could restore his mislayed piece of the conceptual jigsaw, yet there he is sitting with Gurdjieff himself.) Real journeys to Tuapse were less and less advisable: Olghniki had proved yet another false sanctuary; rumours of advancing infantry grew from the faintest of drumbeats

to the most strident and urgent of warnings. Was it not better to
continue?

Round about Christmas 1917, Thomas de Hartmann in Essentuki
answered a knock at the door to find Gurdjieff standing there.
Delighted though he was to have his teacher back safe and sound,
and to accommodate him that night on the living-room sofa, he was
disappointed in his expectation of beginning esoteric work:

> We just went for walks every day with Mr Gurdjieff to the centre of
> Essentuki. He bought sunflower seeds, always giving me a handful, and
> would spit out the shells in front of passersby. Not a word was said about
> philosophy.

Evidently some of the shells fell so-to-say at the feet of Nicholas
Evreinoff – writer, eminent theatrical director (and former lover of
Anna Butkovsky). 'Evreinoff came up to Gurdjieff, inclined his head
towards him and said, "I am a difficult, pretentious man. I am
ambitious. But here, Georgi Ivanovitch, I bow to you ..."' In artistic
and avant-garde circles in Moscow and Petrograd, Evreinoff had met
thousands of celebrities, but he later described Gurdjieff as 'the
unique event'.

From Olghniki Gurdjieff had brought his full nucleus of pupils
but he now chiefly kept company with Dr Stjoernval, massaging
the psychiatrist's bruised confidence with an embrocation of pure
attention. This exclusive liaison inevitably pained de Hartmann and
consolidated on Ouspensky's face an expression of dangerous
thoughtfulness, 'the kind of seriousness which looks out from under
knitted brows, with pursed lips, carefully restrained gestures and
words filtered through the teeth.'

Thomas, hovering on the fringe in an ecstacy of spiritual impatience, found his overtures to Gurdjieff intentionally and comically
misconstrued: 'Doctor, you hear? He's inviting us to the club this
evening. What? Will you invite us for supper? Let's go, doctor.
Thank you for your invitation.'

This was bad. Thomas de Hartmann's private wealth had been
confiscated by the Bolsheviks, and inflation had escalated the cost of
supper to astronomical heights. Gurdjieff began with vodka and
hors d'œuvre and went on to prefer the most expensive courses. 'I
vividly remember to this day', wrote Thomas nearly forty years later,
'the oranges he ordered, because then I knew that my 500 roubles
would never pay the bill.' Like some frantic hero of a Feydeau farce,
Thomas secretly tipped the waiter to run home and get more money

from Olga. The bill eventually came to 1000 roubles – which Gurdjieff fully reimbursed the next morning. In retrospect Thomas viewed the whole experience as a psychological gift.

Throughout the Caucasus and Transcaucasus the waterholes of sanity were running dry; irreconcilable armies marched up and down, and the air was choked with cries of 'infuriated offensive abuse'. The mere existence of a café in Essentuki confirmed it as a precious, if ephemeral, oasis. In February, when Turkish forces began jostling eastward again, Gurdjieff urgently summoned his entire family from Alexandropol. Some complied: his mother, his brother Dmitri with his wife Anna Grigorievna, and his younger sister Sophie Ivanovna with her fiancé Mr Kapanadze. Only when these had arrived were Gurdjieff's worst fears confirmed: his father had proved unbudgeable and his elder sister Anna Ivanovna Anastasieff had remained behind to support him. Swallowing his disappointment, Gurdjieff decided to consolidate in Essentuki. In February 1918 he sent out a circular letter over Ouspensky's signature to all members of the Moscow and Petrograd groups, inviting them to come and work with him again. Although cross-country travel was decidedly risky, forty committed pupils including Zaharoff reached their teacher.

To molify the Pyatigorsk Bolshevik government, which had local jurisdiction, a 'socialist' pedigree was concocted:

'Think out something like *Sodroojestvo* and "earned by work" or "international" at the same time,' said G. 'In any case they will not understand. But it is necessary for them to be able to give us some sort of name.'

So at the back of the beyond, and for reasons of unashamed expediency, there was constituted the 'International Idealistic Society' – a tasteful enough title when Petrov wrote it out in calligraphic script.

By early March the Society's two-storey 'home' was chock-full and a new phase of work began under a rule of stringent discipline. Again there were fasts; again there were interior exercises. For a week Gurdjieff taught an alphabet of arm and leg movements – then suddenly imposed a regime of absolute silence, leaving his more or less desperate pupils to semaphore all their mutual requirements. Perhaps of many such experiments, the most eyebrow-raising was the practical study of counterfeit psychic phenomena. Followers who had risked everything in their search for a quintessential truth, were surprised to find themselves being instructed in sham thought-transference, sham clairvoyance, and sham telepathy. These strangely dedicated hours in Essentuki constituted a wholesome 'initiation of disillusion' and a formidable training in attention, observation, memory, resourcefulness, and role-playing.

In his manifesto *Beelzebub* Gurdjieff defines himself as a 'Teacher of Dancing'. At this second Essentuki 'intensive', rhythms which had their obscure origins in Tibet, Afghanistan, Kashgar, and Chinese Turkestan were first introduced by Gurdjieff on a cheap guitar, taken up by young Shandarovsky on his Guarneri violin, and danced by the untrained émigrés from Moscow and Petrograd. This new emphasis on 'Sacred Gymnastics' temporarily inverted the pupil hierarchy; overnight Mme Ostrowska's marvellous ability carried her to the top, and Ouspensky (willing to give the dances only an embarrassed and perfunctory fling) sank pretty much to the bottom.

But Ouspensky possessed the buoyancy of a large cork. His lucid mind and gravitas came to his aid when Gurdjieff sought pupils to give public lectures on philosophy, mysticism, and occultism. Evidently the author of *Tertium Organum* did some violence to his feelings in speaking to the Essentuki Lazzaroni, though he gave of his best, and his best was admirable. Some of the audience had come for enlightenment and others simply for a cup of tea; a professor from the Military Academy shared homemade sweet rolls with a hairy deacon of the *Raskolniki*; the general preference was for 'tea with a little sugar' but there was a choice of 'very sweet tea with saccharine'. How this peculiar Sunday function in the drawing room of the International Idealistic Society struck Ouspensky (who could picture in his memory the upturned faces of thousands in the Alexandrovsky Hall) is difficult to say, but even the smallest bouquet of self-congratulation shrivelled when Gurdjieff advertised as his next guest speaker the folkloric charlatan 'Dr Black, Bearer of Bad News'.

There is such a thing as the last straw. 'I could not understand,' Ouspensky wrote of this period, 'and *I had to go*.' But dwelling on the question 'Why?', a sense of clinging mystery prevails over a whole family of confident explanations. The absconder himself is vague: 'I do not in the least mean that I found any of G.'s actions or methods wrong . . . I had nothing to say against G.'s methods except that they did not suit me.'

Ouspensky was before anything else a professional writer – had admitted it candidly on first meeting Gurdjieff. As a speculative philosopher of Himalayan earnestness, avid for real ideas systematically advanced with a private elite group, chalk and blackboard meant infinitely more to him than gymnastics or practical work; and the 'sacred' set his agnostic teeth on edge. These factors pretty well explain, on their own level, his ultimate incompatibility with Gurdjieff; who would trouble to deny it? And yet to the heart remotely touched by this separation; to the intellect remotely drawn to teleological perspectives – such 'reasons' are not worth the strand of a woman's hair. They belong with the 'reasons' of Oedipus not to return to Corinth; they are actually worse than useless; they divert our attention from the poetic imperative – the implacable iteration of the myth.

Ouspensky's withdrawal must have sent ripples through the International Idealistic Society and perhaps even saddened Gurdjieff, but all this was quickly subsumed in a more fundamental calamity. In mid-July 1918 there occurred one of the most harrowing moments in Gurdjieff's entire life:

> One rainy morning, while sitting at the window ... I saw two odd-looking conveyances pull up at my door, from which ... shadowy forms slowly emerged ... skeletons of people, with only their burning eyes alive, clad in rags and tatters, their bare feet covered with wounds and sores ... twenty-eight in all ... relatives of mine, among them my own sister with her six little children.

From the broken accounts of Anna Ivanovna Anastasieff and her husband, Gurdjieff pieced together a grim story: two months earlier, at dawn on the 15 May 1918, Turkish sappers had thrown pontoon bridges across the ravine of the river Arpa-Chai and an army thirsting for revenge and plunder advanced into Armenia. Gurdjieff's extended family learned of the impending massacre only one panic-stricken hour before the Turks hit Alexandropol; while the women snatched up their children and fled in terror, Giorgios Giorgiades, in his eighty-fifth year, loaded his ancient rifle and sat in his doorway awaiting his fate. Soon afterwards he died from wounds. Some old men buried him nearby.

Gurdjieff had revered and loved his father all his life: but he had not been able to persuade him to leave Alexandropol; had not been there to help him; had not even forestalled the plundering of his notebooks, that irreplaceable collection of traditional songs and legends. In the majestic psycho-cosmology of *Beelzebub*, an experience of uniquely purgatorial remorse is reserved for developed men whose failings preclude their helping our Common Father Creator. And although Gurdjieff scoffs at the notion of Heaven and Hell, he allows a 'Holy Planet Purgatory', where 'of springs alone, both mineral and fresh which for purity and naturalness are unequalled on any other planet of our Universe, there are about ten thousand.' It is idle to guess how Gurdjieff felt or washed away the sorrow of his father's death, but Mineralni Vodi, where it came to him, has more and purer springs than any spot on earth.

Whatever the degree of Gurdjieff's self-reproach, we catch no hint of anti-Turkish bitterness. The inscription he envisages for his father's headstone breathes a compassion as all-embracing as it is deep:

> I AM THOU,
> THOU ART I,
> HE IS OURS,
> WE BOTH ARE HIS.
> SO MAY ALL BE
> FOR OUR NEIGHBOUR.

Undeflected by rancour, Gurdjieff devoted his energies to practical measures: comforting his mother and sister; feeding and clothing the refugees; and helping his followers in a hundred ways. His much-transported bale of silk came at long last into its own: separate skeins were teased free, painstakingly wound onto paper stars and sold at enormous advantage. Paper was almost as scarce as silk but Gurdjieff blithely commandeered de Hartmann's blank score sheets (for which the composer Prokofiev was also in competition). Dr Stjoernval, 'Old Stingy', was appointed treasurer and de Hartmann – a former protégé of the Tsar – was made door-to-door salesman:

> 'So, Thoma, go tomorrow to Kislovodsk and try to sell this silk.'
> 'But Mr Gurdjieff, Kislovodsk is filled with my Petrograd acquaintances. I cannot sell there.'
> 'On the contrary, so much the better. With so many acquaintances, you will sell the silk more quickly.'

Having eight-five people in Essentuki and sixty in Piatigorsk, half of them in funds and half destitute, Gurdjieff's manipulations were not only psychological and entrepreneurial but frankly redistributive: everyone signed a paper relinquishing their private possessions. 'When we die,' Gurdjieff stressed, 'we won't take our belongings with us ... but something else, if we develop it.' Olga at first could not bear it. 'I was in real torment, caught between conflicting emotions, and I cried all night long.' In the morning she came with red eyes to Gurdjieff.

He sat at a table, his head resting on his hand: 'What is it?' he asked. I told him that he had asked us to bring our jewels to him, so I had brought mine. He hardly moved and said: 'Put them there,' pointing to the little table in the corner. I put the box on the table and left.

I had just reached the garden gate when I heard him calling me. I returned. 'Now take them back . . .' he said.

Gurdjieff's humanity and humour and contrivance were apparently inexhaustible, but by August 1918 it did seem his luck had finally run out. Steel-beaked Russian armies and administrations were pecking at Essentuki like vultures; shots and screams and blasphemies punctuated the intense summer nights. 'Sometimes on getting up in the morning we would not know under which government we were that day and only on going out into the street would discover what politics had to be professed.' The very profession of bogus loyalties – White or Red or Green – was itself a trap, dangerously exposing Gurdjieff's younger men to the risk of impressment and the hideous possibility they would end up shooting each other. Old as well as young were suffering. Money was scarce. Food was scarce. The future on offer seemed nasty, brutish and short.

As to Gurdjieff the *avatar*, Gurdjieff the custodian of a subtle spiritual influence, he was surely checkmated; the clock was ticking; Fate, with a disdainful smile, seemed on the very verge of sweeping all the pieces from the board. Gurdjieff's hand hovered over the table . . . now or never he must find some unexpected resource.

4

❖

THE CAUCASIAN PIMPERNEL

(August 1918–January 1919)

Gurdjieff's revolver perplexes. To envisage him squinting viciously along the sights at another human being is preposterous – he abominated killing. But though the sinister black object itself is anomalous, its accreditation suits the myth.

> The bearer, Citizen Gurdjieff, has the right to carry everywhere a revolver – calibre ... number ...
> Certified by signature and seal affixed:
>
> Secretary:
> SHANDAROVSKY
>
> The President of the Soldiers' and Workmen's Deputies:
> ROUKHADZE
> Place of issue: Essentuki
> Date of Issue: ...

The Essentuki Council of Soldiers' and Workmen's Deputies would cheerfully have hanged 'Prince Ozay', but Citizen Gurdjieff was a bird of a different feather: if they could not trust him with a revolver, whom could they trust? His circle was 'internationalist'; all his followers had made declarations renouncing their personal property; and his protégé the signatory P. V. Shandarovsky (a stirring lecturer on Proudhon and Fourrier), had actually volunteered for work in the Bolshevik legal and passport office, where he was now a Commissar. Citizen Gurdjieff had filthy fingernails and spat sunflower shells and blew his nose with his finger and thumb ... what more could reasonably be asked?

But this particular citizenship would not be exercised much longer. Gurdjieff had audaciously resolved to extricate his company of guards officers, doctors, engineers, musicians, teachers, and other 'enemies of the people', while scope remained; to march them up over the Caucasus range to Sochi where the latest mirage of safety shimmered.

It hurt this decision. With the death of his father, Gurdjieff had become the 'big stick' – traditionally responsible for the safety of his mother, his brother, his two sisters, his in-laws, and his umpteen nephews and nieces. Voices from their family conference are hopelessly out of earshot now; it is futile to conjecture who urged whom to go or stay. What arrangements Gurdjieff made, what palms he greased in aid of his family's safety, are all unknown. The vapours of speculation lift away, exposing the one naked fact that the entire family remained in Essentuki – and Gurdjieff left.

In the event not only Gurdjieff's family stayed put and took their chances in Mineralni Vodi, but so did 80 per cent of his pupils. Some felt the devil they knew was better than the devil they didn't; others (not foreseeing the imminent Bolshevik reign of terror) dreamed of leisurely, feather-bedded exits. Thomas de Hartmann at first demurred: 'Mr Gurdjieff, I know that everything you do and all you require from us, is done for us, for our development. But my wife is at present so tired. . .' Had Thomas stayed in Essentuki a little longer, he and his wife would have rested indeed; with other Guards officers he would have been forced to dig his own grave, then shot and covered with earth alive or dead. Gurdjieff insisted, and just as well.

Marching up and down the garden carrying 50 lb of boulders in a home-made rucksack, is a stoic prescription for the relief of tiredness, but it seems to have worked very well with Olga de Hartmann; Dr Stjoernval was out of condition but he managed 70 lb. Generally the unremitting practices which Gurdjieff instigated not only tuned the body but steeled the will – levered timorous imagination over the mountains to freedom. As Giorgios Giorgiades had long ago impressed on his first-born son, 'Once you can shoulder it, it's the lightest thing in the world.' And yet . . . how to get this well-drilled nucleus away? How to obtain the essential *laissez-passer*?

Even critics who store up instances against Gurdjieff generally miss the fact that he was a pioneer of the planted newspaper story and the rehearsed interview. Late in July 1918 a journal in Pyatigorsk (seat of local Soviet administration) carried a surprising feature: evidently a citizen of Essentuki, G. I. Gurdjieff by name, was urgently preparing a scientific field study; his party of twenty-one would be prospecting for alluvial gold in streams near Mount Induc, while pursuing collateral archeological studies of bronze age and iron age dolmens prevalent in the high Caucasian passes; everyone stood to benefit. As to the question of political reliability, it simply did not arise: 'The expedition intends to go to a remote wilderness, inaccessible to military activities of the civil war. Therefore this scientific work and its discoveries cannot be hindered.'

With amazing effrontery Gurdjieff now harried the Soviets with requisitions for provisions; and the authorities – primed by the newspaper article and further convinced by Shandarovsky's special pleadings – generously complied: despite acute shortages, they sent picks and spades, cooking pans, a big tarpaulin, two large tents for officers, and twenty-one hatchets.

Ouspensky, pursuing with rigorous logic his personal decision to separate, was active in the conspiracy to help the expedition get off; he it was who ingeniously suggested that Gurdjieff indent for alcohol 'to wash the gold'. By now in Essentuki the smallest bottle of alcohol was itself gold-dust, yet Gurdjieff demanded and received two large casks. The clinical stuff was decanted, gallon by gallon, into flasks marked 'Medicine for the treatment of cholera'; the denatured variety, first purified by filtration through baked onions and bread, was labelled 'Medicine for the treatment of malaria'. The latter at least, one supposes, was a 'medicine' which consoled the foot-weary and blended pleasantly with mountain sunsets. Gurdjieff added to his requisition for alcohol a demand for a large black-and-red fireman's belt . . . which was supplied.

In the prevailing chaos, the Bolsheviks unsurprisingly took away with the left hand what they gave with the right. Among this epoch's more poignant cameos is one of Gurdjieff in the streets of Essentuki, flicking the belly of his bay horse Rusty with a rope's end until the poor beast shied in terror. Soon afterwards Red Army soldiers came to commandeer the animals. 'Mr Gurdjieff sat calmly on the garden bench, watching what was happening and interfering in nothing, in spite of the fact that our lives depended on the horses.' An hour or two later, the soldiers brought back both mounts as unfit for service: one had reared taking its rider with him; the other had bitten a soldier's stomach. 'Speaking' softly with his horses, Gurdjieff gradually calmed them; perhaps the vibrations of his voice conveyed something of his unquestionable remorse.

Inflation being rampant, Gurdjieff had converted his personal capital into valuables: some of these he kept, some he distributed among his followers, and some he left with Dmitri (who hid them a little crassly in his basement under the woodstack); to his bemused mother's safekeeping Gurdjieff confided a particularly sumptuous brooch bought from an indigent grand duchess. Slowly but surely, he was drawing all the strands together: he acquired a rifle, two mules, three carts, and a little donkey named Mashka; he taught his men how to walk mountain paths in darkness and convinced his ladies of the North Star's existence and constancy. He emphasized the very real danger and – with dark allusions to the Turkestan Correctional Section of the International Fellowship for Realization through Work – laid down a Draconian rule of obedience; he ran rings round the Bolshevik authorities and (though the railways were chaotic, constipated and even criminalized) somehow drummed up two wagons to start the expedition on its way. When every last moral and material detail had been seen to, Gurdjieff instructed 'Commissar' Shandarovsky to issue them all with Bolshevik passports – and to join them.

On the morning of Tuesday 6 August 1918, the expedition left Essentuki. The sober actuality of this moment and its significance in the Gurdjieffian canon are undeniable ... and yet imagination blends subversively with fact, creating a *mise-en-scène* which is frankly operatic: the nondescript ethnic chorus of bystanders and street idlers, costumed in bright dresses and military uniforms and black *bourkas*, suddenly parts, muttering in amazement, to reveal Citizen Gurdjieff, inexplicable in Astrakhan hat and large fireman's belt, leading forward his motley caravan of carts and animals and 'scientists'; seven of these scientists are men, five women, and two are young children. The free movement of the adults is compromised by penditive kettles, tripods, hunting knives, frying pans, and bottles of medicine against malaria; the men finger their shiny new hatchets, and the women spit out sunflower shells with studious indelicacy. The station is reached. All the paraphernalia is unscrambled and jam-packed into two ramshackle goods trucks – a swirling transformation scene, rich in unintentional burlesque and character cameos and throwaway lines. Where is the lump sugar? How are mules persuaded? A fat sulphurous August sun lights the stage, and the Essentuki municipal band – splendidly oblivious of the civil war – sounds its resolute 'oomp-pa-pa' from the wings.

Gurdjieff humoured this peculiar moment as a psychiatrist might humour a psychopath with a knife; not through engagement with the toad-spotted 'certainties' of 1918 does he give proof of his existential activation, but through his disengagement. Strolling in Essentuki park, filling an hour before the train's departure, Gurdjieff, of all creatures there, is at right-angles to history. But he had nonetheless a heart ... which must somehow have answered to his mother's patient smile, and to the last equivocal glint of Ouspensky's pince-nez. No one required much imagination to see blood on the grass. (The doomed hostage General Radko Dmitrieff approached them: 'If I were younger', he said plaintively, 'I would ask you to take me with you.') After sixty painful, stressful minutes, Gurdjieff and his fourteen 'scientists' re-boarded. Mashka brayed and the engine brayed; then slowly the train started and laboured away, until the regrettable repertoire of the Essentuki municipal band faded forever on the languid summer air.

Gurdjieff and his fourteen assorted companions spent the afternoon and night and all of Wednesday morning jolting along in the goods wagon, which was as cramped, hot and inconvenient as the inside of the Trojan Horse. The train achieved an average speed somewhat over four miles an hour (good going by general freighting standards in Caucasia at the height of the civil war) and Gurdjieff, on finally rolling back the door, found himself 100 miles from Essentuki in the town of Armavir.

Not until Thursday apparently was there the remotest possibility of shunting the train to the requisite Maikop track. Gurdjieff therefore gave the de Hartmanns permission to call on Thomas's maiden aunt – a gesture which nearly cost posterity the Gurdjieffian musical œuvre. For when the two visitors got back to the station late in the afternoon (curiously resembling fugitives from *Cavalleria Rusticana*), the train was nowhere to be seen. The ex-Guards officer and his attractive young wife, with their outlandish disguises and ineradicably upper-class accents, must sooner or later have been detained by Bolshevik foot patrols, had not Shandarovsky noticed them on his way to bully two sacks of sugar out of the commissariat storekeeper. Fortunately Gurdjieff and his other 'scientists' were side-tracked only two miles away, and the trio rejoined him at sunset.

The next day in Maikop the engine shuddered to a halt with an expiring gasp and minutes later the driver simply disappeared. Gurdjieff sent an emissary to the local Soviet to present the expedition's credentials and get permission to continue. Dr Stjoernval –chosen for his seniority, gravitas, and unstereotyped Finnish accent–was away a long time and returned visibly shaken. Not only was the town encircled by fighting Cossacks and Red Army regiments, but an independent faction called the Green Guards had anarchically blown up the railway line; all bets were off.

Two miles from the town on the rim of a wood by the White River

TERRAIN OF GURDJIEFF'S
ESCAPE FROM RUSSIA
August 1918–June 1920

0   50 miles

▬▬▬▬▬ Railway

RUSSIA

Maikop   Armavir

Olghniki

MINERALNI VODI

Tuapse   Essentuki
                              Kislovodsk Pyatigorsk

Uch Dere ●Babakoff Aul
Sochi   Mozdok

                              ▲ Mt. Elbrus (18, 481 ft)

Sukhumi

BLACK SEA   GEORGIA

                    Poti

                  Batoum   Tbilisi

To Constantinople

Trebizond   Alexandropol

          Pontic Alps   Soghanlui Dagh
                                        Kars   ARMENIA

          TURKEY
                    ● Sarikamish   ● Erevan
                        Echmiadzin ●

stood a deserted farm, with hay-filled barns and outbuildings; here the expedition took refuge and gratefully worked the land. Few episodes are stranger than Gurdjieff's pastoral idyll during the three-week struggle for Maikop: desperate battle lines snake and slither about this farm but never quite find it; shadows of tragedy lengthen towards it with military precision, then bend away as if mysteriously deflected; and where Mashka the donkey goes on quietly cropping the grass beneath the big oak tree, actors precipitate who seem to belong to quite other productions. Here Dr and Mrs Stjoernval met a fellow-countrymen en route from India to Finland in Buddhist robes – an authority on *dharma* and the pickling of tomatoes. Here Thomas de Hartmann saluted a fellow Guards officer who had recently preferred the wandering life of the Stranniki: his poor torn trousers reached only to his knees, exposing calves of disturbing elegance. All the men and women went in segregated parties for a daily swim in the White River; there was even a diving board on which we may plausibly pose Mr Gurdjieff in full undress. 'Far away, one could hear gunfire, and sometimes shots whistled over our heads, striking the mountain on the other side of the river and causing stones to fall into it. But we paid no attention.'

White Army savagery, not Bolshevik, brings down the curtain on this lyrical interlude. Immediately General Heyman 'liberated' Maikop, he convened courts martial and raised gallows. 'See', said the Finnish Buddhist in horror, 'they hang there, they hang . . .' Even Thomas de Hartmann's active service in 1917 had not inured him to the sight of 'a two wheeled cart covered with canvas, under which we could discern a heap of flesh and bones, the mangled bodies of people killed in the fighting.' He stood in the street with the sunflower seeds suddenly dry in his mouth. Only when he tried to steady his calloused hands, and noticed his soiled and belted shirt, did it dawn on him that he himself had entered Maikop disguised as a Bolshevik in the middle of an anti-Bolshevik purge.

As Thomas hastily retreated, Leonid Stjoernval, more sensibly dressed, was already in the office of General Davidovitch Naschinski's adjutant, urging Gurdjieff's lifelong political conservatism and the expedition's moral entitlement to White Russian passes. The unforeseen scepticism and resistance encountered was suddenly overcome when an admiral from St Petersburg (as welcome as he was inexplicable in these landlocked mountains) intervened to identify and authenticate Dr Stjoernval personally. The acute scarcity of paper led to one nice historical irony: the Bolshevik certificate empowering

'Citizen Gurdjieff' to carry a revolver was simply turned over and endorsed:

> A certain Gurdjieff is authorized to carry a revolver numbered as indicated on the reverse side.
>   Certified by signature and seal affixed:
>
>   For General Denikin:
>   GENERAL HEYMAN
>   Chief of Staff:
>   GENERAL DAVIDOVITCH NASCHINSKI
>   Issued in Maikop.
>   Date . . .

Gurdjieff was warmly appreciative. He received the admiral for tea at the farm with some matrons from the local theosophical lodge. But even while they were exchanging civilities and homemade chocolate biscuits under the oak tree, the Bolshevik Army was preparing a counter-stroke which, three days later, so thoroughly eradicated bourgeois tendencies that the ensuing history of the Maikop Theosophical Society is not extant.

Characteristically Gurdjieff and his expedition got away one day before the town changed hands, not travelling towards Tuapse as they had misdirected the authorities, but up along the White River pass. They set out at dawn, while the red sun coaxed a thin mist from the harvested cornfields – carts creaking, animals straining, the children excited, the adults serious and watchful. Thomas de Hartmann, who had already dropped a tent pole heavily on his big toe, lost his axe when fording the White River. Soon the party crossed two parallels of shallow trenches, deserted by the men who had dug and stubbornly defended them. But not all trenches were unmanned: before attaining that 'remote wilderness inaccessible to military activities of the civil war', Gurdjieff's expedition was five times constrained to cross Bolshevik and White Army lines.

Where Gurdjieff affirms his general compassion and complete impartiality towards the civil war, it rings sublimely true; where he says 'I and my companions moved under supernatural protection', it breathes authenticity at the metaphorical level; but where he asserts that both sides 'considered us completely neutral', he prevaricates; and where he bald-facedly claims 'I moved amid this chaos without concealing anything or resorting to any subterfuge', he fibs so blatantly that one gasps in admiration.

Neither side considered – or was meant to consider – Gurdjieff as neutral: each identified one of their own. With his double documentation and his double personae, Gurdjieff was the arch-conformable – calibrating his shrugs to a nicety, selecting his accent and idiom, always using his 'language of the smile'. And even so, each sudden confrontation with dishevelled scouts and sentries who might turn out to be White or Red, brought its initial moment of acute danger. How very easily Mme Stjoernval might fluster out the wrong passport; how fatal might be the children's candour. But the Essentuki training in bogus 'thought transference' had not been for nothing. Like musicians intent on the maestro's baton, the 'scientists' watched their leader; if Gurdjieff twirled his right moustache they produced White papers and the manners of the *ancien régime*; if his left moustache, Bolshevik papers and no manners at all. Modern history can scarcely furnish a chapter more complex, more intense, more enturbulated, than the struggle for Caucasia and Transcaucasia between 1917 and 1921. But time is fickle. And when all those serried passions and ethnic psychoses, those utopian dreams and murderous persecutions, have been silted over by the sands of a condign oblivion, there will perhaps remain, protruding inexplicably from the dunes, the two waxed spikes of Gurdjieff's moustache.

After their fifth and last confrontation with combatants, when 'the Cossacks went away, even apologising for bothering us', Gurdjieff and his pupils moved quietly on through lovely late summer days – regretting here and there the smoking ruins of devastated Cossack villages. A vast ancient wood closed protectively around them, in which they gathered sweet wild pears and acorns for 'coffee'. But in the village of Kumichki or Hamishki the road ran out and the bad times began; here the expedition abandoned their carts, shouldered their rucksacks, and 'began to climb the everlasting mountains'.

That evening the advance guard's campfire was built near a deserted hut on an upper slope. 'Now,' said Gurdjieff (prematurely), 'I am peaceful: we do not have to deal with men any more, just wild animals.' Later on however – when he rode back down in darkness to Kumichki with Thomas de Hartmann to collect Mme Ostrowska and the main party – he was nearly shot by agitated peasants, who ironically mistook him for a prowling Bolshevik.

Evidently nothing is easier than to embarrass Gurdjieff's Transcaucasus expedition with a description verging on parody: the gallant women knee-deep in grass infested with vipers and scorpions; the frugal breakfast of baked potato coaxed from the ashes of last night's fire; the glitter of twenty largely redundant hatchets; the shrewd allocation of sugar lumps; Mashka, the rascal donkey, full of guile and pluck – and Gurdjieff pointing (with his revolver preferably) towards the tangled heights; labouring up stiff gradients with 70 lb of destiny in his pack.

Is this pastiche merely *la trahison des clercs*? Or can we conceive that the experience was not altogether unlike that . . . and yet essentially different? The physical topography – the White River pass, the swamp plateau, the green prairie of Luganaky – are plainer to historical view than the journey's psychological dolmens. Yet the heights and depths encountered by this expedition were not all physical – and Mashka the donkey's escapades count for little. In the proof of human character: the painful unravelling of ill-knit loyalties; the emergence of unsuspected virtues; and the implacable separation of the fine from the coarse – herein lies the secret drama and raison d'être of a journey which was quite as dangerous inwardly as outwardly.

At one juncture Gurdjieff became ill; robbers stalked the party, caught and searched and plundered the de Hartmanns at gunpoint; and the horses nearly drowned in the swamp. On another occasion (seemingly almost as grim) the soup was ruined by a mistaken garnish of bitter wild mushrooms. Major and minor crises competed for attention; wandering monks and nomadic Circassian shepherds materialized and dematerialized round the expedition's blue striped tents, offering rumour and white Caucasian cheese. 'I will only add,' writes Gurdjieff, 'that, of all my impressions during this journey, the most outstanding is of the beauty of the regions between Kumichki and . . . the sea; which indeed deserve the high-sounding name of "terrestrial paradise", often attributed to other parts of the Caucasus by the so-called intelligentsia.'

Each dusk Gurdjieff unpacked and assembled the little glass kerosene lamp; he baked delicious bread in an oven contrived of stones; he encouraged, he cajoled, he taught by example. Each dawn he scrupulously repacked the kerosene lamp, supervised the loading of fractious animals, and led his exhausted pupils on through indeterminate stands of oleander and rhododendron. A keen observer standing on the peak of Elbrus (3000 feet higher than Mont Blanc) and pointing his telescope north-west, might just have picked out a climbing column of industrious black ants; and, by night, the tiniest pinpoint of flame in an immense and profound darkness. These – not unfittingly – are images which comprehend Gurdjieff and his entire movement in August and September 1918.

Babakoff Aül, the first village west of the mountains, was reached in a frightful downpour. Gurdjieff had gone ahead and hired rooms in the house of a sympathetic Polish engineer, and soon everyone was gratefully settled in. Gurdjieff was fifty-two. Who would not excuse him a day or two of collapse, a week of complete passivity? But on the contrary! Excited by tales of a solitary dolmen in the surrounding woods, he set off next morning with some pupils and hunters, and climbing vigorously soon came on the seven or eight-foot cube, worked from a single rock and shut fast by a ponderous stone lid.

What was inside? Gurdjieff's unassuageable impulse to penetrate the 'holy-of-holies' could scarcely have received a more simplistic challenge. The box's south-east face revealed a perfect circular hole, too small to give access – certainly to Gurdjieff. But Olga de Hartmann – by now mere skin, bones, and esprit de corps – forgot propriety and, in a flurry of petticoats, insinuated herself through its twelve-inch diameter. In some ways Olga Arcadievna's had been a strange life. She was (on her mother's side) a great-grand-daughter of Kaiser Wilhelm I; she had danced at glittering balls; Princes and High Excellencies had kissed her hand; she commanded all those gentle accomplishments which breeding and old money supply – she played the pianoforte, sang *Lieder*, and spoke five languages; she had attracted as her husband a man of integrity and conspicuous gifts, a protégé of the Tsar; she had followed this husband, who had followed Gurdjieff – and now here she was, almost beyond the reach of rational explanation, on the inside of a Caucasian dolmen.

No concealed artefact or runic inscription justified her athleticism and she struggled out again. But Gurdjieff took measurements, computed a line of advance, projected it by a series of sticks, and cut away into the virgin forest. To his pupils' surprise and the local hunters' utter astonishment, he unearthed a second mossy dolmen from the tangled undergrowth. Then a third. A steep and dangerous slope declined from the prehistoric site, and the de Hartmanns asked nervously how they should manage it. To Gurdjieff's delight the hunters responded gravely, 'By sliding on your arses.'

From Babakoff it proved all descent: down, down, tumbled the scientific expedition from Essentuki, their bodies aching, their reserves exhausted, their cup of suffering and 'medicine against malaria' drained dry; and in the evening they identified the lights of Sochi glimmering over the Black Sea, and, straightening their backs, marched into town and took rooms in the best hotel, and washed and dressed for dinner. 'Sing the Bell Song from *Lakmé*,'[24] said Gurdjieff to Olga de Hartmann. She rose stiffly, went to the piano

and—though perhaps lacking the full range of a coloratura soprano —
gave '*Où va la jeune Hindoue?*'. The restaurant fell silent. And
Gurdjieff (that 'certain Hindu' whose bogus advertisement in *Golos
Moskvi* had long ago raised the curtain on this singular drama)
watched her silently over his black coffee.

This moment was the company's last of full rapport; for in mellow, autumnal Sochi, tenanted by friendly Circassians, Gurdjieff's
group ironically lost its hard-won cohesion and in effect broke up.
Why? Because Gurdjieff had run out of money? Because he had run
out of patience? He does convey that 'certain members ... during
what might be called our "Way of Golgotha"... manifested properties not corresponding at all to the high aim we had in view.' Yet
surely, at the deepest level, the final severance of Zaharoff and Petrov
— pupils dearer than most to Gurdjieff — was neither a dismissal nor
a defection. They went because they went: 'If one thing could be
different,' said Gurdjieff, 'everything could be different.' These sincere and highly intelligent men sugared the bitterness of parting with
pretexts. Had they not professional duties? Had they not mothers?
Was not the Volunteer Army poised to liberate the whole of Mineralni
Vodi? Would not Gurdjieff himself soon return there and resume
formal teaching? Gliding through the myth, downstream towards
their personal annihilation, they kept their spirits up with reasons.

For Gurdjieff this was a strange time. Week after week his entourage diminished: some entrained for Maikop, some for Essentuki,
some for Kiev. He and Mme Ostrowska were uncomfortably billeted
in the house of his cousin, who was coughing his way out of this
world in the final bloody stage of pulmonary tuberculosis. While the
tiny Petrograd nucleus gave continued proof of its unswerving loyalty
(the wretched patient was attended by Dr Stjoernval and died in the
arms of Olga de Hartmann), Gurdjieff himself spent every evening
playing *vint* in the Circassian Officers' Club. He had his extenuating
motive. Under the glittering chandeliers, fiery Georgian spirit loosened
the tongues and wallet-strings of a whole heap of princely and capital-
ist émigrés, and night after night Gurdjieff self-deprecatingly scooped
from the green baize tables the roubles and titbits of military gossip
which he and his remaining companions absolutely needed.

It was warm in the club. Outside, as the months processed, there
closed over the whole Caucasus the coldest winter in forty years; its
superhuman malignity rebuked, but could not wholly forbid, the
brutalities of starving, ignorant armies and the criminal vanity of
their generals. Anton Denikin, whose Volunteers, aided by Cossacks,

had indeed temporarily stunned the Bolsheviks in the north, was now fulminating down the telegraph wires about Georgian incursion in the south; the Dashnakzutiun and many influential Armenians in Sochi were egging him on to 'liberate' the city at bayonet point, but the Green Guards were determined to oppose him. Another fine mess was in prospect.

Yet again however, Gurdjieff was one vital step ahead of calamity. Fill your suitcases he warned his intimates in mid-January 1919, and hurry to the pier immediately you hear a ship's siren. So, two by two, male and female after their kind, the six emissaries of the new age wavered up a narrow, plunging gangplank at Sochi: Gurdjieff and Mme Ostrowska, Dr and Mrs Stjoernval, and Thomas and Olga de Hartmann. Their miserable Ark, already jam-packed with puking refugees from Tuapse and a rich speciation of lice and vermin, fought its way south against a head-wind which threatened to exhaust the bunkers and drive them on a lee shore. They huddled on deck together. The rain drenched them. They did not speak much. What point was there? At long last, on the afternoon of the second day, they disembarked at the little port of Poti, whose palm-trees, mocked by a killing frost, rose along the quayside like florescent crystals of baleful white.

Poti station was congested, disorganized, and gruesomely filthy – a sort of Transcaucasian bedlam with icicles. To inquire there for a train seemed almost frivolous; hope was so obviously cancelled. Even so, Gurdjieff's 'language of the smile' and command of the idiom of railway workers secured them a night's accommodation in an empty compartment. What singular dreams, one wonders, troubled our hero there? (He had, after all, a temperature of 104°.) Did he hear temple gongs straining from the high irrecoverable hills of youth – or the liquid, silver note of camel bells? Did he find himself, to his intense frustration, 'arm-in-arm with the priest Vlakov'? Or endure once again the final, unendurable benediction of Prince Lubovedsky? Did long-discarded, long-forgotten women shake their hair at him in 'their varying manifestations of passion'? Did old Philos (his sagacious and over-contributive dog) fill the entire train with phantasmal artichokes and dead sparrows?

Certainly Gurdjieff woke in the cruel sobriety of a January dawn to no very cheerful perspectives. His purse was light, his face unshaven, his forces and family scattered; the work and resourceful contrivance of a whole epoch had ended merely in the extrication of five bewildered dependents from the 'centre of hell to its edge'. Two

years before, on the station platform at Petrograd, a luminous transfigured Gurdjieff had seemed almost godlike; today on the platform
at Poti he appeared a human being whom fate had brought un-
pleasantly to bay. If Gurdjieff possessed more being than most men,
he suffered commensurately more, though to pity him for this is to
fail altogether in intuition. Hungry and wrapped in a worn and faded
overcoat, he sat on the Tbilisi train digesting his suffering – his sense
of 'I' so powerful and discrete it almost seemed to rattle inside him.

5

❖

AMONG THE MENSHEVIKS

(January 1919–May 1920)

The more things change the more they remain the same. Tiflis had
become Tbilisi in 1917 on a wave of Georgian nationalism, yet
its streets – physically emptied by the intense cold – were for
Gurdjieff populous with memory. Here on the hill were the railway
yards where he had sweated as a young stoker; and here with Karapet,
who worked the steam whistle, he had sung 'Little Did We Tipple'.
Here in frowning disapproval sat the black Theological Seminary.
Here was the parade fronting the old Alexander Gardens, where
decades ago, flitting from bookstall to bookstall, he and Pogossian
and Yelov had fished avidly for knowledge. Round these quick
corners they had lived cheekily on their wits, while nourishing that
discrepant spiritual aspiration which before long called them all
away to 'inaccessible' places. He was back now. Alone. Deepened in
being and embarrassed for hard cash.

Gurdjieff quickly found a roof with his cousins the Turadzhevs.
Although still burning with fever, he felt 'compelled to run about the
city in order to find at any cost some way out of this desperate
situation.' His footsteps turned naturally to Old Tiflis (set in a small
hollow east of the Russian quarter). Here in the Tartar Bazaar he
found little had changed: the same ageless veiled women stared down
from high window grills into the same rat-infested labyrinth; the
tchaikanas were scalding lips with the same fragrantly delicate tea;
and the old caravanserai offered the customary amenities to camel-
drovers. Only the officers of a tiny British garrison, seconded from
Batoum in December 1918, and traipsing around with their Box
Brownie cameras – only these gave due warning of the vacuous
modernism which would soon sweep Old Tiflis into oblivion.

For the bazaar's carpet dealers these were lucky times; even the most dubious kilims and rugs could be funnelled away to Constantinople, where the avidity of undiscriminating young officers of the Allied Occupation Force had produced a splendidly false market. Perhaps no one in Tbilisi in 1919 knew his carpets more intimately than Gurdjieff – knots, provenance, symbolism, style, repair technique and market value; decidedly no one better understood the laws of suggestibility. Friends of Dmitri and of his father-in-law Archbishop Martinian bullishly advanced some risk capital; Gurdjieff bought his first rug cheap and sold it dear; he found apprentices, loyal and active; he taught them to scout for rugs, to wash them, to repair them. Side by side with Mme Ostrowska, he drove himself to a crescendo of activity – and within three weeks 'there was not only sufficient money for all to live on, but a good deal left over.'

With singular speed, the painful decision to quit Essentuki had been vindicated: despite the bleak climate of depression prevailing elsewhere throughout Transcaucasia, the clemencies of the Georgian Menshevik social democratic republic were coaxing through the snow the first unseasonable crocuses of a Gurdjieffian spring. Dr Stjoernval found in the anxieties and maladies of fellow émigrés the basis of a modest new practice (centred in the Russian quarter on the south-west bank of the Kura River). Thomas de Hartmann encountered his old friend the composer Nikolai Nikolaievitch Tcherepnin, who appointed him Professor of Composition at the Conservatoire of Advanced Musical Studies; thus in the twinkling of an eye he acquired 2000 pupils and a place at the centre of the city's cultural life. Olga was cast to sing Micaela in a gala production of *Carmen* at the Tbilisi Opera House – large as the Opéra-Comique in Paris.

The boisterous *Carmen* première in February 1919 was both an ordeal and a triumph for Olga:

> When I entered the scene in the fourth act, I saw a black spot at the back of the hall. Since I knew that no one in the audience would be wearing a black hat, I knew it was Mr Gurdjieff who was there ... He had told me once, 'If you are afraid, just look, and I will be there; sing and think about no one else in the hall.' I really sang my prayer of Micaela quite wonderfully, dropping to my knees and taking a high C pianissimo, holding it for a long time, with feeling.

But the happy young soloist, contrary to appearances, was entering a period of crisis. She did not complain as daily she grew weaker, but she had not been well since nursing Gurdjieff's dying cousin in Sochi.

Had she perhaps – the thought was unthinkable – contracted tuberculosis? A specialist was called in and confirmed lung disease. He could recommend a mountain sanatorium in Austria which offered real hope – but otherwise: he shook his head. Gurdjieff expressed a different opinion. Bacon! Olga should eat bacon every morning; and she should sleep outside on her verandah despite the cold; and, before eating food, she should drink a little glass of red wine from a bottle he had specially prepared. She did so. And when in three weeks' time the specialist again examined her, 'he told me how glad he was that I had listened to him and gone to the sanatorium, as there was practically no trace of infection left in my lungs.'

As the brilliant sets and lighting for *Carmen* had developed in rehearsal, Gurdjieff established that their creator was Alexandre Gustav Salzmann, an associate of Rilke and Kandinsky. This Salzmann – although comfortably at home in Tiflis where he had been born on 25 January 1874 – was a citizen of the world: an artist, inventor, forest ranger; 'a former dervish, former Benedictine, former professor of jiu-jitsu, healer, stage-designer ... an incredible man.' His family was of Baltic origin and the permafrost of an unassuage-able northern melancholy had sunk deep into his face; yet by con-trast his dashing poster-like paintings (redolent of Hieronymus Bosch in their symbolic penetration) shouted out a wholesome optimism and exuberant good humour. His excursions into Sanskrit, Chinese calligraphy, the canons of proportion and the Golden Num-ber, argued a cultivated sensibility – yet, 'In spite of his artistic sophistication, there was something wild and savage in him ... His method of shaving was simplicity itself: he took a dry razor and scraped his face. Even this was a concession ...'

Gurdjieff and Salzmann were brought face to face at Easter 1919 (through de Hartmann's tireless efforts) and interesting exchanges took place. 'He is a very fine man,' Gurdjieff assured Thomas, 'and she – is intelligent.'

The intelligence of Jeanne Matignon-Salzmann was not only men-tal but physical. As a beautiful young woman of twenty-two, she had married Alexandre in Hellerau in 1911, while studying dance at the Eurhythmics Institute of Emile Jaques-Dalcroze. Her passionate interest in movement and rhythm had prevailed through the enforced travels and cruel exigencies occasioned by the war and the Russian revolution; its dimensionality had been enriched by her brilliant husband, and yet she was tormented with a sense of indefinable lack ... which all amounts to saying she was perfect for Gurdjieff. Both

the Salzmanns were people of the highest culture and strongest individuality – hardly less remarkable than Ouspensky – yet in Tbilisi
Gurdjieff transited their lives and swept them imperiously into his
trajectory.

By a happy coincidence Jeanne Salzmann was busy rehearsing for a
prestigious public demonstration of eurhythmics, but on hearing of
Gurdjieff's Sacred Dances taught in Essentuki, she quixotically put
her entire class at his disposal. Jeanne's pupils – a circle of pretty
young girls in Greek costumes – were now due for a series of shocks:

> Mr Gurdjieff greeted them, watched with interest for five or ten minutes
> . . . and at once ordered them, in military tone, to straighten their lines, to
> dress left, to dress right. Then he put them all in one row in front of him
> and said: 'Before beginning any work in "Sacred Gymnastics" you must
> learn how to turn.'

The girls were pleasantly baffled when Gurdjieff produced as class
pianist Thomas de Hartmann, the Professor of Composition at the
Conservatoire; but they were staggered when he ordered him (thirty
minutes before his concert debut at the Town Hall), to demonstrate
one of the six 'Obligatory' dances by putting 'all the weight of the
body on the hands while the feet made very strong rapid movements.'
When Gurdjieff provokingly insisted on paying these idealistic young
amateurs a small fee, the entire class – which had actually wished to
study Dalcroze – was on the verge of rebellion. And yet Jeanne
Salzmann, with 'the whole force of her authority and the feeling of
the rightness of Mr Gurdjieff's Work . . . was able to persuade her
pupils to take part in the new "exercises".'

Shortly after Easter 1919, Dmitri arrived unexpectedly in Tbilisi
bringing eagerly awaited news from Essentuki. Gurdjieff's mother
and sister had suffered in the terrible winter of ice and famine and
typhoid, but they had come through unscathed; they 'embraced'
Gurdjieff but shrank from the risky southward journey to join him;
Gurdjieff's carpet collection had been plundered, but a few recovered
items lay awaiting claim at the public pound; Ouspensky had re-
sourcefully survived the Bolshevik occupation in the guise of 'Essentuki Soviet Librarian', and was now teaching Gurdjieff's ideas to
groups of his own.

Gurdjieff reflected. Someone, he decided, must go to Essentuki
with letters to his sister and to Ouspensky, and to retrieve whatever
valuables remained. Dmitri confirmed that to send a man was out of
the question; a man would be instantly seized by the White or Red
Army. 'When Mr Gurdjieff asked me to go,' recalls Olga, 'I was filled

with terror ... He gave me some gold coins (and) a mysterious little box in which he said there was a special pill that I could take in case of extreme necessity', – otherwise he would like it back. Gurdjieff's intention is transparent: he thrust into life the very pupil whose personality was least equipped to cope – never before had the aristocratic Olga even walked the streets alone – but entirely for her own good. There was sober calculation here, yet equally there was risk.

For an interminable week Gurdjieff endured his private reservations and the eyes of Thomas de Hartmann – and then a radiant Olga returned. By rail and sea, by Batoum and Novorossiysk, by hook and by crook – she had journeyed to Essentuki and back. She had salvaged an Astrakhan coat and eight of her family's priceless Persian miniatures and two of Gurdjieff's antique carpets. Complete strangers had spoken to her and she had responded adequately. No obstacle had defeated her: not bureaucratic spite, nor the unwelcome advances of dirty old men with big black beards, nor even a violent tempest at sea. ('I would use the pill only if the ship went down.') The sense that Gurdjieff was grooming all his protégés – testing them, hardening them while paradoxically sensitizing them, generally mobilizing them to share with him the long daunting struggle ahead – this sense is overpowering.

On Sunday 22 June 1919, in the vast Tbilisi Opera House, the school of Jeanne Matignon-Salzmann staged the first ever performance of the Movements. What was Gurdjieff about? He had indeed created a rich and challenging experience for Jeanne. Yet might he not have done so without compromising his Sacred Dances? This public exposure has raised even some sympathetic eyebrows: after all, the knowledge which Gurdjieff had thirsted for, found and synthesized; the knowledge he had secretly passed on to hand-picked pupils in Moscow, Petrograd and Essentuki – had been esoteric. 'There are things which are said only for disciples.' But now a ticket lifted casually at the box-office appeared to offer anyone entrée to the sanctuary. For us to grasp the sense of Gurdjieff's singular march from inaccessible monasteries to the Opera House, we must ponder deeply. To ensure the future it was imperative he find sufficient good pupils – this inevitably poised him on a tightrope between vulgarization and the exclusivism of clique. Many were called but few were chosen. Gurdjieff's quintessential teaching glided inviolate through the public arena, its exclusivity guaranteed not by locks and passwords and prohibitions but by spiritual capacity; not by social format but by initiatory order.

Thomas de Hartmann was now set a new task. As candidate pianist for the Sacred Dances, he urgently needed to master the distinctive idiom of oriental music; Gurdjieff therefore instigated and fanned in him a passion for Komitas Vardapet the ill-fated Armenian ethno-musicologist and national genius. 'I wish to speak', said Thomas, tightly gripping the lecturn in Tbilisi, 'of Komitas Vardapet who is now in Constantinople, whose mental health is seriously injured and who is kept without money, without moral support, without the warmth of family and without friendship, having lost everything decrying the bloody massacres of the Armenians.' Three months earlier, Thomas had not heard of Komitas but under Gurdjieff's influence he could, for the moment, scarcely think of anyone else.

At the beginning of July 1919, when Olga had gamely brought to concert pitch a repertoire of Armenian songs, Gurdjieff despatched the de Hartmanns to Armenia on a flying cultural visit. They arrived in Erivan debating whether the greatest achievements of Komitas were actually his deciphering of the ancient *neumes* or his harmonic and polyphonic extrapolation of Armenian folk melody. At night they sprinkled round their bed a 'magic circle of kerosene' to ward away lice and vermin; by day, walking to their concerts, they regretted the harrowing and distracting evidence of inefficient flour distribution: 'people sitting like corpses, homeless and starving, awaiting death.' On their final evening, the de Hartmanns were received by his beatitude Archbishop Sarpazan Horen in his house high above the Zanga River:

> When night fell, a full moon shone through the warm southern air and mount Ararat was wrapped in a shroud of mist: an unforgettable sight. To accompany this vision there was real Eastern music . . . different kinds of 'bayati' with 'gap'.

Just as Gurdjieff had intended, Thomas returned to Tbilisi attuned to the beauty, savagery, and immemorial melancholy of his teacher's Armenian heritage, and burning to translate it all into music.

At the end of July Gurdjieff whisked his people away to the mountain resort of Borjom (where the State Theatre company had also gone to escape the summer heat), and there he implacably continued Olga's education. His old coat was worn and faded, and a new one unprocurable. Would Olga now make herself useful and turn it inside out? How? Mark the seams with white thread; rip it open; iron out the old seams; iron in the new; hand-sew the pieces back along the white threads — elementary! But Olga, having never held a needle in her life, was aghast. Suppose she tried and failed and ruined her teacher's coat? Could not Julia Ostrowska tackle it? Yes — and for just that reason should not. So Olga did it, nervously heating her iron on a little primus stove — did it with a difficulty and a determination so great that metaphorically speaking she turned herself inside out in the process. This sort of psychological revolution was evidently Gurdjieff's chief object. A system of self-supportive notional abstractions was simply not on offer: 'Gurdjieff did not draw diagrams on a board and teach from these. His method of instruction was far less comfortable for his class than this. He carved out from us living chunks of experience and taught from them.'

To say that Gurdjieff was pretty well established in the Tbilisi to which he returned from Borjom, understates. He enjoyed there a satisfying variety of roles and backcloths: head of an extended family at Dmitri's fireside; a successful commercial predator in the Tartar Bazaar; a cultural *éminence grise* whose secret influence penetrated the smoke-filled committee rooms and clubs of the establishment; and a jolly bottle companion at the Chimerion. In this risqué under-ground cabaret run by the Tbilisi Poets' Guild, where elasticated negro ragtime singers bawled out their credo of libertinism to a Circassian clientele already inflamed by the novel sight of Lydia Johnson's prancing thighs, Gurdjieff took his 'idiot-delight' among a sprawling entourage which included modernist painters like Sorin and Sergei Sudeikin, and poets like Robakidze and Paul Yashvili. Tbilisi was indeed proving an agreeable interval, an interval it was almost tempting to prolong and indulge *sine die*.

And yet ... beyond the green baize doors of the Chimerion, the sound of gypsy violins and silly-clever intellectual chatter died away, yielding to a deeper and more urgent note. Georgia's recent tumultuous past and problematic future had shaken the burghers of Tbilisi to their core, and many were desperately revaluing their values. Inflation was rising exponentially. The grain harvest was about to fail. A general expectation of new dangers and physical privations provoked a sudden hunger for real ideas. Where had life's meaning gone to? This existential hunger Gurdjieff felt qualified and bound to satisfy.

Seemingly oblivious of past difficulties, Gurdjieff promptly got off letters to his former alumni, inviting them to join him in a new enterprise — but none did. Petrov was now director of a state school in Rostov, and Zaharoff inextricably embroiled in the propaganda machine of the Volunteer Army in Ekaterinodar. Everyone had their reasons. Ouspensky alone declined on principle (though his flying buttresses of self-justification rested ultimately on a straightforward preference to lead his own groups). No, if Gurdjieff were to find help in his latest enterprise, he must solicit it in a more improbable quarter. It was just a year since the Bolsheviks had been persuaded to sanction and provision the scientific expedition of 'Citizen Gurdjieff'. Perhaps the Menshevik administration – which stood so promisingly for enlightenment, for national integrity, for technological revolution, and for the avant garde – and which managed by a sublime chauvinism to perceive Tbilisi as 'the centre of the world's culture' – would prove equally amenable.

The prerequisite for such an exploration was some organizational mask congenial to the times. The subcutaneous reality, which Gurdjieff himself embodied, would never change; nor would the integrity of his nucleus – the devoted Julia Ostrowska and serious disciples like Dr Stjoernval, the two de Hartmanns, and the two Salzmanns. These he convened in September 1919 on the de Hartmanns' sun-baked verandah – where Olga had lain recuperating on her diet of bacon and wine – and confidentially revealed plans for a permanent centre in Tbilisi. 'What name would you give such an Institute?' he queried rhetorically. The little nucleus fell silent. Any title whatever (hinting in words at a spiritual quintessence which by definition lay beyond words) must be a self-caricature. An awkward silence persisted. The name ultimately chosen would be a lightning rod for public reaction: it could garner recruits or invite derision; it might precipitate success or persecution – it would attract its independent fate. 'Finally, as if we had been squeezing a tube of toothpaste, the word "harmonious" came out.'

About ten days later there appeared on the desk of Comrade G. Laskhishvili, Minister for National Education, a petition from a Mr G. I. Gurdjieff, founder and principal of the Institute for the Harmonious Development of Man, commending to Georgia's notice his progressive psycho-somatic system for the development of will, memory, attention, hearing, thinking, emotion, and instinct; a system which:

> was already in operation in a whole series of large cities such as Bombay, Alexandria, Cabul, New York, Chicago, Christiana, Stockholm, Moscow, Essentuki, and in all departments and homes of the true international and labouring fraternities.

The latter claim was preposterous: its nefastarian boasting calculated to set alarm bells ringing in any rational mind. Why did Gurdjieff again and again invite blame? Why masquerade as 'Prince Ozay' or 'a certain Hindu'? Why court the epithet 'charlatan'? Why offer the profoundest, subtlest truth in terms of a thumping lie? Certainly Gurdjieff's sense of humour was highly – extraordinarily highly – developed; his relish for marginal situations strong. The line dividing reality from surreality possesses length but no breadth, and precisely along that line Gurdjieff glided unscathed through a mêlée of blundering challenges. The Circassian national character – as hectically surrendered to poetry as to wine and women – was strangely in tune with Gurdjieff here. Although Comrade-Minister Laskhishvili displayed no special eccentricities (he did not for instance – as did the Assistant Public Prosecutor – jump up on café tables to sing popular comic songs), he promptly directed the mayor of Tbilisi to locate and place exclusively at Mr Gurdjieff's disposal a building 'worthy of such an important establishment of general public significance.'

In 1919 there generally prevailed in Tbilisi an acute shortage of housing and public accommodation. (Prince Orbeliani himself had to queue – and with some impatience – to use one of the lavatories in his own palace.) The mayor wrung his hands in an agony of municipal indecision; he should not, could not, would not be stampeded. But events were acquiring their own momentum. Gurdjieff hired a small hall, bought the dismayed Thomas de Hartmann a rackety piano ('Anyone can play on a good one'), and was teaching round the clock:

> Within a week after the opening of my Institute, all the special classes which had been started ... were filled up, and there were also waiting-lists of two or three times as many people ... In ... temporary premises which were unsuitable in every respect, and under exceedingly trying conditions, 'work on oneself' began to come to life.

All manner of students were attracted, from Princess Obelinski to Able Seaman Tchekovitch. Two of them – Elizabeta Galumnian, a diplomat's wife, and 'Olgivanna' – were gifted dancers.

Gurdjieff saw all prospective pupils and put them his customary searching questions. Was their established life really so unbearable? Had they wish, real wish? His dialogue with Olga Iovonovna Lazovich Milanoff Hinzenberg (to celebrate Olgivanna's full name) was typical:

G. What do you wish for?
O. I wish for immortality.
G. What do you do now?
O. I look after my house and servants.
G. You work yourself? Cook, look after baby?
O. No, my servants do that for me.
G. You do nothing, and you wish for immortality! But this does not
    come by wishing but by a special kind of work. You must work,
    make effort, for immortality. Now, I will show you how to work.
    First tell servants to go and begin by doing everything yourself.

Although a Montenegrin aristocrat, Olgivanna did not find the ideal
of service uncongenial. As a little grave-eyed girl she had led her blind
father through the streets of her birthplace Cettinje to the court
where he presided as Chief Justice. Educated privately in Russia
and Turkey ('she could paint, or sculp, or cook, or dance, or play
and sing'); surprised by the experience of motherhood while still in
her teens; chastened by a failed marriage to the Russian architect
Vlademar Hinzenberg; ... still only twenty-one and yearning now
for a kind of immolation in art – Olgivanna met Gurdjieff, accepted
his hard conditions, and surrendered her willowy beauty to his sacred
dance. Both she and Lili Galumnian had arrived very aptly, just as
the maestro began to dictate his most notable scenario.

The Struggle of the Magicians[11] was more a revue than a ballet:

> The important scenes represented the schools of a 'Black Magician' and a
> 'White Magician', with exercises by pupils of both schools and a struggle
> between the two schools. The action was to take place against the back-
> ground of the life of an Eastern city, intermixed with sacred dances,
> Dervish dances, and various national Eastern dances, all this interwoven
> with a love story which would itself have an allegorical meaning.

Basically the theme was Manichean; and, as an aid to self-study,
the same dancers must enact the pure movements of the White
Magician's pupils and the ugly, discordant movements of the
Black Magician's pupils.

For the next four turbulent years Gurdjieff's work centred on this
improbable ballet. Created and re-created as a living existential
teaching for participants; a vehicle for countless inner exercises;
a provoker and reconciler of unbelievable tensions – it unified
the music of Thomas de Hartmann, the stagecraft of Alexandre
Salzmann, and the dancing of Julia Ostrowska, Jeanne Salzmann, Lili
Galumnian, and Olgivanna. The scenario was completed, tableaux

devised, solo and ensemble dances choreographed and tirelessly rehearsed, properties and backcloths prepared, costumes designed and sewn ... but *The Struggle of the Magicians* was never performed: its première hovered perpetually in some ethereal wave-band like the lost chord; it tantalized and finally disappeared like the grin of the Cheshire cat. There were moments certainly, even as early as 1919, when the production seemed to tremble on the verge of realization; but in such crises Gurdjieff would spring to the rescue and smash some vital stage property with his axe. 'Why are you so astonished? We have done it, so we don't need it anymore. Now it can go to the dump.' Naturally enough, his pupils groped to understand the sense of all this, but as early as 1915 Gurdjieff had given fair warning: 'If I produce the ballet on the ordinary stage the public will never understand these ideas.'

While the ballet veered and wobbled, general conditions ran steadily downhill: autumn came in dank and drear; the harvest duly failed; commodities grew ever more scarce and expensive; and Anton Ivanovitch Denikin – a courageous White Russian general whose slogan 'Russia Great and Indivisible' supplied him with all his best insights – chose this moment to blockade Georgia (not fully appreciating it was on his side). As to the Institute's dream of 'suitable accommodation', this had sunk beyond trace in a quagmire of mayoral ineptitude. Enough was enough, and Gurdjieff protested he would stop all work. Difficult to guess how genuine was his announcement and how manipulative, but no question of its galvanic effect; within days the authorities had allocated the Institute a substantial two-storey house across the Kura River. Alexandre Salzmann had actually been the precipitating factor. He succeeded in planting a bitter cartoon in the capital's satirical magazine, *The Devil's Whip*: Gurdjieff and his entourage were shown bang in the middle of Erivan Place, the city's principal square, huddled round an old stove. 'They have finally moved,' ran the caption ... Strange to relate, the man who in Moscow and Petrograd had blended with the shadows, was now a recognizable public figure.

His footsteps are even easier to track through the snow of early December 1919 because he walks in tandem with a young journalist from London. Mr Carl Bechhofer-Roberts – despite a conveniently misplaced umlaut, despite his inconsequential *Wanderjahre* in Russia, Japan, North Africa and India, despite his linguistic gifts – entered the Chimerion in Tbilisi like an escapee from a P. G. Wodehouse novel. Fattish, red-faced, and irrepressibly facetious, Bechhofer was off to the war zone with little except a scrap or two of editorial encouragement, a great deal of cheek, and his Conway-Stewart fountain pen. Bechhofer's wallet, however, held an important letter of introduction to 'a curious individual named Georgiy Ivanovich Gourjiev' – a figure he speedily identified:

> He was a man of striking appearance. Short, dark, and swarthy, with penetrating and clever eyes; no-one could be in his company for many minutes without being impressed by the force of his personality . . . there was no denying his extraordinary all-round intelligence.

Gurdjieff was affability itself and spared neither effort nor time to show the young newcomer 'some sides of Tiflis that not all visitors see': he led him safely through sinister streets, where 'every second man . . . had a bandage round his head, or at least a patch over his eye'; he fêted him on piquant oriental delicacies in an underground restaurant, 'through the windows of which one looked out upon the swift and muddy waters of the Kura river'; he broiled him to a pleasing lobster-pink in the sulphur baths; he delivered him, gasping and parboiled, into the formidable hands – and feet – of a bearded Persian masseur; he introduced him to Stjoernval, the de Hartmanns, and the Salzmanns; and not least he gave him entrée to rehearsals for *The Struggle of the Magicians*.

The more one ponders the Bechhofer episode the more it intrigues. Obdurate against all 'higher thought', he seems to blunder through the Gurdjieffian diaspora at philosophical right-angles – smiling with vacuous amiability, tipping his bowler hat to a complex situation whose inner dynamic basically eludes him. Whatever his virtues as an amusing companion for 'idiot relief' or as a prize specimen of 'freely-walking guinea-pig', they seem incommensurate with Gurdjieff's largesse. It is tempting to hypothesize that Bechhofer's puzzling letter of introduction bore the signature of his long-time journalistic acquaintance P. D. Ouspensky; that Gurdjieff humoured and helped Bechhofer for the sake of Ouspensky and Zaharoff (now lodged together in desperate circumstances in beleaguered Rostov-on-Don). This, at any rate, is precisely where Bechhofer made for on leaving Gurdjieff in mid-December: 'I fought my way through the crowded station and took a cab into the town. In a few minutes I was knocking at the door of my friend Mr Ouspiensky.'

The ruinous 'vodka' which Ouspensky concocted from pure white spirit and orange peel surely elasticated Bechhofer's tongue as he romanced on Gurdjieff:

If he really wanted to go anywhere, were it even to his mysterious monasteries in Thibet – in one of which, he said, echoing an Indian tradition, Jesus had studied! – I cannot see who would be able to prevent his going.

The notion, however fey, that Gurdjieff might suddenly disappear into the shadowy hinterland of his 'system' was a stimulus to action so powerful that it took an Ouspensky to disregard it. Andrei Zaharoff, more in touch with his original aspirations, made strenuous efforts to get through to his teacher; but having weeks earlier contracted smallpox, died miserably and alone in the bloody shambles of Novorossiysk.

Back in Tbilisi, Christmas 1919 was scant improvement on the year before – the dinner Gurdjieff prepared for the de Hartmanns and the Salzmanns in a cold bare room consisted of rice porridge with honey and dried fruit – and the New Year ushered in more dangers and uncertainties than realistic hopes. The Institute for the Harmonious Development of Man continued to play out its equivocal role but with an air of increasing abstraction: 'When Mr Gurdjieff announced that *The Struggle of the Magicians* would be performed in the State Theatre, it seemed ... like a joke, since we did not even have material for costumes.'

By late March 1920, Gurdjieff was steadily dismantling his Institute, conscious that its host body the Georgian Menshevik Republic was itself living on borrowed time. North of the Caucasus the counter-revolution had been smashed and its miserable remnants 'driven into the sea amidst indescribable circumstances of horror and despair'. A new wave of refugees poured into Tbilisi with grim faces and grim stories. Bechhofer-Roberts passed hastily through with news of Zaharoff's death in Novorossiysk and Ouspensky's escape via Odessa. A Major Frank S. Pinder[18] (referred by Ouspensky) arrived on Gurdjieff's doorstep with dark rings under his eyes and a single bottle of 'Sir Johnnie Walker's spiritual consoler'.

The Major was destined to become an important disciple of Gurdjieff and it would be fascinating to resurrect from the Akashic record their first conversation. Pinder was one who spoke well but never simply. Pithy proverbs, classical tags, scientific formulae, Shakespearean quotations, scriptural quotations, aphorisms, puns and profanities, gellified his conversational broth. Like Gurdjieff, the Major was a polyglot: he commanded Russian and Turkish; could manage in French, German, Latin, and Greek ancient and modern; and interested himself in Hebrew and Sanskrit. While head of the

British Economic Mission to Denikin's Volunteer Army – 'a real Sauchiehall Street haggis' – Pinder had secured Ouspensky employment in Ekaterinodar and paid his salary himself – in effect keeping him and his family alive. Rostov fell to the Bolsheviks on 8 January 1920, but precisely how the Major had extricated himself and got to Tbilisi he preferred not to dwell on; he had seen the future and it did not work. Pinder's best advice to Gurdjieff was to get out while the going was good.

'Begin in Russia, finish in Russia.' Whatever Gurdjieff's riddle means, it hints at the pain of his severance in 1920. A thousand links and memories bound him to greater Russia: in that ramshackle Empire he had been born; his youthful ideal 'Prince Lubovedsky' had been a Russian prince; his mother and brother Dmitri must now remain on Russian soil. But with Georgia outflanked and outmanœuvred; with Lenin, Trotsky, and Mustapha Kemal so unmistakably sharpening their claws, and with his own burdensome mission still to fulfil – Gurdjieff must seize the moment. 'I decided not only to liquidate everything in Tiflis but even to break with everything that up to then had tied me to Russia, and to emigrate beyond its borders.'

Where to make for? In principle Gurdjieff could go east to Turkestan or west, via Batoum and Constantinople, into Europe; in practice he had Hobson's choice. On 27 April, when the Eleventh Soviet Army had made their daring raid on the Caspian port of Baku (and shot the entire Azerbaijani Government), they had effectively sealed the eastward route; only the westward option – to the abominable quarantine ships on the Bosphorus – remained. So be it then. At least powerful friends awaited Gurdjieff in Constantinople: Ouspensky, who had reached there in March, and Prince Sabaheddin, who, from the faded empire splendours of his palace at Kuru Chesme, wielded the dubious influence of a Sultan's nephew.

Thomas de Hartmann's farewell concert (attended by the entire staff of the Moscow Arts Theatre) provided a memorable backcloth to Gurdjieff's very last Tbilisi appearance:

> The hall had many slender columns decorated with tiny mirrors and our ... friends ... brought tall candles. The myriad reflections in the tiny mirrors gave a very beautiful effect. The piano was covered by a magnificent Persian shawl. The music was illuminated by two huge candles entwined with Persian flowers. Instead of chairs, there were benches covered with Persian rugs.

The pace of Georgia's political deterioration obliged Gurdjieff to sell all the Institute's property 'for a mere song'; to convert the proceeds into twenty rare carpets; and to distribute these amongst his people. From Tbilisi it was still possible to reach the Black Sea port of Batoum the easy way or the hard way: the easy way (used by Olga a year before) was by train, and took thirteen hours; Gurdjieff chose the hard way. Within days he and his faithful – thirty souls altogether – were moving through the torrid heat of late May along the Batoum road. Their four pack animals – one especially – baulked at the gullies which erosion and neglect had cut in the path. To Mme Elizabeta Grigorievna Stjoernval – nervous of horses and wondering, yet again, how she had been manœuvred into a false situation – Gurdjieff predictably confided the rogue animal. Despite his encouraging words, progess was slow.

When at last the weary company descended to beautiful, mosquito-infested Batoum, disaster struck: at the harbour gates the so-called 'Special Georgian Detachment', materializing in their gaudy uniforms like a swarm of poisonous fritillaries, confiscated Gurdjieff's precious carpets. Somehow, nevertheless, the refugees scraped together the price of steerage passage to Constantinople. As the ship made way the retrospect was dramatic: above the town's white minarets rose tier upon tier of green wooded hills, and above the hills the indeterminate purple sheen of rugged peaks.

But who can say if Gurdjieff gazed east or west?

6

✣

THE STRUGGLE OF THE MAGICIANS

(7 June 1920–13 August 1921)

Rumour preceded Gurdjieff to Constantinople. In the bazaars and *tchaikanas* there was whisper of the coming of a man of power, a mysterious wanderer, 'reputed by Moslems to be a convert to Islam, and by Christians to be a member of some obscure Nestorian sect' – a true *baba* who knew all the 'one hundred and twenty sciences'. Elsewhere however a different analysis prevailed. In the Gilbertian confusion of General Sir George Milne's HQ in the old Turkish Military Academy at Harbie, Gurdjieff was warily anticipated as a secret agent of the Bolsheviks, or the White Russians, or even the Dashnakzutiun – in any case a very dangerous customer. The object of these conflicting expectations came ashore on 7 June 1920, after strip-search and fumigation on the notorious quarantine hulks; he took the cable car to Péra, the European quarter, and bought some meat cakes and orange juice.

Through the windows of the Greek restaurant Gurdjieff could see the Suleimaniye Mosque crowning the city's arch-dramatic skyline. But though the stage-set was familiar, the cast had been confusingly augmented. Turkey had fought the Great War on the losing side and General Franchet d'Espérey, riding without reins on a white horse, had led the Allies into Constantinople. The dignified and somnambulent ineptitude of the Turks was now subordinated to a brash new ineptitude which wryly amused Gurdjieff and was even regretted in *The Times*:

> The *corpus vile* of Constantinople submitted to Allied medicine is not an exhilarating spectacle. A farrago of High Commissioners, British, French, Italian, Greek, some of them admirals, some civilians, all of them with civilian advisers endowed with nebulous powers . . . no one can see where

they begin or end. Add two Commanders-in-Chief, one French, one British, the former supposed to be supreme in Turkey in Europe but to exercise his control through the British; the latter a bilateral being who is compelled to bestride the Bosphorus with his left leg subservient to the motions of General Franchet d'Espérey, while his right leg is his own. Flavour with a dash of Allenby from Palestine and just a *soupçon* of the remains of a Turkish administration, and you have some idea of the hotch-potch . . .

Gurdjieff was heartily relieved to be away from Tbilisi but the sun which warmed him that first morning in Constantinople was deceptive. The real situation was messy. Fuel was scarce. Transport was chaotic. The police were corrupt. The currency was debased. The population was demoralized. And flitting through the urine-soaked streets and the ghastly hovels around Sirkedji, borne on the miasma which rose nightly from the Golden Horn, a virulent Spanish flu serviced the City's refuse-choked graveyards. The common people anticipated no redress either from their new rulers or their old. Away in distant Ankara, Mustapha Kemal Pasha the hero of Gallipoli was scheming a revolution of incalculable consequence. Behind the triple walls of the Yildiz Kiosk, deep in the sinister labyrinth of the Imperial Palace, Vahdettin the Shadow of God, the last Sultan of the House of Osman, nursed his rheumatism and his mean-spirited anxieties – his bony skull, foundering shoulders, and beaked yellow nose, lending His Majesty the appearance of a pensionable vulture. 'What a catastrophe!' he would sniff to Damad Ferid Pasha the Grand Vizier, 'What a catastrophe!' And the Vizier agreed with some feeling.

Of all Constantinople's environs none was more dispiriting than Péra – with its narrow pavements and vacuous architecture; its maddening clank of trams and its wearisome, heel-bruising cobble-stones; its ominous hill under the Dark Tower. Well might one wonder why Gurdjieff chose to settle there! No doubt, as the traditional enclave of foreigners, infidels, and the dispossessed, it held attractions for a half-Armenian refugee whose father had been murdered by the Turks. But who knows? Perhaps it afforded easy access to friends whose very names have escaped biography. Forty years before, as a raw adolescent, Gurdjieff had explored Péra obsessed with 'all kinds of dervish nonsense', and dived for coins thrown by tourists from the Galata Bridge. Much later, as a 'Seeker of Truth', he had stayed in Prince Lubovedsky's well-appointed house near to the Russian Embassy and the *tekkes* or prayer-lodges of the Mevlevi, Rufia, and Kadiri dervishes. Now in the summer of 1920 he moved quickly to rent an apartment in Koumbaradji Street.

The general speed with which Gurdjieff established himself is all the more extraordinary considering the variety of calls on his slender material resources. He had managed to bring in two small diamonds and two carpets (spirited through Batoum by Dr Stjoernval in the Finnish Consul's diplomatic bag). This was all he had. The entourage which had landed with him was a mixed asset; certainly its nucleus comprised born 'survivalists', able and eager to contribute to the common chest, but its lesser spirits were by now semi-dependents who stood before him like twenty expectant scarecrows. How to respond?

Cynics might claim that Gurdjieff's shift from Tbilisi to Constantinople was essentially a shift from the Chimerion to the Black Rose. This famous café was the general evening rendezvous for White Russians in Péra; here a motley General Staff of Excellencies and Imperial officers refought Denikin's doomed campaigns, recklessly advancing their salt-cellars and pepperpots across the snowy steppes of starched tablecloths. By day, when Gurdjieff made the café his 'office', a more mixed clientele fought off the heat and *accidie* and spleen of Péra with repeated helpings of lemon tea: *soi-disant* countesses, Greek adventuresses, and sloe-eyed Armenian whores made up the necessary complement of pliant but unreceivable ladies. To tell the truth not all the clientele of the Black Rose was fully satisfied with heterosexuality, gypsy violins and lemon tea. Many had recourse to 'very efficient special means, which now exist there under the names of "alcoholism", "cocainism", "morphinism", "nicotinism", "onanism", "monkism", "Athenianism", and other names also ending in "ism".' If these people themselves were too far gone to care, their friends and relatives were often desperate on their behalf. Gurdjieff had only to whisper his undoubted capacity as a 'physician-hypnotist and healer of vices', to divert to his table a remunerative stream of high-born moral derelicts and unreconstructed 'Solovievs'.

To suggest that Gurdjieff's therapy relied on a transference of *hanbledzoin* or animal magnetism is simply to veneer mystery with words: he cured — and that is that. Perhaps forgivably his compassion towards his clientele fell short of pure philanthropy; it was necessarily for a fee that he set them on their feet. As a profession it was certainly far from pleasant; most of his unsavoury patients came to him sulking and 'as irritable as a man who has just undergone full treatment by a famous European nerve specialist.' The diet of human degradation which Gurdjieff accepted at the Black Rose was at least garnished with an amusing sauce of surreality and farce. And *en passant* he struck some good business deals. Sight unseen, he acquired and sold huge consignments of Beluga caviar; he cultivated a preposterous relationship with a Turkish pasha, eager that his son become a champion wrestler; and he received from some tearful Greek parents a half-interest in a ship – long since commandeered by the Royal Navy. All in all Gurdjieff coped magnificently with 'the eternal question of money, so painful for those who have no uncle in America.' Very soon he had freed himself to address his deeper concerns.

Gurdjieff's re-encounter with Ouspensky was emotionally charged. So much had been undergone since Essentuki. Cold, hunger, typhoid, cholera, and even bullets had been outdistanced; Zaharoff was dead; Russia itself, as they had known it, lay dismembered, its intelligentsia and princely classes cruelly remustered as the *dramatis personae* of a thousand picaresque cautionary tales. Ouspensky was brooding – and would continue to brood all his life – over the irretrievable loss of the old order:

> During these last three years the ground had fallen away behind me. It was a quite inconceivable period, when there was no *way back*, when I experienced in relation to places and people the same sensation which we ordinarily feel in relation to time. To no place that I had left was it possible to return. From nobody from whom I had parted did I have any more news.

Genuinely though Ouspensky deplored the social conflagration, he personally was visibly singed by the spirit of revolution. Had he not broken with Gurdjieff in Essentuki? Tried to disaffect Petrov and Zaharoff? Declined to support the Institute in Tbilisi? And inaugurated his own groups without mandate? He was 'very glad to see G'. – but a slightly mixed gladness perhaps (such as the Romanov pretender Grand Duke Cyril might have felt on confronting an exhumed and resuscitated Tsar).

Seated in front of Gurdjieff in the Black Rose, submitted to 'the exacting benevolence of his gaze', Ouspensky melted. It seemed that in the interests of esotericism all former difficulties could be set aside, it seemed that he could work with Gurdjieff as formerly in Petrograd, it seemed he should sacrifice his independence and hand over all his pupils in Constantinople. For Ouspensky had not been idle since arriving in March; by teaching mathematics, which he knew, and

English, which he did not, he was supporting himself, Mme Ouspensky, and her extended family. Their single room in a lodging house on Prinkipo Island in the Sea of Marmara was enviable in many eyes. In Péra, which Ouspensky visited by ferry daily, he had quickly established new groups and although these at their periphery were hopelessly chaotic ('The meetings sounded like pandemonium. Everyone was shouting at once. . .'), a serious nucleus was emerging which met in the upstairs offices of the Russky Mayak, a species of YMCA for White Russians. This core group of twenty to thirty pupils – including the Nietzschean Boris Ferapontoff – Gurdjieff now inherited.

For two or three months the *rapprochement* worked miracles. It sped Gurdjieff across the water to Prinkipo to drink tea with Sophie Grigorievna Ouspensky and her daughter Lenotchka Savitsky, and to dandle on his knee Lenotchka's baby son Leonidas; it set Gurdjieff and Ouspensky strolling, as if spiritually arm in arm through Kapali Tcharshi the grand bazaar; it found Ouspensky working whole nights and days with Gurdjieff at Koumbaradji Street:

> One such night in particular remains in my memory, when we 'translated' a dervish song for *The Struggle of the Magicians*. I saw G. the artist and G. the poet, whom he had so carefully hidden, particularly the latter. This translation took the form of G. recalling the Persian verses, sometimes repeating them to himself in a quiet voice and then translating them for me into Russian. After a quarter of an hour, let us say, when I had completely disappeared beneath forms, symbols, and assimilations, he said: 'There now make *one line* out of that.'

Sharing their coffee and exhaustion after creating twenty-two (strangely abstract) lines, teacher and pupil seemed for a moment in warm reconciliation.

Together they made several visits to the dervishes. Constantinople had 258 different lodges but Gurdjieff, in connection with his ballet, was focusing on one elite order, itself a perennial and potent yeast in Turkish cultural and dynastic life – the Mevlevi or 'Whirling' dervishes. Every Thursday evening he walked Ouspensky to the Mevlevi *Mukabele*, or turning ceremony, in the Galatahane *tekke* at the top of the Yuksek Kalderym. Cerebral as ever, Ouspensky concentrated on the ritual's formal structure as a living orrery or planetary model, while Gurdjieff – though brilliantly illuminating this aspect – strove to awaken his pupil's feelings to the totality of the experience.

The immense œuvre of Turkish classical music offers nothing exceeding in power and poignancy the sixty-six musical settings of the Mevlevi ritual; the emotional impact of this sacred music is direct and no seeker for gnosis can possibly misconstrue the reed-flute's insistence:

> Listen to the reed. It is complaining.
> It tells of separation, saying
> 'Ever since they tore me from the reed-bed,
> My lament has moved man and woman to tears...
> Everyone who is left far from his source
> Wishes back the time of union.'

Ouspensky did not misconstrue it. Nevertheless he remained obdurate against 'beauty' or 'allurement', preferring a dispensation without flavour or aroma: 'I never feel, I *know*.'

Soon afterwards, when Gurdjieff brought the de Hartmanns to the Mevlevi, we may decently suspect that the flute's call indeed 'moved man and woman to tears'. But Gurdjieff's purpose here lay far beyond the mere indulgence of emotionality; the oriental modalities which Thomas breathed in from the Mevlevi or from Komitas, he was meant to employ as he bent all his powers, all his decades of musical experience, to composition for *The Struggle of the Magicians*. The ideal of repayment was very close to Thomas: 'Music has always been for me the "talent" of the New Testament, given to me by God and demanding that I develop and work on it unceasingly.' A unique musical creation[12] was in train — an amalgam of Gurdjieff's being and de Hartmann's sensitivity and technique: the 'Tibetan Masks', 'The Fall of the Priestess', 'Holy Affirming, Holy Denying, Holy Reconciling', the 'Little Tibetan', the 'Ho Yah!', 'The Great Prayer'.

> I saw that, as in Essentuki, the Work was always on strengthening attention. Once as I was watching and playing the piano as usual, Mr Gurdjieff gave me a little piece of paper on which he had written an upper voice as an embellishment. It became impossible to play all the parts with two hands. So he told Madame de Salzmann to play the lower part and me the upper part, and this became the dance of the dervishes. The more the pupils entered into the movement, the more exciting and beautiful it became, full of a magical force characteristic of all orders of dervishes.

By September 1920 Gurdjieff felt sufficiently settled in Constantinople to reanimate his Institute for the Harmonious Development of Man. Surmounting difficulties as big as those in Tbilisi (but in this case with no Minister Laskhishvili up his sleeve), Gurdjieff discovered and rented a rabbit-warren of rooms at 13 Abdullatif Yemeneci Sokak near the Galata Tower. Except for being twenty yards from the *Mevlanahanesi* of the Whirling Dervishes, the place was nothing special. The street commemorating 'Gentle unruffled Abdul, maker of lace, headscarves and slippers' was a shadowy, smelly ravine of aged wooden houses, whose cramped verticality seemed to mock its dedication. Gurdjieff erected a notice board and issued a prospectus of study which contained something to intrigue (and to offend) almost everybody.

On Thursday and Sunday evenings Gurdjieff lectured personally – in Russian, Greek, Turkish or Armenian according to the audience. What was the essential defect of contemporary science? Gurdjieff would indicate it. Was the soul eternal? Was the will free? Gurdjieff would explain. His delivery had a strange texture: a penetrating allusion to Kant, to Freud, or to the newly fashionable Einstein would be deliberately undermined by an allusion to fortune-telling or the 'science of poisons'. Beneath Gurdjieff's seemingly discursive critique of hypnosis, magnetism, fakirism, magic, sleight-of-hand, sacred art, and 'emotionalism' – there still beat the pulse of one tremendous thought – but how seriously was he trying to project it? Did his voice perhaps fall fractionally short of a 'wholly-manifested-intonation', or his dark eyes lack their usual quotient of smoulder? We cannot tell of course. But certainly – compared with Petrograd and Tbilisi – the Constantinople Institute proved a hiatus.

Nevertheless, with his old guard of senior followers, Gurdjieff intensified his work. Three doors away from No. 13, at the Grand Rabbinate, he acquired the use of an austere hall for his Sacred Dances, and here – appropriately enough on a surface of black and white tiles – the Struggle of the Magicians was renewed. The ballet's scenario gives us some picture of rehearsals in Yemeneci Sokak. The White Magician's throne-like chair was surmounted by the enneagram, and in accordance with the dynamic of its inner hexagon, the six files of dancers interwove. Order and purity prevailed: participants had not to transcend their humanity but to infuse it with a luminous attention; and though Gurdjieff might move among them with a feline grace, or even demonstrate some evolution (he knelt like a great planet sinking down), it was chiefly through an iconic stillness that he bore witness to his function and emanated his demand.

In disquieting contrast were the dances of the Black Magician's pupils, who strutted about with jerky angularity and mutual hostility and derision: 'It is seen that the pupils in the chain contort themselves, making convulsive movements; some of them become weak and even fall... As time goes on, the movements ... become ever more violent and terrible.' None of these 'black dances' has passed down to us, but the sense of them is of a libidinal expressionism grown rank. Gurdjieff – picking quarrels and fomenting trouble – brought his own contribution to the essential 'negativity' of these rehearsals, and 'his language on these occasions would have made even Lenin blush.' Given this Manichean dualism, there arose, in one mind at least, an important question: was the 'Teacher of Dancing' himself a white or black magician! Although the moral bias of Gurdjieff's scenario unambiguously aligned him with the White Magician, Piotr Ouspensky remained only half-convinced:

> Mr Gurdjieff is a very extraordinary man. His possibilities are much greater than those of people like ourselves. But he can also go in the wrong way. I believe he is now passing through a crisis, the outcome of which no-one can foresee. Most people have many 'I's. If these 'I's are at war with one another it does not produce great harm, because they are all weak. But with Mr. Gurdjieff there are only two 'I's; one very good and one very bad. I believe that in the end the good 'I' will conquer. But meanwhile it is very dangerous to be near him.

When the Institute opened formally in October 1920, Ouspensky withdrew to Prinkipo. He had personally taken no part in the Sacred Dances but his agonized and protracted hesitation-waltz with Gurdjieff was continuing.

In the dim backwater of the Grand Rabbinate – unsuspected by the great wash of humanity which left its daily tide-mark in Taxim Square and the Grande Rue de Péra – Gurdjieff pursued his strange experiment. Execution of the 'white' and 'black' dances was confided to the self-same pupils – summoned by Gurdjieff to a conscious and alternating appreciation of the 'Holy Affirming' and 'Holy Denying' elements deep within them. The scenario's self-parodying melodrama and pantomimic form – the dark cave, the bubbling cauldron, the pentagram, the stuffed toads and bats – masked a serious and sophisticated morality. For Gurdjieff the prevailing social mores were merely the cardboard stage-properties of history: the eternal and authentic 'ethical drama' turned on consciousness and conscience. The closing prayer of the White Magician puts all moral emphasis on awakening: 'Lord Creator, and all you His assistants, help us to be able to remember ourselves at all times in order that we may avoid involuntary actions, as only through them can evil manifest itself.'

For no refugee in Constantinople was the manifestation of evil a mere abstraction. Since 1915 the entire Caucasus and Transcaucasus had been mired neck-high in the history of crime. A million personal tragedies bore witness to the writhing interplay of greed, nationalism, and warped idealism. On the wheel of humanity's invincible stupidity, Gurdjieff's family had been broken: his father Giorgios Giorgiades, shot by the Turks in 1918, lay buried near his little rose garden in Alexandropol; his aged mother and younger sister Sophie Ivanovna Kapanadze were cooped up in Bolshevik Essentuki, under conditions of grim privation; his brother Dmitri hung on ever more anxiously in Menshevik Tbilisi; only his elder sister Anna Ivanovna Anastasieff, with her son Valentin and her four daughters was safe, having moved in June 1920 to the remote village of Baytar near to Mount Amara (ancestral lands restored to the Dashnak Republic of Armenia). In the first week of November however, the Turkish Nationalist General Kâzim Karabekr Pasha – having swept east through Sarikamish, Kars, and Alexandropol – casually over-whelmed and sacked Baytar, slaughtering Gurdjieff's sister, her husband, and all their daughters. Only the orphaned Valentin escaped, one of thirty survivors in a village of 400 souls.

How soon this dreadful news dressed Gurdjieff in mourning we cannot guess, but the telegram could only confirm his existing abomi-nation of war: 'Don't they really ever see that these processes of theirs are the most terrible of all the horrors which can possibly exist in the whole of the universe?'

Already Péra, hundreds of miles from the bloody arena, had its full complement of casualties. And on 16 November 1920, as Gurdjieff crossed to Kadiköy aboard one of the little bathtub ferries, he found the Bosphorus choked with 126 ships in which Baron Piotr Nikolaevitch Wrangel had extricated from the Crimea the last broken remnants of the South Russian Army. Most of these 145,693 new Russian refugees, sluiced onto the cold marmoreal shore of Constantinople, were exhausted physically or morally – and, as Gurdjieff soon found, desperate for money:

> The young lady had come to me with a dislocated shoulder and her body covered with bruises. While I was busy with her arm, she told me that her husband had beaten her because she had refused to sell herself for a good sum to a certain Spanish Jew. Somehow or other with the help of Drs Victorov and Maximovitch I put her shoulder right, after which she left.

Gurdjieff the good Samaritan, Gurdjieff the disinterested rescuer of nameless 'Solovievs' and 'Vitvitskaias', was steadily encroaching

on Gurdjieff the strictly professional 'physician-hypnotist'. The will
of God could not reach man asleep but Gurdjieff could at least try to
alleviate some pain and instil some hope. Perhaps nowhere more
intensely than in Péra, where he took the blow of his sister's death,
did he suffer from man's inner and outer chaos. Though he firmly
held that a planetary imperative lay at the root of human desolation,
he added a bitter footnote that the reasoning capacity of rulers and
'power-possessors' had attained the level: 'Look! Look! He already
begins to distinguish mama from papa!'

Late on a Wednesday evening in early January 1921, Gurdjieff
went to the palace of Kuru Chesme for dinner. His host Prince
Mehmet Sabaheddin[22] might have chosen his parentage expressly
with 'power-possession' in mind: the bluest of blood (adulterated
only by alcohol') flowed in his veins – he was the great-grandson of
Sultan Mahmud II, the grandson of Sultan Abdul Mejid, and the
nephew of Abdul the Damned and of Vahdettin the present puppet
Sultan. Gurdjieff's innumerable associates and 'freely-walking guinea
pigs' in Constantinople probably boasted no one more singular in
appearance, character, and history: Mehmet Sabaheddin, as he
brooded obscurely amid the faded Empire splendours of his drawing
room overlooking the Bosphorus; as he posed yet again for his
photographer, in fez and frockcoat – diminutive, slender, seagull-
boned – 'gave an impression of a refinement that was too delicate
for this earth.' He possessed, or seemed to possess, a special halo of
eclectic spirituality: educated as a Muslim but drawn to Buddhism,
he often confided shyly to Europeans that 'he had found no satisfaction except in the contemplation of Jesus Christ'... But despite
finding it there, that was not always where he had looked for it.

Like Gurdjieff, Sabaheddin had felt a call – but in a different
direction. From early youth he had searched for the meaning of life,
'and finally, when Edmond Demolin's À quoi tient la Supériorité des
Anglo-Saxons? came into his hands, he felt that his prayers for
guidance had been answered.' He had plunged immediately into the
murky pool of revolutionary politics; had founded the Society of
Personal Initiative and Administrative Decentralization; had cherished through two decades of sanguinary disappointment a hope to
serve his country, preferably as a reformist Sultan or Grand Vizier.
From conference to caucus, on printless elfin Ottoman toe, he had
moved between Constantinople, Geneva, Berlin, Paris, and Athens; in
1908 he had brought back his father's bones from Paris and shrewdly
reinterred them at Eyup; he had entered cynical alliances and hired

various ethnic thugs; in 1913 he slipped out of Turkey, sentenced to death in absentia for contriving the assassination of Grand Vizier Mahmud Sevket. Despite a heinous orchestration of 'personal initiative', 'all the King's horses and all the King's men could not set up Prince Sabahu'd-Din at Constantinople.' Tears sometimes filled his lustrous eyes and in faultless French he would confess that 'The Holy Virgin was for him as much a living reality as Jesus the Son of God.'

Gurdjieff was not the Prince's only guest that Wednesday evening; there were places set for a Temporary Captain John Godolphin Bennett (aged twenty-three) and his mistress Winifred Alise Beaumont (aged forty-seven). In such a seating plan there was rare coincidence, unconscious irony, and plural ignorance. As Head of Military Intelligence 'B' Office, young Captain Bennett was on the lookout for a 'very dangerous Russian agent George Gurdjieff', but he does not seem to have caught the name. Gurdjieff knew nothing of his adverse dossier from New Delhi which lay on Bennett's desk in Military HQ; nor did he know that Mrs Beaumont had just lent her own drawing room in Matchka to Piotr Ouspensky for his afternoon meetings. Neither Bennett nor Mrs Beaumont dreamt that Ouspensky was remotely connected with Gurdjieff. And the Prince did not know how to become Sultan. Within these peculiar constraints, Gurdjieff bore himself impressively: 'I had never before,' mused Bennett afterwards, 'had the same feeling of being understood better than I understood myself.'

Given that even Gurdjieff's social life was consistently purposive, why did he allot time to Sabaheddin? Not to trade theosophical vacuities. Not to solicit funds – the Prince had run out. Not to manœuvre for any advantage which lay within political gift – the Prince was completely passé, equally ignored by the powers at Ankara and the Sublime Porte. His table was certainly renowned for the excellence of its *tcherkess tawuk* (breast of chicken in ground walnut sauce) but Gurdjieff could cook this himself, and even better. Perhaps the explanation is staring us in the face. With westward emigration in imminent prospect, Gurdjieff simply needed to know more about England, France, and Germany from someone intelligent who had actually lived there.

Gurdjieff had in fact just received a letter from Jaques-Dalcroze[21] proposing he come and plant his work at the international centre for *La Méthode Rythmique*, near Dresden. The possibility of staging *The Struggle of the Magicians* at Hellerau, in the lofty colonnaded Bildungsanstalt with its enormous stage and unique lighting system, was strongly appealing to Gurdjieff. He owed this generous invitation from 'Monsieur Jaques' to a pre-war cultural conjunction, when:

> Salzmann's tall, thin, ironic figure might be seen in the corridors of the Anstalt, striding along beside the round little figure of Dalcroze, as he trotted rapidly along to a class, with a sheaf of manuscripts under his arm.

Dalcroze himself had decamped to Geneva in 1915, and deplored post-war conditions in Saxony. Gurdjieff by contrast was evidently undeterred by the prospect of further 'sharp energetic events' in Germany, and could even foresee some advantages in its rampant inflation. It was not the will to go which Gurdjieff lacked, but the indispensable funds and multifarious visas (for Bulgaria, Serbia, Greece, Hungary, Czechoslovakia, and Germany). He must bide his time.

Gurdjieff's 'fundamental rhythm' will probably turn out to be an insoluble biographic *mysterium*, but (judging by Essentuki and Tbilisi) he was inclined to slow down his tempo in late spring and early summer. So it transpired that gradually but inexorably as the returning sun grew stronger, the Constantinople Institute evaporated: popular interest, always fickle, slackened and fell away; European *dilettanti* like Alphons Paquet, Boris Mouravieff, J. G. Bennett and Winifred Beaumont visited Yemeneci Sokak only once, and as observers; Ouspensky maintained his distance; Olga de Hartmann became ill; Mme Stjoernval became discontent; and though the rest of the Russian nucleus could and would have jumped through hoops of fire for Gurdjieff, he abstained from providing any. The hot irritating wind, with its deposit of finely powdered dung, carried the murmur of indifferent doves, the clatter of indifferent trams, and British soldiers' startlingly obscene adaptation of 'K-K-K-Katy'. The city's relics of dead Byzantium added their own sense of futility and historical irony. In mid-May 1921, Gurdjieff closed down the Institute in Péra and 'embarked for Cythera'.

The island of Prinkipo, a few miles off Constantinople, was full of gem-like dragonflies which darted in and out of the papery bougainvillaea. A cheerful yellow carriage hired at the jetty carried Gurdjieff and Mme Ostrowska steeply upwards through the little town, past ragged handkerchiefs of husbandry into the sweet-smelling pine woods, where they settled in a pasha's villa overlooking the Marmara. In this Edenic setting there ensured a sharp tussle between Gurdjieff and Ouspensky for the allegiance of Mme Ouspensky.

Only a day or two before, Piotr Ouspensky had begun to wind up his affairs in Turkey. On 14 May 1921, an unexpected telegram had reached him: 'Deeply impressed by your book *Tertium Organum* wish meet you New York or London will pay all expenses.' Its originator, Mary Lilian, Lady Rothermere, wife of the newspaper magnate (although she chiefly 'utilized her exalted worldly position and vast wealth as a lubricant to living'), was no stranger to adventures of the spirit. Ouspensky, procedurally advised by Captain Bennett and now suddenly armed with her ladyship's patronage, set about obtaining the necessary travel documents for London: four precious visas promptly issued him by the British Embassy (his own, Mme Ouspensky's, Lenotchka Savitsky's and her husband's)... But would all four visas be used?

The fact was that Gurdjieff's invitation to Hellerau and Ouspensky's to London had precipitated an intense struggle, more and more centred on Sophie Grigorievna. Here a curious parallel warrants brief reflection. Dramatically speaking, *The Struggle of the Magicians* is a contest for the soul of the beautiful Zeinab – but Sophie Grigorievna was hardly a Zeinab, either in beauty or virginal purity. And the casting of Gurdjieff and Ouspensky is equally problematical; viewed as contending magicians, could both of them conceivably be white? Eminent critics have thought so:

> Gurdjieff had this lightly tinted whiteness. He never stopped playing with all the colors of life; that is why fools cry out against him. Ouspensky, who was a philosopher, tried to stay in the whiteness he had discovered ...

Yet Gurdjieff always dressed in black at the ballet rehearsals; long ago in Crete he had passed as the 'Black Greek'; and in Ashkhabad had responded instantly when someone saluted him 'Ah! Black Devil!' Although Ouspensky's insight that the Gurdjieff of the early 1920s was alternatively the White and Black magician is sheer heresy among his spiritual posterity, it has the ring of a subversive or forgotten truth.

Gurdjieff held the door open to Ouspensky himself until the very last, but Piotr Demianovich was adamant: 'In the first place I did not believe it was possible to organise work in Germany and secondly I did not believe I could work with G.' A surreptitious plan was gaining ascendancy in Ouspensky's mind: he would proceed to London not as Gurdjieff's pupil but as a 'kindred spirit'; there he would publish all the Work ideas in a book entitled *Fragments of an Ancient Teaching*. Apparently the author of *Tertium Organum* could no longer brook existing in Gurdjieff's shadow – and nor, if he could possibly help it, would Mme Ouspensky!

Ouspensky possessed a mind of singular lucidity; had he not reasoned with his wife for three months in Prinkipo, he might perhaps have kept her. But Sophie Grigorievna beat off the siege of her husband's superior logic from the citadel of an impregnable obscurantism:

> I do not pretend to understand Georgy Ivanovitch. For me he is X. All that I know is that he is my teacher and it is not right for me to judge him, nor is it necessary for me to understand him. No one knows who is the real Georgy Ivanovitch, for he hides himself from all of us. It is useless for us to try to know him, and I refuse to enter into any discussions about him.

When Ouspensky eventually left for London some time in August 1921, he did so alone; Mme Ouspensky and all her family stuck doggedly with Gurdjieff.

Almost simultaneously, Gurdjieff's German visas came through. And not a moment too soon! In Péra the 'run on Homburg hats was over' and more and more fezes appeared every day. Various sure signals conveyed to Gurdjieff a menacing recrudescence of Turkish xenophobia: 'Since ... the wiseacring of the Young Turks began to have a particular smell, I decided ... to get away with my people as quickly as possible, with our skins whole.' Speedily he put together the necessary funds: the ship acquired a year earlier, in payment for curing a Greek dipsomaniac, he managed to 'de-requisition' and sell advantageously; from an indignant Mme Stjoernval he borrowed a very valuable pair of earrings, and pawned them; and a modest supplement he solicited from Thomas de Hartmann. Nor did Gurdjieff forget his non-travelling pupils; these he re-established in Kadiköy (where unfortunately they fell through a hole in history and were never heard of again)... Nothing further detained Gurdjieff; it was closing time in the gardens of the East.

On Saturday 13 August 1921 Gurdjieff assembled his people at Sirkedji Station. On the boiling hot platform he bought a sack of bear meat from a hawker: 'Thank you, Thoma; owing to you I could buy this meat for our trip...' Then, smelling it fastidiously, he threw it away. Subdued amid the crowd's hubbub, the Institute for Harmonious Development of Man entrained once more. The whistle blew, the wheels engaged, and a magician – white or black as history may conclude – began tracking west in a bolted goods wagon.

7

✤

MR GURDJIEFF CHANGES TRAINS

(August 1921–September 1922)

For trains connecting the Sarmoung Monastery with western capi-
tals, timetables are unreliable and even rudimentary amenities
often lacking. Hour after hour Gurdjieff and Mme Ostrowska sat
cross-legged or slept on the goods-wagon floor, until on the second
evening they were jolted into a siding at Sofia. On Gurdjieff's insistence his exhausted party climbed a nearby mountain slope and spent
the night in the forest – his final encampment under the 'imperish-
able' stars. Excepting the Stjoernvals (separately en route to Finland
to liquidate their assets), all Gurdjieff's nucleus ate frugally together
round the fire. A further day's cigarette smoking in the goods wagon
brought them, bone-tired, to the capital of Serbia where the railway
police shouted: 'Russian, go away, entrance to Belgrade is prohi-
bited. Go elsewhere.' Nevertheless, aided by the Russian consul
(whom Lili Galumnian had alerted in advance), Gurdjieff saw all his
followers installed in an hotel and transferred next morning to a
second-class German coach.

> It is impossible to convey the sense of complete assurance with which he
> threaded his way through the complications of countries devastated by
> war and revolution.

A few free days in Budapest – with its enticing museum and world
famous Wiener Café – Gurdjieff infuriatingly allocated to buying
needles and bobbins; then, entrained once more, the company moved
slowly across Czechoslovakia and Germany until on 22 August the
sound of hoarse shouting and a strong smell of cigars and boiled
cabbage confirmed their arrival in Berlin.

The Germany which Gurdjieff had reached was labouring under

Saturnian pressures and strains. The cost of a failed imperialist war and the stiff reparations demanded under the Treaty of Versailles combined to produce a financial cataclysm. Inflation was already ruinous when Gurdjieff arrived, but thenceforward it escalated 'like-a-Jericho-trumpet-in-crescendo'. Progressively, throughout his stay, the social fabric was unwholesomely distorted and natural justice outraged; the thrifty, the pensioners, and the socially immobile were utterly ruined, while a breed of slippery entrepreneurs, tactical mort-gagors and landowners, gleefully paid off their old debts in worthless banknotes. In the cities, despair, nihilism, and sexual licence were the order of the day: 'Even the Rome of Suetonius had never known such orgies as the pervert balls in Berlin.' As the lumpenproletariat strug-gled to survive from one day to the next, the artistic avant garde was gripped by a hectic irrationalism: 'the comprehensible element in everything was proscribed, melody in music, resemblance in portrait, intelligibility in language.'

Who was to blame? The Marxist 'Red International'? A Catholic 'Black International'? Or a Jewish 'Yellow International'? Scape-goats were *au choix* and so were panaceas. As if in validation of Péguy's dictum *'la mystique conduit à la politique'*, a gaggle of reconstructed occultists now proffered social analyses and nostrums: Rudolph Steiner, an acquaintance of Prince Sabaheddin, vigorously urged his solution in *The Threefold Commonwealth* (a book evidently indebted to the ideas of Saint-Yves d'Alvedre); and the ill-omened National Socialist German Workers Union had been founded in the rooms of the quasi-mystical Thule Society in Munich's grand hotel, Vier Jahreszeiten. Gurdjieff's unerring sense of scale preserved him from embroilment in any of this stuff.

Knowing not a word of German except their famous *Nicht*, Gurdjieff moved circumspectly but with growing authority. The in-ventory of his essential needs (an apartment, a Movements practice hall, and a convivial café) had been established in Tbilisi, confirmed in Péra, and was quickly transposed to Berlin. Basing himself with some hospitable old Russian friends, he rented a large hall in the smart district of Schmargendorf, and could often be observed strolling along Kurfürstendamm to a favourite table at the Romanische Café.

On Thursday 24 November 1921 Gurdjieff gave his inaugural lecture in Europe. Noticing that Alexandre Salzmann had invited a number of eminent people from theatre circles, the Teacher of Danc-ing provokingly introduced his theme of man's enslavement and liberation in terms of somatic repertoire:

> Your habitual postures are suited to acting a certain part – for instance a maid – yet you have to act the part of a countess. A countess has quite different postures. In a good dramatic school you would be taught, say, two hundred postures. For a countess the characteristic postures are, say, postures number 14, 68, 101, and 142 ...

The lecturer himself commanded – none better – the characteristic postures of an esoteric teacher, but as an 'authority on the postures of countesses' Gurdjieff was presenting himself in an unexpected light. As a matter of interest, who was his role model?

Our likeliest candidate is Olga de Hartmann. She was not a countess, yet to claim (as she would in old age) that her family 'were some of the best people in Russia', was close to the truth: her sister Nina had married Baron Peter von Nettlehorst; her sister Zöe had married Baron Klüge von Klügenau; and her maternal grandfather, Konstantin Wolfert, was the morganatic son of Kaiser Wilhelm I by his Polish mistress Labounska. The common calamity which brought low the great houses of Hohenzollern, Habsburg-Lorraine, and Romanov had deposited in Berlin (as in Paris) a rich alluvial sediment of counts and princelings; and though Gurdjieff was not in principle receivable in this stratum of society, it was not for want of the de Hartmanns trying.

Their friends Count Valvitz and Princess Gagarin sent Gurdjieff an engraved card requesting the pleasure of his company for dinner at their *Schloss* near Dresden. Both Thomas and Olga were in trepidation that their unpredictable teacher might accompany them in his Tifon-the-Sordid role. Their worries – which only intensified when they were all met at the station by an antiquated carriage drawn by six horses and supported by four coachmen in scarlet livery – reached fever pitch during a many-coursed dinner with a butler positioned behind each chair. Great God! What if Mr Gurdjieff were to belch intentionally or complain about the price of bear meat or say, 'Why are these idiots standing behind me?' But no such fiasco occurred: 'in spite of all the ceremony that greeted us, Mr Gurdjieff behaved as if he had been born at court. The Count and Princess Gagarin were charmed by him, especially the Princess.' Nevertheless it was not a connection which Gurdjieff pursued – the only aristocracy which weighed with him was an aristocracy of being.

Here the importance of Mme de Hartmann was more and more emerging. It was she who now spent every day with Gurdjieff drinking tea in the Romanische Café. Knowing five European languages, she had glided with quiet and formidable competence into the role of her master's interpreter and confidential secretary. Gurdjieff was fifty-five, and in his painful struggle to learn English from Olga we glimpse a rare teacher – one who, in service to his grander aim, submits to becoming his pupil's pupil.

His own disciples – eager to identify and serve this aim – could sense at the time only their master's sinuous opportunism:

> I am sure that when we arrived in Berlin even Mr Gurdjieff did not know what would occur there and in what directions we would have to turn our efforts. He always waited for the right moment for the next step.

We do know he travelled energetically about Germany comparing places suitable for his Institute; we even appear to know that he founded some embryonic group near Munich: but precisely where and when – 'Oh, just there lies their famous Bismarck's "pet cat".'

Winter had come and a cruel Prussian wind was skimming ice-yachts at terrifying speeds across the frozen Wannsee when Gurdjieff left Berlin and went to inspect Hellerau with the Salzmanns. As the tram climbed out of Dresden, he saw to the south and south-east thick snow mantling the Erzgebirge and Saxon Switzerland. Cosmetic dabs of snow powdered Hellerau's self-conscious little houses, and in their sweet-briar hedges various outmanœuvred sparrows gloomily waited for someone to throw them a bit of fat. The focus of Gurdjieff's interest – the colonnaded Bildungsanstalt – rose like some God-awful Greco-Teutonic mausoleum which had wandered into a Victorian Christmas card. Its lapel-gripping classicism gave due warning of a fanatical *idealismus*, Swedish drill, and nut cutlets. Gurdjieff, peculiarly enough, seems to have fallen in love with it.

To fall in love is not necessarily to possess. When Jaques-Dalcroze had left for Geneva in 1915, the Anstalt's ownership had reverted under trust deed to Wolf and Harald Dohrn (its generous donors in the first place). The philanthropic brothers, anxious to mollify a certain Frau Doktor Neustätter (an Australian), had recently leased the complex for five years to a limited company jointly incorporated by her friends the architect Karl Baer and the Scottish progressive educationalist A. S. Neill. The company in turn had drawn triple sub-leases: one for Neill's Ausländerschule, one for Baer's village high school, and one for the shapely Valerie Kratina who – happily oblivious of any legal framework – continued to teach *La Méthode Rythmique* to some forty nubile girls. Such were the marvellous and unappreciated complexities of the situation when Gurdjieff, accompanied by Alexandre, plodded through the snow to meet Harald

Dohrn and fix up an early transfer of the Anstalt, lock stock and barrel, to the Institute for the Harmonious Development of Man.

Like Wolf, Harald was a compulsive giver, a man dangerously impelled to help. But what, he asked weakly, about the prior claims of Baer and Neill and Kratina? 'They don't matter,' explained Gurdjieff, 'my work is of infinitely more importance.' Whether persuaded by Gurdjieff's look or by the crucial letter from Dalcroze, Dohrn acceded – the Anstalt would change hands! This surprising decision bore most onerously on Neill but he was preoccupied by a personal problem (he had not objected when a Russian eurythmics girl had passionately hugged him and cried 'Herr Neill, ich liebe Sie,' until she added: 'I wrote and told my husband and he is coming to shoot you.') Only the stern intervention of Frau Doktor Neustätter – who had her eye on Neill and ultimately married him – persuaded him to fight the Anstalt case in a Dresden court. Dohrn, anxious as ever to please, now changed sides. In the stiff tussle which portended, Gurdjieff was reliant for legal opinion on quite his most egregious pupil – Councillor A. Y. Rachmilievitch, pre-war leader of the St Petersburg legal bar, 'a mournful, dour type, full of prophecies of disaster, dissatisfied with everything'.

We may guess it was not, au fond, an estate agent's Hellerau which attracted Gurdjieff but an ideologue's Hellerau: not the library and sun-baths or even the Great Hall, but a redolence, a title to the attention of civilized Europe. Paradox enters here for the Hellerau which lured Shaw, and Nijinsky, and Stanislavsky was, in various ways, a temple to the 'progressive movement'; Gurdjieff insisted that progress was illusory. Hellerau was a play-pen of artistically sublimated licence, while Gurdjieff was the agent and advocate of tradition. The Wandervögel (assorted sweetness-and-light cases) who camped and kindled ritual fires in Hellerau's summer birch woods seldom wore trousers; Gurdjieff's pupils did. These contradictions need no labouring . . . but had Gurdjieff actually 'captured' Hellerau in 1922, he could have broadcast his call to awaken from the intelligentsia's very own bunker of dreams!

It was not to be. Around the New Year Gurdjieff's attention was abruptly claimed by London. Despite his tendency to visit the sins of Colonel Younghusband upon generations of Anglo-Saxons, he now granted that, at least in parts, the English egg was excellent; he could not deny (when Mme Ouspensky showed him letters) that England was providing her husband with a succès d'estime. The pity was that a wave of interest so genuine, and so surpassing that in Germany,

would meet only the cuttlebone aridities of Ouspensky's dispensation; that the Sacred Dances would not be taught; that theory would
prevail over practice. Nor was this all. Between the lines could be
read a tale of disaffection. From the blackboard of memory Ouspensky
had conveniently dusted off the years 1915 and 1916 and chalked up
instead a reference to 'his synthesis and the method of study and
practice which he had evolved'. When not explicitly fibbing concerning his indebtedness to Gurdjieff, he was a pioneer of economy with
the truth.

And nevertheless the truth prevailed: Pinder (always Gurdjieff's
man) posted off to his friends some uninhibited character analyses;
Bechhofer-Roberts' lively and timely book, *In Denikin's Russia and
the Caucasus*, sketched Gurdjieff as a magus and Ouspensky as the
tragi-comic victim of historical circumstance. Gradually, one way or
another, Ouspensky's pupils were alerted to the genuine hierarchy.
Their antennae were sensitive; they met amongst themselves; they
considered finance; they exchanged letters with Berlin – and long
before Ouspensky himself could isolate and quell this untoward
development, his own hand was forced. Early in February he convened his pupils, extracted a note from his breast pocket, held it near
his nose, and announced in emotionless tones that George Ivanovitch
Gurdjieff would shortly visit London. The turmoil of his private
feelings may be imagined: all the vexing obstacles he had met in
Essentuki and Constantinople would accompany Gurdjieff on the
boat train! To tell the truth 'they had appeared even before he
arrived.'

A dense biographic fog, an authentic London 'pea-souper', has
descended over Gurdjieff's reception there – leaving us to hypothesize from character and circumstance, much like Sherlock Holmes.
'The Affair of the Missing Cameos' is a curious one. Where is
Gurdjieff at Lady Rothermere's table? (Ouspensky on disembarkation had been wined and dined there 'with gold knives and forks
off what seemed solid gold plates'.) Or again, where is Gurdjieff
being greeted at 55a Gwendwr Road – his pupil's maisonette?
(Many memoirs depict Ouspensky framed in that door and stained
a jovial vermilion by its glass panels – but never receiving Gurdjieff.)
Are such lapses innocently explained by the exigencies of the
historical process? Or was Gurdjieff's welcome pared down to the
absolute bone? One thing seems beyond debate: Ouspensky's strong
'territoriality' and impatience for an exclusive Work 'franchise' had
swallowed his wish to learn any more from his former master. At

forty-four he had arguably become what Gurdjieff termed an 'enlightened idiot'.

Gurdjieff was in West Kensington on Monday 13 February 1922. The Theosophical Hall at 38 Warwick Gardens – economical to hire, sited a mere five minutes from Gwendwr Road, and possessing an entrance discreetly masked by a black hawthorn tree – was the ideal venue for Ouspensky's meetings. Even its ambience somehow suited him – though hardly calculated to set Gurdjieff's blood tingling:

> The room is papered in a depressing purplish-grey; purplish Sundour curtains at the windows; on the two mantlepieces there are brass ashtrays and pots with bare branches ornamented with mother-of-pearl leaves. Before the lecturer's chair is a small table covered with an orange cloth . . . these grey walls. What *is* their horrible colour? Elephants? No. Slag heaps? No. Slate roofs in the rain? It is the colour of purplish-grey mud, mud that I have never seen anywhere unless in a bad dream.

That Monday, on sixty-odd seats, smallish and not especially comfortable, a segment of London's intellectual elite perched to hear Ouspensky's mysterious teacher – a 'Conference of the Birds'[25] which, against the ill-concealed wishes of the Hoopoe, was nervously awaiting an audience with the Simurgh.

Never before had Gurdjieff addressed such a concentrated sample of the establishment. Present were Rowland Kenney former editor of the *Daily Herald*, Clifford Sharp editor of the *New Statesman*, and Alfred Richard Orage editor of the *New Age*. Arrived from the world of 'psychosynthesis' were Dr J. A. M. Alcock, Dr Mary Bell, and two former intimates of Jung, Dr Maurice Nicoll and Dr James Carruthers Young. Squarely in the front row sat Mary Lilian, Lady Rothermere,[19] the pneumatic and irrepressible wife of Viscount Rothermere and the sister-in-law of Lord Northcliffe – men who between them controlled most of the newspapers in England. Eric Graham Forbes Adam, Lord Curzon's brilliant young protégé, coped in his best shaving-cream accents with Ralph Philipson, a multi-millionaire of the 'where-there's-muck-there's-brass' school. Yet all, notwithstanding their frailties, had come in a serious spirit, and all settled into a quietness and containment which accentuated the ticking of the clock. At length four people mounted the platform: Ouspensky, Pinder, Olga de Hartmann . . . and Gurdjieff.

Things have been written about Gurdjieff's appearance which are frankly preposterous in their sensationalism. ('His shaved Tartar's skull, sprung from one of Gogol's novels, contains . . . a chaos of forces which cannot even be guessed.') Even so, his unusual bearing and gaze were decisive factors that evening at 38 Warwick Gardens. Olga de Hartmann, beautiful and pale, translated from his Russian but could hardly transpose the warmth and timbre of his voice into the sibilant twittering of English. The question is whether she could even transpose his ideas; Gurdjieff himself perceived English as a blatantly secular language best suited to discussing 'the topic of Australian frozen meat or, sometimes, the Indian question'. In any case he delivered his talk, 'Man is a plural being', aware that his idea of multiple selves had already been promulgated by his pupil. What needed conveying was its truth, its immediacy, its existential relevance. 'You are a machine,' translated Olga tartly, 'and external circumstances govern your actions irrespective of your desires. I do not say nobody can control his actions. I say you can't, because you are divided.' Did Gurdjieff's eyes rest briefly on Ouspensky at this point? – Ouspensky who with his vacillation and ambivalence since Essentuki, had seemed the embodiment of fragmented purpose.

Three or four paragraphs into Gurdjieff's talk, five or ten minutes of his platform presence, and the possibility of his moving permanently to London had emerged as a burning issue for Ouspensky and his pupils – though from converse standpoints. They struggled to decode the lecture but found nothing certain:

> In London I am irritable, the weather and the climate dispirit me and make me bad-tempered, whereas in India I am good-tempered. Therefore my judgement tells me to go to India and I shall drive out the emotion of irritability. But then in London, I find I can work; in the tropics not so well.

What on earth did it all imply? Some of the most thoughtful heads in England leant back against the purple wallpaper (leaving stains of Macassar oil which were still a source of annoyance ten years later). Up upon the platform Gurdjieff reached his finale:

> You must find a teacher. You alone can decide what it is that you want to do. Search in your heart for what you most desire and, if you are capable of doing it, you will know what to do. Think well about it, and then go forward.

Orage at least had searched his heart already, and found it altered: 'After Gurdjieff's first visit to Ouspensky's Group, I *knew* that Gurdjieff was the teacher.'

Considerable importance attaches to this affirmation: the moment when the baton of discipleship limply dropped by Ouspensky is seized by a new and eager hand. Alfred Richard Orage was an unusual man and destined for a role of crucial importance in spreading Gurdjieff's ideas – a task for which he was fitted equally by the richness and the relevance of his gifts: charisma, intellectual virility, a magnetic 'aura', and sheer wizardry in debate. From his tiny, marvellously disordered office at 38 Cursitor Street, Orage had since 1907 exerted a disproportionate influence upon English life and letters. As proprietor, managing director and innovative editor of the weekly review, the *New Age*, he had presided over an unparalleled national arena of cultural and political debate: he knew all the notable figures; he knew the stories behind the stories; he knew the literature of politics and the politics of literature; he knew the urbane mask and the swart backside of a dozen philosophic and artistic 'isms'. Seated in the ABC self-service café in Chancery Lane, brooding over a large black coffee and a dish of prunes, Orage might seem a man complacently surrendered to the values, the issues, the brash horizontality of the 1920s . . . but it was not so.

In early manhood Orage had been conventionally tall, dark and handsome, and even now in his paunchy, round-shouldered, fiftieth year, he retained an inextinguishable charm: 'His eyes were hazel, lively and challenging, and in moments of excitement they seemed to emit a red glint.' Above the nested prunes his imagination climbed like a skylark to the level of an ancient wisdom: to Socrates (whom he particularly reverenced), to Plato, Pantanjali, Aquinas, and the Hermeticists. For years he had worked honestly on self-development, only to see the gap between hope and reality grow wider. He recited the mantra: 'Brighter than the sun, purer than the snow, subtler than the air, is the Self, the spirit within my heart. I am that Self, that Self am I.' His marriage had lapsed, his mistress Beatrice Hastings was gone, and the many idealistic causes which he championed had tended in practice towards 'mad houses, lock-hospitals and ugly accidents'. He refused to give up:

> He was convinced that there was a secret knowledge behind the knowledge given to the famous prophets and philosophers, and for the acquisition of that knowledge and the intellectual and spiritual power it would bring with it he was prepared to sacrifice everything and take upon him any labour, no matter how humble or wearisome or abstruse.

He had come to Gurdjieff at Warwick Gardens bearing the two essential keys: sincere aspiration and a sense that his present life was unbearable.

Though destiny intended a unique role for Orage, he was borne towards it on a general wave of enthusiasm for Gurdjieff which swept the London group after his first visit: an enthusiasm which altered everything – which left Ouspensky and all his barons, and Gurdjieff himself, in a quandary. Gurdjieff still had Germany to think of, and was enmeshed in his Dresden court case; Ouspensky, 'The Man who would be King', found himself suddenly threatened with dethronement; some pupils naively wished to serve two masters, but none were such duffers as to miss altogether the obscure and inexplicable tension between Ouspensky and his teacher. Everything was in painful question.

Gurdjieff's second – and as it turned out final – visit to London took place in March; vis-à-vis Ouspensky, it seems to have begun in an atmosphere of frosty civility, degenerated into a frank and robust exchange, and ended in a minor *coup de théâtre*. Speaking privately in Russian (a language he felt appropriate 'for referring to someone's parentage'), Gurdjieff called his eminent pupil to account.

His precise words are not extant but (thanks to Frank Pinder) we have their gist: despite Ouspensky's command of theory, the groups he had constituted in Ekaterinodar, Rostov, Constantinople, and now London were unauthorized and largely off the rails; he was free as air to propound his own theosophical or philosophical notions, but to transmit Gurdjieff's teaching in all its complementary modalities he was neither mandated nor qualified; he had enjoyed in total only three years direct contact; he knew nothing of the music; he had had only a perfunctory fling at the Sacred Dances; and, not least, he lacked the essential human warmth to insulate his pupils from the bleak ideological climate of the 'System'. In addition there arose the separate matter of his own development. If Ouspensky still sincerely wished to assimilate Gurdjieff's work in his essence and not merely in personality, he must (like his wife Sophie) postpone any pretension to teach and re-dedicate himself as a pupil ... tonic advice but with a taste so bitter that Ouspensky could not possibly swallow it.

The two men were thus already estranged yoke-fellows when, on Wednesday 15 March, in an atmosphere of high expectancy, they together mounted the platform at Warwick Gardens. Orage simplistically inquired (it was to remain his fundamental question) how to attain a radical transformation of being. In Gurdjieff's ensuing lecture on 'Essence and Personality' it is forgivable to suspect some coded derogation of Ouspensky:

Normal human beings are the exception. Nearly everyone has only the essence of a child. It is not natural that in a grown-up man the essence should be a child. Because of this, he remains timid underneath and full of apprehensions. This is because he knows that he is not what he pretends to be, but he cannot understand why.

Hereabouts Ouspensky intervened, claiming that the translation was botched, but Gurdjieff – insisting fiercely that 'Pinder is interpreting for me – not you' – provocatively repeated his private critique on the public platform. To his dying day Ouspensky 'could never forget Gurdjieff's attacking him in front of his own pupils.' From the floor someone mollifyingly asked what it would be like to be conscious in essence. 'Everything more vivid,' said Gurdjieff tersely, and rising with Pinder swept out. On the journey back to Germany, Gurdjieff explained, 'now they will *have* to choose a teacher'.

To Ouspensky's chagrin virtually everyone who mattered chose Gurdjieff – and the means of bringing him permanently to England became their burning question. Lady Rothermere undertook to place at his disposal her superb studio in Circus Road, St John's Wood; Ralph Philipson agreed to provide substantial funds; and Orage to guarantee publicity. Ouspensky himself gloomily resolved to move to Paris or America if the Institute successfully transferred to London ... but would it? Two impediments furrowed the brows of the pro-Gurdjieff lobby and afforded Ouspensky lingering hope. *Item*: could Gurdjieff really be persuaded to settle in England? *Item*: would the Home Office let him?

Ironically, all the resource and combinational skill of Ouspensky's powerful group was now bent to solving Gurdjieff's visa problem. At 86 Harley Street a taxi halted and the Pickwickian figure of Dr Maurice Nicoll emerged to co-opt at breathless speed his friend and colleague Kenneth Walker: 'We have been granted an interview with the Home Secretary in twenty minutes' time and I want you to be a member of the delegation.' Dr Walker, a man rising in his profession and shortly to become a Hunterian Professor at the Royal College of Surgeons, entered gallantly into the spirit of things:

> Half an hour later I found myself explaining to a bored Home Secretary how essential it was to the welfare of British medicine that Gurdjieff (who was only a name to me) should be granted permission to settle in London.

Edward Shortt, the Home Secretary, was a dull dog. Boredom (incidentally his chronic condition after 1929 when cruelly appointed

President of the Board of Film Censors) came easily to him. He yawned. He temporized. He would inquire. He would cause inquiries to be made.

Even today, with the supposed benefit of hindsight, it is difficult to read the entrails in this affair. Certainly the support of Viscountess Rothermere and the personal attention of the Home Secretary made Gurdjieff quite special; neither general quota restrictions on White Russian immigration nor prevailing anxieties concerning the virus of Bolshevism were self-sufficient grounds for a VIP's exclusion. Gurdjieff's exasperating file, ducted through the Whitehall labyrinth in obscure cycles of delegation and cross-referral, passed routinely to the Foreign Office – where Eric Graham Forbes Adam was a star and Rowland Kenney served in the Political Intelligence Department. Back came the opinion that the applicant was not a Bolshevik: had on the contrary just fled Bolshevism (and reportedly considered Lenin and Trotsky dangerous and unconscionable incendiaries.) Unfortunately the groups had no one of substance in the India Office, where the old 'Gurdjieff' stereotype (reinforced by the damning New Delhi despatch to General Milne) was that of an implacable opponent of British interests in Tibet. Of course no one wished to alienate the Rothermeres, but what could one do? Level by bureaucratic level the case rose until it lay again on the desk of Edward Shortt – a minister with a thousand more pressing things to think about than Gurdjieff's real or hypothetical contribution to 'the welfare of British medicine'.

The applicant himself was now back in Berlin – his future problematical, his followers geographically dispersed, and his attention divisively claimed by ballet rehearsals, legal manœuvring, and drafting a third prospectus. Considering Gurdjieff's urgent need to consolidate his position, this latter advertisement was extravagant in tone and content. The Principal of the Institute for the Harmonious Development of Man – notwithstanding his big psychological and ecological insights – deliberately created the impression that he was not quite sixteen annas to the rupee. Dr Kenneth Macfarlane Walker for example discovered he had staked his considerable medical reputation on goodness knows what:

> There has been installed in the main section of the Institute the most modern apparatus and instruments, a collection richer than any ever heard of on Earth before, if we look on it as assembling in one place of 'physico-metric' and 'chemico-analytic', 'psycho-experimental' cabinets ...

Simultaneous English, German, and French issues of this prospectus suggest the fluidity of Gurdjieff's situation in the spring and early summer of 1922. Inflation had reached a surreal level and his legal costs alone could run into billions of marks; Rachmielevitch with melancholy satisfaction brought news of Harold Dohrn's persuasive case that Gurdjieff had hypnotized him. God alone knew where matters would end!

They did end in June: Dohrn won his action and Gurdjieff lost it. The judge's ruling in Dresden slammed the door straightforwardly: foxy, by contrast, but equally conclusive was the stratagem of Edward Shortt in London. 'Permission was refused to the colony, but it was intimated that Gurdjieff would be permitted to enter England alone.' At one brilliant stroke the Rothermeres were thus disarmed yet Gurdjieff still effectively debarred – for never would he abandon his dedicated Russian nucleus. Evidence suggesting that Gurdjieff was denied a third admission to England (to appeal this decision) is unsafe. Conceivably he felt relief! Forebodings of a rebarbative cuisine, an irritating climate, and a stupefying insularity had gradually sapped his enthusiasm for London. Yet neither did Berlin's hectic nihilism nor Hellerau's fundamental provinciality truly suit him. The German episode – not unlike Constantinople – had proved a hiatus: new pupils had not been attracted; funds were depleted; and the Germanic *Weltanschauung* seemed besotted with a ruinous stupidity:

> Blödsin, Blödsin,
> Du mein Vergnügen,
> Stumpfsin, Stumpfsin,
> Du meine Lust.

Then what to do and where to turn?

The myth insists that Gurdjieff entrain for France – for Paris the 'Capital of World Culture'; in this regard teleological causality makes him an offer he can't refuse ... indeed just as the native fisherman stalking his quarry from the riverbank is not deceived by the angle of refraction, but tilts his spear into the breathing fish, so this mythic Gurdjieff has from the outset aimed for France, even while he seemed intent on Germany and England. The historical Gurdjieff of course had sensible pretexts: the French countryside, glimpsed en route to England, was delightful; the French economy (contrasted with Germany's) was splendidly robust; and France's geographical centrality made it a desirable 'cross-roads of all the races and nationalities on earth'. But how to penetrate this latest frontier?

The official Gurdjieff of 1922 was merely a refugee, a displaced person – his Nansen passport[27] of minimal effectuality. 'Let us add,' writes one famously inventive commentator, 'that for services rendered to France during the War, in India and Asia Minor, he enjoyed the protection of Poincaré[28] who personally authorised his establishment in France.' Metaphysical and political wiseacring aside, the blunt facts are that George Ivanovitch Gurdjieff *did* enter Paris on Bastille Day 14 July, bringing twenty or thirty pupils, 100,000 francs, a sewing machine, plenty of material, thread, needles, bobbins, scissors, and a box of thimbles acquired in Budapest. The modest implements of his revolution were now in place.

Alexandre Salzmann, who had gone ahead, met Gurdjieff at the Gare de l'Est; Thomas de Hartmann was urgently tasked to find him a pied-à-terre; Olga to locate a large country house. In the Rue Miromesnil, Thomas quickly discovered the perfect place – living room, bathroom, telephone, separate entrance – and rushed to tell Gurdjieff.

> He listened to me very indifferently and then asked: 'Is there a gas stove?' I had not thought to look. But how revolting of him, I thought, to ask about such a trifle instead of being thankful for what I had found.

Once Gurdjieff had settled in, an informal but pivotal conference took place. The presence of Ouspensky and Ralph Philipson at the Hotel Solferino and Lady Rothermere at the Hotel Westminster hints at its agenda: English money would flow generously to establish Gurdjieff in France, if Ouspensky could retain freedom of action in London.

Fate's assignment of Gurdjieff to France and Ouspensky to England is ironic. Gurdjieff's humour, commonsense, and eccentricity seem so characteristically English, and Ouspensky's logic and formalism French. Paul Dukes, Gurdjieff's first English pupil, enters in 1913, twenty-five years before the French; droves of English cross the Channel while the French will not cross the road; the French intelligentsia consistently ridicules Gurdjieff and his pupils as a *'groupe de théosophes absurdes et agités'*, while the British, many of them, stake their lives on him. Dr Maurice Nicoll borrowed against expectations under his father's will to swell Gurdjieff's funds; Mrs Philipson donated a valuable pearl necklace (which Gurdjieff handed back); Dr James Carruthers Young, eager to commence his studies of 'psychosynthesis' – threw up his lucrative Harley Street practice, caught the boat train to Paris, and tumbled into a milieu which frankly surprised him.

Just as in Tbilisi, so in Paris, the 'Teacher of Dancing' quickly capitalized on local interest in the eurhythmics of Jaques-Dalcroze. The Dalcroze Institute in the Rue de Vaugirard was closed for the summer vacation, and Gurdjieff (aided by his English pupil Jessmin Howarth, choreographer of the Paris Opera) astutely hired it from 10am to 1pm daily. James Young turned up there early in August to find preparations for *The Struggle of the Magicians* in full spate:

> Gurdjieff cut out the materials with great skill and the members were employed in sewing, hand-painting and stencilling designs on them. Metal ornaments for such things as buckles and belts were also fashioned ... Other things were made or improvised, dancing pumps and Russian boots, for example ... This work was carried on with feverish activity and occupied, together with the exercises, thirteen or fourteen hours every day. The keynote was 'Overcome difficulties – Make effort – Work.'

Dr Young – vigorous, handsome, extrovert, cheerfully blasphemous – nevertheless felt himself in a situation more or less incalculable. The company, well outside his social or clinical experience, was composed of 'Armenians, Poles, Georgians and even a Syrian ... a Russian baron and his wife and an alleged ex-officer of the Czar's bodyguard, who afterwards became a very successful taxi-driver in Paris.' His Savile Row suit exchanged for a loose white tunic 'with thick, red-cord piping and tassels, and very large trousers in the Turkish or Oriental style', the doctor began his study of the 'Obligatories' and Sacred Dances under Gurdjieff and his *starotsa* Mr Mironoff. Learning 'No. 19' he found himself suddenly precipitated into 'a reclining position of the body like Canova's statue of Pauline Borghese.' Afterwards – seated cross-legged against the wall and breathing heavily – he observed four older pupils dance and sing a Bach quartet in costumes of flaming red, deep green, indigo blue and light pink. As to the underlying theory of harmonious development, what Young had actually expected to hear is unsure, but certainly Gurdjieff did not mince his words:

> All of you are deformed... A man of such one-sided development has more desires in a given sphere, desires he cannot satisfy and at the same time cannot renounce. Life becomes miserable for him. For this state of fruitless, half-satisfied desires, I can find no more suitable word than onanism.

Through all his personal difficulties and doubts, James Young was sustained by his resolve to grapple with the enigma of Gurdjieff himself: 'He was a man to be reckoned with, an outstanding event in the life of a psychologist – a man whose riddle I was determined, if possible, to read.'

Most applicants in that long-forgotten summer brought their own version of unqualified commitment, their particular rush of blood to the head; many lodged together in spartan conditions in the Rue Michel-Ange and caught the tram from Auteuil to their daily labours in the Rue de Vaugirard. Anna Ilinishna Butkovsky made a brief and tantalizing reappearance. Miss Rose Mary Cynthia Lillard from Houston, Texas – a twenty-one-year-old Dalcroze enthusiast and gifted pianist – became Gurdjieff's first American pupil. Miss Ethel Merston[17] (strictly collectable as Gurdjieff's first pupil of mixed German-Jewish and Portuguese-Jewish parentage) fascinates as a stereotype of English spinsterhood: 'tall, of uncertain age, a bony angular shape topped off by a somewhat untidy nest of fading reddish hair.' Shyly she requested that Gurdjieff take her as a guinea-pig:

> I remember sitting with him on a bench on the Boulevard de la Madeleine, he absolutely silent and I, realising I was being tested, equally silent. I felt a tense atmosphere, perhaps he was weighing up whether to take me or not. At the end of half an hour or so, he rose and said, 'Come'.

Gurdjieff's containment surely masked an exhilaration which was proof even against Miss Merston's idiosyncrasies, the languors of a Parisian August, and all the residual anxieties for his mother and family. He was a teacher. He bore a profound teaching. His need to plant that teaching in the West was felt as an obligation so elemental, so implacable, that modernity can hardly match it. Now, after years of frustration, it appeared he had penetrated not merely the Franco-German frontier but that less negotiable barrier which separates failure from success. He commanded all the actors for a conscious drama and wanted only a fit stage. In requiring Olga de Hartmann to find one, he had chosen well; she had – besides the taste, the wit, the will – an icy hauteur which could reduce the most insolent estate agent to blancmange. She searched unremittingly until she found.

The Prieuré des Basses Loges first emerges from the delicate haze of futurity in mid-August 1922, when Olga reported its providential aptness. Yes, it was handy for Paris – just forty miles away in the village of Avon. Yes, it was big enough – its three storeys and abundant outbuildings could accommodate at least 100 pupils. Yes, it had land to work – forty-five acres of pine trees near the 'chateau' itself and 200 in a walled domain fronting the forest of Fontainebleau. Yes, it had atmosphere – ornate Empire mirrors, oak-panelled walls, a glass 'Orangerie', two fountains, a breathtaking avenue of lime trees, a garden originally achieved by André de Lenôtre, and a history of piety and scandal. Olga's vivid description satisfied a predilection which arguable fringed on precognition – sight unseen, Gurdjieff told her to forge ahead.

The usual protracted negotiations ensued – appearing to Gurdjieff to have all the exactitude of contemporary weather forecasts: 'either snow or rain or something or other'. At issue was a 65,000-franc lease, fully furnished, with an option to buy for 700,000 at the expiration of a year. The Prieuré's owner, Mme Labori, having lost two husbands – the pianist Pachmann and Maître Ferdnand Gustave Gaston Labori (defence counsel for Dreyfus) – clung, naturally enough, to their memorabilia: tapestries, carpets, valuable antique paintings and so forth. To leave these at Fontainebleau unsupervised contradicted her principles. This unanticipated factor, for one surreal moment, cast across the future of esotericism in the West the improbable shadow of Mme Labori's gardener. The lady's insistence that her man remain, in a general custodial role, was quite unacceptable to Gurdjieff; Olga by hook or by crook must dissuade her:

> Mr Gurdjieff told me, 'Even if you speak with her about the most trivial things, but have uppermost in your mind that the gardener has to leave, she will do it.' I took it as an exercise from Mr Gurdjieff and tried to do as he told me. To my great astonishment, after about a half hour's conversation, she said, 'Yes, all right, I will send the gardener away. I trust you that nothing will be ruined in the house.' And I had not even suggested it to her!

With this assurance, Gurdjieff stood on firm ground. Even before the legal i's were dotted and t's crossed he sent in a platoon of shock troops, who – fortified by Mme Ouspensky's bortsch – diligently weeded the Prieuré's paths, sluiced down the glass of the Orangerie, and battled to consolidate a bridgehead. On 30 September the transaction was notarized. Two days later the man from the Sarmoung Monastery finally arrived at Fontainebleau. He hired a *fiacre* which clip-clopped down past the bridge into Avon and out onto the Valvins Road: now, in the pale autumn sunshine, he glimpsed for the first time the low-rising contour of the Prieuré; then the seven little windows set in the steep slate mansard; then the fountain climbing in the courtyard. With what deep feelings did George Ivanovitch

Gurdjieff enter the Prieuré? 'The foxes have holes, and the birds of the air have nests; but the Son of man hath not where to lay his head.' Was he truly home at last? On Sunday 1 October 1922, the wrought-iron gates opened and clanged shut behind him ... and as he confesses, 'From that day on, under specifically European conditions, quite foreign to me, there began one of the maddest periods of my life.'

❖

HAIDA YOGA

(1 October 1922–13 January 1923)

Cigarette in mouth, Gurdjieff wandered through the Chateau and its grounds 'appreciating the situation', while Philos his companionable fox-terrier (large in body, small in head and immense in sagacity) cocked his leg in a baptismal spree. Mme Labori had left the house in a condition so filthy that it surprised even Gurdjieff; the library's mock-Jacobean bookcases were devoid of books, and there was only one bathroom for seventy-odd people. The first floor, with its redeeming elegance, he dubbed the 'Ritz' and chose for himself the first room on the left. The distracting billiard table downstairs must go immediately – Gurdjieff had not handled a cue since Bokhara in 1898.

'When I walked through the gates of the Château du Prieuré,' confides Gurdjieff, 'it was as though, right behind the old porter, I was greeted by Mrs Serious Problem.' Everything that really mattered now depended on him: simultaneously he must counsel, teach, build, lecture, administer, rehearse, choreograph, compose music – and foot virtually the whole bill. He must integrate two flocks of Russian and English pupils, whose disparate experience, expectations and cultural formation, promised all sorts of ripe misunderstandings. He was cramped by his lack of English and French: 'I felt more than ever the need to know European languages, while at the same time I did not have a minute in which to apply myself to learning them.'

Although Gurdjieff's activity during those first frenetic months was essentially pragmatic, earthed in the here-and-now, it nevertheless entailed the creation of a *mise-en-scène* which poignantly linked manhood with boyhood – Fontainebleau-Avon with Alexandropol. On the mantelpiece of the 'English' dining room he set in pride of place a photo of his father; under the old man's penetrating gaze, Gurdjieff surely felt more urgently than ever his obligation to extricate from Bolshevik Russia his mother, his brother Dmitri and his sister Sophie Kapanadze.

Beyond the mystifications of Gurdjieff's singular prospectus, it is clear that the Prieuré was at once his laboratory, his grand advertisement, and his incubator for fledgling missionaries – a radical experiment in communal and holistic living, and an utterly unique school of attention and consciousness. It was also an anomaly. To accuse Gurdjieff of inconsistencies is of course to tiptoe over thin ice (through countless psychological transactions his secret fidelity was to a good sense which discrepantly entailed the moment, the circumstance, the type and state of the pupil); and yet how explicitly, how emphatically, the Gurdjieff of Petrograd had denied the utility of any such 'Prieuré':

> The fourth way requires no retirement into the desert. . . On the contrary, the conditions of life in which a man is placed at the beginning of his work . . . are the best possible for him. . . These conditions *are the man himself* . . . Any conditions different from those created by life would be artificial for a man and in such artificial conditions the work would not be able to touch every side of his being at once.

The case was blatantly altered now. Though Gurdjieff stopped short of becoming the 'Prior of Avon', the milieu he created by no stretch of the imagination mirrored ordinary life: it was removed; it was enclosed; it was quite special in its intensity.

'Hurry-up Yoga', *Haida Yoga* – thus Gurdjieff once sardonically defined his teaching, and even Bechhofer-Roberts' cod-memoir of Fontainebleau presents Gurdjieff as all acceleration: '"Skorry! Queeker! queeker!" he snaps in his broken Russian and English. "Work ver' good; make you better; you start think better; ver' good!"'

The pupil who discovered the Institute's pigs in the tomato patch and went to give warning 'very slowly, to avoid identifying and muscle tension' encountered a Gurdjieff who 'roared at him and leapt, so to speak, about a hundred yards to those pigs.' Again and again Gurdjieff spurred on his flagging pupils with the pointed demand: 'Must be done in half the time.' Just as the staging of *The Struggle of the Magicians* had repeatedly been 'imminent', demanding one 'final' commitment of adrenalin, so Gurdjieff set a fresh goal, a fresh pretext for super-effort. At whatever cost, on 13 January

1923 the Russian New Year, he would throw the Prieuré open, staging some convincing witness to his work's orientation and power. Only three months were available; the clock was ticking; the race was on.

Scarcely had Gurdjieff been engaged a fortnight when (at Orage's request) he received the New Zealand writer Katherine Mansfield: her mood was serious; she was spiritually gifted; she was (incidentally) at the pinnacle of her fame – and she was dying of pulmonary tuberculosis. Bent, breathless, her body ravaged, she had exhausted a range of rashly experimental procedures (strychnine tinctures, iodine injections, X-ray bombardment) which only made her worse. 'I have no belief whatsoever,' she now admitted, 'in any kind of medical treatment.' Dr Young who examined her in Paris on 15 October gave Gurdjieff due warning – Katherine might live perhaps ... three months? With this prognosis the 'Terror of the Situation' suddenly revealed itself: death would keep strict company with life; Gurdjieff's ebullient preparations for 13 January would march step by step, pace by pace, with the young woman's terminal decline. For Katherine herself, spiritual immortality – a potentiality she neither facilely assumed nor facilely dismissed – became the desperate hope: 'More than ever I feel that I can build up a life within me which death will not destroy.' Such was the melodramatic script which fate had provided: the clock was ticking; the race was on indeed!

Present at the start was Mary Lilian, Lady Rothermere, who, like an exotic butterfly, floated cheerfully back and forth across the lawns bringing Gurdjieff cups of black coffee. Profuse in his thanks, he treated his titled benefactress with affable mock-deference and yet at lunch trapped her into gushing appreciation of 'a special trout caught in our own pond' – which was actually a herring. Despite his powers to fascinate, Gurdjieff made no attempt to net (or mount) this rare social specimen; one even infers he shooed her away. After a night or two in the Prieuré's 'Ritz', her ladyship (more acclimatized to the Ritz in Piccadilly) fluttered off, evidently 'to seek spiritual comfort by working for the cinematograph!'. Although without Katherine's existential commitment, she had generously given what support she could and earned her modest niche in Gurdjieffian history.

Gurdjieff's restraint over Lady Rothermere is the more remarkable considering her enormous wealth and his chronic need for money. Only the finer details of Gurdjieff's balance sheet are lost in the haze of distance and the maze of triple-entry book-keeping. His basic predicament is clear enough: he had to maintain extensive buildings in good repair; to repay substantial loans; to amass funds for the Prieuré's outright purchase; and to support an indigent Russian entourage. At the same time, he had to buy kitchen implements; workshop and garden tools; horses, mules, cows, pigs, sheep, goats, rabbits, geese, chickens; bedding and blankets for seventy-odd people. Day after day he had to victual his pupils – and chose to, at first, with reckless hospitality. With these heroic demands on his pocket, the Principal of the Institute yet again drove himself to exceptional exertions.

Sheer pressure obliged Gurdjieff to live as it were two simultaneous Octobers. Working virtually all the hours God sends, he ran backwards and forwards between Fontainebleau and Paris; here in the dubious and unknown streets of Montmartre he launched himself into frenetic business deals, 'always accompanied by inner experiences disturbing the whole of me and demanding an incredible tension of my forces.' As a restaurateur he successively created two atmospheric establishments, worked them up pell-mell, and sold them to Russian émigrés who matched the decor; as a physician-hypnotist he yet again wrestled with a choice clientele of alcoholics, drug addicts and deviants; and as a consultant on the Middle East he made a killing in shares and options for the Azerbaijani oil-fields.

> It is worth mentioning that my external life at this period, when I was spending every night in Montmartre, provided many ... with rich material for gossip. Some envied my opportunities for gay revels, others condemned me. As for me, I would not have wished such revels even for my bitterest enemy.

Back at the Prieuré, the Principal of the Institute snatched his fugitive moments of rest and private reflection in the loft above the stable – Philos the dog at his side, and Dralfit the mule in the straw below.

By now Gurdjieff was struggling desperately to master a rudimentary French. His standby Olga de Hartmann could not be dragged round Montmartre every night and in any case commanded only an inapposite drawing-room parlance.

> The amount of nervous energy I wasted during those first two years in France ... when I felt that what I had said was not being translated correctly, would doubtless have been quite sufficient for a hundred ... novice brokers on the floor of the New York Stock Exchange.

An effort so intense, a regime so demanding, took its inevitable toll. Sometimes Gurdjieff would return to the Prieuré exhausted, to discover his entire body of pupils silently or restively waiting for a lecture. On one such occasion his response was a model of acerbic brevity: 'Patience is the Mother of Will. If you have not a mother how can you be born?'

A certain ambivalence broods over the historical Prieuré, almost as if both White and Black Magician held sway there; perhaps – in unequal measure – they did. Bechhofer-Roberts detected signs of hoofs and horns all over the place; Clifford Sharpe, despite his fundamental sympathy, has Gurdjieff manipulating 'with an ingenuity that is almost diabolical'; and Captain John Godolphin Bennett (a weekend guest) alleges: 'Some people went mad. There were even suicides. Many gave up in despair.' The comment of fringe figures is the comment of fringe figures, but Gurdjieff himself conceded that 'there is something sinister in this house and that is necessary.' Lady Rothermere was pretty lucky to be served herring – many a guest of honour received the unwelcome token of a baked sheep's eye; Dr Young had brought with him an alarming paranoid patient; the task of slaughtering animals for the stockpot was assigned to a man who was phobic of blood; and Katherine Mansfield became day by day a more sobering *memento mori*.

Urgently needed to redress the balance here are two 'parallel Prieurés'. The first bears witness to Gurdjieff's developed sense of humour (uniquely developed one is tempted to say.) It resembles a rustic stage, rich in situation comedy and Dadaesque 'happenings': a Prieuré of tomato patches and 'mystical' pigs; of English gentlewomen labouring uncritically to grub up the roots of trees with tablespoons while memorizing Tibetan verbs; of Philos the dog; of the monkey who refused to be 'trained to clean the cows'; of Miss Merston's and Rachmielevitch's singular misadventures; of peculiar diets of sour cream and powdered cinnamon; of the happy irreverent laughter of children. Such is the Prieuré captured in Katherine Mansfield's evocation:

> The dog barks and lies on the floor, worrying a hearthbrush. A girl comes in with a bouquet of leaves for Olga Ivanovna. Mr. Gurdjieff strides in, takes up a handful of shredded cabbage and eats it . . . there are at least 20 pots on the stove. And it's so full of life and humour and ease that one wouldn't be anywhere else.

But the 'third Prieuré' – infinitely the most important for Gurdjieff

and ultimately for history – is less reductible to our ordinary conceptual repertoire. It is the domain of the Sacred Dances and genuine
transformational experiments; a ground upon which fallible human
beings, 'in a seething atmosphere of speed and tension, of zeal and
high hopes', struggled courageously to transcend their limitations:
struggled and failed, and struggled again – and sometimes succeeded.
It is Gurdjieff's crucible, 'a melting pot designed to reduce to their
intrinsic value the ingredients that boiled and simmered there.'

On 27 October Gurdjieff set his men digging for a Turkish bath.
He swore by the benefits of breathing through the pores and claimed
to experience 'tormentingly' the smells of the unpurged: 'I could
without any difficulty detect to which community the given being belonged, and even by those odours I could distinguish one being from
another.' On the edge of the forest he had found a natural cave, but
to create two additional interior rooms, cement the floors, and install
electricity, showers, drainage, and a recessed boiler was a big work –
all to be achieved at breakneck speed. The soft soil – 'like sand with
small whitey pinky pebbles' – eased excavation but made for an
unstable roof which needed propping by huge beams. Gurdjieff im-
provized the boiler from an old cistern and tackled most of the
brickwork entirely on his own.

It has been cruelly and brilliantly said that 'When Orage arrived at
the Prieuré with *Alice in Wonderland* in his pocket, he found that far
from disappearing down magical rabbit holes, he was expected to dig
them.' Gurdjieff might well have cossetted Orage – after all he was
fifty and already earmarked for a special role. Instead he assigned
him a room in the spartan 'Monks' Corridor', forbad him to smoke,
and threw him into a maelstrom of activity – with effects which
Orage has poignantly described:

> My first weeks at the Prieuré were weeks of real suffering. I was told to
> dig, and as I had had no real exercise for years I suffered so much
> physically that I would go back to my room, a sort of cell, and literally cry
> with fatigue. No one, not even Gurdjieff, came near me. I asked myself, 'Is
> this what I have given up my whole life for? At least I had something then.
> Now what have I?' When I was in the very depths of despair, feeling that I
> could go on no longer, I vowed to make extra effort. . .

Dr Nicoll – who arrived from Harley Street on 4 November with his
wife, infant daughter, her nurse Nanny Nellie, and a supply of goats
milk obtained at the Paris Zoo – was appointed kitchen boy and
spent the next week rising at 4.30am, lighting the boilers, and

washing up hundreds of greasy plates without soap or hot water. Dr
James Carruthers Young had a robust physique but – like others –
'experienced a degree of exhaustion which perhaps exceeds anything
. . . produced even by a prolonged spell in the winter trenches of
Flanders in 1917.' Somehow or other, on the psycho-analytic grape-
vine, news of their involvement reached Freud in his armchair in
Vienna: 'Ah,' he said facilely, 'you see what happens to Jung's
disciples.'

Throughout this turbulence, Gurdjieff proved consideration itself
to Katherine Mansfield. He chose her two especially sympathetic
companions: Adèle Kafian, a young Lithuanian with 'an abundance
of untried strength' and the gifted Olgivanna. 'You take care of her,'
he said. 'Help her all you can.' Delicately, he made a place for her in
his extended family, with a personal entrée which many envied. The
tasks he allotted her were light: 'Eat, walk in the garden, pick the
flowers and rest *much*;' the routine he proposed was simple: 'Not to
think, not to write . . . Rest. Rest. Live in your body again.' Noting
Katherine's unexpected affection for the Institute's four strangely
named cows (Equivoquetecka, Bridget, Mitasha and Baldaofim),
Gurdjieff gave up his own cherished haven in the loft above the
stable, and asked Alexandre Salzmann to convert it into an attractive
bower for his guest. As to the folk tradition that the breath of cows
could help consumptive lungs, it was neither speciously emphasized
nor credulously trusted. Gurdjieff did not – could not – view the pro-
longation of any individual life as commensurate with his obligation
to humanity at large but, beyond this fundamental constraint, he
treated Katherine with an affecting gentleness.

'Double-October' had been hectic beyond description, but at
length Gurdjieff temporarily extricated himself from his Montmartre
embroilments, freeing his evenings for the Sacred Dancing at the
Prieuré. In the ensuing ardently creative period, he choreographed a
dozen or more major pieces which evoked the remote monasteries of
his long search. By 7 November he was working with fifty pupils on
the series known as the Big Seven or Big Group, from a religious
order near Mount Ararat. The Aisor melody was haunting, and
Thomas de Hartmann (having wryly endured a succession of hopelessly inferior instruments in Tiflis, Constantinople, and Berlin),
could at last deliver it on a Bechstein concert grand piano. The six
files of dancers interchanged positions following a pattern mathematically inherent in Gurdjieff's nine-pointed symbol the enneagram;
Katherine Mansfield, seated in her high-backed chair, struggled

'He was extraordinary!' (By permission of Institut Gurdjieff (Paris))

'My Father': Giorgios Giorgiades (*By permission of Institut Gurdjieff (Paris)*)

Kars Military Cathedral: where Gurdjieff was choirboy (*By permission of Prof. Tilo Ulbricht*)

Gurdjieff as professional hypnotist. Tashkent c. 1908 (*By permission of Mrs Elizabeth Bennett*)

Gurdjieff in Kashgar (*By permission of Triangle Inc.*)

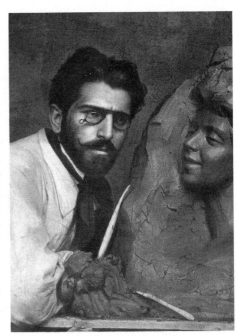

The young Paul Dukes: pioneer English pupil, 1913 (*Copyright unsubstantiated*)

Sergei Dmitrievitch Mercourov: Gurdjieff's famous cousin (*By permission of Mercourov Institute, Gumru*)

Dr Leonid Stjoernval: doyen of Gurdjieff's pupils (*By permission of Institut Gurdjieff (Paris)*)

Mme Elizabeta Stjoernval (*By permission of Institut Gurdjieff (Paris)*)

'Bravo America!': New York, 13 January 1924 (*By permission of the Hulton Picture Company*)

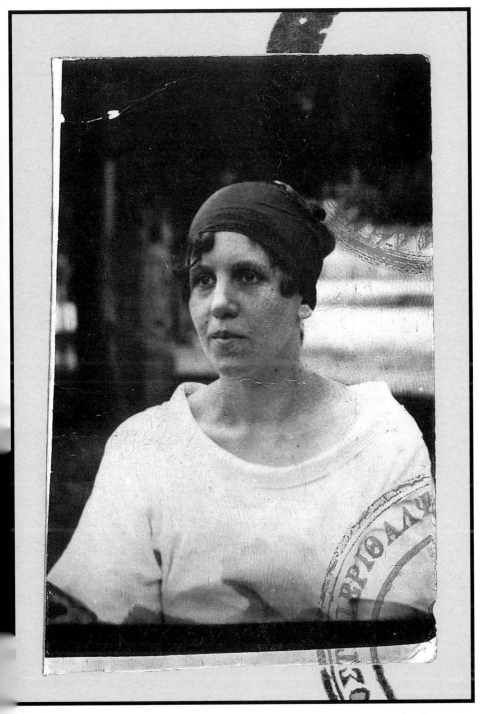

'My uniquely beloved wife': Julia Ostrowska (*By permission of Institut Gurdjieff (Paris)*)

Olga de Hartmann: transcriber of Beelzebub (*By permission of Thomas C. Daly*)

Thomas de Hartmann: the supreme contributor (*By permission of Thomas C. Daly*)

Alexandre Gustav Salzmann: 'Father Sogol' (*By permission of Institut Gurdjieff (Paris)*)

'Ouspensky-Fourth-Dimension' (*Copyright unsubstantiated*)

Fugitive with pets: Gurdjieff at Olghniki (*By permission of Institut Gurdjieff (Paris)*)

Old Tiflis: familiar labyrinth to Gurdjieff (*By permission of Fitzroy Maclean*)

'Olgivanna': from Gurdjieff to Frank Lloyd Wright (*By permission of The Frank Lloyd Wright Archives*)

Viscountess Rothermere: Gurdjieff's benefactress (*By permission of The Hon. Mrs Daphne Mackneile-Dickson*)

Katherine Mansfield (*By permission of the Alexander Turnbull Library*)

The Château du Prieuré, Avon, Gurdjieff's 'Headquarters' (*By permission of Institut Gurdjieff (Paris)*)

The Initiation of the Priestess (*By permission of Institut Gurdjieff (Paris)*)

Study House: Gurdjieff's *Kosshah* (*By permission of the British Library*)

Study in attention (*By permission of The Frank Lloyd Wright Archives and Institut Gurdjieff (Paris)*)

The magnificent obsession (*By permission of Jeremy Finlay*)

Café de la Paix: here Beelzebub was achieved (*By permission of Société Nouvelle du Grand Hôtel*)

Survivor of the Seekers of Truth (*By permission of Institut Gurdjieff (Paris)*)

Mrs Jessie Orage: 'You burn in boiling oil!' (*By permission of Mrs Anne Orage*)

A. R. Orage: 'Ambassador' to the USA (*By permission of Mrs Anne Orage*)

jh: 'Neither a candle for the Angel, nor a poker for the devil' (*By permission of Berenice Abbott, Commerce Graphics Ltd, Inc.*)

Solita Solano: 'Guardian of the thesaurus' (*By permission of The Library of Congress*)

Dmitri Ivanovitch: Gurdjieff's brother (*By permission of Institut Gurdjieff (Paris)*)

René Daumal: pioneer French pupil (*By permission of Institut Gurdjieff (Paris)*)

Gurdjieff's pantry-cum-confessional: 6 Rue des Colonels Rénard (*By permission of Institut Gurdjieff (Paris)*)

Sunset boulevardier (*By permission of Institut Gurdjieff (Paris)*)

Monsieur Bonbon 1947: 6 Rue des Colonels Rénard (*By permission of William Segal*)

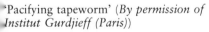

'Pacifying tapeworm' (*By permission of Institut Gurdjieff (Paris)*)

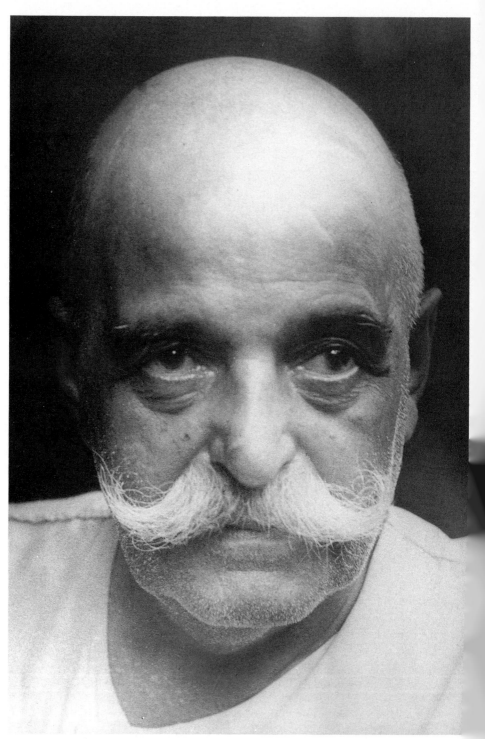

The author of Beelzebub (*By permission of Institut Gurdjieff (Paris)*)

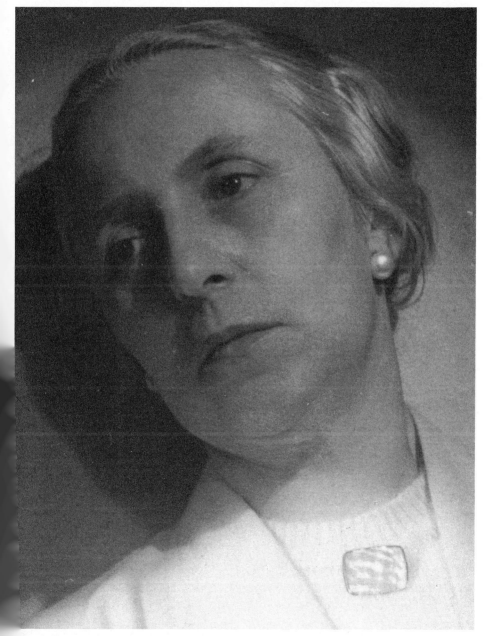

anne de Salzmann in middle age (*By permission of Institut Gurdjieff (Paris)*)

Avon, 3 November 1949 (*By permission of Mrs Elizabeth Bennett*)

The last dolmen: Gurdjieff's grave (*By permission of Bernard Mirwis*)

mentally with these novel 'multiplications', engaging almost as fervently as the participants themselves. That night she wrote to England: 'they are working at present at a tremendous ancient Assyrian group Dance. I have no words with which to describe it. To see it seems to change one's whole being for the time.'

Gurdjieff surely felt the special poignancy of this frail sensitive witness who might have proved such a distinguished cultural herald of his work. That she would not: that on the contrary her imminent death would bring down on him and his Institute the virulent opprobrium of the intelligentsia – was painfully evident. Already autumn was eliding into winter; in the salon grate the sweet-smelling logs spurted, and the brightest sparks flew upward and were gone forever.

Interesting en passant that, despite Gurdjieff's recklessly professed male chauvinism ('He spoke of women in terms that would have better suited a fanatical Muslim polygamist than a Christian'), virtually all his best and most cherished dancers were women; and his dances expressly created for them – 'The Waltz', 'The Lost Loves', 'The Prayer', 'The Sacred Goose' – captured, in their grace and tenderness, a quintessential femininity. Arguably Gurdjieff's perception of woman's special destiny found its deepest expression in his tableau-dance 'The Initiation of the Priestess' (a fragment of a mystery called The Truth Seekers). Olgivanna, cast as the neophyte, was led into the semi-circle of dancers; here she renounced the world, the flesh and the devil; was raised through successive initiatic phases; and at length knelt alone – head bowed, arms crossed on her breast, while the chief priestess (Mme Ostrowska) gave a benediction. Framed within this quasi-religious ceremonial was a psychological glyph, which Katherine Mansfield succeeded in construing.

> There is one which takes about 7 minutes and it contains the whole life of a woman – but everything! Nothing is left out. It taught me, it gave me more of woman's life than any book or poem. There was even room for Flaubert's Cœur Simple in it, and for Princess Marya . . . Mysterious.

On 10 November Piotr Ouspensky (whom from outset Gurdjieff had warmly but unavailingly invited) finally arrived at the Prieuré to find very 'interesting and animated work . . . proceeding there' – and the whole place in turmoil. Gurdjieff, in his role as 'arch-disturber', had abruptly reassigned all accommodation. Orage and Young, who had shared a room in the spartan 'Monks' Corridor' on the second floor, could only benefit – but Katherine not:

My other room was rich and sumptuous. This is small and plain and very simple. When Olga Ivanovna and I had arranged it and she had hung her yellow dance stockings to dry before the fire we sat together on the bed and felt like two quite poor young girls. . .

Far worse affected, however, was Ethel Merston: 'I had a tiny little room to myself until someone had to take in the paranoic and look after her, which fell to my lot – as have mad people ever since!' For a week the Prieuré was like a wasps' nest which has been disturbed. The surrealist component in all this only reinforced Ouspensky's grave prognosis: 'I could not fail to see, as I had seen in Essentuki in 1918, that there were many destructive elements in the organization of the affair itself and that it had to fall to pieces.'

Ouspensky's rider that a 'very motley company' had foregathered at the Prieuré is not entirely unfair. Outside the formidable circle of Gurdjieff's committed nucleus, a subordinate Russian element simply spooned their soup in dreamy, post-revolutionary gloom, and 'like mystical Micawbers waited patiently for something superconscious to turn up.' The equivalent English layer may equally have been Ouspensky's target. They numbered among them some hopefuls whose prior experience – in the Civil Service, the WRNS, the VADs, and even the Theosophical Society – had not necessarily prepared them for Fontainebleau. A handful bordered on the idiosyncratic: Mr Alfred Trevor Barker, a theosophical aspirant (who afterwards compiled *The Mahatma Letters to A. P. Sinnett*), had peculiar little ways; and Miss Merston, as she bent over to serve tea, invariably broke wind with a 'small sharp report, like that of a toy gun' – a phenomenon which, as Gurdjieff charitably observed, was 'so delicate, so refined, that it is necessary to be alert, and highly perceptive, even to be aware of this.'

To catch people's weaknesses was all too easy, but Gurdjieff sternly reminded critics of the pot and the kettle:

When a new person arrives with his luggage, he is at once undressed. And then all his worst sides, all his inner 'beauties' become evident. This is why those among you who do not know about the phenomenon get the impression that we have indeed collected here only people who are stupid, lazy, dense – in a word riff-raff . . . If he is a fool, he does not see that he himself is a fool . . . forgets that he too is undressed . . . imagines that just as in life he could wear a mask, so here he can put on a mask. But directly he entered these gates, the watchman took off his mask. Here he is naked, everybody senses directly what sort of person he is.

It is difficult to avoid the conclusion that Ouspensky accorded himself some privileged exemption.

Nakedness (embarrassing to many of that generation) was soon called for physically as well as psychologically. On 25 November Katherine Mansfield recorded completion of the Turkish bath:

> Now one can have seven different kinds of baths in it, and there is a little rest room hung with carpets which looks more like Bokhara than Avon. If you have seen this evolved, it is really a miracle of ingenuity. Everything is designed by Mr. Gurdjieff.

The boiler was laboriously stoked and fired only on Saturdays, the women bathing in the afternoon and the men in the evening. Though Gurdjieff was unchallenged 'king' at Fontainebleau, he joined in with the rest, delighted in this congenial milieu to discuss 'the four sources of action existing ... under the names of "mother-in-law", "digestion", "John Thomas", and "cash"' – 'Once we had all undressed, it was customary to spend about half an hour, most of the men smoking and talking, while Gurdjieff urged them to tell him stories ... generally ribald or off-colour, at his insistence.'

His little court, convened on tiered wooden benches, was a strange one: Dr Stjoernval, doyen of Finnish hydropathic establishments, had a facial expression which James Young could 'only liken to that of a solemn goat'; Young seemed to Salzmann to resemble an ape – Orage an elephant, de Hartmann a toucan, and Pinder a hippopotamus; Salzmann was himself a cartoon of 'a very surly, angry, and even fierce workman ... haggard, drawn, old-looking, with grey hair cut in fringe on his forehead.' Gurdjieff at fifty-six possessed 'all the requisite number of limbs'; his spine was peculiarly erect and upward-flowing and he was 'hairless as a new-born babe'... (Ouspensky evidently did not bathe with the others and soon returned to his groups in London.)

The end of November marked a brief Indian summer – a golden interval in the octave of muscular spirituality. Workshop and forge were by now running smoothly; paths and ditches were neat and clean; the Turkish bath lacked only a proper boiler; and Katherine suddenly found her bower above the stable an accomplished triumph:

> It's simply too lovely. There is a small steep staircase to a little railed-off gallery above the cows. On the little gallery are divans covered with Persian carpets (only two divans). But the white-washed walls and ceiling

have been decorated most exquisitely in what looks like a Persian pattern of yellow, red and blue by Mr. Salzmann. Flowers, little birds, butterflies and a spreading tree with animals on the branches, even a hippopotamus. But ... all done with the most *real art* – a little masterpiece. And all so gay, so simple, reminding one of summer grasses and the kind of flowers that smell like milk.

A mellower Gurdjieff was suddenly solicitous to protect his people from over-exertion: 'We old men, Nicole, we have coffee'; 'Thomas, now go and burn some leaves'; 'Now, Orage, I think you dig enough. Let us go to café and drink coffee.' From the outset a minority of the English had been tormented by the question: 'Why does Mr. Gurdjieff put so much emphasis on physical work? Is it temporary or permanent?' They had never received a very satisfactory answer, but now their hearts beat again with a good hope.

Alas! – only a day or two later they observed with growing unease the arrival of two big lorries heaped with reinforced iron girders and bolts. According to Gurdjieff, it was the skeleton of a Zeppelin hangar acquired from the French Air Force. A Zeppelin hangar! If the Prieuré's surreality did licence a moment or two of wild conjecture, it soon passed. The jumbled metal had a perfectly serious function: re-erected, it must serve as the framework of the Institute's new Study House, a Maison d'Etudes, a sacred place – which absolutely must be ready by January.

The fervour of the Prieuré's scratch labour force was generally speaking matched by its innocence. Miss Merston in particular proved fearless of dangers she did not perceive: 'eager, as usual, to be in the vanguard, I went forward to help, only to receive a violent kick on the shins from Mr Gurdjieff which stopped me just in time to avoid receiving the girder on top of me.' Gurdjieff could number on one hand his lieutenants with a real practical streak – Salzmann, Pinder, Tchekovitch, James Young and Mme Ostrowska. To most students the Gordian knot probably made more sense than this metal jigsaw; Gurdjieff nevertheless assigned them ten to a girder and stacked the load neatly on site.

To raise and furnish a building capable of seating 300, in little more than a month and with a team of no more than thirty able-bodied men, was on the face of it preposterous – and yet Gurdjieff did it. The creation of the Study House represents the Prieuré's heroic period: six weeks of Haida Yoga which seemed to go on for six years; a disciplined frenzy of shovelling, barrowing, levelling, pounding, rolling, sawing, hammering, tarring, painting; six weeks when

effort grew exponentially and when (in many psyches) the mysterious
energy reservoirs of what Gurdjieff called 'big accumulator' abruptly
opened – living proof of man's extraordinary possibilities.

The work drove on through interminable days and icy lamplit
nights. 'We had no proper tools,' recalls de Hartmann, 'and worked
practically with our bare hands ... when I played the piano later it
felt as if I were playing on needles.' Dr Young diagnosed in himself
the phenomenon which is known surgically as 'snap-finger'. The
burly dishevelled Tchekovitch, high up on a precarious beam, fell fast
asleep from sheer exhaustion!

> None of the others noticed: but Gurdjieff entered, took in the position at
> a glance, motioned to them all to remain perfectly still and climbed like a
> cat on to the truss and along it until he could hold Tchekovitch steady.
> Then we went for him like a fishwife and sent him off to sleep for forty-
> eight hours after which we all went on as before.

Poor Miss Merston (who in any case rose every morning at 5 o'clock
to milk the cows) could not keep her eyes open – as Gurdjieff noted:

> He told me 'You not sleep! You go get black coffee.' So when I felt myself
> dropping off, I would get up, go to the kitchen, drink a whole jug of black
> coffee, return to the Study House and drop right off to sleep again.

The story of the Maison d'Etudes is not, essentially, the story of a
building, but of a human challenge triumphantly accepted. And yet
no emblem of 'super-effort' is more poignant, no comment on the
quest for consciousness more ironic, than the figure of the sleepwalk-
ing Tchekovitch.

Each succeeding day the screw tightened a little; in the 'Russian'
dining room, where all the work-force breakfasted and lunched,
Gurdjieff gradually imposed a more spartan diet until male tempers
particularly began to fray and Miss Merston (taking her turn as
kitchen girl) reaped the consequences: 'One of the Englishmen I was
serving, when he saw the size of the piece of meat on his plate,
certainly no bigger than half a crown, raised his plate and flung it at
my head.'

Yet the Institute's regime never became one of unrelieved privation,
and Gurdjieff's Saturday banquets in the 'Ritz dining room' remained very big occasions. Around his hospitable table (as
of course in the workplace), Gurdjieff established an integration
without distinction of nationality or creed: 'Here there are neither
Russians nor English, Jews nor Christians, but only those with one
aim – to be able to be.' Alcohol certainly helped. But Gurdjieff did

not use alcohol in an unstructured way: from Georgian tradition he now adapted a plan of a feast rendered sacramental by ritual. He himself loomed at the head of the table as *tamada* (the one closest to God); seated immediately on his left, his selected master of ceremonies or *tolumbashi* proposed a succession of toasts to be drunk in calvados or slivovitz – their order so ancient and inviolable that Gurdjieff could hardly resist (and ultimately did not resist) modifying it.

Although *tolumbashi* is construable in Turko-Tartar as the 'superintendent of a fire brigade', it is arguable that the toastmaster stoked rather than extinguished the fires of an intoxication subsumed in the search for consciousness. Gurdjieff himself drank only moderately, and since he could 'see' his pupils far more quickly once drink had rendered their natures 'opaque' to scrutiny, such banquets were less an indulgence than a singular form of Haida Yoga. Peculiarly enough, both 'Hurry-up Yoga' and the provenance of the word *tolumbashi* were lent an ironic literalism when on 16 December 1922 the entire Prieuré nearly went up in smoke:

> We had a fire here the other night. A real one. Two beautiful rooms burnt out, and a real fear that the whole place would go. Cries of 'Vode!' Vode!' (Water!), people, rushing past and snatching at jugs and basins. Mr. Gurdjieff with a hammer, knocking down the wall. The real thing in fact.

The Bolsheviks of Essentuki who in 1919 had so mysteriously provided Gurdjieff with a red-and-black fireman's belt seem in this moment almost prescient (and, for what such coincidence is worth, Rudolph Steiner's Goetheanum at Dornach was totally destroyed by fire only a fortnight later).

The Prieuré was saved just as the Study House arrived at its moment of truth: when the central stanchion supporting the heavy iron fabric, 100 feet long and 40 feet wide, was struck away. 'When the pole is removed,' observed Gurdjieff darkly, 'the House will either stand or collapse.' It stood! But all the ambitious interior work – gallery, stage, railings, windows, boxes, lighting, decoration, and even fountains – had yet to be achieved, and less than a month remained! Turning to Salzmann, Gurdjieff commanded: 'Throw everyone into the work.'

Even with total mobilization, the outcome remained touch and go, especially since Gurdjieff now introduced a sub-plot with huge demands on time and energy. ('We are going to *Fêter le Noel* in tremendous style here. Every sort of lavish generous hospitable thing has been done by Mr. Gurdjieff.') A strange Christmas and a strange New Year! The 'proper' Gurdjieffian historiography with its dry scholastic probity will miss – and arguably suffer from missing – the time's poetic truth: the convergence of two dramatic lines, and their conjunction under the aegis of Higher Forces. A richly human Gurdjieff moils and toils in a sort of elemental fury, faster and faster towards the opening of his Study House – while gliding death (invisible, subtle, disembodied) keeps effortless station. By some concomitant grace, Katherine Mansfield – coughing out the closing sentence of her life's short story towards its inescapable full stop – steadily becomes 'a being transformed by love, absolutely secure in love.' In the biting cold of early January, effort on the Study House reaches crescendo pitch with forty-eight hours of sleepless 'super-effort', and the 'last nail ... finally driven in at 7 o'clock in the evening.'

Katherine Mansfield died suddenly on 9 January 1923. She had never lacked in dignity, never wavered in courage or commitment; Gurdjieff had confirmed in her a witness of the most delicate sensibility, and she in him a real man, a man 'without quotation marks'. He did not go into the room where – haemorrhaging uncontrollably – she failed in the arms of Dr Young. Moments earlier, he had noted her in the salon as she offered her last reserves of attention to 'The Initiation of the Priestess':

> If only I could have just a little place in that group, if I could sit in front of Mrs O. with my arms crossed on my breast, I would listen to the beautiful music. I would feel Mrs O.'s marvellous arms raised above me in prayer. How grateful I could be for it.

In Gurdjieff's personal scheme of things Katherine Mansfield was never pre-eminent: she does not quite tally with his establishment of the Institute, his creation of the Study House, his musical composition with de Hartmann, and his deepening personal relationships with Orage and Jeanne Salzmann. How could she? And yet, if anyone can be said to have died 'directly into' the impressions of Gurdjieff's Sacred Dance, it is certainly Katherine. He never forgot her; he spoke of her as his friend only a month before his own death; he lies buried near her.

On 12 January 1923 Gurdjieff followed Katherine's slow cortège to the Protestant cemetery of Avon. Immortality he had never promised her, yet his thoughts were surely less conformable to the

paraphernalia of conventional grief (the brassy funereal knick-
knacks and the expensive black horses parading their black plumes)
than to Katherine's insight: 'It is not my coffin which is the shell, it is
my body which is the shell.' At the graveside he handed mourners
paper twists of *kootia* – raisins and corn and honey signifying decay,
germination and re-birth.

Though Gurdjieff felt the weight of the event, a crèpe-edged
melancholia was not his style. Preferring to surprise the forces of
darkness and death with a brilliant oppositional flash, he inaugurated
his Study House that very night. Katherine's husband and various
baffled mourners from London mingled with pupils at an unanticipated feast, prepared by Mme Ostrowska and Mme Ouspensky:

> I think I have never eaten food so delicious . . . food from every quarter of
> the world . . . soup, meat with spices, poultry, fish; vegetables of all kinds,
> most wonderful salads whose juice we drank in glasses; puddings and
> pies, fruit of all sorts, dishes of oriental tit-bits, fragrant herbs, raw
> onions, and celery.

We cannot read Gurdjieff's mind nor even detect his facial expression,
since he sat alone in his personal alcove, more or less concealed by its
silk drapes. What did he meditate? – there in his brave new Study
House, so redolent of a huge nomad tent. A blaze of oriental carpets
masked the earth walls and softened the compacted earth floor. ('My
thoughts,' Katherine had written in her very last letter, 'are full of
carpets and Persia and Samarkand and the little rugs of Beluchistan.')
The perpendicular windows which backed the guests' raised divans
were brilliantly painted by Salzmann to mimic stained glass. Gold
and silver fish swam in two pools on either side of the doorway;
coloured lights played subtly on a hexagonal fountain, whose head of
water fell back into a carved stone basin with a soft murmur and a
faint odour of attar of roses.

On the raised stage under the sign of the enneagram the silent
costumed dancers now collected themselves, and gave 'The Initiation
of the Priestess' and the 'Ceremony for a Dead Dervish' from the
Subari Monastery in Thershzas. Perched at the grand piano, Thomas
de Hartmann awaited a final signal from his teacher.

> When the main lights were switched off, and the Study House . . . was
> bathed in a dim glow from the little red lamps, and the illuminated
> fountains, Mr Gurdjieff . . . asked me to play the Essentuki Prayer; the
> pupils led by my wife, hummed the melody. All this created an unforget-
> table impression.

There prevailed a general sense of consummation – an atmosphere of a holy place created for definite inner work ... but, as far as Gurdjieff himself was concerned, the peace which could be felt there was the lull before a force 12 hurricane.

9

❖

RIDING THE TIGER

(13 January 1923–7 July 1924)

'Riding the tiger – difficult to dismount': George Ivanovitch Gurdjieff, astride the yellow beast of media scrutiny, seems alternatively keen to get off and keen to stay on. With Katherine Mansfield's death, various journalists, special correspondents, and literary voyeurs descended on the Prieuré attracted by a story which had everything: a mysterious Russian, a whiff of oriental exoticism, and a beautiful young genius cut off in her prime. Gurdjieff's brush with this tribe of 'slobbering boy reporters' seemingly so vexed him that, twenty years later, he would still scour journalists from his house as if they were rats. But why such vehemence? On the face of it, the newspaper articles of spring 1923 were accurate in substance and remarkably positive in tone. Is it conceivable that some element of self-reproach turned outward here? As phones rang and type-writers clattered, did Gurdjieff recall with painful self-interrogation the Sarmoung Monastery, where there had 'reigned an almost awesome quiet'? We cannot say of course. But in any case there was no going back: Gurdjieff was henceforward engaged in rough trade with the world of cultural *bon ton* – with the contemporary intelligentsia, or 'tramps' as he scathingly called them.

Their initial condemnation was guaranteed. Even before Katherine had arrived at the Prieuré, Wyndham Lewis was sneering at 'the famous New Zealand Mag. – story writer, in the grip of the Levantine psychic shark', and Vivienne Eliot situated Lady Rothermere in 'that asylum for the insane called La Prieuré where she does religious dances naked with Katherine Mansfield.' Now Katherine's widower, John Middleton Murry, fantasizing that she had been a 'princess manifest, a child withouten stain', noisily regretted her reaction 'into the spiritual quackery of Gurdjieff – and death.' Gurdjieff could hardly deny the snakeskin oil ingredient in his prospectus (his physico-metric, chemico-analytic and psycho-experimental cabinets; his grandiose references to hydrotherapy, phototherapy, electrotherapy, magneto-therapy, psychotherapy, dietotherapy and duliotherapy). In public perception, a spectral Katherine – 'very attractive in a dark purple taffeta dress, embroidered with tiny flowers' – lay forever and forever in the gallery above the cow-byre, her wide beautiful eyes focused on Gurdjieff in dumb, unanswerable reproach. From the ordinary view-point, the Institute's French debut had proved disastrous.

How much did Gurdjieff actually care? By and large, the most acidulous personal abuse left him unmoved: 'If a fool has called me a fool, I am not affected inside.' Intriguingly enough, Gurdjieff's earlier poses (as venial carpet dealer or Tifon the Sordid or a 'certain Hindu') strongly suggest the *qalandari* dervish type who – while secretly 'traversing arenas of tranquility of the heart' – is only too eager to court man's blame[6] as the necessary reciprocal of God's regard. Yet just the same, the price which Gurdjieff paid for his simple kindness to Katherine Mansfield was a heavy one, and perhaps for his Institute's sake he did care profoundly.

For better or worse, Gurdjieff was now a figure of intense if ambivalent public interest, and on Saturday 17 February we find him bamboozling twelve different inquirers. Pre-eminent amongst them was Professor Denis Saurat from the Institut Français in London, who, while enjoying a passable lunch, casually regretted his host's absence:

> The door opened suddenly. A large, powerful-looking man burst in . . . His head was completely shaven. His expression was one of habitual ferocity, mixed, at this moment, with a tenderness . . . as he held in his arms a large lamb. . . With great strides he crossed the room, without even glancing at us, and went out by another door.

Saurat's impression of Gurdjieff's ferocity was reinforced that after-noon, when the boiler of the Russian bath was routinely fired . . . and inopportunely burst:

> We could see a crack through which were being sucked long, virulent tongues of flame. No-one knew what to do. Gurdjieff arrived. The heat made it impossible to get near the furnace. So Gurdjieff attempted to stop the crack with balls of cement. He aimed well. He started at the top of the crack, and the balls made a curious sound as they struck the burning casing. His unbuttoned overcoat flapping round him got in the way, so presently he took it off . . . The cement-mixer looked like a slave.

A sense of the sinister, of the ogrish, of indefinable danger, was by now affecting even the most blasé journalists, and the evening's performance in the Study House found them eagerly clutching at Saurat's nervous ironies:

> The *Daily Mail* man was justly frightened. The perfumed atmosphere, coloured lights, rich carpets and strange dances – it was Oriental romanticism at last realised on earth. To reassure the journalist I told him I was a professor in Bordeaux University and that all these people were mad. He thought about it for a moment, and then seemed much relieved; his confidence in himself came back.

Granted a private interview, Saurat went along with mixed scepticism and trepidation – and was disarmed on both counts: 'Gurdjieff had an astonishing courtesy. He gave not the smallest impression of being a charlatan ... His ferocity seemed changed into strength.' However debatable Gurdjieff's softening-up tactics, he had brilliantly succeeded in turning the flank of the first media assault.

That the Institute's public exposure caused Gurdjieff remorse is mere hypothesis, but he certainly embraced a regime of penitential rigour immediately the reporters had gone. The season of Lent in 1923 was marked with a series of 'metabolic' fasts, for pupils to undertake voluntarily and without fear. The programme began with an enema; then a restricted diet of oranges or *prostokvasha*, Russian sour milk; then up to fourteen days complete abstinence (days which seemed endless; days when physical work took on a dreamlike quality; days of unearthly refinement, and days when images of stewed rabbit with *habbur-chubur* rose up irrepressibly and tormentingly); a penultimate day on strong *bouillon*; then finally a day on best beef-steak. The discipline and loyalty of Gurdjieff's 'very motley company' of pupils, his 'riff-raff', was tested and found virtually immaculate. Only Rachmielevitch secretly hid some food in a tree; but just before the experiment started Gurdjieff announced devastatingly, 'Rakhmielevitch need not fast; he already knows too much.'

In May 1923 Gurdjieff began his long love affair with the motor car – a tempestuous embrace which proved near fatal. The Institute's expectation was that Gurdjieff would not need to learn like an ordinary mortal: 'He would be able to drive, so to speak, by inspiration.' And certainly when the huge Citroën was delivered, Gurdjieff does appear to have taught himself entirely by private experiment – but as his nervous pupils listened they heard 'a ghastly sound suggestive of tearing of gear-wheel cogs'. In a matter of days Gurdjieff

could work his new toy and was hurtling down the route nationale –
though if tests had existed in 1923, he must have failed:

> He drove like a wild man, cutting in and out of traffic without hand
> signals or even space to accommodate his car in the lanes he suddenly
> switched to . . . until he was in them, safe by a hair . . . he always got away
> first on the green light even (so it seemed) when he was one or two cars
> behind the starting line . . . the chances he took overtaking buses and
> trucks were terrifying.

The car's frequent repair was undertaken at the Prieuré by young
Bernard Metz, whose dreamy amateurism supplied its own increment of danger:

> That night Gurdjieff had to go to Paris. When the car was taken out and
> he found the headlight had not been changed, he shouted at Metz to sit on
> the bumper and hold the light all the way to Paris. Metz meekly sat on the
> mudguard until Gurdjieff contemptuously pushed him off with his
> favourite word: 'Idiot!'

Gurdjieff's (if one dare say so) Toad-of-Toad-Hall syndrome caused
acute anxiety among his pupils.

By car or rail, everyone who was anyone had seemingly come to
Paris in the fragrant, golden spring of 1923. Even a provisional roll
call is impressive: James Joyce, Gertrude Stein, Picasso, Stravinsky,
Poulenc, Isadora Duncan, Cocteau, Hemingway, Man Ray, Tzara,
and Fernand Léger. Gurdjieff too was there a fair bit, though the
cream-coloured turban he affected throughout this spell warned of
his aloofness from the European mainstream; indeed his considered
opinion of the intelligentsia, the avant-garde and the so-to-say
theatre of cultural *bon ton* could be expressed in a few well chosen
four-letter words. Orage steered one or two hopefuls to Gurdjieff's
newly acquired apartment at 9 Rue Commandant-Marchand, but
nothing significant eventuated. Their clever dismissive sophistication
is epitomized by Ezra Pound:

> Gurdjieff made Persian soup, bright yellow in colour, far more delicate –
> you might say Piêro della Francesca in tone, as compared with bortch
> (tinted Rembrandt). If he had had more of that sort of thing in his
> repertoire he could, had he suspected it, or desired it, have worked on
> towards at least one further conversion.

Albeit Gurdjieff did not desire the conversion of 'tramps', he more
and more appreciated Orage's energy, commitment, and influence.

Back at the Prieuré Gurdjieff suddenly set his indefatigable pupils

to clear a stand of virgin Fontainebleau forest, ostensibly to accommodate a central hall for the Institute. Hacking at the intransigent
roots of trees under a formidable sun, the workers answered with
sweat and dedication Gurdjieff's insistent demand for something
'permanent'. Yet to Dr Nicoll, Gurdjieff had said: 'In a very short
time everything will be different – everyone will be elsewhere.
Nothing can be built permanently at this moment.' The proof of the
Gurdjieffian pudding was again not in the eating, but in the cooking.
On and on toiled the amateur foresters: 'It was a gruelling task . . .
Yet, once again, not a stone of the new building was ever laid. In its
stead, from its unfertile soil sprouted sweet corn and beans.'

Every Saturday Gurdjieff gave an open evening in the Study House
with his well developed programme of music, Sacred Dances, the
'Stop!' exercise, and feats of attention and memory dressed up as
pseudo-occult phenomena.

> Those summer evenings, fading into nights spiced with the aroma of the
> forest, are unforgettable. I can still hear the clanging of the entrance bell
> as the people streamed in, passing by the long flower beds to the study
> house, with the garden fountain a coloured rhythm of changing lights to
> the fitful dancing of the glow worms.

Garlic-exuding dignitaries from Avon and Fontainebleau gave obse-
quious thanks, though secretly confirmed in deepest cynicism. They
'accepted the institute as an economic asset, but dismissed it otherwise as being simply a *maison de fous*.' Cosmopolitan artists of all
complexions and degree looked in: Doris X, a notable dancer at the
Paris Opera, came once and stayed on; Diaghilev himself took time
off from *Les Noces*, finding the Sacred Dances so exciting that he
wanted to incorporate them as a novelty item in his Ballet Russes
season. Sinclair Lewis spoke for the Philistines:

> Some of the dances are imitations of Oriental sacred temple rights [sic],
> some of them stunts requiring a high degree of muscle control . . . But it
> must be a hell of a place to live . . . they have built their own 'gymnasium'
> . . . a cross between a cabaret and a harem.

Perhaps certain Prieuré people whom Lewis met had rattled him?
Though Gurdjieff's phalanx of Russian devotees remained as formidable as ever, some rather peculiar birds of passage had briefly
confused the English ranks: there was 'Bishop' Wedgewood, head of
the Theosophical Liberal Catholic Church (on the run from the
police for homosexual activities); and there was Mrs Finch, mother

of the Everest climber, who tied blue ribbons to the cows' tails and took them for walks in the garden.

Of all these tricky cases, probably the most aggravated was Dr Young's incurably paranoid patient – a problem eventually approached on musical lines. Cradling his harmonium, Gurdjieff 'suddenly began to play a series of notes over and over again. The woman at first fidgetted, then suddenly got up screaming and rushed from the room. Very soon afterwards she left.' Unfortunate repercussions followed: Dr Young himself – who after twelve months felt he had gained all he could – vacated the Prieuré 'with a feeling of supreme satisfaction'. Gurdjieff's regret was undisguised; he had particularly cherished Young's energy, intelligence, and practicality. With this sturdy Laertes gone, the Rosencrantz and Guildenstern set seemed more and more insupportable; on 21 August 1923 Gurdjieff sternly announced: 'For one section of the people here, their stay has become completely useless.' (J. G. Bennett left the following day, after thirty-three days at the Prieuré, and did not see Gurdjieff again for twenty-five years.)

It was a moment to take stock. Olga de Hartmann (treasurer now in place of Dr Stjoernval) frowningly did some sums, and Gurdjieff frankly admitted his alarm: 'My mentation increased to such proportions that there was scarcely room for it in my cerebral cavity.' The message of the balance sheet was brutally clear: 'that if within three months I did not have at least one "cool" million francs, I would go up the chimney . . . forever.'

Careering to and fro between the Prieuré and Paris, Gurdjieff searched desperately for an expedient. Late one autumn night, on a particularly unsafe and unlit track through the Forest of Fontaine-bleau, he nearly killed himself: 'I looked at my watch – it was a quarter past eleven. I put on the large headlights and accelerated. . . From that moment on I remembered nothing . . .' A full twelve hours later, and one kilometre further on, he recovered consciousness to find that 'around me was the forest; the sun was shining brightly; a big wagon loaded with hay had stopped in front of the car and the driver was standing at my window tapping on it with his whip.' Though Fate's warning was prophetic, Gurdjieff's foot was firmly planted on the accelerator of his life and he would not, or could not, slow down.

The plain truth was that the Principal of the Institute was fifty-seven and deadly tired. He needed rest. Complete rest . . . He would therefore work! He would galvanize his dancers. He would give a display in Paris. And another in New York. He would deliver public lectures. He would go to Philadelphia. He would play at Carnegie Hall. Everyone was entitled to some rest ... Night after night at intense rehearsals in the Study House the 'tired man' infused in his dancers a feeling of excitement, of privilege, of ordeal, of service – and a not unjustified sense that everything was at stake.

The formidable Gurdjieff of the gambling tables in Sochi is resurrected here, making an accumulator bet of colossal cheek: he will venture his life's blood on success in Paris; all the cultural proceeds will be restaked in New York; and a triumph there will totally restore his health and fortunes. By early December Orage and Dr Stjoernval were poised to proceed to New York as Gurdjieff's 'Heralds of Coming Good', and he and his company were all but embarked in terms of irretrievable deposits and unbreakable commitments. Yet the Paris demonstration had still to take place – and could prove a fiasco. Visas had been applied for very belatedly – and not yet issued. Gurdjieff and Mme Ostrowska (as others among the gaggle of Russians, Lithuanians, Armenians and Poles) possessed in fact no proper papers at all, resorting to 'Nansen passports' for displaced persons. It was all highly stimulating and problematical.

The *Démonstrations de L'Institut du Développement Harmonique de L'Homme de G. Gurdjieff* were realized at the Théâtre des Champs-Elysées: the dress rehearsal on 13 December 1923, the première on Sunday 16 December, and the final matinée on Christmas day. Gurdjieff had astutely chosen the place for its ambience, its enormous stage, and the congeniality of its director Jacques Hébertot (a friend of Alexandre Salzmann). Early in the month a four-page advertisement in *L'Echo des Champs-Elysées* promised 'tricks, half-tricks and real phenomena observed in religious ceremonies of the ancient East.' *Le Figaro*, building a semi-detached truth on a foundation of blissful ignorance, assured its readers: 'Professor Gurdjieff is perhaps unknown in Paris, but he is celebrated throughout the rest of the world.'

The night before the dress rehearsal all the goat skins, cushions, carpets, and even the three fountains were carted from the Prieuré Study House: 'The foyer became an Oriental palace. For the public there were all kinds of Eastern delicacies, and the fountains were filled with champagne instead of water.' Gravely equivocal ushers, in costumes from *The Struggle of the Magicians*, met the first-night audience in the foyer with trays of perfumed wine (among them, risking his diplomatic career, was the turbaned figure of Eric Graham

Forbes Adam, Companion of the Order of St Michael and St George). Meanwhile, in the pit, Thomas de Hartmann was in agony. He had had to orchestrate the programme while still acting as Prieuré cook, and for the last three nights had not slept at all. His baton commanded only thirty-five musicians and he needed 100; if he compensated with trumpets they would blatantly mask his deficient strings; Nikolai Tcherepnin and Emile Jaques-Dalcroze sat appraisingly in the stalls; and Gurdjieff? – he was down with the choral section indicating how they should add a bass line with unusual flats in the key signature ... Slowly the curtain rose.

The applause which (to Gurdjieff's annoyance) followed each Sacred Dance, signalled a nervous groping for conventionality in the face of the starkly unconventional; critics and hoi polloi alike had the impression of something unique and indescribable: 'the funeral ceremony for a deceased Dervish in the monastery of Souhart at Sarie in Tibet is a moment of grief and grandeur impossible to convey.'

Gurdjieff himself of course remained backstage, all attention focused on his pupils' effort. As the curtain descended, one unfortunate woman prematurely abandoned her 'Stop!' position.

> Mr Gurdjieff scolded her very strongly. He said that the 'stop' had nothing to do with the audience or the curtain ... that it is Work and cannot be finished until the Teacher says; that it has to be held even if a fire should break out in the theatre.

If anything could now conceivably have distracted Gurdjieff's own attention, it might have been his family's expatriation – which is just what occurred. Inextricably embroiled in Paris, he had them met and escorted from the quayside in Marseilles. Five years earlier, on the bullet-scarred platform at Essentuki, he had said goodbye as an imposter-scientist, wearing a red and black fireman's belt and carrying a revolver: now at the Gare de Lyon he warmly re-embraced his family as a fur-coated impresario!

His sister Sophie Ivanovna had hardly changed, nor her husband Georgilibovitch Kapanadze, but Gurdjieff's mother, in her widow's weeds, shocked him with signs of old age and chronic liver illness. Together they all travelled to Fontainebleau. Le Paradou – a compact attractive house – stood in the Institute's grounds, not far from the Orangerie and shielded from the Prieuré itself by maple trees; here (supported by the Stjoernvals and the Salzmanns who occupied the top floor) the family were settled, in what seemed to them unbelievable comfort.

'How did everything go?' asked Thomas de Hartmann when the production at the Elysées was finally over, but Gurdjieff merely smiled. Undoubtedly it had given musicians and dancers a vital experience and inured them against stage-fright in New York; and generally the press had been kind; but the public ... that was a *cheval* of a different colour. The French psyche took this rare vibration not as a spiritual call but as an intellectual provocation; none joined Gurdjieff's ranks.

> The demonstration in Paris ... caused an uproar. The audience ... divided between excitement at the originality of what they had seen, and disgust at what to them had seemed the severe discipline of the exercises. Gurdjieff was now a man of remarkable interest ... But beneath this outward success there were strange rumours.

(Such rumours – for example that Gurdjieff had forced his sexual attentions on his new pupil, Doris X – were indeed strange, but they alone intrigued the French for the next fifteen years, while Russians, English and Americans competed to understand and serve him.)

Although culturally the way to New York now lay open, Gurdjieff's largesse had hopelessly depleted his purse:

> And so I found myself at the last minute in a super-unique tragi-comic situation. Everything was ready for our departure but I could not sail ... This situation revealed itself in all its splendour three days before the sailing of the boat.

The help Gurdjieff providentially received came from the quarter in which he least expected it – his mother. 'Please relieve me of this thing,' requested the penniless old woman. 'I am so tired of always carrying it around.' She unloosened from her neck a little leather bag and extracted a packet which Gurdjieff opened uncomprehendingly: 'But when I saw what was in it, I almost jumped up and danced for joy.' It was the large diamond-encrusted brooch of the grand duchess, confided to his mother's safekeeping in Essentuki. An immediate offer of 125,000 francs made by a Parisian jeweller fell significantly short of Gurdjieff's expectations from a comparable New York sale, so, using the brooch as collateral, he simply borrowed what he needed.

Having appointed Frank Pinder – solid, multi-lingual, and no good at dancing – to hold the Prieuré, Gurdjieff boldly embarked. The s.s. *Paris* sailed for New York in the first week of January and ran into unprecedented storms – which cracked the great mirror in the stateroom, reduced the wretched passengers to a diet of watered orange juice, and rather foreshadowed Gurdjieff's traumas in 1924. With his grand duchess' brooch, his entourage of thirty-six, his stupendous idea, and his minimalist Nansen passport, Gurdjieff was at sea. From the instant in Bordeaux when the coloured ship-to-shore streamers had snapped, his very right to re-enter France was in jeopardy, and his professed intention in these circumstances was 'to eat well, sleep a great deal and read only books whose contents and style were in keeping with the spirit and character of the stories of Mullah Nassr Eddin.'

But the role of lotus-eater did not suit Gurdjieff, and on 12 January 1924 he arranged a shipboard performance of the entire Elysées programme, as an entertainment for the passengers and a benefit for the crew. Thomas de Hartmann recalls how the unique nautical 'Stop!' was achieved 'in spite of the ship's rolling, which was so extreme at one point that the piano slowly, but steadily, slid from one side of the stage to the other, myself following it on my chair.'

The next morning, on sighting the Statue of Liberty, Gurdjieff (so legend goes) threw his passport overboard. Photographs confirm that he came down the gangplank like an emperor who scorns papers, raising his black Astrakhan hat in ironic salute to America and its peaches-and-cream inhabitants; 'these "dollar-foxtrotting" followers of what is called "Christian Science"'. Somehow Orage and his New York coterie talked their unconventional VIP through immigration, and, amid scenes of some excitement and confusion, installed him in a palatial suite in the Ansonia, a big, down-at-heel Edwardian hotel at 73rd Street and Broadway – famous for its baroque Turkish baths.

The America in which Gurdjieff had landed was the America of Calvin Coolidge, Henry Ford, and Alphonse Capone; of 'Fonofilm' talking pictures and Gershwin's *Rhapsody in Blue*; of jazz, of Prohibition, of electrification, of psycho-analysis, and of Gurdjieff's bête noire the foxtrot; a forgotten America where a peculiar innocence sat almost obliviously on the knee of a peculiar corruption. The 'obvious absurdities' which Gurdjieff found so piquant, evidently shocked the conservative Dr Stjoernval into relative inutility. Orage by contrast had thoroughly relished his John the Baptist role, enabling Gurdjieff now to fulfil an almost messianic expectation flitting through the studios and literary covens of Chelsea and Greenwich Village: 'Gurdjieff is coming! He is the master Ouspensky found. Gurdjieff is solid.'

At the Sunwise Turn bookshop near the Yale Club on 44th Street –

'a clearing house for ideas, a meeting place for free spirits' – Gurdjieff was soon giving out copies of his singular prospectus and cordial invitations to dine with him in the Ansonia. Among his guests that night following disembarkation were the dancer Rosetta O'Neil, the writer William Seabrook, and the authoress and architectural critic for the *New Yorker* Muriel Draper ('my first American friend'). Under a deep impression of their host's power, they talked and drank till dawn, by which time Muriel had put at Gurdjieff's disposal her 'peeled gold-leaf and threadbare needle-point salon' in the Murray Hill section of Manhattan; Rosetta had lent him her dance studio in Upper Madison Avenue; and Seabrook had guardedly concluded 'Gurdjieff was not umpiring parlour games. Gurdjieff was turning on the heat.'

A superb venue was providentially available for the inaugural American demonstration on Wednesday 23 January (through de Hartmann's connection with the touring Moscow Arts Theatre). Unaccountably Gurdjieff finessed this trump, preferring Lesley Hall a nondescript affair at 260 West 83rd Street, near the brownstone house accommodating his pupils. The piano was heaved upstairs; de Hartmann's instrumental accompanists were, to his chagrin, reduced to five (violin, cello, double-bass, clarinet and percussion); all tickets were distributed free; and the curtain was set to rise at 8pm. It did not rise. The audience – which included Seabrook, Christopher Morley, Walter Damrosch (composer of the opera *Cyrano de Bergerac*), assorted university professors, reporters and editors from the *New York Times*, *Colliers*, and *Bookman* – waited with an increasingly strained air of indifference. Eventually Charles Stanley Nott, a young English assistant at the Sunwise Turn, ventured backstage to investigate:

> I found Orage behind the scenes swinging a little girl by her hands and talking to ... her parents. When they moved away he told me that the man was a policeman in civilian dress, sent to ensure that no 'erotic' dances were shewn.

Gurdjieff – immaculate in dinner dress and matching aura of Egyptian cigarette smoke – watched sardonically. At 9pm Orage came stage-front and delivered an eloquent preamble (over which the attentive ear could just catch Gurdjieff's prompt, 'Remember yourself, you idiot!'); then de Hartmann, 'a monk in a tuxedo', calmly took his place at the piano. The curtain rose, and for a long telling moment the audience found itself confronted by the ranks of Gurdjieff's silent, gathered, motionless dancers.

A full four-hour programme ensued: Asiatic folk dances and work rhythms; the six 'Obligatories'; 'The Sacred Goose', 'The Waltz', 'The Lost Loves'; the 'Big Seven'; the 'Camel Dervish', 'Trembling Dervish', and 'Ho Yah!' dervish; the 'Pythia', the 'Big Prayer', the 'Initiation of the Priestess' ... A sense of witnessing something impossible – less from Asia than from another planet – pervaded the audience. Some rightly intuited that the exterior 'classicism' of the dances masked a rich inner content; but cruder souls – cheated in their expectation of an Isadora-Duncan-style expressionism – reached for the idiom of Ripley's *Believe it or Not!*. Here is Seabrook:

> What excited and interested me was the amazing, brilliant, automaton-like, inhuman, almost incredible ... obedience of the disciples ... like the soldiers of Christophe who marched without breaking step off the parapet of the citadel on that sheer mountainside in Haiti.

The 'Stop!' exercise in particular was construed in Barnum and Bailey terms. Seabrook again:

> I saw Gurdjieff push a dancer who had been frozen by his command in an attitude of difficult equilibrium. The dancer tumbled and rolled over several times, then rolled upright and was back again, apparently without volitionally *assuming* it, in the original frozen position.

The argument is increasingly persuasive that Gurdjieff's 'time-span-of discretion' was vast; that he did not plan days ahead, but decades perhaps even centuries ahead. If he cast his pearls before swine in Paris and New York in the early 1920s, he did so with calculation. He suffered nevertheless – surely he suffered – from the irrelevance, vulgarity, and ignobility of reaction in certain quarters. The 'Left' (routinely preferring the Commissar to the Yogi) was vaguely hostile, but those 'slobbering boy reporters' of the gutter press were outrageous. The *American Weekly*, under the banner headline, "DR" GURDJIEFF AND HIS MAGICAL SECRET OF LIFE – HOW TO BE A SUPER-MAN OR SUPER-WOMAN BY FEEDING PIGS, DANCING WEIRD DANCES ALL NIGHT AND OTHER FANTASTIC ANTICS, gave a spurious account of Gurdjieff's ecstatic nights at the Prieuré: ' "Dance!" he cries from behind the curtain. "Dance as your souls dictate! Dance-dance-dance to freedom!" ' Weak-minded and credulous readers compounded the tale with rumour. 'I understand,' said someone to Stanley Nott, 'that Mr Gurdjieff lives in the Forest of Fontainebleau with Katherine Mansfield and that they call themselves "The Forest Lovers".'

One week later, on 2 February 1924, Gurdjieff answered his critics
with surely the most productive performance he ever gave. Among
New York's intelligentsia, the little Neighborhood Playhouse on
Grand Street in Greenwich Village had a special reputation for
'progressive' drama and for a musical repertoire which ranged
from Prokofiev to Hindu *ragas*. It enjoyed the patronage of the
influential and narcissistic literary coterie dominated by Waldo
Frank; of the writers, publicists, and self-publicists constellated
about Herbert Crowly and the *New Republic* magazine; and of the
significantly lesbian entourage of the ultra avant garde *Little Review*
edited by Margaret Anderson and Jane Heap ... And Gurdjieff –
that uncompromising advocate and agent of tradition – took it by
storm.

Admission that Saturday evening was by prior invitation, but
Gurdjieff himself stood in the cold outside the theatre dispensing
supplementary tickets on impulse. The poet Hart Crane, 'jobless and
dependant, alcoholic and homosexual', was admitted drunk;
Georgette Leblanc, ex-consort of Maeterlinck, took her seat wearing
a gold wig. Toomer, Heap, and Munson (though time would prove
them the real fruits of that evening at the Neighborhood Playhouse),
were, at first sight, an ill-assorted and improbable trio for Gurdjieff
to recruit.

Jean Toomer[20] – tall, magnetic, swartly handsome – was a social
conundrum: the grandson of a former governor of Louisiana, he
nevertheless vociferously claimed to speak for the world's dispossessed;
though his blood-lines were in fact marvellously entangled (Jewish,
Welsh, Indian, Dutch, German, and French), his best-seller *Cane* had
paradoxically canonized him as the *avatar* of a negro literary renaissance. Jane Heap had surmounted appalling problems. Of relatively
straightforward English and Lapp extraction, she had grown up in
the claustrophobic and hallucinatory atmosphere of a lunatic asylum
(where her father was warden); as a turbulent adolescent, she had
discovered she was a 'full-blown Lesbian case'; and as a relatively
young woman had contracted an intransigent form of diabetes.
Three Februaries before she had stood (with Margaret Anderson) in
the criminal dock, convicted for serializing Joyce's *Ulysses* in the
Little Review – and from all this she had emerged with monumental
force.

Gorham Munson was a critic.

The performance apart, Gurdjieff's personal body-language on
stage spoke convincingly to Toomer:

I saw this man in motion, a unit in motion. He was completely one piece. From the crown of his head down the back of his head, down the neck, down the back and down the legs there was a remarkable line. Shall I call it a gathered line? It suggested co-ordination, integration, knitness, power ...

Munson was galvanized by the dancing – 'sleepless for hours afterwards, such was its awakening effect'; Jane Heap was completely won over, and invited Gurdjieff to lecture at her studio-apartment at 24 East 11th Street; and Toomer was so affected that he began to speak with a Russian accent. All three would bear witness, in different degrees, to the underlying sincerity of their conversion.

This one evening's impact on 'thinking' New York was remarkable: 'All that spring and into the summer months the question of Gurdjieff – a new Pythagoras or a charlatan – was the most controversial topic at intelligentsia gatherings.' No softening in Gurdjieff's demeanour suggests that he cared tuppence either way. In sixteen lectures (delivered between 13 February and 16 March) he ranged confidently over such themes as art, the actor, essence and personality, God the Word, the education of children, and means for prolonging life. Confronting some of the crème de la crème of New York café society – people like Theodore Dreiser, Llewellyn Powis, Margaret Anderson, Rebecca West, Carl Zigrosser, John O'Hara Cosgrave, Waldo Frank, Margaret Naumburg, Zona Gale, Gloria Swanson – his timekeeping and platform manner became, if anything, more provocative:

> The meeting was timed for nine, but it was almost ten before we saw Gurdjieff. He came in from another room, wearing a grey suit and an old pair of carpet slippers and holding a large baked potato. Everybody became frigidly silent.

Nor was there anything emollient in the way he handled his distinguished clientele: 'You have nervous restless movements,' he explained to one inquirer, 'which make people think you are a booby ...'

In the vivid, auspicious month which followed success at the Neighborhood Playhouse, Gurdjieff prowled happily round New York. He cultivated a good Jewish butcher; he gave away his wallet to an astonished journalist; he mystified various jewellers; he aided the recovery of Muriel Draper's son Paul (felled by a bus); he established his now traditional 'café-office' at Childs on the corner of Fifth Avenue and 56th Street. Here, thanks to an amiable social gangsterism, his ritual of the toasts could proceed unembarrassed by Prohibition:

> In these New York restaurants, various alcoholic liquids called 'Arrack', 'Doosico', 'Scotch whisky', 'Benedictine', 'Vodka', 'Grand Marnier' . . . made exclusively only on what are called 'old barges' lying at sea off the shores of that continent, are to be had in any quantity you please . . . if you point your fourth finger and, covering one half of your mouth with your right palm, utter the name . . . that liquid is served at table – only in a bottle purporting to be lemonade or the famous 'French Vichy'.

The man who had ostensibly come to America to rest scarcely seems to have slept, assigning his evenings to rehearsals and lectures, and his nights to intimate talks; his caravan's hazy itinerary (involving shows at the Lenox Theater, the Knickerbocker Theater, Webster Hall, the Astor Hotel, and St Mark's-in-the-Bowery) ultimately regains sharp definition at the city's cultural Mecca.

Gurdjieff's final New York performance at Carnegie Hall on Monday 3 March was the first, last, and only occasion when he charged for tickets. Grandiose plans for four pianos and full orchestral backing ran into last-minute trouble with the Musicians' Union, leaving Thomas de Hartmann, as so often, to cope alone. Thanks to Zona Gale's strenuous PR work, the famous auditorium was packed; just the expensive front-row seats stood empty – until Gurdjieff beckoned forward delighted people from the back. His own debatable transfer from the Sarmoung Monastery to Carnegie Hall had been self-propelled – but had it not entailed (as Olga, peeping out from the curtains at a pretty mixed audience, ventured to suggest) a mistaken preference for quantity over quality? Gurdjieff sharply demurred:

> How can you judge? Perhaps those who seem asleep today, in twenty years something will be awakened in them, and those who now seem so eager will forget in ten days. We have to let everyone hear, and the result does not belong to us.

Although Gurdjieff had landed in America essentially looking for pupils, he also needed money, and positively trumpeted his 'avarice':

> I have ventured to come to this 'dollar-growing country' and here, breathing this air saturated with the vibrations of people who sow and reap dollars in a masterly fashion, I, like a thorough-bred hunting-dog, am on the scent of certain and good game.

His free demonstrations and private informal lectures had hardly made him a cent, and with forty-six dependants and New York so expensive, his funds steadily evaporated. He sold the grand duchess' brooch very shrewdly but again the proceeds evaporated. In mid-March 1924 Gurdjieff regretfully asked his people to fend for themselves, and Thomas de Hartmann went off to an employment agency: 'I offered myself as a musician; but only cooks were in really great demand.' In this grim hour unexpected help came from Illinois.

Adolph Bolm, an eminent ballet-master who had danced for Diaghilev in *Firebird* and *Carnival*, unexpectedly wrote to offer Gurdjieff the hospitality of his studio in Chicago. Accepting with warm appreciation, Gurdjieff entrained his company for Philadelphia and Boston. ('The ways are different, but all must get to "Philadelphia" – this is the basic aim of all religions.') On to Boston, where a performance in Judson Hall – attended by Harvard faculty members and students – went tolerably well, yet the academic big fish escaped Orage's net ('Coomaraswamy was fast asleep in his work, and had no attention for other worlds than the long dead.')

Buying the cheapest possible ticket to Chicago from an agent in Hoboken, Gurdjieff now pressed on ahead of the company. On 25 March he met Bolm, evidently with some prevailing sense of the ridiculous: 'This Chicago Mister turned out to be very amiable and obliging. His name was "Mister Bellybutton".' A 'petting party' misconceivedly arranged by Bolm in Gurdjieff's honour misfired completely:

> In the midst of the conversation, the American as they say 'young lady' suddenly, for no earthly reason at all, began stroking my neck. I immediately thought, How kind of her! She must certainly have noticed a 'flea' on my neck and is now stroking the place to allay the irritation.

The following evening found Gurdjieff in more refined surroundings at the French Consulate, where he warned the diplomats against the dangers of unsupervised *pranayama*:

> All Europe has gone mad about breathing exercises. For four or five years I have made money by treating people who had ruined their breathing by such methods! Many books are written about it . . . I am very grateful to the authors. . .

Gurdjieff's star dancers – Julia, Olgivanna, Elizabeta and Jeanne – finally turned up in Chicago only a hair-raising two hours before a preview specially commissioned by the Consul. The unwanted applause was echoed and amplified next evening at a larger, more prestigious Chicago venue . . . the clapping swelled, then faded, and was subsumed in history's grand silence. The 'Teacher of Dancing' never gave another public performance.

Gurdjieff had come and seen and conquered. He returned to a New York constituency where Muriel Draper, Gorham Munson and Elizabeth Delza, Jane Heap and Margaret Anderson, Zona Gale (to say nothing of Orage) were eager and active agents on his behalf. On Tuesday 8 April he founded the New York branch of his Institute for the Harmonious Development of Man; he was fêted at a Russian restaurant and spent the night conversing with pupils at an apartment on 49th Street. Answering a seemingly indiscreet question about his budget, he told with astonishing verve and candour the story of his life — all its rich exigencies subordinated to his search for consciousness. Dawn, grey in the East, dimly lit a wreck of coffee cups and liqueur glasses. 'Mr. Gurdjieff remained silent a long time, as though immersed in heavy thoughts. Suddenly he looked tired. His eyes rested for a moment on each one of us.'

The general company from the Prieuré, including Dr Stjoernval and Julia Ostrowska, returned to France aboard the s.s. *Washington*, but Gurdjieff lingered on in New York like some huge erratic boulder stuck on an alien shore. Avoiding many patrons and well-wishers, he lived reclusively in two small rooms, existing 'on beans mixed with thumbtacks'. Only in June 1924, when Orage's lectures and Mme Galumnian's Movements classes had furnished the wherewithal; only when he had redeemed a ring tearfully pawned by Olga de Hartmann; only when he had cast about for a New York 'ambassador', and Orage 'with great excitement began to affirm his ableness to do it brilliantly'; only when Bechhofer-Roberts had published his evocation of the Prieuré in *Century* magazine — only then did Gurdjieff embark, first class, for Cherbourg. A big clutch of new American pupils sailed with him; no fewer than eighty had applied to work at Fontainebleau that summer. Throughout the voyage Gurdjieff contrived many intimate exchanges: 'We always returned from a meeting with him jubilant and hopeful. It was a very special time.'

In Paris Major Pinder met Gurdjieff with news that was, none of it, particularly good. A gaggle of undesirable voyeurs had visited the Prieuré, including D. H. Lawrence (who thought it a 'rotten, false, self-conscious place of people playing a sickly stunt'), and Aleister Crowley, the Beast 666 (who supposed Gurdjieff was 'a tip-top man . . . a very advanced adept'). Piotr Ouspensky intended an imminent visit to glean Americana directly from Gurdjieff's lips. The snag here, as Pinder diffidently pointed out, was that back in January with Gurdjieff safely quarantined on the high seas, Ouspensky had formally broken off relations and forbidden those English pupils he could influence (Maurice Nicoll and J. G. Bennett) ever again to communicate with Gurdjieff or even to mention his name! Two subsidiary matters: the lease on the Paris flat at 9 Commandant-Marchand would fall in (virtually tomorrow) at the end of June . . . and he, Frank Pinder, would be grateful for a very long break.

With all these pressures, it seemed inconceivable that Gurdjieff should find the time or the charity to receive Ouspensky, but he evidently did: 'We were curious about Ouspensky. He sat on Gurdjieff's left and acted like a small boy, laughing more than he meant to, saying what he meant not to, flushing with the armagnac forced on him.'

In Fontainebleau and Paris Gurdjieff quickly picked up the rhythm of his life. Again he composed, again he choreographed, again – shaded by fringed parasols and green leaves – he sat on the terrace of the Grand Hôtel-Café de la Paix, watching (from his strange transhistorical viewpoint) the world go by:

> That tall man pretending to be an important gentleman, sitting alone in the corner, making eyes at a lady who sits with her husband . . . is he not a real 'Veroonk'? And these waiters, exactly like dogs with their tails between their legs . . . are they not Asklay-slaves? . . . And again it is the same . . . shoutings, uproar, laughter, scoldings . . . the same as in the city Babylon, or as in the city Koorkalai, or even in Samlios, their first centre-of-culture.

Was Gurdjieff at peace? Or dubious finally that an esoteric work, nourished in immaculate silence, had been publicly staged – precipitated in this very domain of shoutings, uproar, laughter and scoldings? He sipped his Armagnac. Perhaps from a seed necessarily sown in malodorous ground would rise up a tree of wisdom which in a hundred or two hundred years would give a green refreshing shade. Time would tell. Meanwhile, at the junction of the Paris–Fontainebleau highway with the N168 road from Versailles to Choisy-le-Roi, Gurdjieff had a rendezvous to keep – with Nemesis.

10

❖

DEATH AND THE AUTHOR

(8 July 1924–23 April 1928)

The 'punctuation' of a life such as Gurdjieff's strongly affects the rhythm of contingent existences. By 1924 the drastic exclamation marks of former years (virulent diseases, bullets 'plunked' into him) had softened into commas of relatively modest incident. But at 4.30 pm in the torrid heat of Tuesday 8 July, an event occurred which looked to be – and practically was – Gurdjieff's culminating full stop. From the blow he took, a hundred lives suffered a collateral insult; and he himself had painfully to remould his strategy of evangelism. In the spectacular ruin of large and legitimate hopes his work ended . . . and his work began.

The accident report is basically straightforward: the heavy Citroën, going at 90 kilometres an hour, hurtled with a 'charge-and-crash' into a thick tree; the axle was buckled, steering-column snapped, radiator crushed, and engine shorn from its seating. Mr Gurdjieff, the car's only occupant, was thrown providentially clear and lay unconscious on the bloodstained grass, his body 'so battered and everything in it so mixed up' that for months it looked like a fragment of a general picture which might be described as 'a bit of live meat in a clean bed.'

There is ample room for prosaic explanation: Gurdjieff was over-tired; his driving was appalling; he had enjoyed a big Armenian dinner at the restaurant Chez Simonian; and the sun was hot. So far, so rational. It is only when we backtrack and place that particular Tuesday under the microscope that little animancules of an exotic doubt swim into view. Why – precisely then – had Gurdjieff given his secretary Olga de Hartmann power of attorney? Why had he unprecedentedly insisted she return to Fontainebleau by train? Why did he have his mechanic triple-check the car – nuts, bolts, lights, and especially the steering? Why. . .?

Some 'memory' of events to come, some secret intimacy with the myth, might offer – to certain temperaments – an explanation for Gurdjieff's actions. Unfortunately for this notion, his very precautions are part of the myth sequence – tending directly towards the tree, not away from it. Did he then crash accidentally-on-purpose? This unexpected hypothesis, believe it or not, enjoys a modicum of support. Well . . . Gurdjieff was indeed a ruthless enemy of habit: 'If today is like yesterday, tomorrow will be like today.' Yet it takes a bit of swallowing that a man of his resource needed to purchase his brave new tomorrow at the cost of so agonizing and hazardous a today. Was Gurdjieff then the victim of malignant and retributive forces? Either mundane sabotage by some spiteful nonentity, or mysterious intervention by theosophy's 'dark brethren'? (The more Ouspensky thought about it, the more the latter seemed the likeliest explanation: 'I'm frightened . . . this is dreadful . . . Georgeivanitch's Institute was established to escape from . . . the law of accident . . . Has he not gone too far? – I tell you, I'm terribly afraid.') In the end none of these rhetorical questions proves answerable – except tautologically in the haunting mood of *Glimpses of Truth*:

> Strange events, incomprehensible from the ordinary point of view, have guided my life. I mean those events which influence a man's inner life, radically changing its direction and aim and creating new epochs in it.

Discovered on the off-chance by a bicycling gendarme, Gurdjieff was urgently whisked away in an ambulance to Fontainebleau hospital where the duty surgeon Dr Martry could not grasp how he had not been killed outright. Shock, multiple body lacerations, and loss of blood were the least of his problems: what rendered his condition critical – very possibly terminal – were severe head injuries and major concussion. The pulseless, asthmatic, almost mummified figure of the bandaged Gurdjieff roused Olga de Hartmann to a paroxysm of emotion:

> I really felt as if, without him, the forces of life would stop, and that if he died, all that lives would die. I felt that his whole life's work would be undone. Such fright overcame me at this idea that, at the same time, another feeling rose up and I told myself, 'If God exists, it cannot happen. If God exists, Mr Gurdjieff lives, so he will not die.'

On Wednesday 9 July, Gurdjieff was released into the care of his two personal physicians Dr Alexinsky and Dr Sirotine, and brought home to the Prieuré. As he was tenderly carried upstairs to his room on a stretcher, he was heard to murmur faintly, 'Many people, many people.' Dr Stjoernval felt obliged to warn the family that the chances of recovery were marginal: Georgeivanitch was sinking.

But Georgeivanitch did not sink. For five days and nights he hung in the twilight between two worlds. His wife Mme Ostrowska (evidently herself in the early stages of cancer), and his sister Sophie Ivanovna nursed him devotedly. His lips were moistened with a damp cloth, and oxygen was repeatedly administered. Dr Martry prescribed morphia but this Gurdjieff wordlessly refused. From the whole Institute there arose a silent, desperate petition for his life: 'every night, two or three of the Russians were on their knees in front of Gurdjieff's door.'

Mme de Hartmann bravely assumed charge of the Prieuré – but a Prieuré chastened beyond recognition:

> There was silence . . . we spoke with lowered voices; the bell in the belfry no longer rang, there were no dances or music in the Study House, and everyone wished with his whole being for Gurdjieff's recovery . . . it was as if the mainspring of a great machine had broken and the machine was running on its momentum. The force that moved our lives was gone.

At the end of the sixth day, Gurdjieff opened his eyes and asked Mme Ostrowska, 'Where am I?' Amnesic, virtually blind, and in acute pain, Gurdjieff was registering that hard shock when 'to my misfortune, into my totally mutilated body there returned in full force, with all its former attributes, my consciousness'.

With Gurdjieff's enforced inactivity, the Institute's financial situation quickly grew desperate. Ouspensky – established in upholstered comfort in London – held aloof, but Gurdjieff's tiny nucleus surrendered everything, including any vestiges of false pride: Alexandre Salzmann, the associate of Kandinsky, tackled murals in Montmartre cafés; Thomas de Hartmann, musical protégé of Tsar Nicholas II, turned out film scores under the pseudonym 'Thomas Kross'; and Olga Iovnovna Lazovitch Milanoff, daughter of the chief justice of Montenegro, became an attendant in a women's lavatory.

Many decent people visited Gurdjieff in his room on the Ritz corridor, but their well-meant solicitude left him feeling that they 'came, sucked me out like vampires, and went away.' Defying doctors' orders, he soon made tremendous efforts to get up. By August he could be seen hobbling painfully in the garden, propped up by Julia Ostrowska and Olga de Hartmann – a piebald, almost dehumanized figure, with the familiar black Astrakhan hat perched on his completely bandaged head. Soon he was managing alone (though squired by Fritz Peters the eleven-year-old nephew of Margaret Anderson, who carried his chair and prevented him from falling into ditches). He wore dark spectacles now, equally to conceal his purple bruises and to filter the caustic light.

An unaccountable appetite for burning and smoke overtook him. 'He asked in a very serious tone to give him one cigarette after another, saying that he *needed* them.' At his further insistence, giant trees were felled and bonfires built: 'This continued until it looked as if we should have to cut down half the forest to keep the fires going.' Silent, swaddled in a black coat, he would gaze for hours into the urgent, spurting logs and the blue smoke rising. What did he see? The transition of energy states? The shining tents of nomads? Or the obstinate hope of consciousness which – nested in flame – rises again and again from its own ashes?... Very gradually, Gurdjieff's sight and strength and memory returned to him.

The pupils had barely recovered from the earthquake of Gurdjieff's accident when, on Tuesday 26 August, they were hit by the secondary tremor of his changed disposition:

> I was very ill. Now, thank God, I feel better ... In principle, I had to die, but accidentally I stayed alive ... I will liquidate this house ... the Institute is closed. I died ... inside of me, everything is empty ... I wish to live for myself. I don't wish to continue as before, and my new principle is – everything for myself. From today the Institute will be nothing.

The Institute will be nothing! Was it possible? – Dr Stjoernval, the de Hartmanns, and the Salzmanns – after so long service – expelled from the magic circle? The poorer dependent Russians thrust onto their own economic resources? Miss Ethel Merston obliged to tout her fidelity elsewhere? And the present influx from America – Jean Toomer, Margaret Anderson, Carol Robinson, Jessie Dwight, Stanley Nott – sent packing in the very moment of their hopeful new adherence? Was this the end of the affair? Would Gurdjieff never transmit the essence of his teaching?... A profound, almost indescribable, gloom settled on the Prieuré.

Perhaps if the pupils had been able to remember 'The Initiation of the Priestess' the old dispensation might have continued. but unhappily:

> none of the movements and steps had been noted down, since Gurdjieff carried everything in his head; and when we tried to reproduce the

Initiation ... we found, to our dismay, that we could not do it. We could remember our own parts, but no one could recall the sequence.

The Teacher of Dancing had given the world a work of objective art ... and the world had mislaid it. A terrible extrapolation followed. What if, without him, his entire teaching likewise evaporated? What if (worse still!) his œuvre were corrupted, as copyists set up their 'Schachermacher-workshop-booths' and 'began manufacturing out of various unfortunate naive people, "candidates for lunatic asylums"'? Gurdjieff was now fifty-eight and reminders of mortality pressed all about him: liver disease would soon claim his mother; Julia his wife was cruelly ill; and he himself had escaped violent death by a fingernail's margin of grace. Slowly – mirrored in the shifting patterns of the great pine-wood fires – the collapse of Gurdjieff's former hopes settled into a new resolve:

> Since I had not, when in full strength and health, succeeded in introducing in practice into the life of people and beneficial truths elucidated for them by me, then I must at least, at any cost, succeed in doing so in theory, before my death.

At any cost – but how?

The diaspora of Gurdjieff's 'parasites' in early September 1924 was pretty elastic. At the outset everyone disengaged except his family and those nursing him. Within days however, most of his Russian Old Guard had tiptoed back; then came a handful of English, Miss Merston, Miss Gordon, Miss Alexander, and Bernard Metz; then eight Americans – in all about a third ignored the dismissal and reconvened. Just two of his nucleus left permanently: Olgivanna ostensibly for New York and Mme Ouspensky ostensibly for London. Both ladies scrambled their itineraries: Olgivanna went to Chicago (where on 30 November, she captured the heart of Frank Lloyd Wright and entered a completely new life); Sophie Ouspensky – refusing point blank to place the Channel between herself and Gurdjieff – settled in Asnières.

From all standpoints, the argument for selling the Institute's reserve Citroën seemed overwhelmingly persuasive – but Gurdjieff insisted on driving again. His first attempts were sensibly frustrated by Olga de Hartmann, who surreptitiously cut the accelerator wire with a pair of scissors. Before too long however Gurdjieff's whim prevailed and the tradition of his singular excursions through France and Switzerland began. Incorrigibly he 'drove his car as if possessed' and particularly enjoyed mountain roads; Alexandre Salzmann –

sighting a village cemetery half a mile below – remarked on its convenience; without exception everyone agreed that 'travelling with Gurdjieff was not an ordinary experience.'

Among Gurdjieff's white-knuckled passengers, history can just identify the hunched figure of Alfred Richard Orage – who re-crossed the Atlantic in October for a brief conference. The pre-crash Gurdjieff had built enormous hopes on the USA – planning to be back in New York in the winter of 1924; the post-crash Gurdjieff could not entertain the notion. Thus it transpired that Orage came to France with a pocketful of newspaper clippings and left with a de facto mandate to supervise the Work throughout America. But why Orage for this stupendous task? He had been with Gurdjieff a mere two years, and his well-rehearsed familiarity with the Sacred Dances was entirely verbal; even his indisputable strengths – rapport with the intelligentsia, command of literary sources, fluent rhetoric, and delight in the manipulation of ideas – situated him nearer the Work's public face than its heart.

Perhaps it counted most that Orage was ensconced in New York – well liked (as Gurdjieff put it tartly) 'on account of his smart appearance which, as might be easily understood, has great importance in all business relations especially among ... Americans.' Perhaps a loyal, presentable, and eloquent proconsul was all Gurdjieff required *pro tem*; perhaps the mandate given Orage was less than explicit. (Ouspensky's had been marvellously inexplicit – mere recognition of a teaching role already commandeered.) One thing alone is certain: Orage's appointment was a piece in a much bigger jigsaw. In late 1924 an impulse of wholesale delegation – verging on the capricious – saw Gurdjieff's business in antiques, carpets, cloisonné, and Chinese porcelain confided to a 'secret partner', and the raffia-entwined figure of Miss Ethel Merston appointed 'director' of the Prieuré. On all sides Gurdjieff was disengaging; retracting his wounded energies; drawing back, the better to spring forward ... but in what direction?

'Could you write what I will dictate to you? Are you sleepy?' With these straightforward questions to Olga de Hartmann, Gurdjieff set out on his last great journey to 'inaccessible places'; only his practised recourse to the 'big accumulator' of energy promised him even a slender chance of safe arrival. At fifty-eight, shaken in health and thronged about by material problems, he had taken a decision: 'I, who have lately been considered by very many people as a rather good teacher of temple dances, have now become today a professional

writer.' His eyes were now focused on the Himalayan peak of a work
of objective art: a 'legonomism' which would transmit to generations yet unborn real information of an initiatic order.

The wastepaper basket received his regrettable apprentice pieces:
'The Cocainists', 'The Three Brothers', 'The Unconscious Murder'
and 'The Chiromancy of the Stock Exchange'. But if Gurdjieff could
fail, he could also persevere – late in the night of Tuesday 16
December 1924, in his flat at 47 Boulevard Péreire, he set off again
on a new tack:

> It was in the year 223 after the creation of the World, by objective
> time-calculation, or, as it would be said here on the 'Earth', in the year
> 1921 after the birth of Christ.
>   Through the Universe flew the ship *Karnak* of the 'trans-space' com-
> munication ... On the said 'trans-space' ship was Beelzebub with his
> kinsmen and near attendants.

So was born Gurdjieff's celebrated work *Beelzebub's Tales to His
Grandson*. Well might he register in that moment 'the-fear-of-
drowning-in-the-overflow-of-my-own-thoughts'; through the point
of his stumpy pencil must flow into the future all the gleanings of the
Seekers of Truth and all his own profoundest insights.

Gurdjieff wrote stoically through seven plagues of distraction;
through the inane chatter of the Café de la Paix and Fontainebleau's
Café Henri IV, and the self-contrived turmoil of roadside breakdowns:

> These delays were a great annoyance to everyone except Mr Gurdjieff
> who ... would settle himself comfortably at the side of the road ... and
> write furiously in his notebooks, muttering to himself and licking the
> point of one of his many pencils.

Fuelled by strong black coffee, Khaizarian *bastourma*, and Château
de Larresingle Armagnac, Gurdjieff's new occupation quickly assumed
'the character of a "not-to-be-trifled-with-enthusiasm".' From the
beginning his Space-Odyssey format served him well – imparting an
'extra-terrestrial' dimension to his social and historical critique,
and dramatizing his key analogy between the outer space of the
starry world and the inner space of man's psyche. His eponymous
'Beelzebub' was superbly achieved – an original and heroic archetype
whose presence indicates Man as he might be; aware with gratitude
of the divine spark within him, and striving by conscious labours and
intentional suffering towards his fulfilment of his true place in the
cosmic scheme ... There was only one snag: the first instalment (sent

to Orage in translation for critical evaluation) was returned in March 1925 as completely unintelligible.

Beelzebub is an undoubted masterpiece: yet for barbarous syntax, dislocated sequences, parabolic digressions, tautological indulgence, onomatopoeic conceits, improbable laminates, and sheer ear-grinding advocacy – it has scarcely its fellow in modern literature. Evidently, as the reified precursor of a 'New World', Gurdjieff's first book signals a complete and imperative rupture with all prior canons – certainly with what he scathingly terms 'the *bon ton* literary language'. But what a gambler! Here was a strategy which simply leap-frogged the jejune problem of publication, and took the success of an impenetrable book by an unknown writer buoyantly for granted.

Perhaps it means something that Gurdjieff wrote his first drafts in Armenian, his mother-tongue. Composing in the Prieuré gardens he would watch impotently while 'in the company of two peacocks, a cat and a dog, there slowly strolled down the path my unforgettable old mother.' She was dying. Her husband and most of her grandchildren had been massacred, and her eldest son critically hurt in a car accident; now her own long life of bleak material privation was ending painfully in exile. To observe her unfailing noonday rendezvous with Julia Ostrowska (in whom the symptoms of cancer grew more pronounced) was a torment to Gurdjieff. Had he been a 'good son'? He had done what he could within the framework of his 'peculiarly composed life', but his overriding sense of mission had radically interfered: his *Wanderjahre* had occupied twenty-five years; duty had compelled him to leave his mother in Essentuki in August 1919, and to sail for America once she reached France. Only in part could he share his filial dismay with his sister Sophie Ivanovna and his brother Dmitri (newly arrived with his wife Astra Grigorievna). Gurdjieff of the Prieuré garden in 1925 is an intensely lonely figure, aware he must drain a bitter cup.

Mme Giorgiades expired at the end of June 1925. Although she had lived and died with stoic reticence, her's was not a hearse destined to be drawn by felt-shod horses. On the contrary, Gurdjieff arranged in the Study House a spectacular ceremony, which took place at the height of a summer thunderstorm. He had the great tombstone cryptically – and splendidly – inscribed:

> Ici Repose
> La Mère de Celui
> Qui se Vit par

Cette Mort Forcé
D'Ecrire Le Livre
Intitulé
Les Opiumistes

Born in utter obscurity, the poor old woman had some very distinguished mourners at her graveside – most notably Eric Graham
Forbes Adam CMG, the epitome of youth and success. (Mr Adam
departed the Prieuré to take up a diplomatic posting in Constantinople
– where on 7 July 1925, to everyone's surprise and mystification, he
shot himself.)

On 29 July, Gurdjieff entered an intensive period of musical composition with Thomas de Hartmann. Since he certainly had neither
time nor energy to wheel and deal commercially, responsibility for
the Institute's budget increasingly devolved on the Russian nucleus
and enthusiastic New Yorkers. In mobilizing and canalizing the
generosity of Gurdjieff's 'dear, for the time being, unconditionally
respected dollar-holders!', Orage was resource and delicacy personified (time and again a cheque for 1000 dollars would reach the
Prieuré), yet over the sunny landscape of his loyalty had appeared a
shadow no bigger than a woman's hand. It belonged to the high-born
co-proprietor of the Sunwise Turn bookshop, Miss Jessie Richards
Dwight. 'Tall, fair-haired and hardly half [Orage's] age, the strong-
minded scion of generations of Connecticut clergymen and scholars,
she fell in love with him at first sight.'

Although the editor had basked in *Schwärmerei* all his life
('women in his presence were liable to develop what Marchbanks in
Candida calls "Prossy's complaint"'), he himself was now smitten.
Gurdjieff from the outset frowned on the tempestuous liaison as
discrepant and diversionary; Orage was his 'super-idiot', while Jessie
on the contrary – 'a young American pampered out of all proportion
to her position' – fell in the 'squirming idiot' category.

Fritz Peters (whom Gurdjieff had adopted as a sort of juvenile Man
Friday) was momentarily witness to a celebrated row when Orage
and Jessie descended on the Prieuré that summer:

Gurdjieff was standing by his bed in a state of what seemed to me to be
completely uncontrolled fury. He was raging at Orage, who stood impas-
sively, and very pale, framed in one of the windows. I had to walk
between them to set the tray on the table. I did so feeling flayed by the
fury of Gurdjieff's voice ... Orage, a tall man, seemed withered and
crumpled as he sagged in the window, and Gurdjieff, actually not very

tall, looked immense – a complete embodiment of rage … Suddenly, in the space of an instant, Gurdjieff's voice stopped, his whole personality changed, he gave me a broad smile – looking incredibly peaceful and inwardly quiet – motioned me to leave, and then resumed his tirade with undiminished force. This happened so quickly that I do not believe that Mr. Orage even noticed the break in the rhythm.

Conceivably this melodrama was prompted by money matters or editorial differences; more likely it was Jessie who lit the blue touchpaper of Gurdjieff's firework display – she seldom missed an opportunity to signal to him an ambivalence which fringed on dumb insolence.

Orage's personal analysis of the triangular relationship is both shrewd and self-extolling. Gurdjieff, he concluded, 'regarded me as someone who had … come with him from another planet with a task to carry out. But I had fallen in love with a native, and this interfered with his aim.' Orage and Jessie sailed for New York on 3 October 1925, with both 'task' and 'native' vying congenially for the editor's energies.

New Year 1926 delivered to Gurdjieff the sudden and singular possibility of a link with the smallish cultural colony at Taos, New Mexico – even of his featherbedded existence there. It all came out of the blue: Mrs Mabel Dodge Luhan (an associate of D. H. Lawrence, and the presiding spirit at Taos) had for two years nourished a dilettante interest in the Work. Now she concluded that her sharp spiritual and sexual necessities could be reconciled only if Gurdjieff set up a full-blown branch of his Institute at Taos – with virile and handsome Jean Toomer as principal. On 8 January she wrote personally to Gurdjieff and waited.

Correspondence reaching the Prieuré was strictly monitored on empiric lines. Some letters contained no money; these fell under Gurdjieff's instruction 'to destroy them in such a way that not even their "astral smell" should remain in my house.' More apposite letters were graded: if the accompanying cheque or bank notes reflected one zero, the letter was simply burnt and the money given to the children for sweets and toys; if two zeros, Olga de Hartmann would acknowledge the donation and pass the money to the kitchen fund; if three or more zeros, she would refer the letter to Gurdjieff personally. Of hundreds, perhaps thousands, of letters received since his accident Gurdjieff read fourteen and actually replied to six: one of these was Mabel Luhan's. The lady had volunteered 15,000 dollars and even offered to throw in her ranch.

Toomer's covering note to Gurdjieff was cautionary: Mrs Luhan certainly had strength of a sort, but a heart which had already warmed to four successive husbands. 'I can hope for her,' wrote Toomer sententiously, 'just in so far as she will persist in her present idea of following your method – but I could not persuade myself to certainty in regard to her constancy.' Toomer himself was someone Gurdjieff could barely recall, let alone license to transmit his teaching (their contact thus far had been minimal – four months at the Prieuré in summer 1924 when Gurdjieff was convalescent and virtually incommunicado). Accordingly on 1 February 1926 Gurdjieff tendered Mabel his profuse thanks and excusals ... he did not add that the Taos option was almost offensively discordant, a frivolous squib touched off during his personal *Götterdämmerung*.

Gurdjieff's overriding and passionate concern was the illness of his wife. Julia Ostrowska's once fluid figure had become locked and stooped; she who had danced the High Priestess now hobbled to the terrace leaning on a stick. Gurdjieff could hardly bear the spectacle: 'Each time I noticed it there arose in me a feeling of revolt and my heart pounded like that of a baulking horse.' He felt his moral burden as intolerable; had his accident not depleted him, he might (so he genuinely believed) have 'energized' and cured her. But on the contrary, 'the process of the terrible disease flowed in her at an accelerated tempo, chiefly because during his illness she took constant and anxious care of him without sparing herself.'

His late and reluctant sanction of orthodox X-ray treatment had merely caused Julia's disease to ramify – bankrupting any final hope. Although the prognosis was now unbearably clear to Gurdjieff, yet he would try to the last.

Early in February 1926, Mme Ostrowska was given two weeks to live, but Gurdjieff fought for her with a resolve so elemental that it is difficult to calibrate with normal human experience. The motive too (as confided to Fritz Peters) lay beyond any recognizable impulses of compassion and palliation:

> If she alone, already she be long time dead. I keep alive, make stay alive, with my strength; very difficult thing. But also very important – this most important moment in life for her. She live many lives, is very old soul; she now have possibility ascend to other world. But sickness come and make more difficult, make impossible for her to do this thing alone. If can keep alive few months more will not have to come back and live this life again.

For better or worse, Julia did not die in two weeks, nor in two months, but by spring was suffering unalleviably and had taken to her bed.

The whole sobriety and sense of the Institute seemed for the time being concentrated in the mysterious sick-room, while beyond its curtained privacy the values of the Sarmoung Monastery had undergone a peculiar translation. Gurdjieff had bought all his pupils bicycles, and insisted they ride everywhere: 'Whatever his reasons ... the results were shatteringly colourful. . . For days, and in the case of many of us, weeks, the grounds rang with the sounds of bicycle bells, crashes, shouts of laughter and pain.'

At a table on the sunny terrace, a German touch-typist, latest of Gurdjieff's acquisitions, banged out *Beelzebub*, 'gazing triumphantly off into space'; and with each dull carriage return, Mme Ostrowska's remaining span grew shorter.

Summer came with no remission. In the Prieuré kitchen Gurdjieff carefully supervised the preparation of all his wife's meals; when her throat seemed hopelessly constricted, a glass of water, first cupped in his hands for five minutes, enabled her to swallow, and in the last harrowing period her diet included blood, hand-pressed from specially selected meat ... Day after day, week after week, Gurdjieff and Julia were alone together. The inscrutability of their final transaction is subsumed (at least in the Gurdjieffian canon) in mysteries which range from the true identity of 'Countess' Ostrowska to the very nature of death itself. Not least at issue is the existence, character, transmissability, and effect of certain indescribably fine energies. To intrude more into that area would be a reckless impertinence ...

Thomas de Hartmann sometimes came to the failing woman in the beautiful room on the Ritz corridor and played tenderly for her on the old upright piano: not only the compositions of her husband but of her compatriot Chopin. As with the passing hours hope darkened on hope, Julia urgently requested the ministrations of a Polish priest and showed great joy when he came; soon afterwards she fell into a coma and her long ordeal was over. Mme Ostrowska, the wife of Gurdjieff, died at the Prieuré at 3.30 in the morning on Saturday 26 June 1926, just as the birds began to sing. She was thirty-seven.

'Go bring Dr Schernvall right away. Madame Ostrowsky is dead. Better tell.' The unfamiliar Gurdjieff who alerted Fritz Peters appeared 'impassive, very tired, and very pale'. He had been alone with Julia when she died. Now he returned to his room, where (jealously guarded by his old dog Philos) he refused to speak or eat. How Gurdjieff coped that day we cannot guess, but since he viewed death as an attenuated process, not an incisive event, his efforts on Julia's behalf surely did not cease with her breath. During his seclusion, Mme de Hartmann made the necessary registration with the Mayor of Avon, Christian d'Aleyrac, Baron de Coulange; had the body removed to an improvised catafalque in the Study House; and sent urgently to Paris for the Russian Orthodox Archbishop.

Generally speaking, the element of slapstick which so often perversely intrudes into the usages of domestic bereavement is adventitious. But not here one suspects. Certainly Gurdjieff's view that 'The question of death is just that question which supersedes all the established and subjectivised conditions of our life', did not make for conventionality. When at dusk he finally emerged from his vigil he unexpectedly asked his brother Dmitri to fire the boiler for the men's Turkish bath. Young Peters, scampering in a trifle late, was surprised to find everyone still wearing their underwear – which Gurdjieff insisted they remove, and the scandalized Archbishop that they retain:

> The argument must have gone on for about fifteen minutes after I arrived, and Gurdjieff seemed to be enjoying it immensely ... The Archbishop remained adamant, and someone was despatched back to the main house to find ... a large number of muslin breech-cloths...

This ecclesiastical victory, however, proved hollow: once in the steam-room, Gurdjieff gradually removed his breech-cloth, and every single man excepting his Right Reverence followed suit. By now the occasion bafflingly juxtaposed laughter and solemnity: blue jokes and a serious disputation on ritual cleanliness – all the more poignant because of Mme Ostrowska's impending obsequies. The mood of paradox prevailed late into the night, when at an incongruously festive banquet in the salon, 'the Archbishop turned out to be a convivial and well-mannered hard drinker.'

Next morning, as Gurdjieff led the long winding procession to Avon cemetery, he was gravitas itself: there 'were no manifestations of sorrow, no tears, just an unusual heaviness about him, as if it required great effort to move.' He walked bareheaded, revealing for once his impressive shaven skull (which 'rose to an immense height above the level of the ears, reaching its zenith at a point midway between the frontal region and the occiput.') Piotr Ouspensky had come for old time's sake, but little passed between him and his former teacher. Gurdjieff had lost in swift succession two beings uniquely near to him; small wonder that he seemed abstracted, 'silent and withdrawn ... as if only his body were actually present among the mourners.'

Although the double bereavement only reinforced Gurdjieff's determination to write, his life-style at the Prieuré exposed him to a hundred distractions which pitilessly gnawed on his time and energy ... With Julia gone, Mme Stjoernval's long-simmering resentment boiled over: she refused to speak to Gurdjieff, while feverishly supplying 'proof of his unreliability and even of his evil nature' to anyone disposed to listen. Had he not grossly 'exacerbated' the Russian revolution? Stolen her husband Leonid? Obliged her to drive a flatulent horse along the road to Batoum? Failed to return her best earrings (pawned in Constantinople)? And most cruelly prolonged his dear wife's suffering, to no conceivable purpose? ... He had.

Gurdjieff – for Dr Stjoernval's sake – felt obliged to repair matters. Summoning Fritz Peters, he deplored the vagaries of women but announced his determination to stand again in Elizabeta Stjoernval's good graces.

> He then handed me part of a chocolate bar in a torn box, as if someone had already eaten the other half, and told me to take it to her. I was to tell her how he felt about her, how much he did respect and value her friendship, and to say that this chocolate was an expression of his esteem for her.

Mme Stjoernval's all too predictable reaction of nettled disdain vanished when she explored the box to find, hidden in the silver paper, her long-lost earrings. To Fritz's amazement:

> She burst into tears, hugged me, became almost hysterical ... made up her face, put on the earrings, and [said] that this was proof of what a wonderful man he was, and how she had always known that he would keep his promise to her.

Gurdjieff had indeed put himself to inordinate trouble: five years of vexatious inquiry to locate the owner of the jewels (a Turkish usurer), and an inflated sum to recover them.

Scarcely however was Mme Stjoernval pacified and harmony restored, than a discordant note was struck by the brief unwelcome visit of Aleister Crowley – 'The Master Therion', 'The Great Beast', the 'King of Depravity'. Scuttling between Paris and Tunis to shake off his creditors and find new ones, Crowley closed in on the Prieuré from his Fontainebleau hotel, Au Cadran Bleu. How he actually gained entrée is a mystery; 'Gurdjieffians' who had previously met him (Orage, Pinder and Stanley Nott) would never have sponsored him. Nott felt discomforted when:

> to my surprise, he appeared there . . . and was given tea in the salon. The children were there, and he said to one of the boys something about his son whom he was teaching to be a devil. Gurdjieff got up and spoke to the boy, who thereupon took no further notice of Crowley.

The I Ching oracle had counselled the Great Beast to be 'patient, tenacious, modest, ashamed, friendly, affecting, tremulous and grateful', but this did not come easily; with his fishy eyes, rubbery androgynous face, outré dress, sinister rings, and 'sweet, slightly nauseous smell', Crowley was a noxious guest. Immediately he lost the protection of that status, Gurdjieff showed him off the premises in decided terms: 'You filthy, you dirty inside! Never again you set foot in my house.'

For all Gurdjieff's renewed authorial drive and the unstinting editorial help of Orage and Jane Heap, the fate of Beelzebub went unelucidated in the autumn and winter of 1926. Sometimes Gurdjieff felt it so near completion that he had best get out his newly acquired Fiat and motor at top speed down to Dijon to settle the format with a printer: sometimes he felt he had barely begun. In his volatile analyses, one stable datum was the onerous expense of maintaining the Institute – a nettle largely left for Orage and his New Yorkers to grasp: 'Gurdjieff is really quite extraordinary about money ... I'm only sorry I cannot give him a million if only to see if he could be impecunious within a month or so of receiving it.' Whatever the funds actually placed at Gurdjieff's disposal and the calls actually made on his purse, he personally did not live lavishly; on 16 April 1927 he was obliged (for lack of no greater sum than that spent on bicycles) to relinquish his modest flat at 47 Boulevard Péreire. A fortnight later, on 1 May, Gurdjieff completed his very last composition with Thomas de Harmann.

In summer 1927 Gurdjieff found himself seasonally pestered by the swarming attentions of his ever-generous trans-Atlantic disciples and voyeurs: Jean Toomer was at the Prieuré, genuinely eager to support publication; Gorham Munson with Elizabeth Delza; Carl Zigrosser, Melville Cane, Schuyler Jackson, Edwin Wolfe; a splendidly entangled lesbian quartet – Margaret Anderson, Georgette Leblanc, Jane Heap, and Solita Solano; Payson Loomis with Lincoln Kirstein (whom Gurdjieff ironically dubbed 'Little Father' because he affected the dress of a seminarian); Waldo Frank with his second wife Alma ... and a dozen more. 'They take too many baths', said Gurdjieff, with superbly inverted logic: 'All Americans dirty!'

Gurdjieff's 'acting' bespeaks an intention to discard all creatures superfluous to his plan. He seemed particularly keen to alienate Waldo Frank (eminent poet, armchair mystic, and associate of Gide, Romains, Ortega y Gasset and Unamuno). In Solita Solano, Jane Heap had aroused a hope so exhorbitant ('There you will see not one man, but a million') that disappointment was in any case assured: 'The magnitude of this interger [sic] excited me. I hoped for a demi-god, a superman of saintly countenance, not this "strange" écru man about whom I could see nothing extraordinary except the size and power of his eyes.'

If any Prieuré voyeurs gave Gurdjieff the benefit of the doubt, he generally pulverized it in the restaurants of Montmartre; his favourite table at L'Ecrivisse (or 'Madame Crayfish' as he termed it) became a point of departure for many esotourists. Here is Solita's memoir: 'He seated me next to him and for two hours muttered in broken English. I rejected his language, the suit he was wearing and his table manners; I decided that I rather disliked him.' The waiters at L'Ecrivisse – sweetened with chocolates and peppermints from Gurdjieff's pocket – became inured to stormy and incalculable scenes: 'Go back to your hell, you devil,' screamed Waldo Frank, shaking his fist, 'and leave us alone.' – What angry man say? asked Gurdjieff blandly. 'I not understand.'

To say the ensuing autumn took a sober colouring to Gurdjieff's eye, is to understate. Orage's allegiance was being slowly eclipsed by Jessie Dwight (whom he married in New York on 24 September). At the same time a shadow was lengthening over Gurdjieff's creativity; no longer was he able to compose his virile and haunting music. To tell the truth he was desperately tired and ill:

> All the functions of my organism which previously had been as my friends said, 'steel-cast', had gradually degenerated, so that at the present moment due to constant overworking not one of them was, even relatively, functioning properly.

Surely – he felt – he would soon blend with his mother and wife in the cemetery at Avon; the precise time depended on 'the self-willed Archangel Gabriel', but in any case 'there remained to me but one or two or perhaps, at the most, three years more of life'. Fearless of death itself, but appalled by the consequence that his work would remain uncompleted, Gurdjieff cast about for a solution.

The crisis had come in mid-October: having goaded himself almost night and day for three years to create *Beelzebub*; having achieved a prodigious first draft; and having set his heart on publication in 1928 – Gurdjieff suddenly realized that he had missed the right tone of voice. The problem itself he had always perceived ('to write my book for conscious man would be easy but to write it for donkeys – very hard') . . . but the solution evaded him. Between a voice too popular and a voice too obscure, the novice author trod a hair's-breadth line. How often had he unwrapped a subtle and important idea only to recoil from its naked exposure? And when his long-suffering editors Orage and Jane Heap enquired if he intended in principle to bury the bone deeper, he corrected them: 'Bury the dog deeper,' he explained. Aiming thus simultaneously at a book of revelation and of mystery; a book of rustic simplicity and Hegelian opacity; a book so plain it could be read aloud in working men's clubs, and yet so deep it would exact a formidable premium of attention and pondering – Gurdjieff had affected to square the circle. Now evidently – at the cost of God knows how many more years – absolutely everything would need to be rewritten. With this grim realization, 'there just then appeared before me, in all its splendour and full majesty, the question of my health.'

Gurdjieff's sense of being trapped overtook him on 6 November 1927, as he sat disconsolate and alone in an all-night café in Montmartre, 'tired already to exhaustion from my "black" thoughts.' But was it a veritable trap, or a 'Yezidi Circle'? His characteristic resolve to test the case and prove some exit was linked – for the first and only time in his life – to a contemplation of suicide: 'If unable to discover this means then, on the evening of the last day of the old year, to begin to destroy all my writings, calculating the time so as, at midnight with the last page, to destroy myself also.' But even as he harboured this terrible vision, a countervailing voice sounded in him with the force of trumpets: 'I wish . . . and will be!! Moreover, my Being is necessary not only for my personal egoism but also for the common welfare of humanity. I still wish to be . . . I still am.' Gurdjieff's life-force was formidable (it is telling that in that same black night when he meditated self-destruction, he wrote generously to Orage, urging on him a regime to regulate his angina pectoris).

The beleaguered author's first small breakthrough came in late December. After drinking Armagnac in some provincial hole of a café, he succeeded at least in clarifying his tripartite aim: to rewrite everything in a form he more or less intuited; to infuse the work with a deeper understanding of man's psyche; and to recover his health.

By Christmas he had become intrigued and emboldened by hints of a direct causal link between his literary output and his conscious suffering – strangely enough, he had written best and most prolifically while painfully empathizing with his mother's and wife's travails. Supposing he could now generate and embrace fresh personal sufferings, surely his enhanced 'labour-ability' would match the task. By the fateful New Year's Eve of 1927, the notion of suicide lay well behind Gurdjieff. Some blessed allotropy had reconstituted his predicament as an intriguing challenge: just how to revise? – just how to engender the necessary suffering? For the resolution of these twin problems George Ivanovitch plucked from the calendar a doubly potent date – his own 'nameday' and Julia Ostrowska's birthday: '23rd April by the old style of the real year, that is ... the day of St-George-the-Victor, which ... counted throughout the period of the existence of the Institute as, so to speak, its "Coronation-Day".' Minimizing his writing, he pondered deeply; he sought advice from Asia; he waited on the time.

Scarcely had the portentous New Year begun to unfurl, than it worryingly confirmed Orage's divided loyalties. The newly-weds turned up at the Prieuré in mid-January 1928, bringing Atlantic squalls: if Miss Dwight had felt irritated by her lover's deference to Gurdjieff, Mrs Orage found her husband's subservience unbearable; in a hundred feminine ways she signalled her contrariness and proprietorial claim. The couple's stay was brief and occasionally splenetic – indeed their departure for New York in February provides one of those rare if apocryphal incidents when Gurdjieff the Black Magician manifests. He fixes Jessie with a Basilisk gaze: she cannot move; she cannot breathe – will she faint? Probably. Then, as if from a great distance, she hears his words: 'If you keep my super-idiot from coming back to me, you burn in boiling oil.'... Perhaps in some meta-biographical inferno there is room for the image of young Jessie languorously toasting on the buttered side – Alfred Richard Orage, for better for worse, for richer for poorer, never again returned to the Prieuré.

By the eve of St George's day, Gurdjieff had half resolved his *Beelzebub* problem. Helped by a mysterious letter containing 'some wise advice from one of my oldest friends', he was clearer than ever as to the necessary idiom and corrigenda. This alone generated a palpable excitement. No one had sympathized more during Gurdjieff's literary crisis, or was more sensitive to its abatement, than his faithful amanuensis Olga de Hartmann. Summoned to him, she hurried with eager expectation into a moment of unimprovable bathos: what Gurdjieff confided to Olga, after months of charged silence, was his chagrin that English kippers were unobtainable in France, since he fancied a pair for supper on his name day.

Olga said nothing and her feelings remain conjectural. Within minutes however she had discreetly phoned London; ordered a large case of best quality kippers, arranged its collection in Paris and urgent delivery to the Prieuré. Her innocent impulse – so typical of a hundred supportive acts, so at variance with Gurdjieff's quest for intentional suffering – revealed to him, in a magnesium flare of insight, the missing key:

> I ... locked myself in my room, and ... having brought myself into a suitable state, took ... this ... solemn vow ... under the pretext of different worthy reasons, to remove from my eyesight all those who by this or that make my life too comfortable.

It had come to this: in service to the purpose of his writing, the very flower of Gurdjieff's companions must be banished; his round table dissolved ... that night at the feast of St George, Mr Rachmilievitch raised a prophetic vodka glass above the kipper bones, and, looking at Gurdjieff, said in a voice charged with emotion: 'God give you the strength and the manhood to endure your lofty solitude.' It would certainly be needed.

11

---- ❖ ----

SCATTERING ACORNS

(24 April 1928–Summer 1931)

Infinitely more addictive, more corrupting, than greed for money, is the greed for disciples; the bearer of spiritual gifts becomes all too easily the miser of souls – binding even as he liberates. On this count Gurdjieff is not indictable. In his vow of St George's day there is more than an author's impatience for elbow-room: there is sacrifice and largesse – a remarkable insistence that his pupils should go free to realize their own destiny; that the subtlest of imparted influences should measure its effectuality in the vortex of life.

Already in spring 1928, absentees predominated at the roll-call of Gurdjieff's entourage. The engaging duo of Gurdjieffian pre-history, Lev Levovitch and Paul Dukes, had vanished from view; the first Moscow aspirants had other avocations now – Vladimir Pohl as a musical 'survivalist' in Paris and cousin Mercourov as a rising sculptor in Moscow (fabricating his Leninist credentials along with his huge granite statue 'The Death of the Leader'). Of the 'Petrograd Six', Anthony Charkovsky and Nicholas R. had disappeared 'at the time of the great agitation of minds in Russia', Anna Butkovsky had settled for prosaic domesticity, Piotr Ouspensky was nursing his London constituency, Andrei Zaharoff lay in an unmarked grave in Novorossiysk – and only Leonid Stjoernval had withstood the proof of events. The Transcaucasian climbers – Petrov, Zhukov, and Shandarovsky – had drifted north again into oblivion; Frank Pinder had bolted from the Prieuré in 1924; the beautiful Olgivanna had danced away into the West; Miss Merston had left for an Indian ashram; and Captain J. G. Bennett was in Athens' jail.[15]

The socio-political *mise-en-scène* of summer 1928 was bland as milk broth: no revolution or singular upheaval seemed in prospect.

Gurdjieff would need to invent his 'worthy reasons' for banishing further pupils, unaided by history's 'sharp energetic events'. His grand strategy admitted wide tactical variation: flattery and insult; roses and thorns. Precisely how he inveigled away Margaret Anderson and Georgette Leblanc is not extant, but within a month of his vow, they broke the cycle of their visits to the Institute. From Gurdjieff's standpoint, these two had never been exactly model pupils, not because they were lesbian but because both were 'enlightened idiots' – temperamentally distanced from understanding by an *a priori* certitude that they possessed it already. It was virtually impossible such inflated personalities should acclimatize to the Prieuré. The singer and dancer Georgette, in her heyday, was a construct of almost sinister perfection; Jean Cocteau euphemistically defined her as 'the model for a lyric saint – one of those strange great beings who move through the crowd, headless and armless, propelled only by the power of their souls, as immutable as the Victory of Samothrace.'

As for the editor Margaret, hers was a life dedicated less to the toilsome quest for consciousness than to the rhapsodic titillation of 'an elaborate old-fangled euphoria'; her implicit claim of a full-blown Gurdjieffian transformation may be easier to swallow if we add a pinch of salt. Gurdjieff had changed them both – that is admitted: he had captured the citadel of their idealism – then gently restored them to their equivocal sphere as his articulate and passionate witnesses. No one had lost by his practicality.

Scarcely however had Gurdjieff disembarrassed himself of Margaret and Georgette, than their formidable associate Jane Heap turned up from New York, longing – who more sincerely? – to live and labour at the Prieuré. Gurdjieff refused. Whether he felt any temptation to have her monumental strength and editorial verve immediately to hand, who can say? Instead he 'placed her' in a Montmartre apartment among the flower girls, negroes, arabs, liveried doorkeepers, pock-marked touts, *chansonniers*, pickpockets, disposable pageboys, whores, and inebriates in evening dress; among the talented and narcissistic café society of English-speaking writers and artists, whose self-adulation is so patent in the photographs of Man Ray and Bernice Abbott; and above all (dare one add) among the women of special tastes who merited inclusion in the *Ladies Directory* compiled by Jane's intimate friend the authoress Djuna Barnes.

Despite her relative inexperience in the Work, Jane was mandated by Gurdjieff to give a weekly lecture on his ideas in her apartment-salon, attracting whom she could – while he himself got on with his writing. He noted ironically that Jane almost immediately 'magnetized' the woman who twelve months earlier had rejected his language, suit, and table manners: Solita Solano (featured in the *Ladies Directory* as the lubricious journalist 'Tuck') became almost overnight a clandestine Gurdjieffian, with an aim – of whose integrity she would later give touching proof – to become a 'fully conscious, developed human being'.

In early summer 1928, Gurdjieff turned his attention to Mme Sophie Grigorievna Ouspensky. Hers was a case more complex and more delicate than the stereotype which some have unkindly assigned her (a cross between Clytaemnestra and Mrs Beaton) might suggest: her amazing energy, hauteur, violent temper, and unsurpassable way with bortsch were awkwardly bundled with the pale, imponderable, spiritual huffiness of Piotr Ouspensky.

Based since 1924 at Asnières only three miles from Paris, Mme Ouspensky had not been a total stranger to the apartment at 47 Boulevard Péreire, or to Gurdjieff's table at L'Ecrivisse and the Café de la Paix. From her lips and from Boris Ferapontoff's, Gurdjieff had a shrewd idea of the highly theoretical dispensation prevailing in London, and the peculiar spirit brooding over the flat at 55a Gwendwr Road, West Kensington. In Ouspensky's self-willed isolation and mounting depression, there had lately seized on his imagination (never subsequently to loosen its teeth) the obsession that he must contact 'Higher Source' – an entity he situated sometimes on the supernal plane and sometimes in a mythologized Asia. Mme Ouspensky (a 'majestic figure, dressed entirely in black, with dark chestnut hair and flashing eyes') might be expected to exert in England a tonic influence, revitalizing the Work's practical aspect and conveying something of *Beelzebub* ... Ironically it was Sophie Grigorievna's very loyalty to Gurdjieff which enabled him to hurry her onto the London boat train.

Gurdjieff's vow being secret, Sophie Ouspensky viewed herself as a powerful trump rather than a discard. Scarcely however had her train pulled round the bend, than Gurdjieff set up another such diversionary mission: he sent both the Salzmanns to Germany. There lived in Frankfurt, in amity with his wife and numerous daughters (and in communion with the Beautiful and the Good), Herr Alphons Paquet, a sympathetic Quaker and Whitmanesque nature poet. Paquet and Salzmann had met twenty years before in Munich, in the circle round Rilke and Kandinsky, and briefly renewed contact in 1920 when Paquet stumbled on the Institute in Constantinople. Behind Gurdjieff's primary intention – to initiate a modest German group – evidently lay a stratagem to create for Alexandre a separate personal domain, but neither this nor subsequent visits to Frankfurt bore fruit; Jeanne was soon reclaimed by the Prieuré, and Alexandre by his favourite boulevard café where he drank, not always in moderation, a mixture of beer and calvados.

Within the Gurdjieffian firmament Alexandre's erratic star still twinkled – but perhaps less crisply than hitherto. He was not a well man and looked poignantly older than his fifty-four years; events had not, by and large, turned out as he originally envisaged. Ouspensky's intellectualism, Thomas de Hartmann's musical powers, and Jeanne's flair for dance – all these Gurdjieff had wonderfully developed and elevated: but the artist's formidable gift had somehow been marginalized. The transformation of Katherine Mansfield's loft in the cowshed, and the invention of a decorative script[4] (for encrypting aphorisms formulated in English), were tasks which did not really test his true stature and capacity. As Alexandre looked at the world, as he looked at the Institute, and indeed as he looked close to home – his mordant humour found ample and rich material. An immaculate loyalty left room in Salzmann's voice for a sarcasm vented on everyone except his master.

Not that Gurdjieff lacked critics. By 1928 he had stirred up a hydra-headed enmity among the intelligentsia. The genesis and tearaway development of the Katherine Mansfield cult apparently demanded a Bluebeard; French rationalists stigmatized him as a charlatan and Catholic apologists (not least François Mauriac) as an irritant to Mother Church. Overall however, the most potent influence contra Gurdjieff – because the most intelligent and sustained – was that which the French occultist René-Jean-Maria-Joseph Guénon exerted from his apartment at 51 Rue St Louis.

To envisage two characters, or indeed two authors, more preposterously contrasted than Gurdjieff and Guénon exasperates the mind. Guénon's exquisite prose style was smooth as a mill pond, but, gliding just beneath its surface like a cruel pike, his spiritual paranoia snapped at the anti-traditional and counter-initiatic forces, which a trick of parallax caused him to detect in virtually every modern renewal. Gurdjieff (so near, so practical, so full of being) attracted Guénon's special anathema:

> This man, of Greek extraction, is not purely and simply a charlatan, but this only makes him the more dangerous . . . the truth is that . . . Gurdjieff exercises on those who go to him a kind of grip of a psychic order which is quite astonishing and from which few have the strength to escape.

A psychic grip . . . when ironically Gurdjieff was exercised to shed his entire echelon of senior pupils!

For all Guénon's sublime spiritual gifts, for all his vast and rabbinical erudition, he emerges as a theorist with a personal blind spot. Proud yet humble to have begun as a pupil of 'Papus', he was humble yet proud to have been initiated (by a Swedish painter) into an order of African dervishes; the more Guénon achieved in the domain of writing – and he achieved much – the more ostentatiously modest he became. Frankly there were moments (as a smile of self-deprecation played over the occultist's sensitive yet goat-like features, and he murmured '*Il n'y a pas de René Guénon*'), when his pride in his humility seemed almost excessive. In late summer a pale figure joined Alexandre Salzmann's table in the Boulevard St Germain, and spoke disparagingly of Gurdjieff. Salzmann feigned confusion: had he the honour of speaking to M. René Guénon? '*Il n'y a pas de René Guénon*,' the apparition replied. Salzmann was instant commiseration: '*Il n'y a pas de René Guénon? Helas.*' In future Guénon avoided Salzmann; perhaps it signifies something that, in *Beelzebub*, the solar system 'Salzmanino' is full of gaseous cyanic acid – utterly lethal!

Gurdjieff's revision of his major work was going apace, though whether he ever fully resolved *Beelzebub*'s inherent stylistic contradiction is a moot point. More than once he felt he had; more than once he dictated the 'very last line'. Olga de Hartmann, at this, became so emotional that he was obliged to comfort her: 'We have a whole other book to write so be peaceful.' Before tackling – indeed before plotting – this new project, Gurdjieff took a breather:

> I intend to rest for a whole month, to write positively nothing, and for a stimulus to my organism, fatigued to the extreme limit, s-l-o-w-l-y to drink . . . fifteen bottles of 'super-most-super-heavenly-nectar' called at present time on Earth 'Old Calvados'.

In the fumes of calvados, there rose up before the 'Black Greek' the cherished images of youth: his father and Dean Borsh; Prince Lubovedsky and Professor Skridlov; frail cross-eyed Pogossian burning with intensity. What men; and Vitvitskaia, what a woman! So many gone! So many irreplaceable mentors and friends committed to obscure graves in Alexandropol, Kars, Samara, the Olman monastery, and the Taklamakan desert.

Gurdjieff himself was now sixty-two: who, if not he, could rescue these vivid, meaningful lives from the encroaching sands of historical oblivion? Who better celebrate their resource, self-restraint, and empathy? Surely there is passion in his decision to embark on an 'autobiography' – some echo of Katherine Mansfield's authorial affirmation: 'You are not dead . . . All is remembered. I bow down to you. I efface myself so that you may live again through me in your richness and beauty.'

To work then! Even as the ageing Gurdjieff hustles away his flesh-and-blood disciples, his busy pencil summons the Seekers of Truth to testify at a last and companionable rendezvous. On the ground which the awesome critique of *Beelzebub* had swept clear of the accumulated rubbish of centuries, *Meetings with Remarkable Men* must lay the foundation of a New World.

In autumn 1928, Mme Ouspensky, who cordially disliked the English, returned from London to France where (in common with others) she found Gurdjieff more and more elusive – more and more engrossed in his writing. With funding and editing in mind, the author's thoughts were gravitating not towards England and Ouspensky but towards America and Orage. Early in the New Year therefore, Gurdjieff summoned his energies and struck out on his long-deferred return visit to the United States. Thomas and Olga de Hartmann – his only travelling companions on the s.s. *Paris* – found themselves closeted with the 'Arch-disturber of Complacency': far from humouring their sense of privileged intimacy, Gurdjieff, from the very first day, astonished Thomas by urging on him the imperative need to leave the Prieuré, and carve for himself an independent musical career. Day after day, as the *Paris* steamed remorselessly west towards the Statue of Liberty, the de Hartmanns grappled with the horrible spectre of freedom.

On 23 January 1929 when Gurdjieff entered for the second time into a frigid New York harbour, Alfred Richard Orage also felt himself trickily placed – his five-year stewardship under scrutiny, his groups over-excited, and his wife Jessie heavily pregnant. As compère he was not disappointed: rich and characteristic moments ensued at Muriel Draper's salon, Child's Restaurant, and Gurdjieff's suite on the corner of 7th Avenue and Central Park South. This apartment (overlooking the marquee of the Al Jolson Theater) was rented furnished from the Shubert Theater Corporation, and 'the rugs, drapes, and wall decorations looked like a conglomoration of stuff left over from some long ago Shubert theatrical disaster.' Against this pantomimic backcloth, Gurdjieff blossomed: 'G. is more himself than ever – that is to say, he is more impossible than ever. But certainly New York needed a shaking up ...'

The vibration was strangely familiar: although the Master was full of fire and insight, he pushed the impression of his veniality to the point of self-parody. Since practically all his American flock were 'power-possessors' of some sort, and the Calvin Coolidge administration was ushering towards its fatal dénouement the nation's greatest ever peacetime boom, Gurdjieff cheerfully demanded 10,000 dollars within three weeks. Meanwhile on Olga he piled an impossible administrative work load, stressing her almost to breaking point – 'Often I was on the brink of leaving everything and running away.'

A hidden intention to nourish Orage's and Toomer's doubts, to reinforce Jessie's antipathy, to frighten Olga into retreat, and to keep the New York groups quivering between enthusiasm and mutiny – such might explain Gurdjieff's demeanour. On 5 April he embarked for France with his wallet a good deal heavier and his vow dangerously nearer attainment; the de Hartmanns sat chastened in their cabins, while on the quayside Orage danced for joy: 'Thank God I'm free again!'

The golden epoch of ocean-liner socializing, dollar supremacy, and the 'American-in-Paris' phenomenon was nearly over. Few if any sensed it and no one dreamt of apocalypse. The well-oiled Parisian cultural apparatus gave a convincing imitation of perpetual motion. Scarcely however had Gurdjieff returned, than the expatriates' cosy sense of 'being geniuses together' was shaded by the inexplicable closure of the *Little Review* – a journal to which many contributed and virtually all read. Perhaps the most jarring aspect was the insurrectionist tone of Jane Heap's editorial *vale*:

> I am bringing the *Little Review* to an end ... we have given space ... to 23 new systems of art (all now dead) representing 19 countries ... Self-expression is not enough; experiment is not enough; the recording of special moments or cases is not enough. All of the arts have broken faith or lost connection with their origin and function ... it would be more than an intellectual adventure to give up our obsessions about art, hopelessness, and *Little Reviews*, and take on pursuits more becoming to human beings.

Whatever Jane Heap did in 1929 Gurdjieff countenanced if not instigated; his surely (granted this one premise) is the man's hand which comes forth at Belshazzar's non-stop literary party and writes *Mene, Mene, Tekel, Upharsin* on the wall; his is the whim which here so curiously intermingles the credos of the high and mighty (James Joyce, Ernest Hemingway, Aldous Huxley, Gertrude Stein, Wyndham Lewis, Bertrand Russell) not only with those of sacramental Gurdjieffians (Margaret Anderson, Alfred Orage, Georgette Leblanc, Gorham Munson, Solita Solano) but of the near certifiable Elsa, Baroness von Freytag-Loringhoven; his the black humour which binds together within the same cover Jean Cocteau's professed ambition of 'creating love' and Fritz Peters' (aged fifteen) of 'continuing to work with Mr G.'s method'. For Cocteau's sincerity one cannot answer, but Fritz's endorsement was certainly a half-truth; by now he was hankering to leave the Prieuré and return to his mother Lois and step-father Bill in Chicago, and only the adamantine opposition of Jane Heap, his legal guardian, held him back.

The more one reflects on this whole affair, the more intriguing it appears. Cached within the *Little Review* – a vehicle created by Anderson and steered by Heap – Gurdjieff might for years hence have smuggled explosive barrelfuls of his own ideas into the domain of cultural *bon ton*. Now however, at minimum, he assented to the journal's destruction, and to the irreversible decommissioning of Jane Heap as his cultural gladiator.

In early summer Madame Ouspensky was again urged off to London. Then – far more significantly – the protesting de Hartmanns ran the gauntlet of Gurdjieff's glowering insistence to the Prieuré gates ... and out at last into the world beyond. Olga Arcadievna, settling dazedly into a congenial house in Courbevoie on the outskirts of Neuilly, was scarcely able to comprehend the new situation: 'I was very unhappy and nervous. Mr de Hartmann, who was so much more sensitive and individualistic by nature, could not endure it and was on the edge of a nervous breakdown.' And Gurdjieff? His state of mind is unknown, but consider: a whole œuvre of music, more than 300 compositions, bears witness to the mutuality of his and de Hartmann's sensitivity; in escaping from Essentuki they had crossed the mountains virtually arm-in-arm; and when Thomas had contracted typhus, Gurdjieff had saved his life ...

In June 1929 a Miss Louise Goepfert appeared at the Prieuré gates, rang the bell marked *Sonnez fort!*, was admitted by Fritz Peters and assigned a room in 'Monks' Corridor' with a skull and crossbones painted above the door. Miss Goepfert – twenty-nine, Roman Catholic, and expensively educated as an art historian – had been commended to Gurdjieff by Robert F. J. Schwarzenbach the Swiss Consul in New York, as an eminently suitable person to translate *Beelzebub* into German. (Albeit Swiss herself, Miss Goepfert answered so perfectly to a certain German stereotype that Gurdjieff nicknamed her 'Sausage'.) The impending translation task was monumental, but – to older pupils' amazement – Gurdjieff further appointed the newcomer his secretary. 'If you help me now,' he assured Sausage, 'later can buy half Germany.' As to the banished de Hartmanns, they had been inexcusably provocative explained Gurdjieff: 'She impertinent, husband also.'

Needless to say this was purest fiction; month after month Olga divided her dutiful attention between her shell-shocked husband at Courbevoie, and her teacher whom she still loyally visited at the Institute. Whenever she came, Gurdjieff shouted at her relentlessly until the Prieuré shook and 'Sausage' concluded that her predecessor was a horrible person ... Gently Dr Stjoernval drew Miss Goepfert aside: 'May I say something to you? How to explain it? Mr Gurdjieff tries something that no one has tried. He tries to put people born under certain stars, under another constellation. And that is, in general, impossible.'

Because Olga's 'adhesion' only grew more tenacious with each attempt at dislodgement, Gurdjieff finally found it necessary to play the Black Magician and conjure up a spate of unforgivable scenes. He appeared suddenly at the house in Neuilly and urged on Olga's protesting parents, Arcady and Olga Constantinova Schumacher, the necessity of their returning to the Prieuré, adding darkly: 'Well, if you don't come in a week's time, a coffin will be in this room and your daughter will be in it.' Practised in Gurdjieff's ways and perceiving the provocation as subterfuge, Olga refused to panic.

Meanwhile the industry of Sausage was proving beyond belief; by autumn 1929 Book 1 of *Beelzebub* had been sensitively translated into German and was ready for appraisal in Frankfurt and Berlin by Alphons Paquet's handpicked audience. Gurdjieff wickedly brought both his lady secretaries on the ensuing train journeys, and created an atmosphere which left Olga with very painful memories. As winter advanced, each week brought accentuated demands on her sang-froid, until eventually she confronted excruciating moments when 'Mr Gurdjieff asked me to do something that I felt I could not do.' The campaign began in a first-class compartment on the train to

Berlin, and took impetus when Mme de Hartmann visited the Prieuré late one night. If she would not do 'it', explained Gurdjieff, something bad would happen to her husband ... Yet again, however, Olga kept her balance.

Contrasted with Mme de Hartmann's long and complex service, young Fritz Peters' contribution to his master's creature-comforts (tidying his room and ensuring a perpetual flow of black coffee) must seem trivial. Yet he too had qualified himself for 'banishment', and in late summer Gurdjieff intervened magisterially in the boy's stalled campaign to break free: 'The effect of Gurdjieff's decision ... was remarkable. Not only did Jane capitulate, but came to the Prieuré and announced that all the details – tickets, passport, legal papers, etc. – had been arranged.'

Page and monarch parted in September 1929. On both sides there was feeling: just as Peters had led by the hand the concussed and half-blind Gurdjieff of 1924, so Gurdjieff had led Peters with great psychological delicacy towards many important insights. In Gurdjieff's rhetorical question, 'So you decide to go?', there is sorrow as well as irony ... and Fritz could not speak: 'I was only able to nod my head at him. Then he put his arm around me, leaned over and kissed my cheek, and said: Must not be sad. Sometime maybe you will come back; remember that in life anything can happen.'

Late in October 1929 the momentous crash on Wall Street closed the era when Gurdjieff could count on facile help from the USA; no longer was the atmosphere of New York saturated with the vibrations of dollars. On the contrary, Stanley Nott reported a parlous state of affairs:

> Shops were empty of customers, streets unswept, shabbiness everywhere; soup queues, bread lines. Twenty million people without money to buy food lined up each day to receive a dole to keep their families from starving. It was as if a terrible war or famine or plague had passed over the country.

Immediately Gurdjieff felt drawn there – to see for himself; to confront Orage; and to explore *Beelzebub*'s publication.

In February 1930, the evening before setting out from the Prieuré on this his third trip to the USA, George Ivanovitch Gurdjieff burnt his personal papers. In the space of perhaps ten minutes, all those passports, memoranda, certificates and correspondence, which might have illuminated (or perhaps undermined) the author's self-depiction in *Meetings*, were obliterated forever. Only Olga was

present as Gurdjieff's clever spatulate fingers dropped his mysteries
one by one into the flames; only Olga had had access to the little
chest which held the evidence, and she (to the intense annoyance
of every right-thinking historian) had never pried. 'Happily,' said
Gurdjieff, 'you had not that awful quality of curiosity.'

Early next morning, Gurdjieff called his faithful disciple to his new
Paris flat in the Rue Marchand. Through all the vicissitudes of her
long and arduous life (she lived to ninety-four) Olga Arcadievna
remembered their final dialogue there as 'wonderful' – and its
dénouement at the railway station as a bad dream. For the last nine
months she had contrived with marvellous ingenuity to serve two
masters – her husband and her teacher: now she was compelled to
choose. The mechanism was diabolically simple: relying on circumstance and the 'law of resistance', Gurdjieff demanded the very thing
which contradicted his vow – that Olga bring Thomas to join him in
New York. She could not of course. Thomas was in no fit state.
Together Gurdjieff and Olga walked the level platform in ominous
silence; looking down from the steps of the dining car, the man
renewed his demand – and, looking up, the woman excused herself.

> Nevertheless, with a cold, icy tone, Mr Gurdjieff repeated, 'Come in a
> week's time, or you will never see me again.' I told him, 'How can you ask
> of me such a thing, you know I cannot do it.' He repeated with the same
> tone of voice, 'Then you will never see me again.' Although I had the
> feeling that a thunderbolt had struck me, a voice in me said, and I
> repeated, 'Then . . . I will never see you again.'
>
> The train moved. Mr Gurdjieff stood motionless looking at me. I
> looked at him without moving my eyes from his face. I knew it was
> forever . . .

Olga went home and did not get up for four days.

Whatever Gurdjieff's sorrow at his self-inflicted loss of Olga;
whatever his remorse at its ruthless contrivance – he wasted no time
in re-focusing his spoiling tactics on New York. The cables beamed
ahead from the s.s. *Bremen* ranged from the mildly idiosyncractic
(IF LOVE NOT DISSIPATED, ARRANGE BATH AND PARTY.
SIGNED GRANDSON AND UNIQUE PHENOMENAL GRAND-
MOTHER) to the downright bizarre (BREMEN BRINGS THOUSAND
KILOS DISILLUSION; HUNDRED KILOS MOMENTARY HAPPI-
NESS, AND TEN POUNDS RETRIBUTION. SIGNED AMBASSADOR
FROM HELL). When the liner berthed on 15 February, the crowd of
welcomers – stamping their feet and blowing their fingernails against

the extreme cold – did not include Orage; he did not witness the dockside furore under the letter 'G', as Gurdjieff heatedly forced through Customs twenty-five illicit melons ('They special from Persia'); nor was he even at the Great Northern Hotel to welcome his teacher.

This foretaste of a fuller alienation suited Gurdjieff perfectly. As his visit progressed, he subtly deposited in Orage an alluvial sediment of resentment: a sense of having been cheated; the feeling of a deserved initiation perversely withheld. How fully he succeeded is only too clear from Orage's correspondence:

> I told Gurdjieff in New York that I'd come to the end of my patience and that, without a new initiation, I was as good as dead about the Prieuré ... in despair, frankly, of Gurdjieff doing any more for me than he has done for Stjernval, Hartmann, etc., however faithfully they have given up all to follow him.

Gurdjieff's resolve 'to press the most sensitive corn of everyone I met' played havoc with Orage's network of literary contacts; a carefully stage-managed meeting between the unpublished author of *Beelzebub* and Alfred Knopf was turned upside down when Gurdjieff growled: 'First clean house, your house, then perhaps can have my book!' By the time the 'Unique Phenomenal Grandmother' sailed for France in April 1930, not only was Orage more than ever disaffected, but amazing whispers were heard that 'Gurdjieff himself was a great stumbling block to the understanding of the system.'

Summer of 1930 saw Mme Ouspensky yet again hopefully despatched to England, and by autumn (when she obstinately returned) the Prieuré's ranks had thinned again: Alexandre Salzmann had more or less disappeared from the Institute. The artist's salty wit, humanity, stark masculinity, and preposterous range of experience were irreplaceable; often – even in the darkest hours of the long recession from Georgia – we catch Gurdjieff, 'his frame shaking with laughter at some story told by Mr Salzmann.' All Gurdjieff's separations from his nucleus were bitter-sweet, but this one (for private and personal reasons) had a special poignancy.

A veil descends to obscure the moment of Salzmann's actual parting: one moment he is solidly there in the 'Monks Corridor', painting over the lintel the words *In Memento Mori*; the next moment he is gone. Allegory hints that he left the Prieuré transformed by Gurdjieff's teaching: 'That night I took the train to Paris. I had entered the monastery under the name of Brother Petrus. I came out with the title of Father Sogol, and I have kept that pseudonym.' More than ever he was hopelessly lost to conventionality: 'I can't bring myself to fall in with this monkey-cage agitation which people so dramatically call life.' By day an interior decorator and antique dealer, and by night a fixture at his café on the Boulevard St Germain, Salzmann burnt his candle at both ends; he ate little and drank his old mixture of beer and calvados; his lungs were increasingly affected by pulmonary tuberculosis.

There remained to Alexandre one crowning contribution to the Gurdjieffian myth: his 'magnetizing' of René Daumal (first Frenchman to enter the Work). It would be a dangerous over-simplification to claim that Daumal was to Salzmann what Soloviev was to Gurdjieff, but the process of reclamation bears comparison. Late in 1930 Daumal arrived at Salzmann's table with a spiritual search more vehement than wholesome; his experimental mysticism (alcohol, hashish, carbon tetrachloride, etc.) had led him by way of chimerical ecstasies to attempted suicide. The young man's flair for extremes was abetted by a prodigious intelligence: he had published avant garde poetry; he had mastered Sanskrit; he was co-founder of *Le Grand Jeu* (a review supposedly dedicated to a grand convergence of poetry, philosophy and initiation, though in practice surrendered to an obscure polemic about the parameters of Dada and surrealism). At twenty-two René Daumal was a huge success: he suffered from fatigue, anaemia, violent migraine, and various chemical addictions.

Salzmann's long years of experience under a real teacher enabled him to wean Daumal from drugs, while pointing an alternative avenue to the noumenal; he turned the young man from the hot-house literary influence of Nerval and Rimbaud, and alerted him to Gurdjieff. Daumal wrote excitedly: '[He] restores my hope and purpose in life. I see that the hidden knowledge, which I had dreamed of, exists in the world, and that someday I may, if I deserve it, attain it.' Gurdjieff – preoccupied with his writing – held aloof. Avant garde poetry and poets had no *prima facie* appeal for him, judging by his caustic parody in *Meetings with Remarkable Men*:

> Green roses
> Purple mimosas
> Divine are her poses
> Like hanging memories

Evidently he preferred to live surrealistically – as his fourth trip to America makes almost too plain.

Alfred Richard Orage – tried, condemned, and sentenced *in absentia* – was on extended holiday in England when, on 13 November 1930, Gurdjieff arrived again in the USA. The entire New York group met that evening in Studio 61 of Carnegie Hall to hear Gurdjieff's secretary read from *Beelzebub*, but their forgivable sense of excitement, privilege, and even self-satisfaction was brutally curtailed by Gurdjieff's personal intervention:

> While sitting in the corner and observing out of boredom the expressions on your faces, it seemed clear to me that there stood out on the forehead now of one, now of another of you, the inscription 'candidate for the madhouse'.

And if Gurdjieff's American followers had indeed become candidates for lunatic asylums; if their artificiality provoked in him 'a cold shivering similar to that which takes people who are afflicted by the so-called "yellow malaria of Kuska"'; if the technique of 'self-observation' had become for them a disastrous *idée fixe*; if they were hopelessly confused about the Sacred Dances; if they wandered in a labyrinth of wiseacring about 'The Local Map', 'The Boat', 'The Greater Map', and 'Destination' (concepts unknown at the Prieuré) – it was all culpably due to the titillation of Mr Orage.

Worse portended. At Gurdjieff's fateful lecture on 1 December he scattered Orage's already demoralized company with a psychological hand-grenade. In a pronounced German accent, Louise Goepfert read out the notorious 'oath' which all must sign within thirty-six hours on pain of strict expulsion from his work:

> I, undersigned, after mature and profound reflection, without being influenced by anyone else at all, but of my own free will, promise under oath not to have, without instructions from Mr. GURDJIEFF or a person officially representing him, any relations whatsoever, spoken or written, with any of the members of the former group existing till now under the name of 'Orage's group' of the followers of Mr. GURDJIEFF's ideas and also not to have any relations without special permission of Mr. GURDJIEFF or his substitute with Mr. Orage himself.

Conflicting hopes and loyalties threw the defenceless New Yorkers into a terrible quandary: some signed, some refused, some equivocated. A clutch of frantic telegrams reached Orage at his old stone farmhouse near Rye, and, without a moment's delay, he took passage for New York on the s.s. *Washington*. Arriving on 10 December, he urgently requested audience with his teacher. Gladly, Gurdjieff sent reply ... on one condition: that 'you also M. Orage, will sign the obligation I proposed.'

If Gurdjieff had counted on his super-idiot's refusal, he had mistaken his man; taking up the fountain-pen which had served Gurdjieff so magnificently, Orage without hesitation vowed to ostracize Orage. News of this *coup de théâtre* reached Gurdjieff in apartment 'Q' at 204 West 59th Street just as he was cooking supper ... and had its effect:

> I suddenly ... instead of a pinch of ginger, dumped into the casserole with the left hand the whole supply in the kitchen of cayenne pepper ... then flung myself into the room, fell on the sofa and, burying my head in the cushions which, by the way, were half moth-eaten, began to sob with bitter tears.

Whether Gurdjieff wept particularly at Orage's magnaminity, or because he had lost Orage, or failed to lose him – who can tell? His cruel succession of self-inflicted wounds might have excused more general tears.

It was easier for the faithful Dr Stjoernval to restore Gurdjieff's equilibrium with a large bottle of Scotch whisky than for anyone to prescribe for the scrappy Work situation which ensued in New York. And the confusion now prevailing in the centrum of East Coast esotericism subtly communicated itself to a wider circle of sceptics and intellectual voyeurs – even arousing press interest. Gurdjieff's manipulations had become a matter of minor public interest – what was he up to? The light shed on the question by the *New York Herald Tribune* was unsatisfactory: 'Mr Gurdjieff said that he was in America to "shear sheep" among other things, but he declined to elucidate his meaning.'

In January the eminent behaviourist, Professor John Watson, with several friends and colleagues 'whose intelligence was strictly in the nine-minute egg category', came to see for themselves. The ambiance of room 'Q' – wobbly steel-framed chairs, bubbling cooking pots of stewed goat, and a grand piano piled high with liqueur bottles – unsettled their nerves. 'I write book,' announced Gurdjieff darkly from his shabby, liver-coloured couch. 'But who here can read?' At three the next morning, when he stopped the ensuing reading with a whispered, 'Enough, enough,' an elderly gentleman with a red ribbon across his starched shirt-front burst into tears and the company dispersed. 'You see what called "intelligentsia" in America,' said Gurdjieff. 'Can you imagine. Such empty thing. Intelligentsia they are called. Such nonentities.'

Beneath the stoicism of Orage's letter of 14 March 1931, there is real and natural hurt: 'Gurdjieff sailed last mid-night, leaving behind him an almost hopelessly scattered and hostile group.' The two men never met again (and Orage abandoned America for good on 3 July). Gurdjieff's apologia for his sabotage – in so far as he volunteered one – was blatantly designed to drive more people away. When C. S. Nott sought explanation at the Café de la Paix, almost any reply would have satisfied him, except the one Gurdjieff gave him:

> He listened quietly until I had finished, and with a sardonic grin said,
>   'I needed rats for my experiments.'
> 'What?' I asked.
>   'I needed rats for my experiments.'

Such 'rats' or 'freely walking guinea-pigs' were still available to Gurdjieff – albeit his old 'king-rats' were mostly gone. New and collectable specimens still poked their whiskers into view, but Gurdjieff generally took care to singe them. Thornton Wilder's is an interesting case in point. Meeting the celebrated author of *The Bridge of San Louis Rey* at Fontainebleau in the spring of 1931, Gurdjieff assured him genially: ' "I idiot, too. Everybody idiot. I idiot *type vingt-et-un*: I" – holding his forefinger emphatically pointed upward, "I the *unique* idiot" – with convulsions of . . . laughter.'

Wilder – tensely on guard against being fleeced – was confronted with a Gurdjieff who exuded venality: 'He sniffed at me. "Yes, I smell him. I think that he have money." ' Again and again Wilder confronted in Gurdjieff a Dadaesque distorting mirror:

> I sing song to you . . . When I sing in Paris, in Berlin it cost two hundred dollars. I give you two hundred dollars . . . I let you read my book. When my book published it cost five thousand dollars. I give you five thousand dollars.

At last, summoning the Prieuré gate-keeper to take Wilder home, Gurdjieff reassured his rich guest: 'He drive you to hotel. You no pay him. I pay him – by showing him money.' He extracted a large note from his wallet and passed it slowly before his pupil's appreciative eyes.

That Gurdjieff actually needed money – more desperately than ever since alienating New York – was undeniable. Had he courted Piotr Ouspensky, who commanded the purse strings of the wealthy London group, it might just have materialized. But Gurdjieff did nothing of the sort. Indeed when Ouspensky unexpectedly set out for the Prieuré in midsummer, he found its gates effectively barred against him. The powerful, equivocal liaison begun in 1915 in Moscow, 'at a small café in a noisy though not central street', ended forever in 1931 on the *terrasse* of the Café Henri IV in Fontainebleau.

The two men's final deadlocked meeting is out of earshot, and imagination is a treacherous lip-reader. That Gurdjieff pressed heavily on Ouspensky's pet corn is pretty clear, since more and more, as grey years passed, a 'mad', hubristic and even 'criminal' Gurdjieff became a stage property of Ouspensky's apologetic. To anyone disposed to listen, Ouspensky would just add that Gurdjieff's 'failure to contact Higher Source' was a catastrophe greater than the Russian revolution. Gurdjieff's feelings are less transparent: 'Ouspensky very nice man to talk to and drink vodka with,' he said, 'but he is weak man.' Weak or strong, Ouspensky's final estrangement polarized the Work, embuing it for decades with a priceless and painful vitality.

The decisive explosion at the Café Henri IV furnished a blast which deposited Sophie Grigorievna Ouspensky at 'The Dell', Sevenoaks – and this time she did not return. Gurdjieff was sixty-five. His writing – profound yet seemingly unpublishable – lay chaotically about him in typescript bundles and mimeographed copies; his aphorisms were peeling from the Study House walls and 'an air of intolerable melancholy streamed from those uneven white surfaces, those brilliant garish blues and sombre reds'; under the dripping maple trees the ghosts of former hopes stalked unkempt paths – the Prieuré was running down, and its Principal, for all his incredible inner reserves and Rabelaisian bonhomie, wore a faint aura of desolation:

> We said farewell to Gurdjieff under the lanterns of the château entrance . . . he turned away and walked off through the gardens . . . hands clasped behind his back . . . I thought that he looked like the loneliest man in the world.

Late in his collaboration with Thomas de Hartmann, Gurdjieff had composed the piece, 'As if the Difficult Years had Passed', but the difficult years had obviously not passed . . . to tell the truth they were just beginning.

12

❖

Holy Denying

(Summer 1931–6 May 1935)

If a man's being attracts his life (and Gurdjieff says it does), it is answerable for lean and fat years. And if Gurdjieff had attained inner unity (and he says he did), he nevertheless now opposed, now accepted, and now exacerbated, the rotten difficulties which overtook him. A curious double image – of a man defeated and a man invincible – dominates this four-year period. 'He had grown fat; he looked untidy; time had turned his long, black ring-master's moustache to grey; but he was unmistakenly a personage, and the old, arrogant, undaunted look shone forth from his eyes.' Not only do efforts to establish the 'real' Gurdjieff founder on a baffling impression of *dédoublement*, but (as Jean Toomer bitterly complains) his Tweedledum is the mirror image of his Tweedledee: 'for every fact there is a counter-fact, for every reason a counter reason, for every bit of "bad" behavior another bit of "good" behavior, for every son-of-a-bitching thing, a counter saintly thing.'

Of the five founder members of the Institute for the Harmonious Development of Man, just two now remained at the Prieuré: Leonid Stjoernval and Jeanne Salzmann. Three young Americans, two visiting Germans, and the repressed English gentlewoman Miss Elizabeth Gordon, were the sum total of subordinate pupils; Gurdjieff's dependent family hung on in Le Paradou; Mme Stjoernval and Rachmilievitch guaranteed a peevish chorus ... The seeming contraction of Gurdjieff's work was actually a corollary of its diffusion; those whom he thrust from the Prieuré, he did not thrust from the Work – on the contrary. In autumn 1931 Payson Loomis, a youngish American translator, announced his intention to decamp to Paris, and Gurdjieff gladly acquiesced: 'This is alright, only I give you exercise.'

But when Loomis unexpectedly spurned further tutelage, Gurdjieff startled him by brandishing his big black revolver: 'Take this with you,' he suggested helpfully. 'You will want to shoot yourself.'

In Gurdjieff's undeniable theatricality, actor and impresario merge imperceptibly, and the audience itself is sucked willy-nilly into the drama. The American Work-stage to which he briefly and unashamedly returned for a fifth performance in the winter of 1931 was much reduced; various minor players nervously trod the boards (the writer Gorham Munson, the actor Edwin Wolfe, and the poet Schuyler Jackson) but New York without Orage was like *L'Aprés-midi d'un Faune* without Nijinsky.

History cherishes one contemporary dinner-party scene (hosted by John O'Hara Cosgrave, former editor of the *New York World*), which has Gurdjieff playing opposite a certain Nadir Khan. Although this guest, who earned his living by incontinent authorship under the pen-name 'Achmed Abdullah', had a tendency to preen himself socially, he seems genuinely a man with a biographic hinterland: in 1903, as a regular officer attached to Colonel Younghusband's Expeditionary Force to Lhassa, the twenty-two-year-old Captain Khan had pitted his energies and wits against those of the formidable Lama Aghwan Dordjieff – and putatively against those of George Ivanovitch Gurdjieff. Now facing Gurdjieff directly across Cosgrave's generous dinner-table, 'Achmed Abdullah' made his famous and wildly erroneous ellision: 'I was convinced that he was the Lama Dorjieff.[3] I told him so – and he winked. We spoke in Tadjik.' (Few winks one might think have cost more ink.) As to the substance of what passed in Tadjik we shall never know, but here is Nadir Khan's tribute: 'I am a fairly wise man. But I wish I knew the things which Gurdjieff has forgotten.'

Despite such diversions, Gurdjieff did not linger in New York. The Work spotlight had refocused on Chicago where Jean Toomer's groups – less blighted by last season's problematical 'oath' – cherished, in 'an atmosphere of grim, humourless, devotion', the hope that Gurdjieff would return to consummate Orage's work. Orage himself had hoped it: 'What I pray for is that ... through me, like another Moses, they may find themselves led to Jordan and transported over by Joshua Gurdjieff.' Whether the adventist spirit prevailing in Chicago had been realistic, would be tested by Gurdjieff's coming, as inevitably would his followers' financial stamina.

Jean Toomer's personal fervour was beyond question, and arguably outran his competence and his commonsense. In the preceding summer, under the patronage of Zona Gale, he had conducted a rash Prieuré-style experiment at Portage, Wisconsin, which attracted much spiteful publicity; according to a reporter from the *San Francisco State Journal*, 'they were climbing trees out there just like squirrels.' Gurdjieff made light of this, indeed he seemed the soul of affability and understanding; even the fundamental misconception of Toomer's groups ('based on the assumption that life at the Prieuré must have been indiscriminately "free", meaning "licentious" '), he handled correctly and with tact. Yet immediately he had accumulated the money he needed, he raised his Astrakhan hat in farewell, and – wasting no time in New York – sailed for France aboard the s.s. *Bremen* on 16 January 1932.

With his wallet temporarily restocked, Gurdjieff plunged back into his writing regime at the Café de la Paix. The explanation that he 'liked to find there the sepia taste of his travels in Trans-Siberia' seems a little hard on Le Grand Hôtel, but certainly it remained for decades his Paris 'Headquarters'. It was there in February 1932 that the American writer Kathryn Hulme, already a junior member of Jane Heap's special group, first spotted him: 'With one leg pulled up beneath him Oriental-fashion on the banquette, he looked from a distance like a broad-shouldered Buddha radiating such power that all the people between him and me seemed dead.'

Once Gurdjieff had accepted Miss Hulme's tenuous credentials ('Geep?' he rumbled. 'Mees Geep?'), he bore her away to visit the Prieuré. Their pell-mell course down the route nationale – he in his black sedan, she in a following Packard – was notable equally for its dangers and lyric interludes: 'Here we make pause,' said Gurdjieff, pulling up at a frog pond, 'we listen to *grenouilles*.' The Prieuré itself and Kathryn's one night there, lodged in her memory as 'a dream, singular and inexplicable, a vision of trespass through a haunted house.' For if Miss Hulme had missed at the Café de la Paix the 'ghost' of Olga de Hartmann, perched forever and forever at Gurdjieff's little round marble-topped table, she was not so insensitive at the Château du Prieuré. Here she could sense the presence of Katherine Mansfield; dimly intuit spectral dancers in the empty Study House; and catch subliminal echoes of Gurdjieff's long-silenced music.

Month by month the Institute for the Harmonious Development of Man was settling into its final decline. Stanley Nott, visiting in spring 1932, was shocked at the Prieuré's condition: 'The gardens were neglected, the orangery in ruins ... the precious carpets ... damaged by rats and mice.' Gurdjieff's personal badges of affluence (Karakul hat, gold-topped walking stick, etc.) had been discarded, and however fast he drove to Paris with Nott and Jeanne Salzmann, he seemed overtaken by melancholy:

> He was dressed in a shoddy ready-made brown suit and cloth cap. When we stopped at a café, instead of talking and joking, he sat silent or answered with a word or two. We ... could feel his state of inner suffering ... the bigger the man, the bigger the burden; the stronger the man the stronger the suffering.

Deprived by his own will of virtually all his most effectual allies, Gurdjieff was desperately placed vis-à-vis the Prieuré. It was heavily encumbered, and neither his darting business ventures nor sluggish American donations came remotely near matching expenditure. The old lawyer Rachmilievitch was one of the few Prieuré residents actually contributing to the budget – and he had been reduced to peddling bric-à-brac from door to door, and working in a road gang. Trying for a second mortgage (to redeem the first), Gurdjieff persuaded a banker down from Paris and dined him memorably ... but Stanley Nott records the ominous sequel:

> Afterwards Gurdjieff took him with Stjoernval and myself to a raised bank behind the orangery; Persian carpets and cushions were spread, and we sat in bright hot sunshine drinking coffee, while Gurdjieff spoke of the value and possibilities of the Prieuré. Then we walked round the grounds, and as we walked the face of the financier became blanker; finally he left, promising to write after he had consulted his partners. But as I went to the gate with him, he muttered, '*Impossible, pas possible!*'

The camel's back was finally broken by the slenderest straw. A local coal merchant (owed 200 francs by Gurdjieff) sold his outstanding bill to a debt collecting agency; the agency pressed Gurdjieff, who perversely dug his heels in; and the alarmed mortgagees took fright and foreclosed ... On 30 April 1932 at supper Gurdjieff shockingly announced that this was 'the *last* Saturday, the *last* Armagnac'. Above the arrested knives and forks, eloquent faces betrayed their owners' diverse reactions: Elizabeth Gordon conveniently disbelieving, Elizabeta Galumnian fatalistic, and Bernard Metz cheerfully cynical. But the following day, when the kitchen was officially closed, at least one young American became incensed, threatening Gurdjieff 'with lawsuits and even bodily harm'. There ensued a week of turmoil: of rumours and counter-rumours, of impassioned unforgettable dialogues and frantic trips to Paris. 'Do quiet yourself,' said Jeanne Salzmann to Louise Goepfert.

Gurdjieff was never more the rounded, perfect host than on 7 May – only regretting again that this was the *last* Saturday, the *last* Armagnac. The Toasts to the Idiots were solemnly given by Papa Svetchnikoff and the ever-faithful Dr Stjoernval. On Monday after dinner the company adjourned to the beautiful salon and there, beneath the photograph of his father the *ashokh*, Gurdjieff played the harmonium for a long time. 'Can I do anything for you?' whispered Sausage hopelessly. 'Now only money, money,' Gurdjieff replied. 'One hundred thousand francs I need at once.' But no one had a purse so deep, and on Wednesday 11 May 1932 a melancholy silence settled at last over the Chateau du Prieuré: the Institute for the Harmonious Development of Man had ceased to exist.

No one can define with precision the absolute nadir of Gurdjieff's missionary hope but it is surely hereabouts. Although the Prieuré's impending closure had been staring him in the face for months, even years; although it had been accelerated by his own policy of isolationism – it nevertheless eventuated as a brutal shock. That the querulous Rachmilievitch and the querulous Mme Stjoernval would at last pass out of earshot was paradoxically a deprivation for Gurdjieff; that Leonid Stjoernval – the very doyen of his pupils – would retire to Normandy a disappointed man, raised awkward and painful questions; and that Jeanne Salzmann's companionship would soon end dispirited him. Gurdjieff himself cut his connection emphatically. He went to Paris, abandoning to fate his personal memorabilia, and trunks loaded with irreplaceable sheet music . . . all these, but for Jeanne's resource, would simply have vanished.

From a cramped room at the back of the Grand Hôtel Gurdjieff faced the wreck of former hopes and the fragility of future hopes. He was sixty-six but could not rest. In August he surprisingly telegraphed London urging his 'dear Anglo-American delicatesse' to come to him for one day, but Orage – infuriatingly true to his imposed vow to have no further commerce with 'Orage' – replied: 'There was a time when I would have crossed oceans at your bidding. Now I would not even cross the Channel.' As to Gurdjieff's motive, there are tell-tale signs of his desperate need for literary guidance. He had roughed out the plan of a third book to consummate *Beelzebub* and *Meetings* – the awkwardly titled *Life is Real Only Then: When 'I Am'*, but the urge to get something into print immediately was hot upon him. On Tuesday 13 September 1932, sitting in the Café de la Paix, Gurdjieff drafted at breakneck speed *The Herald of Coming Good: First Appeal to Contemporary Humanity*.

The mystery and heated debate surrounding this production – the only one Gurdjieff published in his lifetime – does not extend to its literary quality. That, by common consent, is abysmal. Half autobiography and half tract, *Herald* is a structural jumble, and the writing so marvellously bad it is almost 'good':

> The little book was an amazing publication. It gave you in many instances the impression of the work of a man who was no longer sane ... The style itself exhibited the same signs of strangeness, amounting almost to insanity, that were manifest in the subject matter. Reading the *Herald* was like the progress of a cart over cobblestones ... The first sentence contained no fewer than two hundred and eighty-four words.

Why did he do it? To drive away more pupils? To mock the *bon ton* literary language? To shock Ouspensky? To court blame (in the way of the *qalandari*)?... Or simply to appeal – with a drowning man's strident insistency – for help in rescuing the Prieuré?

The 'Coming Good' he promises is essentially the majestic *Beelzebub* (here falsely proclaimed to be 'completely finished and given to the printer'). Yet if anything on earth was likely to besmirch *Beelzebub* and hinder its publication; if anything was calculated to drive an obstinate nail into the coffin of Gurdjieff's literary reputation – it was the ironically titled *Herald of Coming Good*. Failing, predictably enough, to find a publisher, Gurdjieff circulated copies privately among his consternated followers.

Hardly less counter-productive than *Herald* – in fact arguably more so – was Gurdjieff's disastrous sixth visit to the USA. Arriving late in 1932 he made straight for Chicago: he was obese; he was difficult; he was (or took care to appear) blatantly venal. He distributed unwanted sweets, and on the packets were stuck 'postage stamps' portraying a highly unflattering 'Mister Gurdjieff'.

'Every person you see,' he explained to Fritz Peters, 'including yourself, is shit. You learn this and then when you find something good in such shit people ... you will feel good inside.' Jean Toomer watched with dismay the impact of this deconstructed Gurdjieff on his following; watched them recoil 'with disgust and anger and the conviction that he was using his power merely in order to obtain money, money and more money without cease.'

Everywhere he went, Gurdjieff was disruptive. At a literary reception in New York he roguishly anticipated Claude Bragdon, who was
busy cultivating a prominent woman novelist:

> Gurdjieff caught her eye, and we saw distinctly that he suddenly began to
> inhale and exhale in a particular way . . . A few moments later I noticed
> that my friend was turning pale; she seemed to be on the verge of
> fainting . . . 'That man is uncanny,' she whispered. 'Something awful
> happened . . . he looked at me in such a peculiar way that within a second
> or so I suddenly felt as though I had been struck right through my sexual
> centre.'

By the time Gurdjieff sailed for France at the end of February 1933,
Toomer was wonderfully disenchanted: 'To me he seemed a changed
man, changed for the worse. I felt his work was dead . . . It was a
travesty and hollow mockery of the Work I had entered in 1924 with
all my heart.'

The 'Supplementary Announcement' to *Herald* (which Gurdjieff
wrote at the Grand Café Fontainebleau on 7 March) is if possible
even more bizarre than the main text. Thanks professedly to very
recent socio-political developments of crucial significance, Gurdjieff
predicts for *Herald* 'an unusually large and moreover rapidly increased circulation'. Undoubtedly the two outstanding socio-political
events of 'the last few weeks' (Hitler made Chancellor on 30 January;
the Reichstag fire on 27 February) cast a long shadow. Yet what
responsible biographer could conceivably read here the entrails of
Herald's circulation figures? Wilder and wilder grow Gurdjieff's
claims: on St George's day 1933 (five years after his vow) he will
solemnly lay the foundation stone of an ambitious new Study House:
besides its three unprecedented laboratories – the 'Magnetic-Astral',
the 'Thoughthanbledzoin' and the 'Mentaloethero-winged' – it
will boast a 'Luminous-Key-Board' and a 'Retro-Rebounding-
Echoraising-Organ' . . . Across the Atlantic, Toomer forgivably
rehearsed his exasperated despair over Gurdjieff: 'He seemed to be
tearing down everything he had created . . . His life was a blight, he
was alienating people and throwing them off right and left.'

By 23 April Gurdjieff's big material preoccupation was not the
laying of a new foundation stone but salvage from the Prieuré's
wreck. At this low point in his fortunes, his friend Alexandre
Salzmann unexpectedly materialized in a Fontainebleau hotel,
coughing out harrowing days behind shuttered windows. He 'was
extremely emaciated and ghastly pale; in fact he looked like his old

nickname for Fraulein Gorter: "*Der wandelde Tod*".' This last perceived transaction between Gurdjieff and Salzmann is an enigma
(dangerously smudged by speculation). We know that halva and
other delicacies from Gurdjieff's table reached Alexandre, who rose
from his bed and struggled to the Café Henri IV for a poignant
meeting. We know Gurdjieff's unextinguished warmth towards
Salzmann, and his conviction that, in the sense of objective art, he
was 'the greatest of living painters' ... The rest is silence.

With cruel irony the long-awaited publication of *Herald* coincided
with the formal loss of the Prieuré, when, with all its contents including seventy dented bicycles, it was repossessed and sold to the French
manufacturer M.L. at the knock-down price of 200,000 francs.
Meanwhile Gurdjieff's unfortunate tract was 'Achieved printed on
the 26th August Nineteen Hundreds [sic] and Thirty-Three by La
Societé Anonyme des Editions de L'Ouest, 40, Rue du Carnet,
Angers, France.' Thus the Principal of the Institute for the Harmonious Development of Man lost his headquarters with its unique
Study House; lost his home where his wife and mother had died; and
gained a booklet of eighty-seven pages which would place his reputation in perpetual jeopardy. All the husbandry of the last decade had
borne this single strange fruit: priced idiosyncratically at 8 to 108
francs, according to the buyer's whim, *Herald* was 'bound in a most
curious sort of paper: it resembled suede leather and yet gave a
harshness to the touch that almost set one's teeth on edge.' Hundreds
of copies were sent to Ouspensky who had them burnt (hypothesiz-
ing that the author had contracted syphilis and gone mad). Even to
Gurdjieff himself it seemed that he had stayed in France too long for
any good that he was doing. He entrusted to Mme Salzmann's care
her husband's brilliant protégés René Daumal and his young bride
Vera; he made practical dispositions for his own family ... but an
autumn morning came when his emblematic figure was missing from
its accustomed place at the Café de la Paix: Monsieur Gurdjieff was
gone.

The strange man with heavy foreign accent who registered at the
Henry Hudson Hotel in New York toiled upstairs carrying cheap
black suitcases; he was alone and seemed exhausted. But although
Gurdjieff had re-entered the United States without fanfare, retinue,
or clear-cut programme; although indeed he bore all the trappings of
ignominious failure – he had not lost his extraordinary power of
attraction. The moths who fluttered back to his flame on slightly
singed wings (Muriel Draper, Jean Toomer, Gorham Munson,

Lincoln Kirstein, Edwin Wolfe, Schuyler Jackson, Nick Putnam, Paul Anderson) were valuable specimens: yet how far did Gurdjieff actually welcome their renewed attentions? There are signs he was suffering acutely from didactic fatigue.

Certainly no 'spiritual' claimant ever presented a less attractive or ethereal image to the American press. Reporters and feature writers predominated among the fifteen glossily veneered New Yorkers whom Gurdjieff invited for dinner within days of arrival. For an hour he wined and dined them royally, in the role of a poor, humble, and utterly unworthy host – then sadly observed how humanity had degenerated into 'pure shit':

> He indicated one very well-dressed, handsome woman, complimented her on her coiffure, her dress, her perfume, etc., and then said that . . . her reasons for turning herself out so elaborately were because she had a strong sexual urge (as he put it 'wish to fuck') . . . especially strong because she had a very fertile imagination and could already picture herself performing various sexual acts . . . 'such as, how you say in English? "Sixty-nine?" '

Egged on by more Armagnac and four-letter *conversazione*, and catching the apparent spirit of the thing, his guests were soon coupled in various stages of undress. At this point Gurdjieff suddenly:

> told them all, in loud, stentorian tones, that they had already confirmed his observations of the decadence of the Americans and that they need no longer demonstrate for him . . . he deserved to be paid for this lesson and . . . would gladly accept cheques and cash . . .

Surprisingly he collected several thousand dollars!

New York's familiar rituals and landmarks gently reclaimed Gurdjieff; he could be spotted through the plate-glass windows of various Child's Restaurants eating pancakes and squeezing lemon into his coffee; here he counselled pupils and (as in more exotic cities) treated a subsidiary clientele of psychological and physical derelicts. On the anxious Jean Toomer he fathered a brawling family of rhetorical questions: 'Who and what was he? What were his purposes? What aims did he have for me, if any? What aims for the people of the world? Was I a mere tool?. . . was he the supreme egotist? Was he, as some claimed, insane?'

In spring 1934, when Toomer nervously conveyed his intention to marry the well-to-do Marjorie Content and virtually leave the Work, his teacher misleadingly responded that he himself was leaving for France next day and would be glad of 200 dollars. And although

Gurdjieff did not in fact budge an inch except to extract a further 300 dollars, the sheer weight of his presence soon overrode all Toomer's doubts:

Insane? He was in full possession of every one of his extraordinary faculties. Debauched and slovenly? Nothing of the sort. Afraid of the dark and being alone? It was ridiculous. Whatever he had gone through, the thing that showed plainly was a decided improvement in every respect.

In May this remagnetized Toomer prevailed on Gurdjieff to set off for Chicago.

In the theatre of train departures Gurdjieff is a nonpareil: just as the noble 'transfigured' wisdom-figure of Petrograd is offset by the desperado 'scientist' of Essentuki, so the Greek tragedy of his parting from Olga de Hartmann in Paris finds its perfect counterpoint in the black comedy which opens at Grand Central Station, New York. Reaching the platform with seven suitcases, umpteen well-wishers, and just ten minutes in hand, Gurdjieff ordered his travelling companion Fritz Peters to hold the midnight express; and, despite his young adjutant's best efforts, had finally to be shoved by main force onto the moving train.

Growling and cursing over his shoddy treatment, he slowly banged his way towards his reserved berth, infuriating the dozing occupants of thirteen Pullman cars. Through a night that seemed to Fritz (and fellow-sufferers) interminable, Gurdjieff tossed and turned, moaned and groaned, clamoured for water and cigarettes; at breakfast he fancied nothing on the menu and embroiled the waiter and head steward in 'long irritating conversations ... about the possibility of procurring yoghurt and similar – at that time – exotic foods, accompanied by vivid descriptions of his digestive process and its highly specialised needs.'

Etched forever in Peters' memory were the hours which followed:

I have never, in my life, spent such a day with anyone. He smoked incessantly, in spite of complaints from the passengers and threats from the porter; drank heavily, and produced, at intervals when we seemed threatened with peace, all kinds of foods, mostly different varieties of strong-smelling cheeses.

Fritz reached his destination suffering from something like a nervous breakdown – Gurdjieff fresh as a daisy.

Although Peters' forgivable outburst of fury – bitten back until the very moment of arrival – scandalized the expectant groups, his

invective evidently had as negligible an impact on Gurdjieff as
Gurdjieff himself had on North Side Chicago intellectual circles. In
actuality it was not on Peters or even on Toomer that Gurdjieff's
mind was concentrated; pressing on quickly from Chicago, he ab-
jured all his recent levity: 'Now must change, we are going to special
place.'

In June 1934 Gurdjieff, his beautiful pupil Olgivanna, and her new
husband the American architect-genius Frank Lloyd Wright,[23] converged decisively at 'Taliesin', Spring Green, Wisconsin. Never since
parting from her master a decade earlier had Olgivanna's allegiance
wavered; Gurdjieff's teaching had been her rod and staff, as (through
a dispiriting vale of injunctions, attachments and writs alleging conspiracy, illegal immigration, desertion, alienation of affection, moral
turpitude, abduction, and adultery) she and Wright had painfully
extricated themselves from previous marriages and come together.
Gurdjieff's methodology had guided her as she and Wright jointly
devised their 'Taliesin Fellowship' for residential architectural
apprentices on their 1000-acre estate in the hills near the Wisconsin
River; and Gurdjieff had been strenuously defended in her simple
and moving memoir *The Last Days of Katherine Mansfield*. The
alarming question now was which 'Gurdjieff' would present himself
for inspection – and how Olgivanna's spiky, self-willed, and opinionated husband might react.

Our few extant memorials of Gurdjieff at Taliesin invite questions.
Billed as a profound savant, he seems to have walked in and nabbed
the role of chef:

> He asked them to bring him the oldest and toughest fowls they had ...
> took out of his pockets a number of little bags of spices and peppers and
> herbs and put pinches now and again in the pot, and produced a superb
> meal.

Wright's young apprentices happily accepted their incalculable guest
on his own terms. As pianist Edgar Tafel admitted: 'The thing we all
remembered most clearly afterwards – more than his music or
philosophy – was that he taught us how to prepare sauerkraut.' Yet
such a two-dimensional cartoon can hardly explain Gurdjieff's impact upon America's greatest contemporary architect.

Frank Lloyd Wright, with his blue beret and operatic cloak, was a
man who reserved most of his bouquets for himself; approbation
from him was praise indeed. Gurdjieff however elicited a Niagara of
endorsement: he was 'the stuff ... of which genuine prophets have
been made'; he was a builder in the truest sense; he was 'Organic

Man' (Wright's *summum bonum*); he resembled Augustine, Lao Tse, and Jesus:

In the work of this remarkable man ... we have for the first time a philosopher distinguished from all the others: a man ... sacrificing much during his life-time to make the ancient wisdom of the East not only intelligible to the thought of the West but to make it a way of WORK.

The stamp of the Prieuré, already set on the wax of Taliesin by Olgivanna, was now confirmed: Gurdjieff's 'moving, emotional, and intellectual centres' re-emerged as Wright's 'hand, heart, and head', and Gurdjieff's 'super-effort' as Wright's 'adding tired to tired' ... only the disruptive and surrealist element (the infusion say of seventy bicycles) was lacking.

Olgivanna's eyes with their 'yellow wildcat sparkle' presumably signalled her satisfaction and relief; true her husband's acceptance of Gurdjieff fell one important ratchet sort of discipleship, but there was a happy consensus that as Wright was to architecture, Gurdjieff was to philosophy. If Gurdjieff felt any temptation to outstay his welcome at the Fellowship – to play the ornamental hermit there – he resisted it. He nevertheless liked and respected Taliesin, 'The Shining Brow', as the acceptable face of America – almost as an entity in America but not of it. The notion of his creating a 'Prieuré of the Far West' had once seemed utterly ludicrous to him ... slightly less so now.

Any thought that the emissary from the Sarmoung Monastery might have settled in Taos, 120 miles north of Albuquerque; that his new echelon of pupils might have been Hispanic-Americans, with a sprinkling of Hopi, Navajo, Apache, or Comanche Indians – is somehow awkward to handle. The fact remains that, from Taliesin in the blistering summer of 1934, he did send out urgent overtures to Mabel Dodge Luhan to give him the ranch in New Mexico which she had originally volunteered (and he declined) in January 1926. But considering that Mabel was now fifty-five and her ardour for Jean Toomer had cooled, and considering that her friend D. H. Lawrence had worked so assiduously to undermine her trust, it was hardly surprising when on 18 August she signified that her offer was null and void ... Adios Gurdjieff!

Reappearing in late September at the Great Northern Hotel in New York, Gurdjieff had to cope with a new episode of media intrusion. The lightweight sculptor and writer Rom Landau arrived at room 217 greedy for copy, primed with sensational hearsay stories, and fatally complacent ('I am not easily influenced by "telepathic" enticement ... no doctor or hypnotist has ever succeeded in hypnotizing me.') Gurdjieff swung immediately into action with a surfeit of unnerving hospitality: 'I give you wonderful cigarettes,' he insisted, 'real cigarettes, Turkish and Russian. Say what?... Come, come, they good, *prima, prima*. If not smoke these, can give you ... what calls itself non-smoking cigarettes.' Although Landau held out, his sceptical temper did not armour him against Gurdjieff's 'emanation':

> I was beginning to feel a distinct weakness in the lower parts of my body, from the navel downwards ... After about twenty or thirty seconds ... the feeling inside my stomach was one of acute nervousness, amounting almost to physical pain and fear ... I was sure that if I tried to get up my legs would sag under me and I should fall to the floor.

Incidentally, the copy of *Herald* which Gurdjieff gave Landau must have been one of the last he distributed; within weeks he had turned against his own book. Since, on reflection, its very raison d'être was inexplicable without allusion to radiography, telepathy, 'telepsi', and the entire science of black and white magic, Gurdjieff resolved – arguably not a moment too soon – to suppress it: 'If you have not read this book entitled *Herald of Coming Good* then thank the circumstances and do not read it.' In Landau's case the prohibition came too late; Gurdjieff, as 'Black Magician', had already filled the mould of his lurid journalistic expectation.

A day which began very well for Gurdjieff and ended badly was Monday 6 November 1934. Getting up early he went to Child's Restaurant at Columbus Circle and began drafting his introduction to *Life is Real Only Then: When 'I Am'*: 'That morning I felt like a "mettlesome horse" let loose after having been confined for many months in the stable.' What a dramatic and happy contrast to his state precisely seven years before, when, lying 'sleepless in a whirlpool of oppressive thoughts' about his writing, he had actually contemplated suicide. At 11 am in the heat of a stimulating philological discussion about the distinction between 'voluntary' and 'intentional' suffering, Gurdjieff was called to the phone and told that during the night Orage had died of a heart attack.

For the next two months Gurdjieff did not write a word. Whatever may have been his private grief for his 'super-idiot', it was intruded on to an extent which almost drove him to distraction; virtually no one approached him without parroting: 'Oh, I am sorry about Mr Orage's death.' In New York – where Orage's ghost hovered so palpably – Gurdjieff found uninterrupted work out of the question. His vigorous evasive action took him first to Washington, then Boston, then Chicago, then the South. It was hopeless. Wherever he fled bands of well-wishers ambushed him with their predictable condolences, 'learned by heart from the list of "sympathies" .' The vacuous mechanicity of their recitation rendered it stuff and nonsense: 'Among the people of the Southern states who expressed their world famous "sympathy" were those who had not only never seen Mr Orage but had never even heard of his existence.' Only in January 1935 was Gurdjieff able to slip quietly back into New York and his dual role of professional writer and physician-hypnotist.

Gurdjieff's final weeks in America in spring 1935 are perhaps most intelligently approached as a kind of Rorschach Test, revealing more about the biographer than his elusive subject: their smudged motivation, symmetrical tensions, and blood-stained coincidence, license extraordinary projections. On 9 April, as Gurdjieff finished the Prologue to *Life is Real* and commenced his module, 'The Outer and Inner World of Man', he seemed exultant – his writing task virtually accomplished, his health recovered, and his grasp of 'deep-rooted minutiae of the common psyche of man' gratifyingly extended. Moreover he understood from Leonid Stjoernval that the Prieuré was again on the market; and his American pupils Nick Putnam and Paul Anderson were busy looking for a financial backer. But then on Sunday 14 April, Gurdjieff's eyes chanced on the émigré newspaper *Russky Golos*, and somehow or other all his hopes were re-patterned by that mysterious modifier: 'Begin in Russia, finish in Russia.'

Evidently what struck Gurdjieff so powerfully in *Russky Golos* was a little feature article entitled, 'The Problem of Old Age'. But how? And why? The style is pedestrian and nothing in its bland and unconvincing praise of contemporary Soviet scientific studies into longevity seems remotely on Gurdjieff's scale. So what secret factor caused him to lift this entire piece and plunk it (with attribution) into 'The Outer and Inner World of Man'? Is it conceivable that a single clause, suggestive of some coded warning, holds a vital clue? At the end of an otherwise anodyne passage these grim words are inserted: 'Death is doubtless in too great hurry to reach man.' Two weeks passed. Then a telephone call from Paul Anderson brought news that an eminent politician was expressing serious interest in backing Gurdjieff financially.

In Bronson Murray Cutting, Republican Senator for Santa Fé, New Mexico, providence seemed to have concentrated all that was

ideally and quintessentially American. A Harvard Phi Beta Kappa, a
leader of the Bull Moose movement, a member of the Knickerbocker
Club, and an Episcopalian, Cutting had already self-deprecatingly
declined the office of Secretary of the Interior, and, at forty-six was
widely mentioned as of presidential timbre. Gurdjieff was predisposed towards such types: 'Americans more receptive because not
closed up inside yet; they naive, stupid, perhaps, but still real.' In a
spirit of practised confidence, he set off for Washington to rendezvous with this heaven-sent benefactor. Soon, however, a small hiatus
(Bronson was unexpectedly detained in Santa Fé) found Gurdjieff
uncharacteristically impatient and even defensive: 'enemies with an
unusual inner attitude to me are multiplying in great numbers.' After
a tense day or two in his hotel, he delegated a drop-jawed Anderson
to go to the Soviet Embassy and explore if he could return to Russia
and teach there.

Astounding! What of Dmitri and Sophie Ivanovna in France?
What of Jeanne Salzmann? What of the unpublished *Beelzebub* with
its ill-disguised diatribe against Lenin? What of the Prieuré waiting to
be recouped with Bronson's funds? And what of Gurdjieff's mission
to the West? Add to this that the Russian scenario was then particularly appalling: the assassination of Sergei Kirov in December 1934
had just set in motion the wave of terror which, cresting in Stalin's[30]
Great Purge, swept away ten million lives. Only the sharpest necessity could have induced Gurdjieff to think of going to Russia – if for
example death were in too great hurry to reach his teacher. The final
indeterminacy of this singular Rorschach card must prevail over
every subjective interpretation, but one honest datum invites consideration: it was in 1934 that that remarkable man the Lama
Aghwan Dordjieff was exiled from Buryat-Mongolia to Leningrad;
he was eighty-one, in black disfavour, and death was indeed in a
hurry to reach him.

While Gurdjieff awaited Moscow's decision, the Senator telegraphed a firm date for his arrival in Washington: he would be there
on 6 May to vote on the veterans' bonus. The augury was golden.
The 6 May, by Gregorian computation and contemporary usage, was
tantamount to the 23 April by the old or Julian calendar, which
Gurdjieff invariably used for events high and holy. By his reckoning,
the crucial meeting was thus set for the Prieuré's 'Coronation Day',
the nameday of Saint-George-the-Victor, and the birthday of Julia
Ostrowska. Unfortunately for augury however, on 6 May 1935 –
seven years precisely after Gurdjieff's vow to 'remove from my

eyesight all those who by this or that make my life too comfortable' – tragedy struck.

The twin-engined Sky Chief No. 323, lofting the Senator to Washington from Albuquerque, was scheduled to set down at Kansas City at 2.56 am to refuel; frustrated by 'soupy' air conditions, it turned desperately for the emergency field at Kirksville, and crashed into a cow midden near Atlanta, Missouri, just before dawn. Identified among the dead by an outstanding telephone bill and a photograph of his mother, was Bronson Cutting ('He never knew what hit him,' testified Linwood Butler, who pulled out the crushed and mutilated body.)

By the time Gurdjieff was up and about in Washington on 6 May, the Stars and Stripes were at half-mast on the Senate Office Building and various politicians were lamenting into microphones: Senator Borah said he could not find words to express himself; Senator Hiram Johnson said Bronson had been more like a son to him; and even President Roosevelt confessed himself 'greatly grieved to learn of the untimely death of my old friend.' Doubtless he was, doubtless they all were, but whether anyone (except Bronson's mother) was more grieved than Gurdjieff seems remotely improbable. A day or so later, fate cruelly foreclosed on Gurdjieff's alternative option: 'He may return to the Soviet Union, only if he will accept work where he is assigned,' pronounced the Embassy darkly, 'but he must not teach anything.'

In this intensely bleak moment, Gurdjieff the professional writer ceases to exist; he breaks off 'The Outer and Inner World of Man', and jettisons his promised and eagerly anticipated revelations as to the Sarmoung Monastery and the secret needs and possibilities of man's body, spirit, and soul – the very kernel of his esotericism. His own narrative freezes and the frame collapses – Gurdjieff simply disappears.

13

❖

MODALITIES OF HEALING

(7 May 1935–2 September 1939)

It is a long, long time from May to September, but that is the duration of our missing patch in 1935 when Gurdjieff vanishes. Did he go to Germany? Even visit Leningrad? Conceivably penetrate Central Asia? All are variations entertained in the Gurdjieff apocrypha and not inconsistent with his passport. What alone is certain is that one morning in September the sweet-toothed waiters at the Café de la Paix found him installed again at his favourite seat beneath the striped parasol on the *terrasse*: 'Monsieur Bonbon' had returned.

Gurdjieff's brother Dmitri, Leonid Stjoernval, Jeanne Salzmann (Jeanne de Salzmann now),[29] Jane Heap, and even Rachmilievitch quickly updated him. His old friend Alexander Gustav Salzmann had finally died from tuberculosis on 3 March 1934, at Leysin near Geneva. In Paris – small consolation – new pupils were now at Gurdjieff's disposal, in two contrasting flocks: Jane Heap's preponderantly lesbian conclave, now in Montparnasse, and Jeanne de Salzmann's embryonic French group, six miles away at Sèvres. The name 'Sèvres' was inauspicious (the Treaty of Sèvres in August 1920 having inflamed Kâzim Karabekr Pasha and prompted the massacre of Gurdjieff's sister and her family). Nevertheless, at the Sèvres establishment in its derelict park, the wholehearted Work engagement of René and Vera Daumal, the orientalist Philippe Lavastine and his young wife 'Boussique' (Jeanne de Salzmann's daughter), signalled the first exciting breach in the wall of French hostility to Gurdjieff.

News from England was bad. Rom Landau's spiritual *tour d'horizon*, *God is My Adventure*, published in September by Ivor

Nicholson and Watson, had proved a rampant bestseller with explicit and unprecedented reference to the Work and its teachers: 'Never before,' acknowledged Landau, 'have I met anyone working more directly and logically to help people conquer the phantoms of sleep and to lead them into consciousness.' The snag was that this accolade was awarded to Ouspensky! As to Ouspensky's master, Landau was of a different opinion: his teaching was chaotic and 'his personality, however strong, failed utterly to convince me. I had been unable to perceive in the man George Ivanovitch Gurdjieff the harmonious development of man.' The cauldron of Landau's pique boiled and bubbled as he stirred in the story of Gurdjieff's hypnotic aggression, his appalling book *Herald*, his 'telepathic rape' of Bragdon's novelist friend, and his political manœuvres as 'Dordjieff' ... This unsavoury and preposterous muddle was to remain the most drastic critique of Gurdjieff published in his lifetime; it reached many minds and closed them against him.

Free of dependants, of his Institute, and of the authorial grind, Gurdjieff had not been so temptingly accessible since early 1924. It almost seemed – but the semblance was delusive – that Jane Heap's hour of golden intimacy had come. The extraordinary paradox of her move to London on 18 October 1935 is certainly not construable in terms of disaffection on either side: rapport between her and Gurdjieff proved strong and enduring (for years she was the only pupil he sanctioned to read out-loud his apotheotic chapter from *Beelzebub*, 'The Result of Impartial Mentation'.) Why then? Did Ouspensky or Landau's book figure in this riddle? We cannot guess. But certainly on arrival in England Jane modestly applied to enter one of the groups of Ouspensky – who rejected her in principle as an incorrigible lesbian.

To do Ouspensky justice, his repudiation of 'such types' faithfully echoed Gurdjieff's own dicta:

> Only a person who is completely normal as regards sex has any chance in the work. Any kind of 'originality', strange tastes, strange desires, or, on the other hand, fears ... must be destroyed from the beginning. Modern education and modern life create an enormous number of sexual psychopaths. They have no chance at all in the work.

And did Gurdjieff's rule apply to homosexuality? Fritz Peters (somewhat of an expert witness) leaves not a shadow of doubt: 'He was puritanical, even a fanatic about homosexuality, and condemned it vigorously ... he felt that homosexuality – as a career – was a dead-end street. . .' And yet (theory and practice once more at logger-heads), Gurdjieff now extended his sheltering wing not over the pupils of Sèvres but of Montparnasse.

Although Jane Heap had disbanded her group without explicit referral, its members needed no encouragement to try their chances with Gurdjieff. Kathryn Hulme, quickest off the mark, sought him out at the Café de la Paix on her way back from seeing Jane off at the Gare St Lazare, and that same Friday afternoon found herself in his small, cluttered room in the Grand Hôtel, reading aloud from *Beelzebub*: 'I was agonisingly aware of the author sitting opposite me on the sofa . . . listening with a concentration that seemed to burn up all the oxygen in the air between us.' By that evening, she and Louise Davidson and Solita Solano were dining with their master in the Brasserie Excelsior:

> Gurdjieff cried 'Oie, oie!' when the huge platter of crimson 'river lobsters' were set before him steaming in a thin reddish sauce . . . There was a pause while Gurdjieff poured Armagnac into the six glasses . . . four for himself and party, one each for the patron and the waiter.

Events were developing with astonishing speed.

Gurdjieff's first Parisian group (comprising this adventitious trio of American spinsters) convened on Monday 21 October 1935 in room 6 of the Hôtel Napoleon Bonaparte, a dwarf establishment, which, if it lacked in amenities, certainly reeked of atmosphere. Sited at No. 36 Rue Bonaparte, close by the Ecole des Beaux-Arts, a block away from the Café des Deux Magots and the Café de Flore, and equally convenient for the church of St Germain-des-Prés and the Brasserie Lipp, the Hôtel Bonaparte had briefly roofed any number of literary bigwigs: Djuna Barnes had wept out emergencies here; Scott Fitzgerald had slept it off in the hall ('Margaret! Help me!'); a spring-heeled Ernest Hemingway had run up these stairs with James Joyce 'over his shoulder, a featherweight of brittle bone and brilliant brain.' Solita Solano currently lived in room 16 on the fifth floor; in room 15 (taken by her partner Janet Flanner, the columnist 'Genét'), Jane Heap and Margaret Anderson had – years since – wound up the *Little Review*, spilling editorial green ink all over the sheets. Room 6 had been appropriated by Kathryn Hulme when Jean Cocteau vacated it for one of his period 'cures' of opium addiction – and now Gurdjieff sat there, 'Perrier water and ashtray set out for him beside the sagging sofa that he occupied completely, like a Buddha on a pedestal.' So often and so unpredictably did *Monsieur le Professeur* reappear at the Hôtel Bonaparte in November and December 1935, that the bald-headed patron M. Louis 'consented to signal his approach by three quick warning rings of the house bell.'

After recent – somehow anaemic – years Gurdjieff re-entered his teaching role with Gargantuan relish. His three unlikely pupils were first assigned their 'inner animal': Solita a canary, Louise a stranded sardine, and Kathryn a crocodile. ('Crocodile meat I do not like, never eat, but crocodile I like, I can send ahead of me to swallow enemy, can be *useful* to me.') The unexpected and problematical toast, '*A la santé de tous les idiots ordinaires*', plunged them without preamble into the *science d'idiotisme* – a typology of twenty-one 'idiots' or archetypes, saluted successively in Château de Larresingle Armagnac, with formularies and improvisations. Eagerly 'Canary', 'Sardine', and 'Krokodeel' groped towards the sense and sequence of these idiots: ordinary, super, arch, hopeless, compassionate, squirming, square, round, zigzag, enlightened . . . and so on up to No. 21, the Unique Idiot, God himself. Small wonder if the women sometimes gazed about them with a wild surmise: 'We had become habituées of the incalculable.'

At Christmas 1935, Gurdjieff moved from the Grand Hôtel to an apartment in Rue Labie just inside the old fortifications of Paris. Its distance from the Café de la Paix and relative proximity to the Salle Pleyel (by the Alexander Nevski Cathedral) rather confirms Gurdjieff's reversion from professional author to 'Teacher of Dancing'. The little menagerie from Hôtel Napoleon Bonaparte encountered in Rue Labie a more oriental Gurdjieff in carpet slippers, baggy trousers, and tasselled red fez, who combined the role of spiritual exemplar with that of cook and paterfamilias:

> When you do a thing, do it with the whole self. *One thing at a time*. Now I sit here and I eat. For me nothing exists in the world except this food, this table. I eat with the whole attention. So *you* must do – in everything . . . To be able to do *one* thing at a time . . . this is the property of Man, not man in quotation marks.

On really big culinary occasions Gurdjieff was helped by Gabo his strapping Russian aide-de-camp, and fussed over by his temporary secretary Miss Elizabeth Gordon, whose repressed emotionality sometimes erupted 'in the form of quick flushes and small livid angers'.

Early in January 1936 Gurdjieff constituted 'The Rope': a special group comprising Miss Gordon, Solita Solano, Kathryn Hulme, and her American friend the voguish milliner 'Wendy' . . . What is one to make of Gurdjieff here? Perhaps, despite his catholic experience, there was novelty in sustained, close-quarter, transformational work with four successful, ambitious, middle-aged lesbians? Perhaps, simultaneously, the White Magician reveals his essential benignity (love without limits as Fritz Peters once expressed it), and the Black Magician a value-free experimentation upon a variant breed of 'trained and freely moving "Guinea-Pigs" '? Allowing this ambivalence, one must stress that the expression 'rope' was Hulme's not Gurdjieff's, and carried entirely innocent associations:

> We were going on a journey under his guidance, an 'inner-world journey' like a high mountain climb where we must be roped together for safety, where each must think of the others on the rope, all for one and one for all.

As best we can guess, Gurdjieff's seventieth birthday fell on 13 January 1936. He did not look seventy or act like it. The silver in his beard was contradicted by his general animation and virile expression. Besides his intensifying work with The Rope, he was sticking a practised thumb into various entrepreneurial pies, and treating on the side a shadowy clientele who complained of arthritis, alcoholism, and psychic depression. In one coup of exceptional complexity he managed to get a brand new car without down-payment – helped, purportedly, by a Faustian contract with Saint-George-the-Victor: 'But he is a very *expensive* saint. He is not interested in money, or merchandise like candles. He wishes *suffering* for merchandise, an *inner-world* thing.' And immediately St George had delivered transportation, Gurdjieff pressed down hard on the accelerator and was off on those hair-raising weekend jaunts – to Germany, the Low Countries, Vichy, the Riviera, Geneva, and Normandy – which he felt essential *changer les idées*.

By May 1936, The Rope was received every day in Rue Labie. Stanley Nott, though eager for entrée, was bluntly refused – no heterosexuals need apply. Report of Gurdjieff's orientation spread though pertinent circles and in June three better qualified personnel arrived: Georgette Leblanc, Margaret Anderson, and their elderly *bonne a tout faire* Monique ('a fairy-tale nurse, a character met only in books with coloured illustrations, a nature without an angle'). A nurse was indeed sadly apropos, for the once beautiful Georgette was barely recognizable. At sixty-seven, and after three grave illnesses in as many years, she was ravaged physically though strangely exalted spiritually: 'During my struggle with death I had thought, "If I am to live, I swear to myself to go further than before . . . I do not give myself the right to come out of danger in the same state in which I entered it." '

Gurdjieff met her more than halfway: whatever could be provided by way of encouragement, attention, and unrestricted access, he freely gave her. Georgette read voraciously from the unpublished writings in his flat, and within weeks her pain had begun to abate: 'Physically I am living a springtime in this cold month of July. I feel charged like a dynamo.'

But for Georgette, Margaret Anderson would not have endured Paris a single week. Her memoirs shriek out her sense of alienation:

> In town, in the middle of July, walking through the noxious gases of the exhaust fumes of automobiles, my throat burning, my ears crackling with the loudspeaker city, my head fainting with fury, my heart failing, my eyes trying to see what they saw but, instead, distant hills.

At the end of the month, when summer belatedly arrived, Gurdjieff mercifully declared a three-month break. He dismissed his enlarged entourage (ironically dubbed 'Knachtschmidt and Company' since Margaret's, Monique's and Georgette's arrival) with one of his big feasts: specially imported rice steamed with raisins and apricots, roast baby lamb, *fraises des bois* with fresh cream, Syrian loucoum and Latvian chocolates. 'Let the food you eat here stay in memory only, but the *other* kind of food . . . carry with you.'

The Americans' sabbatical gave Gurdjieff time for a first token contact with the French. A haze of conflicting allusions obscures his encounter with René Daumal, but probability situates it in Geneva in summer 1936. Certainly Jeanne de Salzmann's group customarily worked there in those months when heat made Sèvres oppressive, and certainly in mid-1936 René's view of philosophy (already transformed by the Salzmanns) was lent an exciting new quotient of practicality:

> At last I have met someone with whom I work, who has dedicated his life to that problem and can help others to find the solution to it. It is a work at each moment, in which the whole human being (with his body, his instincts, his feelings and his intellect) experiences and realises himself . . .

As with Ouspensky ages ago in Moscow, so now, the sheer force of Gurdjieff's individuality reversed the cultural pecking order: he was after all, in French cultural estimation, an old man with nothing particular to show, while Daumal, at twenty-eight, already had *Le Contre-Ciel* – poems just awarded the Jacques Doucet prize by Valéry, Giradoux, and Gide. Yet so enthusiastic was René's discipleship (and so fragile his constitution), that Jeanne de Salzmann urged him to conserve his physical health or break with the teaching ... he did neither.

Gurdjieff did not linger with the Sèvres group that summer, not simply for psychological reasons but because, with indomitable hope, he was scouring about for a new country seat. The likeliest he found was a château on the Marne, rentable at 12,000 francs per annum – but unfortunately he had not got sufficient of what his American pupils called 'dough' or 'oof'. Finally he settled for a place even nearer to the Salle Pleyel – an apartment at 6 Rue des Colonels Rénard.

Gabo and 'Our Dear Esteemed, Our Reverence, Miss Gordon' – that stalwart be-hatted monument to British reliability – bore the brunt of transferring Gurdjieff's paraphernalia from Rue Labie. Not that he had a lot in August 1936. The days when Apartment 6 would dominate the Gurdjieffian myth as a *mise-en-scène* perhaps more extraordinary than his Moscow apartment on the Bolshaia Dmitrovka, lay in the future. In estate agent's terms it was merely a 'compact' first-floor flat handy for the Etoile, comprising a dining room, lounge, two bedrooms, kitchen, pantry and the usual amenities. Indistinguishable from its fellows in a grey nondescript block, it was a modest and even improbable setting for the grand seigneur of the Prieuré, as Gurdjieff himself conceded: 'Such a place we have now is not convenient. We must have more *solid* place.'

In late October Gurdjieff remustered his formidable regiment of women. He found them all refreshed except Georgette Leblanc, who, during the long summer break, had been physically shaken by alternating tempests of hope and despair. The entry for 2 November 1936 in her little red diary suggests the volatility as well as the intensity of the forces at play:

> A great emotion today. When I arrived at Gurdjieff's apartment it was he himself who opened the door. I said immediately, 'I am completely well, I am in a new body.' The light that came from the little salon illuminated him fully. Instead of avoiding it, he stepped back and leaned against the wall. Then, for the first time, he let me see what he really is . . . as if he had torn off the masks behind which he is obliged to hide himself. His face was stamped with a charity that embraced the whole world. Transfixed, standing before him, I saw him with all my strength and I experienced a gratitude so deep, so sad, that he felt the need to calm me. With an unforgettable look he said, 'God helps me.'

Despite Gurdjieff's solicitude for Georgette, Margaret, and Monique; despite his acknowledgement of their relative seniority – he did not admit them into the holy-of-holies of his present work: they belonged to 'Knachtschmidt and Company' but never to 'The Rope'. In a sense, Margaret Anderson's exclusion was self-inflicted. By successive phases of explosive dissent, bilious fuming, and mute rage, she had become a rebel without a cause, brooding over Gurdjieff's table like some heavily lipsticked Rachmilievitch:

> Must we all eat burning food in a burning flat and walk the burning streets to develop a soul? . . . So this is the higher life! . . . I should think that if any life could produce authentic neurasthenia it would be just this unmanaged, mismanaged, struggling, squirming, torturing, uninteresting, uninspired succession of days that now present themselves to my numbed personality.

Margaret's obtuseness, her breathless emotionality, and her dumb insolence, constituted a sort of gritstone on which Gurdjieff honed his transcendental patience.

The Rope's long readings from *Beelzebub* were supplemented by serious tasks of interior attention. In November, as if saluting their effort, Gurdjieff gave each member a chaplet of black beads and a special sensing exercise to go with it:

> You see men – Turk, Greek, Arab, Armenian – sitting all day in the coffee house with such chaplets. To you they make a picture of the lazy man, but what they do with these beads creates an inner force you cannot imagine.

Although the evidence-in-chief for Gurdjieff's own inner force was his silent, monumental presence, he still bore ample witness to a capacity for action. Despite suffering from a badly infected right hand, he made Christmas 1936 an enormous event – a celebration, a housewarming, and general rendezvous. To get his fifty ill-assorted guests, adults and boisterous children, into a 'compact' apartment was one thing, but to jam-pack them into a lounge already containing a fabulously decorated Christmas tree was another. Proximity must have enforced some unlikely relationships. Did the Scrooge-like Rachmilievitch mellow to some long-forgotten Tiny Tim? And how did the alienist Dr Stjoernval react when suddenly confronted with seven lesbians? Everyone received superb food . . . and banknotes . . . and presents: 'Ikons, underwear, toys and perfumes are plucked from the boxes and waved aloft, then thrust safely back amid flurries of thanks in Russian . . . *Spasiba*, Georgivanitch! *Spasiba, spasiba*!'

Exactly how the host with his Hédiard tastes and 'perenially flat pocket-book' had managed it all was anyone's guess, but the evening smacked of that universal charity which Georgette had intuited. As she left at midnight, the Russian maid told her: 'From one o'clock till dawn the poor will be coming.'

According to Gurdjieff, 1936 had resembled a garbage pail: 'Another *swallach* year is ended. I deserve a rest. *Truth*, Miss Gordon?' In spring 1937 (as the savage and unprecedented bombing of Guernica ushered in an entire *swallach* epoch), Gurdjieff often filled his motor car with picnic basket and passengers and gunned it south – to Vichy, Cannes, Monte Carlo, and the Alpes Maritime. Although he himself blended rather choicely with the Riviera setting, his fantasized 'final solution' for its raddled habitués was drastic!

> Paint them, and then with ceremony, throw them in the sea. Like old automobiles, you paint them and make them look like new; but *still* they are good only for throwing into the sea. But of course with ceremony ... big ceremony.'

These heroic outings in Gurdjieff's sedan (a privilege often visited on his brother Dmitri and Miss Gordon) typically reduced the passengers to rag dolls – as this Vichy cameo suggests: 'Gurdjieff stopped the car with sudden application of brakes before the hotel. Then the mimosas heaped on the back seat parted and Dmitri's white face appeared like a death mask; he groaned "*Je suis mort!*" ' Although the complainant was nothing more than car-sick, his exclamation was grimly prophetic, for in just four months Dmitri was laid in his coffin.

On 4 May 1937, Kathryn Hulme and Wendy sailed for America (supposing their master was hard on their heels) but the struggle for Dmitri's life – that all too familiar struggle with cancer – dominated the ensuing months and overturned all Gurdjieff's plans. His tragic impotence in the fate of Julia Ostrowska's illness he had ascribed to his convalescent frailty; he was strong now – perhaps as psychically strong as any man could hope to be – but he was not as strong as cancer. Saint-George-the-Victor was exacting in the coinage of suffering full payment for his favours. In August, as Kathryn and Wendy were poised for Gurdjieff's arrival in New York, they received instead his regrets and the news that Dmitri was dead. With characteristic hyperbole they cabled back 'Your brother is our brother.' ... Had Dmitri even been Gurdjieff's brother? Yes indeed in blood and amity, but how startlingly the two sons of Giorgios Giorgiades differed in scale and orientation. Dmitri Ivanovitch Gurdjieff, sometime proprietor of the first cinema in Tiflis, had gone now to whatever sphere is reserved for such as he. He had never – one is led to believe – worked on himself spiritually in his life. Had he then 'perished like a dog'? Was he simply 'wiped off'? Or did some incalculable grace cradle him?

Whatever Dmitri's life had amounted to, his unexpected death was a *memento mori*, a prompting to more intense and authentic work. On 20 October 1937, Margaret Anderson and Georgette Leblanc (already fifteen years in Gurdjieff's circle) went to him and asked if they could actually begin: 'We have spent our lives', they had concluded, 'walking about under parasols.' Gurdjieff gave them a line of work so powerful that Georgette soon professed, 'I am almost afraid – life rises in me like the sea.' ... Yet the sober truth was that the heyday of The Rope and Knachtschmidt and Company was over, virtually before it had begun: Miss Gordon for one was not getting any younger; Kathryn Hulme's professional obligations allowed her only three weeks in Paris in the next seven years; Wendy never returned from America, drifting out of the Work altogether; and by early spring 1938, the born-again Gurdjieffians Margaret and Georgette had retreated to Normandy with the spoils of their new insights:

> It was afternoon when the lighthouse emerged for us, again from the trees and the river. The tide was high, birds were singing, flowers blooming ... Inside I looked once more at the rooster plates, and the cracked ones with roses ... Air from the forest entered. I sat down. Everything was the same. But I was not ... A blessing was upon me, I felt it on every side.

In the burnt-out landscape of Gurdjieff's singular lesbian experiment there nevertheless still loomed two statuesque and impressive figures: Jane Heap of course and Solita Solano.

Although when Solita became Gurdjieff's private and confidential secretary in 1937 she was forty-nine, the years had scarcely touched her operatic beauty. The incisive fringe of her dark bobbed hair instantly evoked Katherine Mansfield – a likeness only contradicted by Solita's big blue eyes. Where Olga de Hartmann had brought to her role as Gurdjieff's secretary a touching and strangely efficacious innocence, Miss Solano brought rather the converse: she had lived to the hilt as an actress, reporter and dramatic critic; she had published four novels; she made one triangle with Janet Flanner and the heiress Nancy Cunard, and another with Flanner and Ernest Hemingway; she was 'Tuck' in the *Ladies Directory*, and had enjoyed such a catholicity of experiences (from Grosse Pointe, Michigan, to

Constantinople, Turkey) that she spoke of herself as '*guardian* of the thesaurus: birth to retirement'.

Despite Solita's verve and utility, she happily acknowledged a contemporary whose shoes she was not worthy to unlatch. Mme de Salzmann's command of Sacred Dance, of music, of Russian – these alone would have elevated her to an unchallengeable position. But beyond such considerations, Jeanne 'Begins-to-Understand' was now, in Gurdjieff's eyes, living proof of the transmissability of his Work: her inner search, sustained through many vicissitudes since 1919, had brought its law-conformable result, expressible in the words – 'She is someone!' In preparation for a new phase, Jeanne was gradually winding down her group at Sèvres, and at the same time reaching out for luminaries like Luc Dietrich, author of *Le Bonheur des Tristes*. A gauge of her leonine confidence was the sheer ruthlessness of her critique. On 29 January 1939, she attacked the complacent young Dietrich in the presence of his Work friends:

> Good speaker, bad doer. You must draw up a balance sheet, kill the old man in you. You prostitute everything with your words ... you and your secrets, your MOTHER, your FRIENDS, your WOMAN ... And then you lie all the time. Your lies make me disgusted with you ... what you give has no value. You give what you have too much of, what you no longer want. You give your excrement.

At forty-nine, and brimming with energy, Jeanne de Salzmann was emerging as Gurdjieff's de facto deputy. As to Dr Leonid Stjoernval – that decent Petrine rock on whom no church was destined to be builded – he had died near Reims in April 1938, as unostentatiously as he had lived.

Early in March 1939, accompanied by Solita Solano, Gurdjieff arrived in the s.s. *Paris* on his penultimate visit to the USA. What begs analysis is less his going there than his coming back. Daily the newsboy's 'Read all about it!' confirmed Europe's slide towards reciprocal destruction: soon after Gurdjieff arrived, the US Ambassador was recalled from Berlin; a week later Hitler repudiated Germany's non-aggression pact with Poland – the entire trend was consistent and ominous. Gurdjieff had already warned Stanley Nott of 'horrors on an enormous scale that were about to take place. When war did come, he said, it would be a "nasty mix".' Small wonder that his influential American followers – who had aided him for fifteen years and who cherished his every word – begged him to sit out the war in New Jersey. What made him refuse? Was it his long-unrealized aim to build a significant following in France, or his inveterate taste for 'sharp energetic events'? ... Perhaps there is a clue of sorts in Gurdjieff's response to a youngster who enquired in general terms about the 'good life': would it make sense to retire to the country, build a log cabin, and literally cultivate one's garden? 'Yes,' said Gurdjieff acidly, 'that good life. For dog. For man, no. You eat, you sleep, live in dream. How could that be life of a man?'

Under the 'No Cooking' sign in his small suite in the Wellington Hotel, Gurdjieff created his usual aromatic feasts: a Sterno coffee machine performed noisily in the bathroom, stewing pots simmered, Pyralin soup bowls encumbered the bookshelves, and cleavered carcasses of lamb swung provocatively from the fire escape. Failing to find any Château de Larresingle Armagnac, and detesting American 'bourbon whiskey', Gurdjieff concocted his own brew 'from triple-distilled alcohol shaken up with lichee nuts and small pieces of toasted lemon skin ... a frightful drink, so strong it ate up all the varnish off the table.' The New York group's struggle for self-observation assumed a new dimension: 'Never lose the Self,' counselled Gurdjieff, 'even when drunk. He can be drunk, but never can his "I" be drunk.'

Beyond the renewing of old ties, it is difficult to see quite what Gurdjieff had achieved when he and Solita sailed for France on the s.s. *Normandie* on 19 May 1939: the huge white liner shrugged off her tugs, hesitated a moment in mid-stream, and began to strike foam; the New York group — still affected by last night's farewell dinner — gazed avidly until it passed from sight. Who could foretell how the Ark of the Work would fare in the coming deluge, or on what stony Ararat it might alight?

Gurdjieff reached France only to hear from Jeanne de Salzmann a melancholy litany: Georgette Leblanc (in Paris again with Margaret Anderson) had just contracted cancer; an X-ray of René Daumal had revealed irremediable tubercular infection in both lungs; and in England Mme Sophie Ouspensky, that once dynamic woman, was 'stricken of the palsy, grievously tormented' and had taken to her bed. An English intuition that only Gurdjieff himself could now help Sophie Grigorievna was conveyed to him by Stanley Nott: 'He listened gravely and quietly, thought a little and then said, "If possible I will come. But she must also make effort." '

What had Ouspensky himself to fear from this? Regally established at 'Lyne Place', Virginia Water; possessed of 1000 pupils; materially secure; culturally chic; and supported by distinguished lieutenants – he seemed almost excessively qualified to cope. So it seemed. But the private man was less sanguine; desolated by his continued failure to contact 'Higher Source' and acquire the noetic insights of a decisive mystical experience, he had surrendered himself to the lethal consolations of nostalgia and drink. Twice before he had seen Gurdjieff sweep in and capture virtually his entire flock. This time he retired behind a Maginot Line of prior engagements -- he must first convene the Council of the Historico-Psychological Society; he must first complete a bomb-proof air-raid shelter; he must first contact the hereditary chief of the Mevlevi Dervishes; he must first ... he knew not what! In its own minor key, Ouspensky's manœuvring to frustrate Gurdjieff's reception at Lyne echoed the diplomatic frenzy to restrain Adolph Hitler.

July came ... but Ouspensky's creative procrastination shunted Gurdjieff's visit further and further to the right. August came ... and with it a sickly atmosphere of war phobia. It was a time of farewells and consolations: 'I have given you enough for years,' Gurdjieff would growl reassuringly. Margaret, Georgette, and Monique fled to the village of Orgeval, their car packed with the barest necessities: winter clothing, soap, candles, iodine, toothpaste, aspirin, two revolvers, and Rachmaninoff's Second Piano Concerto. Late in the evening of 27 August Jeanne de Salzmann offered to rush Luc Dietrich to meet Gurdjieff before it was too late (though not having slept for forty-eight hours, the young man demurred). Paris was convulsed by rumour. Gas masks were distributed. As Neville Chamberlain served Hitler final warning that, come what may, Britain would stand by the Poles, it seemed for one fascinating moment that Ouspensky had exhausted his repertoire of excusals and that Gurdjieff would indeed establish his personal beach-head at Lyne. The situation was grave. Only on 1 September 1939 when the Wehrmacht's tanks charged into Poland, only then did fate and history confirm that Gurdjieff's landing in England was *streng verboten*: in occupied Paris sterner challenges, sterner ordeals, awaited him.

14

---- ❖ ----

C'EST LA GUERRE

(3 September 1939–14 August 1945)

By the end of the Second World War the entire map of so-to-say 'Gurdjieff-land' had been redrawn. Although no triumphalism marked the ascendancy of the French Gurdjieffians over their English and American predecessors; although, on the contrary, they bore themselves with studied modesty – Napoleon himself might have envied them their dazzling victory. Entering this period as the merest platoon of bright recruits, the French emerged as a large, powerful, and cohesive group, on whom – by virtue of their unique access to Gurdjieff during a golden teaching phase – the mantle of his work fell with a justice all too apparent. And how peculiar it was. The Gallic temperament had cold-shouldered the Work for seventeen years, and even the general wartime renaissance of interest in the noumenal, which at long last did deliver the necessary quota of French intellectuals, was perceived on the Rive Gauche as entirely aberrative: 'In desperation, people turned to the predictions of Nostradamus, of Saint Godefroy, Saint Odile. The irrational reigned as it always will when reason vacillates in the face of desperate facts.' Surely Gurdjieff's French were phenomenally lucky; but undeservedly lucky? – that would be an entirely different proposition.

In September 1939 the phoney-war opened with deep anxieties and unintended burlesque: as young French conscripts converged on the Gare de L'Est with their steel helmets, fretful parents, clean underwear, and postings to obscure northern fortresses; as Chopin waltzes, *études*, preludes and mazurkas poured from the PTT radio – the civilian populace wrestled with government gas masks furnished in one adult size only. Many found them too large: Gurdjieff (who did not bother of course) would have found his too small. His personal preoccupation in these first surreal days was evidently the plight of various ailing pupils: Sophie Ouspensky, to whom he sent generous gifts, and René Daumal at grips with the disease which had doomed Katherine Mansfield.

Of most immediate concern was poor Georgette Leblanc. On 12 September Dr Thierry de Martel operated on her cancerous arm in his clinic in Rue Vercingetorix, and a fortnight later she began her convalescence in the Hôtel Napoleon Bonaparte. The proprietor Monsieur Louis gamely sought to reassure her: 'What if the Germans do come to Paris, madame? What if they come to this hotel? I will meet them at the door and I will stop them. I will say *Messieurs, je suis chez moi.*' But Georgette's devastation related to warfare on a different front:

> First with opération, thing of the earth, I was very down, terrible down. You understand certainly. A little after, the second stade arrive – she his more spirituelle and disparing because she said me – 'Now I have lost Gurdjieff; impossible learn; my times is broken. Finish all the miracles, they are finish.'

At the end of the month Georgette left Paris with Margaret Anderson in frantic search of rural sanctuary; she and Gurdjieff never met again.

While month after month the war stood still, Gurdjieff waited actively, gradually stocking his pantry until it bulged. Shelves which rose to ceiling level eventually groaned under the weight of dry goods: sugar, salt, flour; preserved fruit, raisins, sultanas, dates, Corinthian currants; split peas, beans, and assorted spices ... Forays into the countryside (there was still petrol) yielded Gurdjieff cured hams and bacon, and sacks of goat cheese. Hédiard, his favourite emporium behind the Madeleine, could still – at a price – supply exotica: Beluga caviar, Smyrna halva and dried figs, guava jelly, Turkish *loucoum*, crystallized fruit, chocolate, peppermint balls, and sugared almonds. Bottles of vodka, calvados, and Larresingle Armagnac competed for pantry space with whole cartons of Gauloise cigarettes. The entire ceiling was festooned with onions, scarlet peppers, dried eels, smoked sturgeon, and thin, indecipherable sausages, purportedly made of camel's meat. 'By what grocer's miracle, with what cash and for what esoteric-culinary fantasy are they gathered here?'

Although the recurrent air-raid alarms of 1939 and 1940 almost always proved false, the stringent 'black-out' restrictions chimed in with Gurdjieff's personal whim: he had closed his apartment's blinds and shutters for the duration – not of the war but of his entire life. Henceforward he would keep house in an atmosphere of fragrant eastern spices, yet under the discrepant glare of naked electric bulbs: day and night, East and West, no longer signified at 6 Rue des Colonels Rénard.

The nucleic French group under Mme de Salzmann was meeting now at Philippe Lavastine's house, 54 Rue du Four, near the Hôtel Napoleon, where impressive figures convened – Henri and Henriette Tracol, Marthe de Gaigneron, Pauline de Dampier, Bernard Lemaître. To René Daumal Gurdjieff gave privileged access – less because of his seniority than his desperate need. The young poet had accepted the blow of his medical prognosis with incredible gallantry, embarking immediately on the first French testament to Gurdjieff's teaching: *Mount Analogue: A Novel of Symbolically Authentic Non-Euclidean Adventures in Mountain Climbing.* For the rest of his short life Daumal would pursue his task, under cruel difficulties and against the clock. Although in the prevailing intellectual climate, his was a discipleship which dared not speak its name, his sustained tribute to Alexandre Salzmann is easy to decode.

On 10 May 1940, when Hitler invaded the Low Countries and turned the Maginot Line, it was suddenly appreciated in Paris that national calamity had had a nine-month gestation period. On 14 May the Germans pierced the French defence at Sedan; on 29 May a nondescript flotilla of little boats began evacuating the British Expeditionary Force from the beaches of Dunkirk; on 3 June air-raids on the outskirts of Paris triggered a mass exodus; Daumal left for Pelvaux in the Alps; Solita Solano reluctantly left for the USA; on 8 June Margaret, Georgette, and Monique failed in a frantic attempt to board the s.s. *Washington* at Bordeaux; on 11 June Paris was inexplicably cloaked by an ominous, sooty cloud; on 12 June it was declared an open city: of its 2.8 million inhabitants, 2.1 million were now streaming west and south along roads strafed by Stuka divebombers, a myriad urgent specks of mortality polarized by history – and one of them was Gurdjieff.

He had set out very unwillingly under fierce pressure from anxious and protective pupils. But twenty-four hours later his better judgement had prevailed and he was struggling back towards Paris against the human tide. The 14 June dawned with the Germans at the city gates. Le Chabanais, the capital's most famous brothel, closed its doors with the terse reassurance: 'The establishment will re-open at three o-clock.' They had confidence that the more things changed the more they would remain the same. Elsewhere however tragic events precipitated. Dr Thierry de Martel for example would be unable to supervise Georgette Leblanc's recovery, having availed himself of a *piqûre* of strychnine from his own medicine cabinet; 'I am over sixty. I expect nothing more from life, and I don't want to see the Germans march down the Champs Elysées.' Gurdjieff, at seventy-four, did nothing so foolish. Our myth has him re-entering his apartment at 6 Rue des Colonels Rénard more or less as the swastika is raised over the nearby Arc de Triomphe – he is travel-weary but undaunted by the future. It is the first of 1533 nights under a curfew which he will not always observe.

Overnight the Parisian stage set was crowded with new and un-popular actors: the German Army – the *emmerdeurs corrects*. At the Café de la Paix S.S. officers toasted their victory in champagne – doubtless at the very table where Gurdjieff had written *Beelzebub*. They massed there especially thickly on Sunday 23 June, when Hitler swept into Paris in a black Mercedes to visit the Opéra (and the doorman earned his crumb of immortality by disdaining the Führer's 50-mark tip). With the peremptory banning of private cars, Gurdjieff's career as a motorist was suspended *sine die*, and a strange and not unpleasant calm settled over Paris. Taxi-bicycles with bright plywood coachwork advertised *Vitesse-Confort-Sécurité*; the air tasted purer; horse-drawn cabs reappeared to the delight of the ancient fraternity of sparrows, whose distinctive viewpoint Gurdjieff himself had long ago articulated:

> Suddenly down in the street there would be heard a noise, a rattling and a rumbling, and soon after that an odour would be diffused, at which everything inside us would begin to rejoice ... without food, as you yourself will understand, it is difficult even for sparrows to bring forth a healthy posterity.

That summer, there were ancient streets where only the Gestapo's gliding black Citroëns, *traction avant*, spoilt a scene which bordered on the lyrical.

A turn of fate which suited sparrows fell cruelly on the average Parisian – who from lack of nourishment would lose 40lb weight during the occupation. Gurdjieff's ration card, received on 23 September 1940, was in the 'V' category for those over seventy. Armed with this (like nursing mothers and pregnant women) he could buy milk in a surreal market: 'Parisian housewives stood outside dairy shops for hours with rented babies in their arms, or with pillows under their apron fronts, or with borrowed grandparents hanging on their shoulders.' Such deceptions were the new order: as chronic malnutrition tightened its grip, society polarized – there were those who manipulated and those who succumbed.

The 'D' system (D for *debrouillardise* or making do) accommodated different forms. The innocent substitution of dried nettles for tobacco and charred barley for coffee, tailed off into practices more bizarre: shamefaced old gentlemen snared pigeons in the Jardin du Luxembourg; breeding pairs of guinea-pigs were marketed as 'the flat-dweller's rabbit'; and newspapers carried hygiene warnings 'Cat-eaters beware!'. If there were Parisians who dwindled down to bone in uncompromising honour, there were also women with hungry children who became 'horizontal collaborators', and men who struck deals they could never rightly remember. The fundamental resilience of French agriculture, the proverbial slyness and cupidity of the peasants, the sclerotic formalism of the German administration, the corruptibility of Vichy officialdom, the conspiratorial networks surrounding the communist Maquis Rouge and the non-communist Maquis Blanc, and, above all else, the ordinary Parisian's desperate ingenuity – all these together guaranteed a milieu in which Gurdjieff was born to thrive.

In October 1940 Jeanne de Salzmann anxiously presented her French protégés at 6 Rue des Colonels Rénard. Not since escaping from Russia had Gurdjieff taught in riskier conditions; although the curfew had just been relaxed from 9 pm to midnight, it was brutally enforced, and (as one pupil admits): 'No-one would have dared, on pain of death, to go out into the deserted streets.' To hold group meetings of any sort was to flirt with danger. In nearby Rue Lauriston, former Police Inspector Bonny, officer-in-charge at the sinister French 'Gestapo' HQ, began each day by sorting through a pile of anonymous letters of denunciation. M. Gurdjieff was already 'known' to the authorities, and – albeit his moustache was now as white as Marechal Pétain's ('purest white, colour of virtue') – his character had been officially logged as grey. Smiling neutrally on French and Germans; serenely impartial towards Christians and Jews; equally involved with White Russians and Black Market; the recipient of numerous letters from America; dealing in carpets and foreign currencies; and owner of a mysterious business purportedly manufacturing false eyelashes – Gurdjieff fell rather naturally under surveillance. Bureaucratic factions who could agree on little else, concurred that an eye should be kept on G. I. Gurdjieff, and appropriate dossiers were opened with the Sûreté Publique and the Préfecture de Paris.

The winter of 1940–41 had set in early and was exceptionally harsh: Thomas and Olga de Hartmann (their house at Courbevoie commandeered) were among thousands shivering in abandoned and derelict buildings. For seventy days the temperature hung below freezing, and the oldest and weakest Parisians simply began to die. Every afternoon – come ice, come snow – the German Power made its parade to the Arc de Triomphe, and the faint blare of martial music beat against the glazed shutters at 6 Rue des Colonels Rénard. Of Gurdjieff's ruthless intention to survive there is no doubt. For the sake of others he had to survive. His esoteric mission apart, he alone could defend the defenceless within the circle of quite ordinary people accessible to him:

> My family very big ... old people who come every day to my house, are, also, family. They my family because have no other family ... For such people ... impossible even to find any way to eat. But for me, not so. I not interested in who win war. Not have patriotism or big ideals about peace ... all have ideals, all have peaceful purpose, all kill. I have only one purpose: existence for self, for students, and for family, even this big family. So I do what they cannot do, I make deal with Germans, with policemen, with all kinds of idealistic people who make 'black market'. Result: I eat well and continue to have tobacco, liquor, and what is necessary for me ... I can also help many people.

In this epoch of grey austerity a privileged niche in Gurdjieff's scheme of things was occupied by the deprived child: 'I understand him. I understand his language. It's this language I love. Only to hear it, only to see this real impulse, I give out 5 kilos of sweets everyday – for which I pay 410 francs a kilo.' His charity to adults was marked by considerable delicacy of feeling. At the time when the Germans were systematically plundering the art treasures of the Rothschilds and other eminent Jewish families; when Vermeer's *Astronomer* was expropriated by Hitler and van Gogh's *Bridge at Arles* by Reichmarschall Goering – Gurdjieff also began interesting himself in this sector. Seated comfortably on a red moleskin-covered bench at some bistro in the Rue des Acacias, he would pay starving artists for their daubs – discussing each picture appreciatively while riffling his huge wad of francs with the dexterity of a bank-teller. To his final choice he brought a connoisseur's eye for the absolutely worthless: 'I have the worst collection of paintings in Paris – perhaps in the whole world.' One nail – sometimes in the dead centre of these 'creations' –

sufficed to exhibit them in the dim peculiar gallery of 6 Rue des Colonels Rénard.

Was it history pure and simple, or was it the myth, which held Gurdjieff in Occupied France? After all urgent promptings to extricate himself were coming both from Olgivanna and from New York City; and proven avenues of exit existed through Unoccupied France, Spain, and Portugal. America and Germany were still at peace. Solita Solano had mobilized the alarmed Oragean groups, and Schuyler Jackson had even begun looking for a suitable New Jersey property ... but it was not to be. Gurdjieff absolutely refused to abandon Jeanne de Salzmann and his new French following. His stance resembled Jane Heap's who held on in beleaguered London:

> Many bombs have fallen around our house – the last terrible raid nearly got it – five hundred planes over from 8–45 until 5a.m. ... It is good to feel unafraid ... I am reading the religions of the world – not the man-made ones, only the divine ones of which Gurdjieff's is one.

Piotr Ouspensky by contrast – after a deeply meditated (and wholly erroneous) political analysis – forsook his pupils at Lyne Place on 29 January 1941 and sailed for New York on the s.s. *Georgic*. This, if anything, only strengthened Gurdjieff's resolve to discard the American option.

In spring 1941 (when Jean Paul Sartre extricated himself from Stalag XII and turned up at the Gare de L'Est) no end to hostilities seemed remotely in sight. A grim prospect generally, but not one which particularly daunted Gurdjieff: 'It does not refer to us,' he had pronounced decades ago during another phase of mass insanity. 'War or no war it is all the same to us. We always make a profit.' Although humanity's reciprocal destruction was the abomination of abominations, it at least shattered the carapace of conformity which sealed off the world from its animic substratum – provoking urgent questions, liberating vital energies, attracting sincere pupils. Gurdjieff's Paris had been rehearsed long ago in Moscow and Petrograd ... And in any case nothing lasted forever; on 22 June when Hitler invaded Russia fate had clearly hedged its bets.

In the raw October of 1941 cancer finally claimed Georgette Leblanc. Her last grim and honourable days at 'The Chalet Rose' cottage, near Cannes in the Unoccupied Zone, were not sustained by morphine, Sédol, and *Der Rosenkavalier* alone; every morning she read from *Beelzebub* and every night offered The Lord's Prayer in French and English. During the delirium of Friday 18 October she became obsessed with the hope that Gurdjieff was coming, indeed that he was already with her, sharing her suffering: '*Il vient, je le sais, il est déjà là – il est entré par en bas.*' But Gurdjieff had no car, no petrol, no *permis de circulation* – he was seventy-five and time had run out.

> In the evening mail there was an inter-zone card from Paris, with a message: that Gurdjieff had said she had '*beaucoup de courage*' and called her 'friend'. With a transfigured face she said '*Il a dit cela?*' And then she made her last statement: '*Alors ... nous allons mourir sans mourir?*'

She died two days later and was buried in the cemetery of Notre Dame des Anges.

From his 'compact' apartment, Gurdjieff watched the war unfold with dispassion, as if from an observatory on the planet Mars. Not for him the French artistic world's delicious moral hesitations, at a time 'when the dividing line between resistance and treason was as narrow as that between genius and madness'; not for him the intelligentsia's scramble to build post-liberation credentials (which escalated when America declared war on Germany on 11 December 1941). The immediate realities sufficed ... It was cold. Young Germans were skiing on the slopes of Montmartre. Electricity supplies were erratic (on 23 and 24 January 1942 Gurdjieff had to rely wholly on candles). Charcoal for his stove was hardly obtainable; his pupils brought bits of coke salvaged from ashcans and sometimes briquettes of compounded sawdust; occasionally one might present him with the treasure of a solitary lump of coal. Official food rations had been reduced to 1200 calories a day – half what nutritionists considered necessary to sustain life. Even the stocks of his famous pantry were running low ... It was at this point that Gurdjieff went to Hédiard: 'I tell how letter from New York brings such good news.' A rich American pupil – he explained – had given him a Texas oil-well, and he would appreciate a credit account until the war ended and his gushing dollar surplus could be uncapped. It speaks volumes for his acting ability that Hédiard and various local shops gave him the benefit of the doubt.

The spring of 1942 came with cruel reluctance and cruel qualifications. On 29 May, when a German edict was posted obliging all Jews to wear the yellow Star of David, Gurdjieff urgently advised those closest to him to escape to the Unoccupied Zone or 'go underground'. The appalling risks of the latter option cut a broad swathe, affecting the Jews in hiding, the Gentile group members who loyally harboured them, and Gurdjieff himself who had instigated the arrangements. The ration books of the clandestine Jews were useless now. In cramped attics and cellars they worked – mostly with unpractised fingers – making small artefacts which their protectors hawked in the streets to buy food on the black market. The expedient was desperate but so were the times. The virulence of 'The Jew and France' exhibition at the Palais Berlitz was matched every week by the virulence of the anti-Semitic, anti-Free Mason journal, *Au Pilori*:

> Death to the Jew! Aye, we say again! Death! D.E.A.T.H. TO THE JEW! There! The Jew is no man but a foul-smelling beast. We pick off fleas. We fight epidemics ... we defend ourselves against disease and death – why not against the Jews?

Over a glass or two of cognac at a lakeside villa in Wannsee, Eichmann and Heydrich had already schemed the 'Final Solution' to the Jewish problem.

Since the Milanova family into which René Daumal had married was Jewish, he and Vera were permanently cut off from Gurdjieff, wandering the Unoccupied Zone – reduced sometimes to drinking hot water to stave off the pangs of hunger. René, who had now reached Chapter 4 of *Mount Analogue*, struggled every day to evoke Gurdjieff:

> Remember the man who came, who shattered everything, who took you with his bare hands, who drew you out of your dreams and set you down on thorns in the full light of day; and remember that you do not know how to remember.

All too rarely the Daumals had a vital but equivocal contact with fellow writers in Mme de Salzmann's sphere of influence – Luc Dietrich and Lanza del Vasto.

In late June 1942 (when the grieving Margaret Anderson sailed for New York from Lisbon on the s.s. *Drottlingholm*, with tickets paid for by Ernest Hemingway), Mme de Salzmann finally presented Luc Dietrich at 6 Rue des Colonels Rénard. 'I have been able to approach M. Gurdjieff,' Luc wrote to René. 'Now I sense what it is to have confidence ... The other things (this mountain of orange peel), it is necessary to put them in their place ... now I see myself very often resolved on another road, a completely different road.' Yet, however much Luc's enthusiasm fanned the Daumals' longing to return to the source, history brutally confirmed its impossibility. On 16 and 17

July operation 'Spring Wind' saw 900 squads of French police fall on the Jews of Paris and consign them, via the concentration camp at Drancy, to the gas chambers at Auschwitz – close to 120,000 French Jews were deported and only 1500 lived to return ... a profound human tragedy had vindicated Gurdjieff's seemingly alarmist precautions of May.

In November 1942 when the Germans abrogated their agreement with Vichy and overran the Unoccupied Zone; and in February 1943 when they instituted forced labour for young Frenchmen – philosophical collaborationists like André Gide and Jean Cocteau ('Long live the shameful peace') found themselves increasingly out of fashion. The clear ascendancy now lay with Resistance writers like Camus, Jean Bruller, André Malraux, and Sartre – with those clustered round the underground journal *Combat* ... There was however a third force invisibly at work in ideological Paris, a tiny minority who – declining their turn on history's merry-go-round – stood sobered by the necessity of personal transformation. From this neglected company came those who arrived – by way of Mme de Salzmann – at Colonels Rénard.

By mid-1943 more and more French pupils were finding their place in the complex mosaic of Gurdjieff's teaching. At the Salle Pleyel he was giving Movements classes of great vitality, based largely on the enneagram; where decades ago Julia, Olgivanna, Jeanne and Elizabeta had stood, a new and promising generation was ranked before him – Pauline, Marthe, Boussique, Solange, Nicole. At 6 Rue des Colonels Rénard the wrinkled concierge – noting the daily influx of men and women – could only marvel at the capacity of Monsieur Gurdjieff's apartment. The little wooden stools in the salon made for spartan sitting during the two-hour readings from *Beelzebub*. On Thursday evenings, the dining room regularly saw forty people crammed in, with juniors eating from plates on their knees, or on the chimney piece or even on the piano:

> One had squeezed oneself in as best one could between a shin-bone, a knee and two thighs – that is to say three neighbours: but more were arriving ... They stood hesitantly as if overcome with giddiness ... these poor herons, balanced precariously on one leg, searched in vain for a resting place.

Gurdjieff's ceremonial meal had been translated into a French usage startlingly at variance both with the pre-war *élégances* of Paris and with the impoverished world just beyond his door, where rice now enjoyed a pharmacopoeial status and was given out only on a doctor's certificate. The food – bought, cooked and carved by Gurdjieff – was rich and memorable: 'That, special Georgian dish, little chicken, rice and onion, must eat with fingers,' or 'That, Kurdish desert; when suitor proposes and has been accepted, next day he sends this dish to future bride.'. . . To the left of Gurdjieff's brooding, mahogany presence sat the *Directeur* or master of ceremonies, who at intervals rose to his feet and with real or feigned aplomb proposed the successive 'Toasts to the Idiots'.[14] It demanded a peculiarly fine memory and sense of timing, exercised under Gurdjieff's gaze and to his exacting specification:

> If you take on the role of '*Directeur*', you should control all aspects of it . . . While you are carrying out all your obligations, nothing else should matter. Even if you have business worth millions, you must forget about it.

To the Director's left sat *Verseur* (the 'Butler') who charged the glasses with Armagnac and vodka. To Gurdjieff's right sat *Monsieur Egout* (Sewer), an 'Esteemed person' on whom periodically the host himself lavished various equivocal titbits – for example, a 'half-denuded roasted calf's-head, with the brains still bubbling under the sawed-off apex of the calvarium.' To *Egout*'s right sat *Monsieur Poubelle* (Dustbin) who helpfully coped with the superfluities from *Egout*'s plate. *Egout pour Sweet* – generally a pretty girl – came forward if required, to help Gurdjieff in that department. His gathered presence and the sheer incongruity of his hospitality lent to these feasts an incalculable quality: 'A chain reaction took place in which nothing any longer made ordinary sense. Eating and speaking became momentous acts and remarks exchanged across the table seemed like stabs of a knife.'

The Gurdjieff who 'would have seated a Nobel prize winner next to a roadsweeper, a "lady" next to a prostitute' had unusual scope for witty juxtapositions: Tchekhov Tchekhovitch a former champion wrestler, and Pierre Schaeffer the inventor of 'concrete music'; the delicious 'Brioche' and René Zuber, austere observer of different cultures; the vulpine, womanizing Dietrich and Louis Le Prudomme a rustic old Breton woman . . .

Eventually – across a bridge of sobering silence – the meal elided into a formal group exchange. Gurdjieff's 'Have you anything to offer me?' cast everyone back on themselves. 'Squeal, squeal!' he insisted helpfully . . . Had any pupil a question? A real question? A

question which exposed his chief internal blemish? Let René Zuber
speak for those who dared: 'All eyes were turned towards me, and I
found myself suddenly confronted by infinite space, just as I imagine
an astronaut, in a state of weightlessness, would if he opened
the door of his capsule.' If an observation indeed had substance,
Gurdjieff would respond like a caring father; if it merely showed
promise, he might nod the duty of response to Jeanne de Salzmann;
but if it were 'invented', the thunder of Zeus fell – 'You not understand. You complete idiot. You candidate for lunatic asylum. *Vous
merdité! Vous absolue merdité!*'

Between 10 May 1944 (when the Germans requisitioned all dogs
more than eighteen inches tall at the shoulder) and 25 August, when
Dietrich von Choltitz surrendered Paris to General Leclerc, Gurdjieff
lost both the young authors whose endorsement might have secured
him some recognition in post-liberation France. René Daumal – his
physical access to high altitudes progressively forbidden by his insidious illness – had never ceased striving to master the poetic
gradients of *Mount Analogue*; and yet, on his terminal relapse at the
age of thirty-six, had only reached Chapter 5, 'Which is that of
setting up the First Camp'. Luc Dietrich had concluded his novel
L'Apprentissage de la ville with a coded tribute to Gurdjieff, and –
on the slenderest basis of experience – had even started his own
'Gurdjieff group' in Marseilles.

On 21 May when Daumal drew his last tortured breath in Paris,
Dietrich underwent a crisis of nerves. In company with the French
psychiatrist Hubert Benoit (another of Gurdjieff's pupils), Dietrich
sought peace and quiet on the Normandy coast, a fortnight before
D-Day. Wounded by misadventure in the massive destruction of
Saint-Lô, he was brought back to Paris, where, in the Clinique
Lyautey on 12 August, he succumbed to maladies variously described
as gangrene and an abscess on the brain. He was thirty-one . . . When
Gurdjieff, pink and fresh, had visited his pupil two days earlier, he
brought two oranges (items virtually unobtainable) and placed one in
each of Dietrich's hands, with the assurance: 'All your life has been a
preparation for this moment.'

One week later, on Saturday 19 August, the Paris uprising commenced, and the ragged gunfire of Germans at bay and Gaullists and
Communists vying for street honours, hindered Gurdjieff's regular
visit to the Turkish bath. At least he was saved the greater inconveni-
ence which would have ensued if von Choltitz had complied with
Hitler's order to blow Paris up. By Thursday, Gurdjieff could read

(with conjectural feelings) an airborne leaflet: 'Hold fast, we're coming! – Leclerc'; and by Friday the 25th the instrument of surrender had been signed at Police Headquarters. Great forces had arisen and passed away; the octave had deflected; Germany and Vichy no longer signified in the 'Capital of World Culture'. . . . The big chocolate fish, scaled in silvery-blue tinfoil, which swung gently from the pantry ceiling at Colonels Rénard had so-to-say failed to rise to history's bait. *Les républiques passent. Gurdjieff demeure.*

In the following three days, with the colloquialism 'Vive La France!' extrapolated as 'Pétain to the gallows!', thousands of perceived collaborators met summary retribution – sometimes condign and sometimes not. No Parisian arrondissement was lacking its tearful women with shaven heads and worse, its taciturn men with bullets in their chests or knives in their backs . . . Gurdjieff – despite his commercial transactions with German 'idealists' – was wholly indemnified by his grandfatherly humanity and his support of Jewish group members.

The French police however with demonstrable hypocrisy, chose this moment to activate the *Dossier Gurdjieff* and secure a warrant to search 6 Rue des Colonels Rénard for illicitly held foreign currency. Thanking the pupil who tipped him off, Gurdjieff reassured him: 'They can never find anything in my apartment.' . . . That afternoon when the squad arrived they looked under his mattress and found heaps of dollars. To Jeanne de Salzmann's consternation, Gurdjieff was carted off to police remand cells, where a petty criminal put him the initiatic question: 'Old boy, how many times have you been inside? '*Dix-huit!*' Gurdjieff replied grandly, to warm approbation . . . Next morning however, the magistrate discharged an entirely different 'Gurdjieff': a citizen with an unblemished record and many character references – 'a poor old man who understood nothing about foreign currency, and could scarcely speak French'. (Gurdjieff relished telling this story, and on reaching the bit about hiding the money under the mattress, would hesitate, survey his audience with child-like naivety and say 'Good place? Hein?')

His serious work continued. In post-liberation Paris the strengths of the new French nucleus were tested as much by their exacting and incalculable teacher as by unrelenting privation. The winter of 1944–5 was yet again harsh – electricity unreliable and food paradoxically more scarce than ever (with gangsterish appropriations by the Mauvais Maquis). The Rue des Colonels Rénard became glazed with ice like a skating rink, and there was no plaster-of-Paris in the entire city to set the broken bones of old gentlemen who fell. As if from nightmare, Paris emerged into the dusty, beautiful spring of 1945; on 30 April came news of Hitler's suicide; and on 6 May the bacchanal of VE Day ... The 'Teacher of Dancing' had come through.

In Parisian post-war estimation Gurdjieff counted for nothing. As spring elided into the crippling summer drought of 1945, the masses' attention was captured by the drama at the Palais de Justice, in which the aged Marshall Pétain was finally answering for his treasonable proposition: 'You have only one France, which I incarnate.' The intellectual centrum had meanwhile shifted from the Café des Deux Magots to the more humdrum Café de Flore, where Sartre (increasingly habituated to drugs) had a telephone specially installed at his table ... As to the little apartment at 6 Rue des Colonels Rénard, it never entered any French mind, except those of Gurdjieff's entourage and his creditors. Nevertheless by the end of July it had twice given proof of its extraordinary magnetic power.

First to return was the formidable Kathryn Hulme, who arrived by milk train at the Gare Montparnasse in UNRAA officer's uniform, looking like a para-military bus conductress. With ungovernable feelings of trepidation and *déjà vu*, she negotiated the terrain of memory. What if Gurdjieff's apartment proved as inaccessible as the castle of Count West West or as ephemeral as the castle of the Fisher King? But no, there it was! 'In the dim foyer one low-voltage electric bulb gave just enough light to see the old familiar out-of-order sign hanging on the elevator door.' She rang the bell a second time in an ecstasy of hope and foreboding – perhaps he would rebuff her ('You have lost too much'):

> Another long wait, then I heard steps, slow, heavy, shuffling, behind the tall door ... there stood Gurdjieff looking out with a slight scowl at the unknown figure on the landing. I had forgotten that my uniform would be a regalia strange to his eyes.
> 'It's Crococdile, Mr. Gurdjieff...
> 'Kroko-*deel*!' The door swung wide. I rushed into his arms and began to cry. He also seemed moved, saying over and over, 'Not expect ... not expect!' in a hoarse voice.

In the saffron-scented pantry Gurdjieff made Kathryn thick black coffee: ' "*Vrai café!*" he said in French, "only place in Paris you can have such." ' Compulsively Kathryn poured out her hotch-potch of news: Solita Solano was alive and well and in the American Woman Volunteer Service; Mont St Michel had escaped destruction; the

Germans had gassed and burnt millions of Jews. As he took in the enormity of the holocaust, Gurdjieff's 'face darkened and a vein in his forehead swelled and beat. I saw the wrath of God in that clouded countenance, a righteous fury that seemed about to explode ... holy wrath for man's repetitive inhumanity to man.' When Kathryn's hour was up and she left en route for Germany, Gurdjieff gave her a box of loucoum. 'The houri on the label lay on her side on a purple divan, her painted eyes looking out invitingly from under long hair twined with roses ...' She was everything which Kroko-*deel* and the members of The Rope would never be.

The loucoum-donor was now in his eightieth year but no attempt to domesticate him biographically, to serve him up as a kindly, soft-gummed, old eccentric, would even approach the truth. The second surprise visitor at his apartment encountered warmth indeed, but also an experience which the Monsieur Bonbon of sentimental iconography could never have provided ... Fritz Peters, as he slumped exhausted in the concierge's armchair in crumpled American Army uniform, desperate to intercept Gurdjieff, was suffering an acute nervous breakdown – in his own words, half mad. After an hour's wait, he heard at last the tap of a walking stick on the cobblestones of Rue des Colonels Rénard:

> I stood up, rigid, and Gurdjieff ... appeared in the doorway. He walked up to me without the faintest sign of recognition, and I simply stated my name. He stared at me again for a second, dropped his cane, and cried out in a loud voice, 'My son!' ... we both threw our arms around each other, his hat fell from his head, and the concierge ... screamed.

In a celebrated dénouement, the Gurdjieff of the Sarmoung Monastery – the Gurdjieff with access to the 'Big Accumulator' of energy – materializes in the kitchen of that stifling Paris flat, leaning against an old refrigerator. Surely Peters' dramatic account provides an essential clue to all those cases where, down the years, Gurdjieff had mysteriously cured people of psychosomatic illnesses:

> I could not take my eyes off him and realised that he looked incredibly weary – I have never seen anyone look so tired. I remember being slumped over the table, sipping at my coffee, when I began to feel a strange uprising of energy within myself – I stared at him, automatically straightened up, and it was as if a violent, electric blue light emanated from him and entered into me. As this happened, I could feel the tiredness drain out of me, but at the same moment his body slumped and his face turned grey as if it was being drained of life. I looked at him, amazed, and

when he saw me sitting erect, smiling and full of energy, he said quickly:
'You all right now – watch food on stove – I must go' ... He was gone
for perhaps fifteen minutes while I watched the food, feeling blank and
amazed because I had never felt any better in my life ... I was equally
amazed when he returned to the kitchen to see the change in him; he
looked like a young man again, alert, smiling, sly and full of good spirits.

These flying visits of Kathryn and Fritz signal the end of Gurdjieff's
five years' enforced parochialism, and (more than Japan's surrender
on 14 August 1945) raise the curtain on the next dramatic act in the
Gurdjieffian myth ... Had it been a good war? As good perhaps as
the curate's egg. The sheer effrontery with which Gurdjieff had
managed the 'Material Question' left him in frantic need of an
American oil-well. Fate, which had swept away his supporters René
Daumal and Luc Dietrich, had preserved his critics Lanza del Vasto
and Pierre Minet. Jeanne de Salzmann – her worth triumphantly
reconfirmed in the crucible of the Occupation – had emerged as the
chief guarantor of his posterity; yet *Beelzebub* was not a jot nearer
publication. As to the small miracle which Gurdjieff had achieved at
the Salle Pleyel, that also was ambivalent. Onto the grander Work
stage (thronged with sturdy old troupers from England and America)
Gurdjieff must somehow usher a new French group which displayed
all the dangerous modesty of an infant prodigy – any number of
piquant 'misunderstandings' seemed guaranteed. In his heyday he
had deliberately provoked friction, but now, approaching his eightieth birthday, the tactic was unthinkable. On the contrary, the good
shepherd, at whatever personal cost, must gather his scattered flock
into one fold ... everything was finally at stake.

15

❖

HOLY RECONCILING

(15 August 1945–30 October 1948)

To reconcile, to harmonize, to repair the past and prepare the future – Gurdjieff's prospectus was impeccable. Yet would its implementation run on greased wheels? Far from it, apparently. Leaving aside the delicate problem of French integration, the English and American constituencies were internally at sixes and sevens. From his discreet 'Observatory' at 6 Rue des Colonels Rénard, Gurdjieff surveyed a world scene of dispiriting fragmentation.

To pillory the various Work grandees, as they emerge into the austere post-war light, would be dangerously facile. Obstructed by the highest motives, divided by a common ideal, and puffed into mock-heroic proportions by their pupils' adulation – they fulfil the only roles which destiny has assigned them. The Oragean old guard holds New York tenaciously against Ouspensky's repeated sallies from Mendham, New Jersey. At Lyne Place, Virginia Water, the dignitories of the Historico-Psychological Society (Kenneth Walker, R. J. G. Mayor, and Dr Francis Roles) protect the 'System' within a grim stockade of rules and regulations – one of which forbids the very utterance of Gurdjieff's name. Behind their respective ramparts at Great Amwell House, Ware, and Coombe Springs, Kingston-on-Thames, Dr Henry Maurice Dunlop Nicoll and John Godolphin Bennett nurse a satisfying mutual disapproval; Jane Heap is mewed up in spiritual quarantine; and Ouspensky has actually retained a solicitor to communicate with his protégé Bennett . . . They are human, all too human – surely evoking biographic compassion as they jostle for precedence in the margins of the great myth from which they draw their contingent importance. Their essential brotherhood shows through in their vulnerability, in their genuine strivings, and in their common ideological homage to a 'very wise old man sitting in his rich pantry of foods and thoughts' in Paris.

On 13 January 1946, Gurdjieff celebrated his 80th birthday. At one moment he seemed prey to 'the lawful infirmities of old age' and at the next gave 'a massive impression of contained energy – leonine, alert, watching and capable of springing up.' His hoar years repeatedly licensed the mischievous experiment of 'choosing his successor'. A portentous silence, which he himself had engendered, he would break with the formula: 'In life is only necessary for man to find one person to whom he can give accumulation of learning in life. When find such receptacle, then is possible die.'

Slowly his raised arm and pointing apostolic finger would circle the expectant room until it finally rested on some goggle-eyed candidate, whose reaction was devoured by the senior pupils – not least Jeanne de Salzmann – as an infallible index of his egotism. (Evidently the only person to swallow his 'selection' hook, line, and sinker was distinctly un-*papabile* Fritz Peters.)

Between Gurdjieff and the world of cultural *bon ton* there was to be no conciliation, no giving and no asking of quarter. The fact that in post-war Paris the three dominant ideologies (doctrinaire Communism, boulevard existentialism, and the Gaullist/Roman Catholic coalition) ignored Gurdjieff totally, did not insulate him from critical attention. Even in venerable old age he was still dogged by the Bluebeard stereotype – that macabre consequence of his unselfish kindness to Katherine Mansfield. On 19 January 1946 the periodical *l'Illustration* ran Roland Merlin's article, *'Le drame de Katherine Mansfield'*, which relied for its effect on a stage villain preposterous even by the standards of French popular journalism:

> Then Gurdjieff seemed to concentrate his powers of spell-binding. His eyes, from which emanated an insidious intoxication, passed slowly over the foreheads of his pupils ... everybody fell into a cataleptic state. The sleepers, among whom figured Katherine Mansfield, seemed to savour the voluptuousness of their state of prostration.

A month or two later this Beauty and the Beast legend received a new and unwelcome impetus with the publication of Irène-Carole Reweliotty's *Journal d'une jeune fille*. Young, gifted, consumptive, seagull-boned, Irène was startlingly in the Katherine Mansfield mould; she had entered the Work through Luc Dietrich's well-tenanted bed and left it in a coffin on 11 August 1945. Seduced both physically and mentally by Luc, Irène soon transferred to his teacher the negative feelings in which she died tragically from heart disease at Salanches ('Dear mother, I shall end by believing that Gurdjieff has cast a spell on me.')

Upon Gurdjieff's power to cast a spell of sorts, to remain a 'poet of situations', very much depended the enterprise of reconciliation; and time it seemed could lay no finger on this faculty. In June 1946 when Kathryn Hulme returned from 'Gair-*man*ia clutching a bottle of Polish vodka and her new female companion Chouka', she found, admittedly, a frail Gurdjieff: 'I heard a kind of phlegmy rattle in his respiratory passages, not a very healthy sound I thought with a pang.' A man nevertheless whose power to subvert the mundane had not slackened . . . Chouka was a lapsed nun, guilt-tormented and desperate to conceal her personal history from Gurdjieff's penetrative look. When he appeared to pass from reverie into sleep, her pity mingled with relief and she opportunistically whispered to Kathryn, '*On doit partir . . . il est très fatigué.*':

> At that moment Gurdjieff opened one eye, looked sideways at her. His face came alive with a slow spreading smile that lifted up all its tired lines. He nodded at Chouka and said hoarsely in French: '*Petite Sœur de* —', naming her former religious order exactly.

Kathryn's gift of vodka and cigarettes had, incidentally, been superfluous. She need not suppose, said Gurdjieff, gesturing with heavy irony at his overloaded shelves, 'that I do not have very, *very*, good relations with the American Army.' The ever-faithful New York groups had also renewed their donations: how like a Texas oil-well was their generosity, and how painless in consequence had been the redemption of that big debt to Hédiard . . . yet again Gurdjieff had kept one short step ahead of insolvency.

If New York supplied the dollars, it was London which infused new blood, and initiated the *entente cordiale* between French and Anglo-Saxon 'idiots'. Jane Heap who (from her home in Hamilton Terrace and her celebrated craft shop, The Rocking Horse, in St John's Wood) had carried the banner of Gurdjieff for nearly twenty years, eagerly coached her people for the trial of direct contact. 'He is a multitude,' she warned them. 'But, if you watch, sometimes you see the sage pass by.' In autumn 1946 her committed people – including Michael Currer-Briggs, Annie-Lou Staveley, Dr John Lester, and Elspeth Champcommunal – climbed the stairs at 6 Rue des Colonels Rénard for the first time and in natural trepidation. 'Do not be afraid any more,' Gurdjieff insisted. 'You are at home here. I am your new father.'

Perhaps Jane's artistic nature and practised agility in side-stepping
social norms had prepared her pupils, more than others, for the
surreal component in Gurdjieff; certainly the poetry of situation
found in them a ready and unsurprised appreciation. 'Mr. Gurdjieff's
implacable regard rested upon us. Considerings receded. He spoke
from an immeasurable distance with great force . . . "I – invite *you* –
to my next marriage!" he said.' No one from St John's Wood even
wished to translate the gnomic into the mundane.

Helpful in smoothing their path was Gurdjieff's improbable facto-
tum at the flat – the young Lise Tracol, whose poise and singular
adaptability qualified her as a 'universal type'. Require Lise to double
as the President of the United States, explained Gurdjieff grandly,
and 'from now three hours' she would do it; if necessary he added,
raising the stakes, she could even play the role of Mme de Salzmann!
One morning, assembled in the hall nervously anticipating entrée to
the salon, Jane's pupils found the door locked. 'Oh, is scandal!'
protested Gurdjieff. 'Such important people to be kept waiting!
Where is Lise? Where is key?' Returning from the kitchen with a
gigantic screwdriver and minuscule tack hammer, he made a pantomimic attack on the hinges, 'precisely like any clown you might see in
a circus, embarrassed and apologetic.' Eventually Lise appeared
laden with shopping, and, after enduring Gurdjieff's explosion about
her stupefying lack of consideration, calmly took the key from above
the door lintel and let them in.

Jane Heap's return had been axiomatic; so was Solita Solano's and
the New York Orageans – but in the path of any grander *rapprochement* there stood, like some grey, forbidding, philosophical dolmen,
the personage of Piotr Demianovich Ouspensky. When in January
1947 he finally crossed the Atlantic to England, Gurdjieff had quick,
accurate report – and what he learned grieved him. Ouspensky's
despair of ever contacting 'Higher Source' had long since been translated into a pattern of punishing drinking; his once towering intellect
was crestfallen; his integrity, by his own admission, was compromised; and as he was hastened along icy roads from Southampton to
Lyne Place (in the Buick of a Mr Basil Tilley), he was suffering from
progressive kidney failure and terminal disillusion.

Gurdjieff was far from indifferent to his old protégé's haemorrhage
of hope (a hope moreover which had been imparted to thousands of
English pupils); within days of Ouspensky's disembarkation from the
s.s. *Queen Elizabeth*, Jeanne de Salzmann conveyed to him a cordial
invitation to the table at 6 Rue des Colonels Rénard. Ouspensky

refused. The personal script he had in mind did not include a grand reconciliation, still less a deathbed repentance; it featured instead a spectacular catharsis – the public sacrifice of his lifetime's work and all his pupils' aspirations ... At six momentous meetings held at Colet Gardens, West Kensington, between 24 February and 18 June, the author of *In Search of the Miraculous* pounded every question with an amazing and obdurate nihilism.

To mock Ouspensky's public admission of spiritual bankruptcy; to deny him a consolation prize for supreme (if late-flowering) honesty – would be to trivialize a life of inordinate strangeness. No one at Colet Gardens had posed him the crucial question: 'Should we go to Gurdjieff?' Perhaps they were too quick to put a negative reply in the mouth of that shabby, ill, and incorruptible figure. Who can tell? Ouspensky's inevitable and imminent death, his abjuration of the System, and his stress on Eternal Recurrence, created in the closed circle at Lyne an indescribable atmosphere, no less electrifying than that prevailing at 6 Rue des Colonels Rénard. The Gurdjieffian myth had reared up and become a kind of dangerous psycho-drama, reaching an incalculable caesura when Piotr Demianovich died on 2 October 1947.

To say that the executive Council of Ouspensky's Historico-Psychological Society felt nonplussed after the mandatory requiem service, understates the case. How should they lead – where should they lead – the heavy-footed faithful streaming out from the Russian church in Pimlico? They were inclined to think that the surest guidance would emanate from 'Franklin Farms', New Jersey, where the widowed Sophie Grigorievna Ouspensky lay prostrate in a dim room, guarded by her grandees and a mangy, aggressive chow dog. The powerful three-man delegation which left London for Franklin Farms to elucidate Mme Ouspensky's mind, met there a smokescreen of Russian ambiguity, through which they could just identify the silhouette of a vast and unsafe question: 'What would you do if a Higher Teacher came?' For Sophie Grigorievna herself – in the middle passage of Parkinson's disease – this query was rendered poignant by its irrelevance. Nevertheless she took an initiative in sending her old master in Paris 300 dollars and a roll of silk – tribute which the French urged him to repudiate as provocatively inadequate. Gurdjieff rounded fiercely on these critics: 'No. You out of mouse make elephant.'

As months passed tension mounted. Lyne's sense of spiritual devastation translated itself into a hundred soul-baring and circumstantial pleas for Mme Ouspensky's direction. Early in January 1948 she

hesitated no longer: ringing imperiously for her secretary, Sophie
Grigorievna dictated the cable which sets on her head an imperish-
able Gurdjieffian crown. Some sense of Piotr Ouspensky's ghost –
pale and forbidding – is needed to appreciate both her independence
of spirit and the dramatic reaction at Lyne Place: 'The message for
which we had been waiting was of such a potent nature that it split
the council of the Historico-Psychological Society in twain. It was a
very simple message: "Get in touch with Mr. Gurdjieff in Paris." '

Torn between conflicting allegiances, Lyne writhed exquisitely on
the rack of conscience. A late and cruel spring elided into summer.
Early in June 1948, in the midst of seeming interminable conferences,
fracas, and exploratory dinners, there arrived the telegram which
finally closed the magic triangle between Lyne Place, Franklin Farms,
and 6 Rue des Colonels Rénard. It was from Gurdjieff himself and
read bluntly: 'You are sheep without a shepherd. Come to me.'

No imputation of self-aggrandisement holds water here. Gurdjieff
was stoically committing to the goal of reconciliation all his slender
physical reserves. An eloquent witness is Dorothy Caruso (Enrico's
widow), who arrived from America in late June as Margaret Anderson's
newest companion. Her head was fully primed with Andersonian
romanticism: cloudy notions of Hermes, the Gnostics, the Essene
Brotherhood, the School of Pythagoras.

> But when I saw Gurdjieff all my preconceived ideas vanished. For I saw
> an old man, grey with weariness and illness, yet whose strength of spirit
> emanated with such force from his weakened body that . . . I was galva-
> nised to a zenith of attention: every expression of his face and each small
> movement of his body I found heartbreaking.

Despite her intuitive understanding, Dorothy developed a huge in-
feriority complex at the apartment ('Everybody here seems to have a
soul except me. Haven't I a soul?'). Sensitive to her alienation and her
difficulties with *Beelzebub*, Gurdjieff drew her aside, poured her
some coffee from his battered old thermos flask, and astonished her
altruism with the injunction: 'You must help your father.' Mrs Caruso
politely explained that her father was dead.

> I know. You tell already. But because of your father you are here. Have
> gratitude for this. You are your father and you owe to him. He is dead. Too
> late to repair for himself. You must repair for him. Help him . . . You must
> work on yourself . . . And what you do for yourself you do also for me.

Beyond the mystery of these words, in which Dorothy sensed
'something rich and strange and full of meaning', was the heartening

fact that Gurdjieff had not rejected her ... he was not rejecting anyone, but attracting more and more candidates to his table.

Whether or how Gurdjieff approached Maurice Nicoll is not extant. The good doctor (no longer young nor in perfect health) could count on a welcome in Paris but felt it improper to 're-enter his mother's womb'. Thus during the last fiercely dramatic months of Gurdjieff's life, the group at Great Amwell held aloof and cultivated its own well-manicured certainties ... The only other independent player of note, John Godolphin Bennett, was not approached directly by Gurdjieff; the epoch's exciting potentialities opened to him by accident, when on 7 June 1948 he paid a casual visit to Franklin Farms, New Jersey. Speaking deferentially to Sophie Grigorievna, Bennett confided his sense that, on the day Ouspensky died, Coombe Springs had been visited by a presence which 'might have been some angel or even greater Being'. Mme Ouspensky's speech and hearing were impaired. She said: 'Now that Mr. Ouspensky has gone, what will you do?' When Bennett indicated he could have wished Mr Gurdjieff himself were not mad or dead, Madame replied tersely: 'He is not mad. He has never been mad. He is in Paris now. Why do you not go to him?'

Here as elsewhere, Bennett experienced no moral or intellectual difficulty in switching track; he had repudiated Gurdjieff in 1924 to suit Ouspensky – now he sensibly re-embraced him ... When, early in July 1948, Gurdjieff received Bennett's written offer of 200 pupils from Coombe Springs, together with a farm called 'Donkerhoek' in the northern Transvaal near the source of the Crocodile River, we cannot easily enter his feelings. One thing however was plain: the Anglo-Saxon current – silted up for years by secondary fidelities – was now flowing strongly back towards him.

Bennett was fifty-one and his second wife Winifred Alise seventy-five, when in early August 1948, they presented themselves at 6 Rue des Colonels Rénard. Even by the standards of that 'world centre of piquant situations', the tall Englishman was curiously and bravely circumstanced. For decades 'Gurdjieff' had been to him a shadow, a memory, an unutterable name: the deceased originator of a marvellous teaching (kept on a life-support system not least by his own lectures, seminars, and expository writings). Now, against all reasonable expectation, Gurdjieff in person – his head crowned with a tasselled magenta fez; his feet in kid slippers; his cunning hands cupped and mottled with age; his triumphal belly jutting through a stained and flabbergasted waistcoat – appeared in a cloud of

Gauloise cigarette smoke, and stood confronting his apologist with undismayed attention, 'as dangerous as Everest or the Orinoco, as expensive as aureomycin, as exacting as a lover.'

While Jeanne de Salzmann, effecting the reintroduction, made kindly allusion to Bennett's Prieuré experience (thirty-five days, culminating in 1923), Gurdjieff held him in a long, searching gaze. 'No, I not remember,' he said finally. Yet, supposing those eyes could indeed insinuate themselves into a man's psyche and find out his secret levers and delinquencies, Gurdjieff was surely reading in the man from Coombe Springs a very particular challenge ... The rich spirituality of John Godolphin Bennett was not one submitted to Dean Borsh's 'Calm Light'; on the contrary it moved almost too excitingly through a terrain of fasts, vigils, ordeals, temptations, signs, portents, special graces, and mystical climaxes. He had repeated the Lord's Prayer a thousand times a day for the last nine years (adding the words, *Fiat Voluntas Tua*). His restless activism grew from two largish ambitions: he yearned to play Paul the Apostle to some new Christ, to preach, to compose Epistles, to appoint *episcopoi*, and to convert multitudes; and he wished to become immortal. He came to Gurdjieff now offering numerous people, influential contacts, high organizational ability, fluency in Turkish and Russian, and an impatient and headstrong commitment ... and Gurdjieff used him.

'Polly' Bennett, to employ her sobriquet, had come less as a spiritual aspirant than a physical casualty; Harley Street was lucratively baffled by her grave disorder, which might have been her spine, her kidneys, or even cancer. Behind a well-bred stoicism (she was the daughter of Elliot of Baroda), Mrs Bennett concealed, or supposed she did, her pitiable distress. It was not a mask which convinced Gurdjieff:

> After a time he stopped eating and spoke to my wife in English: 'You are in pain?' 'Yes.' 'Bad pain?' 'Yes.' He left the table, and returned with a small flask from which he took two pills, saying: 'Eat. If pain goes, I will know what to do for you. If not, you tell me.'

Her near instantaneous remission was followed by a whispered exchange which hints intriguingly at a self-sacrificial element in Gurdjieff's therapy. He asked: ' "Where is your pain now?" She answered: "It is gone." He insisted: "I ask you where *is* it now?" Her eyes filled with tears and she said: "You have taken it." He replied: "I am glad. Now I can help you." '

On Saturday 8 August 1948, Gurdjieff set out by car for Cannes.

Old age had neither sapped his enthusiasm for driving nor improved his skills. The crash occurred as he was passing through Montargis and it killed outright the drunken lorry driver involved. Gurdjieff – ribs smashed, face cut, skull fractured, sternum broken, and lungs choked with blood – was pinned in the wreckage by the steering shaft. Throughout the interminable hour in which the emergency service fought to extricate him, he remained conscious, even directing them in order to avoid fatal bleeding. Jeanne de Salzmann – with feelings which may be imagined – drove to Montargis at frantic speed, promptly discharged Gurdjieff from hospital into her own care, and drove back to Paris at a snail's pace.

As she reached 6 Rue des Colonels Rénard at dusk on Sunday, Bennett was a chance and eloquent witness:

> The door of [the] car opened, and Gurdjieff came slowly out. His clothes were covered with blood. His face was black with bruises ... I was looking at a dying man. Even this is not enough to express it. It was a dead man, a corpse, that came out of the car; and yet it walked ... He walked into his room and sat down. He said: 'Now all organs are destroyed. Must make new.' He saw me and smiled, saying: 'Tonight you come to dinner. I must make body work.' A great spasm of pain passed through him and I saw blood flowing from his ear.

Images of a dinner agonizing beyond description were implanted in the memories of the appalled guests. Gurdjieff – his face a purple shadow and his throat bound with surgical gauze – presided with a beautiful and terrifying weakness. His lacerated fingers painfully divided and distributed a trout: 'You like? Then take!' One of the two doctors present believed he might live; the other despaired; both urged he take morphia and sleep.

The Director rose to his feet, lifted his glass, and in a tightly controlled voice said: 'To the health of all Ordinary Idiots!' The grim-faced company swallowed down an emotion which burnt more than the vodka. The Director hurried on: 'To the health of all Super Idiots!' *When would he go?...* 'To the health of all Arch Idiots!'... Morphia was brought but he refused it; in great difficulty he took a mouthful or two of melon. Against the Director rose:

> To the health of all Hopeless Idiots subjectively and objectively! That is to say, to the health of all those who are destined for an honourable death, and to the health of all those who are candidates for perishing like dogs!

Never perhaps, before or since, did this toast sound more awesome and proximate. Even so, Gurdjieff motioned for the full addition:

Addition: by the way it is necessary to add that only those can die honourably who have worked on themselves in life. Those who do not work on themselves will inevitably, early-lately, perish like dirty dogs – even sometimes like rabid dogs.

Here, at Mme de Salzmann's quiet but formidable insistence, the guests dispersed and the casualty was tenderly confided to a bed from which there was no certainty that he would ever rise.

Gurdjieff was an appalling patient – spurning X-rays, spurning rest, spurning penicillin ('It is poison for the soul of man.') *'Veut-il donc mourir?'* protested the visiting nurse. *'Il se tue.'* But he did not die. 'It hurts: great suffering I have,' he conceded to Dorothy Caruso, but still refused morphine, having discovered 'how to live with pain'. On Wednesday the 12th – scarcely able to walk – he extended to Bennett and his 200 pupils a breathtaking invitation: 'Let all come. Now my French group are away on holiday. Necessary not to lose time. Go home and bring whoever wishes to come.' Seven days later Gurdjieff had unaccountably cured himself. He could be found again at his favourite cafés, immaculately dressed with gold-topped walking-stick, and panama hat shading his eyes from the hot sun. He was eighty-two, 'yet his recovery was so complete that he looked younger after his accident than before, as if the shock had strengthened his whole organism instead of weakening it.'

The ten-month hiatus which commences with Ouspensky's death ends with Gurdjieff's accident. As this remarkable August closed, no fewer than six unequal tributary streams had begun to mingle uneasily in the Rue des Colonels Rénard: via London, Frank Pinder, Stanley Nott, and Jane Heap's group; from New York, Margaret Anderson, Dorothy Caruso and Solita Solano; from Lyne, Kenneth Walker and his family; from Mendham, Aubrey Wolton, Reginald Hoare, and Basil Tilley; from Coombe Springs, J. G. Bennett and sixty-odd pupils, including Elizabeth Mayall and Dr Bernard Courtenay-Mayers – and from the *campagne* the sunburnt French, confronted as never before by the Work's perilous diversity and historicity.

Heresy, apostasy, schism, anathema, excommunication, the elect and the damned – the Work thesaurus offers no accommodation for words which tend to bonfires. For the words, no: but for the referents which they encode? That is arguably another matter. The quest for harmony and universal brotherhood was far too serious for instant back-slapping camaraderie at 6 Rue des Colonels Rénard. The one New Testament dictum which all-comers had for years tacitly held in common was not exactly conciliatory: 'Strait is the gate, and narrow is the way which leadeth unto life, and few there be who find it. Beware of false prophets, which come to you in sheep's clothing, but inwardly they are ravening wolves.'

The light shed on such an attitude by a supercilious and entertaining rationalism dazzles more than it illuminates. To meet Gurdjieff and be burnt by him; to stake a lifetime's energy and resources on a slender but objective hope; to calibrate one's flawed and brief existence with a vast and exacting critique; and to support all this with real 'being-effort' – left one opinionated at a level of quite peculiar validity. In August 1948, the several Work leaders – despite their best resolutions of amity – strained their initial affabilities through their teeth.

As the newcomers entered Gurdjieff's little salon, they observed – cunningly lit and ramified by mirrors – a collection of figurines: Nubians on camels, Guards officers in *droshkies*, mounted Hussars, pirouetting ballerinas, galloping Arab sheikhs. Yet Gurdjieff the collector of figurines was as nothing to Gurdjieff the collector of 'sons and daughters'. He yoked together his quarrelsome spiritual offspring by the force of a unique paternalism: he taught untiringly – by private interviews, telling looks, and whispered intimations – taught while he drank and swore and played the harmonium and told repetitious and 'pointless' jokes and robbed Peter to pay Paul. He did not rely on rhetoric but on audacious salads, peppered vodka, and surreal car trips; he did not raise his glass to a man's past but to his quotient of presence. And as to the 'differential calculus' undeniably employed at his table, it did not entail the pupil's nationality or Work itinerary but his indicative 'idiocy'. . . . To the health of all Squirming Idiots and hysterical women! To the health of all Zigzag Idiots! To the health of all Enlightened Idiots! To the health of all Patented Idiots! This strange speciation of a universal idiocy proved, paradoxically, to have powerful cohesive effect.

Ouspensky's familiars, who had acquired (more by osmosis than formal study) 'the chapel-going faces of Plymouth Brethren', suddenly found themselves perched on smallish stools toasting a variety of idiots. A high and fastidious intellectuality, the very fulcrum of their trust, was challenged by Gurdjieff's insistence: 'You must feel, you must feel, your mind is a luxury. You must suffer remorse in your feelings.' Where the diorama of their expectation had most relied on memory, there it proved most deceptive. Where were the familiar chalk and blackboard? Where were the diagrams of the enneagram, the Ray of Creation, the Table of Hydrogens? 'All who come to me,' declared Gurdjieff alarmingly, 'must have enema each day. Very necessary have apparatus for this always. If do not have such apparatus come here very early tomorrow morning and I will give such. Five o'clock'. . . This was not at all what had been expected.

The transit from Ouspensky to Gurdjieff first presented itself as a transit from the saturnine to the jovial: ' "*Le Patron*," he said, rubbing his hand over his rather prominent abdomen, "is demanding instant attention, and *le Patron is une personne très importante*, to be treated always with the greatest respect. He asks to be fed . . ." ' Yet the ensuing dinners were hazardous – hard on the behind and liver but even harder on the conscience. The differentiation of objective and subjective Hopeless Idiots, for example, was loaded with scarcely bearable significance:

> No description can convey the terrifying reality of this distinction as it was conveyed by Gurdjieff, with the burning eyes and the vibrant tones of a Jeremiah. I saw old men break down and sob who perhaps had not been so moved since their childhood.

Many younger men at that unique table were shaken by the richness and extremity of their predicament. 'Now,' wrote Basil Tilley to his wife Irène at Mendham, 'is really the harvest of our lives, but here, we are beyond the harvest, right in the mill – so God help us!'

Especially poignant was the case of Kenneth Walker, who since 1924 had invested his bankable integrity and formidable inner strength in Ouspensky and the 'System'. Now, at sixty-six, his life was sadly changed: none of his distinguished friends and colleagues – Dr Francis Roles, R. J. G. Mayor, and John Sinclair, Lord Pentland – would accompany him to Paris, and he himself arrived there bowed down by Ouspensky's alteration and death. 'Gurdjieff received him with true compassion, restoring his faith and hope. It was a great joy to watch the transformation taking place under our eyes. Within a few days, Walker was rejuvenated . . .' His wife Mary, who described the apartment's ambience as indescribable and Gurdjieff as the most astonishing man she had ever met, soon concluded he was not really a man at all but some species of magician.

Early in September 1948, Gurdjieff tossed into the melting-pot of 6 Rue des Colonels Rénard his professed need of a 'more solid place' – a country seat where, in a milieu at once atmospheric and physically challenging, his pupils' private hopes could be subsumed in a common aim. The quest for this idealized 'Prieuré' evoked a French enthusiasm withheld from the real thing twenty-five years before.

Willing parties scoured left and right, and with amazing speed a possibility glimmered to acquire the magnificent Château de Voisins at Rambouillet, twenty-eight miles south-west of Paris; and, what is more, on providential terms. The owner, a millionaire sugar baron, felt inclined to lease it cheaply to minimize his tax liability, and upon this inclination Jeanne de Salzmann and J. G. Bennett leant strenuously.

Why did Gurdjieff start this hare? Surely, at eighty-two, he had neither the full capacity nor the motive for such a venture? Distinctly more important now in the grand strategy of his mission was the long-deferred promulgation of *Beelzebub's Tales to His Grandson*. Here was his quintessential teaching: a text helped into being by the devotion of Olga de Hartmann and the wit of Orage and Jane Heap; a text which had once driven him to the brink of suicide as he strove, against failing health and time's merciless arithmetic, to communicate his profoundest insights. A text, yes ... but not a book. Typed, mimeographed, copied overtly and surreptitiously, hoarded from hand to hand – *Beelzebub*, after twenty years, nevertheless remained unpublished; a scripture in tedious gestation; an influence waiting to be born.

That the book indeed counted more than the château emerged when the chimerical negotiations at Rambouillet were peculiarly transposed into a grander scheme to urge forward *Beelzebub*'s publication. The shift in emphasis carried a disturbing corollary: that once *Beelzebub* was actualized, Gurdjieff himself would 'disappear'. His more naive pupils protested that they would follow him wherever he went, but he replied soberingly: 'You will not easily find me.' Frank Pinder – perhaps more sensitive to the situation's human dynamic – argued for delay: 'Why do you publish *Beelzebub's Tales* now? Every page has grammatical errors, faulty punctuation and even mistakes. It ought to be properly edited.' But Gurdjieff overrode him: 'It is a rough diamond. There's not time now to edit it. It will have to go.' Just as *Herald of Coming Good* had been priced from 8 to 108 French francs, so *Beelzebub* was planned to cost its readers a small fortune or virtually nothing: Gurdjieff's disciples must dip deep into their pockets to produce a book for issue gratis to deserving members of the public; the work would appear simultaneously in four languages, be distributed everywhere, including Russia, and be read aloud by prepared pupils in workmen's clubs. J. G. Bennett – keenly enthusiastic – placed in *Everybody* magazine an article he considered appropriate.

The weakness, and simultaneously the strength, of the 'Voisins –
Beelzebub scheme' lay in the financial area: to lease the château or
launch the book would demand big money – 'many zeros' – and
where would that come from? From France?. . . Perhaps. But, as Paul
Schaeffer conceded: 'We French . . . are the stingiest of people . . .
also the most incredulous.' From England?. . . Unfortunately,
August's huge outpouring from English wallets had already fallen
through the chronic hole in Gurdjieff's pocket . . . Old but indomitable, the Teacher of Dancing caught on the air the faint and faraway
whiff of requisite dollars, and thus, on 9 September 1948, let slip his
intention to prepare eighteen people (three rows of six) to demonstrate his latest Movements in New York.

Albeit the French 'Demonstration Class' could have carried with
distinction this entire enterprise, Gurdjieff sacrificed their technical
perfection on the altar of integration. 'How you situated?' he asked
Basil Tilley jovially. 'You are English? Can you come to America
with me for a month?' Soon the floor of the Salle Pleyel (and indeed
the floor of the Hotel Belfast) shook to the stamp of uneducated
English feet in desperate rehearsal. 'You first cousin to elephant,'
Gurdjieff told Tilley pointedly: 'Necessary to become first cousin to
cat.' It fell on the Paris group to coach the English, and especially on
such luminaries as Alfred Etievan, 'a fervent young Frenchman with
the nervous intensity of one whose inner fire is too hot for a frail
body and who is destined to die young.' The instructors' goodwill
was exhaustively tested and abundantly proved (though each English
dancer selected for New York meant one fewer from France). The
awesome – the near impossible – standard to which the English must
aspire, was rammed home on 18 September, when, under the exacting
gaze of Gurdjieff and Jeanne de Salzmann, the French gave a full
programme to an audience of Bennett's pupils.

As a Nansen passport holder and a social black sheep, Gurdjieff
encountered yet again those Kafkaesque complications which did not
so much inhibit his foreign travel as embellish it with peculiar human
incident. The Paris *gendarmerie* was pleased he would go to America,
but had no intention whatsoever of issuing him a re-entry permit;
without a re-entry permit (and clear intent to use it) he could not
expect a visa from the United States Embassy. Here was an impasse
which no tactical distribution of bonbons nor even of banknotes
seemed likely to resolve. Yet if at the bureaucratic level Gurdjieff
was immobilized, the secret influence which he commanded through
his pupils clambered to the diplomatic heights. All the vital papers

were eventually issued on the personal guarantee of a former Prime Minister of France.

It was on Saturday 30 October 1948 that Gurdjieff sailed for New York with Jeanne de Salzmann. Ahead he had sent Alfred Etievan to initiate Movements classes, and behind him he was leaving a company whose astonishing, if fragile, cohesion is hinted at in the memoir of Dorothy Caruso:

> as I sat observing, absorbing, rejoicing, I grew aware of a swelling sense of harmony that related everything within the room to everything else — gestures, faces, voices, food, my thought vibrated in unison like a chord in music.

At the farewell lunch in 6 Rue des Colonels Rénard, the role of Director was assigned not to the trusted Bernard Lemaitre but to Bennett – who broke the ritual of the toasts by proposing Gurdjieff's own health. 'No,' interjected Gurdjieff quickly. 'I will propose myself health of English. Thanks to the English I sail to New York free from all debts. Pure *comme bébé*.'

Embarking at Le Havre, Gurdjieff once more 'produced himself' amid the ritual and paraphernalia of the theatre of departure: yet again the crucial messages, the adroit, slanted asides, the frontal silences pregnant with meaning; again the serio-comic bits of 'business' with caviare, Armagnac, *zakushki* and smelly cheeses; again the contrived altercation with a nettled purser. The old man's salty engagement in life, his ferocious relish for its rich and surreal specificality, seemed to promise him endless tenure . . . Did no one catch in the seagull's alien cry the omen of an inescapable estrangement? One year precisely this very Saturday, one revolution of the earth about the sun, and the singular traveller would set out on a longer more mysterious journey: George Ivanovitch Gurdjieff would be dead.

16

AU REVOIR, TOUT LE MONDE

(31 October 1948–29 October 1949)

Through the vast labyrinth of Gurdjieff's myth there runs, like Ariadne's thread, a curious quality of *intentionality*; the secret intimation that he somehow composed his own life, both in its incident and symbolism, bestows on its final chapter a biographically awesome significance.

'I am Gurdjieff. I *not* will die!' This notorious affirmation (which bamboozled to almost equal degree his most credulous pupils and thick-headed detractors) can only be construed ideologically. Not for an instant did Gurdjieff imagine death convertible from its *idée fixe*, or that he personally could escape his wooden box. He trod the way of everyman advisedly, and on a sumptuous carpet of experience: creating Movements, playing music, toasting 'eedyots', concocting new salads, scattering bonbons, distributing Hershey bars, inhaling Gauloises and burping Perrier bubbles; en route through cafés, night clubs, Turkish baths and high mountain passes; joking with children, tormented by *gaz*, swamped by pupils, nourished by sheep's heads and an exhorbitant vision ... until in the end he delivered himself with Socratic dispassion to the moment when death, one hopes, was swallowed up in victory.

'You move like worms in shit!' In November 1948 Gurdjieff entered the studio in Carnegie Hall to challenge the American pupils of Alfred Etievan. Although he was old and had driven straight from the jetty, he seemed the very epitome of evergreen activity:

> dictating movements, changing rhythms, spotting mistakes, lashing orally ... changing from one number to another, giving fast explanations on the spot, never compromising, demanding more and more effort, playing no favourites, urging understanding.

As Gurdjieff re-evoked *The Struggle of the Magicians*, pupils who had translated Piotr Ouspensky's New York lectures into a sclerotic puritanism had suddenly to fling themselves about exhibiting the most revolting symptoms of envy, vanity, lust, pride, fear and anger: 'Everybody began to move back and forth in a frenzy of changes in positions and tempo, whirling past one another with satanic fury, making detestable faces.' A moment later the same dancers were required to evoke in flowing harmony feelings of piety, awe, and compassion.

Reoccupying his small suite in the Wellington Hotel, Gurdjieff resumed his perpetual *peek-neek* under the 'No Cooking' sign. His day was pleasantly crowded. After breakfasting lightly at Child's Restaurant on tomato juice, applejack and eggs, he would hold court in the Luxor Baths on West 46th Street, drinking judicious quantities of Perrier water and turbanned by an iced towel:

> His abdominal girth was heroic and his presence in the Turkish bath ... at least the match of Rodin's Balzac ... Other patrons must have wondered at the enigmatic, caramel-colored, fiercely moustached figure of Gurdjieff picking his way with feline grace from the hot room to the steam room to the Russian room ...

A business lunch, the briefest siesta, countless tête-à-tête with eager pupils and clients at Child's, on to Carnegie Hall for Movements, a long ceremonial dinner at his Wellington apartment with scores of guest-idiots ... until at length the eighty-two-year-old would ask brightly: 'Who have idea for night?'

During his 'last hurrah' in New York, Gurdjieff's swirling entourage had dizzy variety: it blended Prieuré originals, Orage's lieutenants, a couple on 'The Rope', several French aides-de-camp, nervous escapees from Mme Ouspensky at Mendham, and a miscellany of hopeful latecomers. Dinners at the Wellington found notables and nonentities packed together like herrings in a barrel. Sitting near Gurdjieff under an enneagram made of large leaves, and wearing an insurrectionist porkpie hat, might occasionally be identified the venerable figure of Frank Lloyd Wright. Sometimes the great architect's mind wandered to the laboratory tower he was building for S. C. Johnson & Son, and sometimes to his ailing gall bladder. 'I, seven-times doctor,' Gurdjieff interjected. 'In Paris I have two hundred *élèves*, all doctors.' With Olgivanna's connivance he amazingly prevailed on Wright to abandon his prescribed diet and substitute mutton, avocado and peppered Armagnac. Humour and gravitas rubbed shoulders here. And when the host fingered the keys of his battered harmonium he seemed (not least to Wright) to bring echoes of another, better world. 'This music I play you now,' Gurdjieff explained, 'came from monastery where Jesus Christ spent from eighteenth to thirtieth year.'

Though Gurdjieff dubbed Paul Anderson his 'American Secretary' and Edwin Wolfe his 'Minister for Finance', his actual choice of favourite son was a 'political' upset; he loaded prime responsibility for furthering the Work throughout America onto the angular shoulders of Henry John Sinclair, Lord Pentland. Criteria of intrinsic merit apart, the choice looked variously improbable: Pentland was relatively young and not American; he was not a protégé of Orage; he had neither been to the Prieuré nor even to 6 Rue des Colonels Rénard; in fact he had never met Gurdjieff before in his life. Forty years old, tall, cadaverous, with a keen bird-like gaze produced beneath militant eyebrows, he was a distinguished product of Cambridge, Heidelberg, Lyne Place and Mendham – a man, one might think, peculiarly unsuited for the roles of *Monsieur Egout* or *Monsieur Poubelle*. How could Pentland's Savile Row sensibilities not be affronted by Gurdjieff's latest taste in orange tweed suits? How could that famous Pentland eyebrow not rise subliminally when Gurdjieff passed round photos of the Château de Voisins and guaranteed a permanent suite there to anyone who would donate 5000 dollars in cash? How could his Lordship's effortless *politesse* adjust to the new mode of after-dinner conversation? ('You know for me,' said Gurdjieff thoughtfully to an over-confident priest, 'that collar you wear is like red carnation prostitute wears when she menstruates.')

Pentland's impeccable antecedents as a lieutenant of Ouspensky only compound the mystery of his preferment ... It was a pity about Ouspensky (so Gurdjieff informed an expectant gathering of his New York followers): had he not slunk off to manipulate on his own, he need not have 'perished like a dog'. But, protested one plucky young man, it was solely due to Mr Ouspensky that they were there. 'What is the use of your being here?' retorted Gurdjieff magisterially. 'You also are candidate for perishing like a dog.'

In what spirit, one wonders, did Sophie Grigorievna Ouspensky actually invite Gurdjieff to visit Mendham in the dead of winter 1948? In what spirit did he accept? And what transpired in the widow's magnificent curtained room with its desolate stack of medicine bottles? Beyond the renewal of an old amity, beyond the now forlorn question of Sophie Grigorievna's health, there lay, demanding urgent resolution, the future of a singular document. *Fragments of an Unknown Teaching*, Ouspensky's recapitulation of Gurdjieff's ideas, was a masterpiece of objective reporting, but its publication had been detained for eighteen years. Ouspensky's editor at Routledge, who could smell a hot property a mile downwind, hankered to set it in type in 1931, and so in certain moods did Ouspensky himself. But not in the mood which prevailed. As, through the late 1930s, the author patrolled his delightful grounds at Lyne Place astride his portly horse Jingles, his mind was painfully divided. In compiling his testament he had acknowledged with exemplary candour his overwhelming debt to 'G.' but whether the time was ripe to expose that debt to a wide pupil-readership – pupils moreover whom he had forbidden to mention Gurdjieff's name – that needed the further and more responsible thought which Ouspensky was doubtless still applying when overtaken by death in October 1947.

It has its poignancy – that moment at Mendham when Sophie Grigorievna, with shaking mutinous fingers, confides to Gurdjieff the manuscript of her husband's book. Gone forever the epoch which gave it birth; scattered or dead the first Petrograd group . . . yet here, like a beautifully pressed flower, is the great psychological and cosmological glyph which had bloomed so suddenly and mysteriously in a lost world. To the stricken Mme Ouspensky – acutely aware that Gurdjieff's direct speech constituted four-fifths of the manuscript – now fell the delicate task of seeking his permission to publish. No foregone conclusion, for if *Fragments* were hastened into print and *Beelzebub* for any reason foundered, an undesirable confusion of provenance might fasten on the entire Work. What mattered basically was this: did *Fragments* resonate, both in its mundane and inner octaves, the note which Gurdjieff had sounded? He sampled it and, pausing, pronounced: 'Before I hate Ouspensky; now I love him. This very exact, he tell what I say.' This endorsement effectively concluded the long relationship between Sophie Grigorievna Ouspensky and the man she called 'X', the unknown quantity. She was far gone in her unalleviable disease and he 'racked by a spasmodic cough, a deep, gurgling, tracheal rumble that reflected . . . a chronic inflammation of the lungs.' Time was measured out for both of them . . . but the sleeping giant of the Work had begun to stir and on the legs of *Beelzebub* and *Fragments* would soon proceed to walk.

Neither book could expect good reviews: the American and English ideological establishment, the grandees of cultural *bon ton*, the entranced proponents of trance – these could not, in Gurdjieff's estimation, do other than oppose him. He was nevertheless determined to set his pupils marching under the banner of *Beelzebub* towards the sound of the guns. J. G. Bennett (who was there for Gurdjieff's birthday on 13 January and took an adjacent room at the Wellington) found himself ominously received as the 'esteemed representative for England'. He was enjoying the privilege of morning coffee with his teacher at Child's Restaurant, fronting 5th Avenue below 57th Street, when Gurdjieff said peremptorily, 'You now write letter.' Game for virtually anything, Bennett fell to composition without the slightest hint as to theme and treatment:

6, RUE DES COLONELS RENARD
PARIS, 17

13th January, 1949
This circular letter is addressed to all my present and former adepts . . .

So, in Gurdjieff's name and under Gurdjieff's mesmeric gaze, Bennett proceeded. His fountain-pen – like the broom of the sorcerer's apprentice – seemed self-propelled. Unmeditated words positively jumped from its gold-plated nib; they heralded *Beelzebub*'s impending publication and urged each 'adept' (a noun which particularly grated on Bennett) to buy a first-edition copy for £100 so that others might receive one free.

> By means of this action, it will be possible for those who have gained personal help from contact with my ideas to do something to repay and to help to reap the harvest which I have sown.
>
> G. Gurdjieff

Without a word Gurdjieff folded the paper and put it in his pocket.

Kathryn Hulme, who had flown in from Frankfurt the day before, arrived for lunch at the Wellington just in time for the wry dénouement. Taking the folded letter from his pocket, Gurdjieff handed it to Bennett (as though Bennett had never seen it) and urged: 'Read, read – is for everybody.' Throughout a lengthy and even boisterous lunch served on paper plates, the room hummed with excited comment. 'All those present were loud in approval, saying that it was exactly right: only Mr. Gurdjieff could have written it, and so on.' Gurdjieff himself sat silent – except to nominate three literary executives: René Zuber for France, Pentland for America, and Bennett for England.

On a blustery afternoon early in March 1949, Gurdjieff embarked on the *Queen Mary* for Cherbourg. Goodbye America! Goodbye New York! Goodbye to a long and Runyonesque relationship . . .

To have arrived in the Coolidge administration and be leaving in Truman's; to have sampled the Golden Twenties, the Prohibition Era, the Stock Market Crash, the Great Depression, the New Deal, and the Fair Deal; to have registered, with irony, successive increments in the hyperbole of altitude (the Woolworth Building, the Chrysler Building, the Empire State Building); to have tasted Jack Daniels straight and deprecated the foxtrot; to have visited Coney Island and played Carnegie Hall – all this had been the strangely inflected consequence of a pilgrimage to the Sarmoung Monastery ... Astern, against the winter sunset, the Statue of Liberty dwindled and the Wall Street elevation of Manhattan Island slowly telescoped back into its solid granite foundation. How many 'bucks', how many 'fins' – indeed how many 'grands' or 'gees' – had Gurdjieff consecrated to higher purpose? How many exotic birds (vivid as Audubon's) peopled the America of his singular memory?

Gurdjieff had embarked a heftier entourage than ever, yet if imagination were to assign him just three companions at his first-class dining-room table, they would be Jeanne de Salzmann, Lord Pentland, and Iovanna Lloyd Wright. After some hesitation the great architect had joined Olgivanna in encouraging their precious daughter to go. 'Yes,' approved Gurdjieff with debatable parallelism, 'I have many sons away in monasteries.' Iovanna (with half-a-dozen more, like Tatiana, Mme Ouspensky's grand-daughter) had become one of Gurdjieff's 'calves' – a sorority of decorative young women, whom he planned, if time permitted, to instruct in Sacred Dance and who in any case would come in handy as *Egout pour Sweet*.

April in Paris! Although Gurdjieff is marvellously inconformable to the cliché of lovers under budding chestnut trees, perhaps some intimation that this was his last spring, did lend a special bite to his senses and poignancy to his camouflaged feelings. He had delegated Jeanne de Salzmann away to London to counsel and appraise Kenneth Walker's pupils at Colet Gardens. Despite her enthusiasm, she could not persuade her master to cross the Channel; it was evidently not disdain, not an insistence that the English mountain come to Muhammad, simply that France monopolized his attention. Besides, having now without a blush quietly dropped all plans for the Château de Voisins, he was on the look-out for a smaller place.

Gurdjieff's travelling *peek-neeks*, which facilitated this quest, were a sort of university on wheels. Huge uncertainty gripped the pupils. What hour – what day – would wheels roll? Where would they make for? Who would be chosen to come? (Basil Tilley recalls how rudely conditional was the place assigned him: ' "Mr Tiggey" was to be the passenger of Mrs. Sutta on the trip to Vichy and when my smell became intolerable I was to be passed to another car.') Early in the morning the frantic loading of hampers and watermelons in the narrow canyon of Rue des Colonels Rénard heightened the tension: 'Finally, Gurdjieff himself would appear, smoking a cigarette in a big black holder, with his red fez at a jaunty angle on the back of his head and a pocket book bulging with thousand-franc notes.' From start to finish, money was liberally if eccentrically spent. On 12 June – loaded with gifts of exotic confectionery and rejuvenated by Vichy's famous *massage sous l'eau* – Gurdjieff drove back to Paris and his favourite café in the Avenue des Acacias, where he distributed to all-comers 'a fantastic cake in violent colours'.

The summer solstice found Paris boiling hot and Gurdjieff in a handsome Panama hat. He was hinting capriciously at new and more heroic journeys: he would come at last to London; thence to America; there hire a fleet of Citroëns and toot his way in stupendous cavalcade through the mid-West. Sometimes, in the thick of his pupils, he admitted a more modest and poignant hope: 'I would like to go to Chamonix – to hear water running; there I could sleep.' In any given day now, he was speaking *tête-à-tête* with forty 'clients'. His inveterate sharing of cake and bonbons, food and banknotes, symbolized a far more costly apportionment of his time, energy, and final reserves. His pupils were not conscienceless. 'The kind of force he is using is wearing him out,' observed Dorothy Caruso. 'Why must he go on doing it? Why do they let him? We should go home, we should not ask this tired man for anything.' But Gurdjieff himself had built the atmosphere where most of his 'adepts' confronted some tormenting personal riddle and prowled around him desperate for the tiniest window of legitimate access: 'This man, I know, is going to die – to die before I can ask him *my* question.'

As in New York, the general mêlée mostly featured newer people. A spiritual link between the Sarmoung Monastery and the delicious 'calves' was not corroborated by any surprise visitor from the deep hinterland of Gurdjieff's past. Even survivors from his early ministry were rare: Savitsky *père* had come out of Russia; Jeanne de Salzmann and Frank Pinder evoked the memory-haunted streets of Tbilisi; and three British ladies in sensible shoes (Elinor Crowdy, Gladys Alexander, and Dr Mary Bell) were faded snapshots from the Prieuré scrapbook ... A scene so crowded and a purpose so intense forbad Gurdjieff scope for nostalgia; the 'good old days' were now. In just this spirit, late in July, he set off for a final invigorating brush with his oldest 'pupil-adversary'.

To a brutal crashing of gears and labouring of engines, Gurdjieff's three-car convoy ascended into Switzerland by the Col des Faucilles – while in Geneva Elizabeta Grigorievna Stjoernval (who thirty years since had gloomily crossed the northern Caucasus on foot), prepared her coiffure. Hers had been a singular story: titanic revolutionary forces had tumbled her from the warm cocoon of the *haute bourgeoisie*; she had fallen in with a magician; kicking and protesting she had been dragged along a transformational road – now in the dull, sanitized city of Calvin, she had recovered the sanctuary of the completely mundane. With what shiver of trepidation did she now pluck those special earrings from her jewellery box?

The meeting eventuated in a baroque station buffet, where a Swiss string ensemble, elbowing at full pelt, impeded conversation. Gurdjieff himself seems to have become nettled:

> After a time he called the head waiter and gave him a large tip to stop the music. Anyway, he said, it was not music, but masturbation, and all the musicians were masturbators. The head waiter, probably expecting a compliment to the orchestra, said he did not understand the word – what did it mean!

On this embarrassing note, Mme Stjoernval passes forever from biographic earshot, while Gurdjieff – after a brief remission by Chamonix's cool mountain streams – drove back to the heat of Paris.

Among Gurdjieff's entourage at 6 Rue des Colonels Rénard, the Salle Pleyel, and in the haunts round the Réna, the Belfast, and the San Remo hotels, there grew with every week that passed a mood of unbearable tension. The whole pace must accelerate explained Gurdjieff, because he needed to go in a day or two to Tibet. 'Tibet, Monsieur?' asked a perplexed disciple. 'Or Dieppe?' 'Mr G. gave a particularly wicked and sly smile and said, "Either way very expensive", as though apart from that the destination did not matter much.'

Sometimes he renewed his intent to go to America – if only someone would stay behind and safeguard his figurines. 'All this,' he said, gesturing affectionately at Cleopatra with her asp, and a woman with a pigeon biting her ear. 'All this very valuable thing is.'

Wearing a burgundy-toned fez, Gurdjieff presided in his dining room against an Oxford-blue curtain ruined by symmetrical clumps of red flowers. His stomach (or, as he called it, his 'valise') was impressive – but so, he pointed out, was Buddha's, from eating too much tripe. Comedy? Indeed he brought ample comedy, broad and subtle. Yet who, in this final year of Gurdjieff's life, could study his face and not see there the sovereign, potent dignity of an immense and unassuagable sorrow. Never did the attention he bent on his pupils waver; nor, for the most part did theirs on him: 'At the end of a meal, when *Egout* gave him a cigarette and *Poubelle* lit it for him, he said, "See now how my life is roses, roses. And I – only a poor old dancing teacher." '

Beyond this ironic self-deprecation, how did Gurdjieff – after a lifetime's inner work – categorize himself? Man No. 4? Man No. 5? Man No. 6? Or even Man No. 7? Faithful as ever to paradox, he evinced both humility and breathtaking self-esteem. René Zuber celebrates this first aspect: 'Compared with the behaviour of any of us, or of my family, or of anyone I came across in public, he was a monster of *modesty*.' And to Edwin Wolfe he admitted quietly: 'Many men on earth more than me. I have long way to go.'

Yet in coded language, his confessions arguably took a different tack. 'For a long time now,' he whispered, 'I can write cheque with 7 "*zéros*". . . Even your King cannot do that.' To J. G. Bennett at least, the meaning was transparent: Gurdjieff had adroitly calibrated his numerical typology with the thieves' argot – '*zéros*' of £1000 and 'hunchbacks' of £500; his actual import was not that he was a millionaire but Man No. 7 – possessed of an objective and completely practical knowledge, and immortal within the limits of the solar system . . . At this point in Bennett's reflections he was told to collect 'three *zéros* with hunchback', while Gurdjieff was in America.

Whatever Gurdjieff's meaning and rank of attainment, he undoubtedly went on wrestling for a 'New World' he personally could never hope to see. His body was worn out. Very soon his life's overall effect must rely on his pupils' struggles and on the kinetic energy in his unknown dances, music, and writing. Half in earnest and half in self-mockery, he drank to the moment when *Beelzebub* would begin its slow, corrosive action on the mechanical world of obvious absurdities. On 24 August, when Bennett adduced Gurdjieff's ideas at the 1949 Montessori Conference in San Remo, and Italian radio picked up his speech, Gurdjieff affected an exaggerated delight: 'Perhaps Pope Rome heard. One day *Beelzebub* will be read in Pope's Palace. Perhaps I will be there.'

That Rome would embrace *Beelzebub* was a singular idea, yet one more exhorbitant was flickering across the upper room at 6 Rue des Colonels Rénard:

This great feast – can I say it without shocking? – reminded me of another. It was impossible not to think about the Last Supper. Bludgeoned into life, we were taking part in tragic agapes. We dipped our hand in the dish with a Master. The figure of Judas and of the favourite disciple was enough to give one a fit.

Yes! . . . Who would betray and who serve Gurdjieff's purpose in the dubious but inescapable years beyond the horizon? Who could fathom the essence of his 'New World' and help to realize it? Who would minister wittily to his extravagant evangelism: '*All* English must become followers of my ideas . . . all or nothing'?

Immediately the Master was dead, history would start recording the all-too-human acts of his apostles. Everyone would contribute according to their understanding (blunt instruments of a slow but inescapable deflection). Even Jeanne de Salzmann, who had accepted the taxing role of Saint Peter, must somehow accommodate Gurdjieff's heretical vision of Judas Iscariot as the best and closest friend of Jesus, and the very saviour of his work: 'Because of Judas, your Christ has been God for 2000 years.'

As to Tibet, Gurdjieff did not return there (or even to Dieppe) but his final 'expedition' – to the cave paintings of Lascaux – was in the line of the Seekers of Truth. The old man drove south through the heat by way of Nevers, Vichy, Clermont Ferrand, Mont Dore, La Bourboule, Ursel, Tulle and Brive – arriving at 9 pm on 31 August at the Hôtel Soleil d'Or in Montignac. Next morning he was still tired and his legs so ominously swollen that Bennett ferried him to the cave's entrance in his Vauxhall. The dark, sudden air was almost shockingly cool. A great bull, twenty feet across, confided to the contours of the rock millennia ago with the easy flow of ink on silk, was lit suddenly by torchlight. To the grazier's son from Alexandropol and the habitué of the Café de la Paix, how close – and then again how distant – was that image. Who had created this objective art? When? And why? Deep in the earth, by what light and under the stress of what impulse? The brochure's answers, however buttressed by science, meant nothing to Gurdjieff: an imagination which had created the vast 'anti-history' of *Beelzebub's Tales to His Grandson* saw on the rock the faint but unmistakable imprint of Atlantis . . . Gurdjieff bought a special album to go to Frank Lloyd Wright, urging his daughter Iovanna with eloquent simplicity: 'Tell him that such place exist.'

By early September, Gurdjieff had resolved to concentrate his entire effort in France and consolidate at some suitable chateau a 'Beelzebubian world centre': perversely he had also resolved to sail for New York on 20 October aboard the s.s. *America*. Sometimes at dinner he would produce from his pocket a little wooden snake painted with yellow and green spots, which wriggled now this way, now that. By 22 September he had actually acquired a visa for the USA and exchanged contracts to purchase the station hotel at La Grand Paroisse.

Set among marigolds and unkempt rose bushes on a steep, stony slope above the railway, this 'poor man's château' commanded, between tall chestnut trees, a prospect of the gliding Seine. Its large kitchen, wild garden, and ill-maintained outbuildings gave promise of a physical demand familiar to Gurdjieff's English pupils (and novel to the French). All at La Grand Paroisse was now at Gurdjieff's disposition – except the essential; numerous and devoted followers stood poised to translate into concrete terms intents he could never realize. By 8 October he had entrée. Despite the intrusive autumnal sun and the urgent hiss and spurt of flame from the pinewood fire – Gurdjieff sat wordlessly in the château dining room, gathering round his shoulders his heavy greatcoat with its Astrakhan collar. His legs (which only the day before had received the cunning attention of an Armenian masseur), were nevertheless, painfully swollen and propped on a stool; his lunch, on medical insistence, comprised a few rusks soaked in milk, cream and yoghurt . . . To envisage a second Prieuré at La Grand Paroisse, or indeed a trip to America, demanded an increasingly heroic suspension of disbelief.

Three days afterwards, during a reading in the Paris apartment, Gurdjieff gave his first notarized yawn. Less and less now could he disguise or retard his decline. When Dorothy Caruso made her final farewell in the Avenue des Acacias, she felt overwhelmed by her teacher's suffering:

> 'Does something hurt you?' He moved slightly in his chair and for the first time I heard from him a sound like a groan. 'I must take habit of pain,' he said. Then he held out his hand and I said good-bye, and left him sitting there, alone, in the shrill sunlight.

Nor was pain his only companion: the old man was supporting a near insupportable fatigue; the Teacher of Dancing could scarcely walk. Yet walk he still often did, across the studio floor at the Salle Pleyel, entering with all his force into the 'being-effort' of the class as they worked on No. 17, the Multiplication.

The Sarmoung Monastery lay aeons away on the disputed frontier of memory and hypothesis, but for thirty years Gurdjieff had proved himself 'a rather good teacher of temple dances'. Was there (as some have alleged) disdain in his long and tireless dispensation? Could one justly impute to him a possessive esotericism – 'You are nothing but the hieroglyphs of an inexhaustible language that I shall continue to speak through you and whose secret I shall guard with my life'? Or had he, on the contrary, marched generations of dancers between bayonets to communion with a subtle and energetic truth which transcended verbal explanation? Long ago he had promised the French a repertoire of forty Movements, and had already given thirty-eight. Now, unexpectedly, he delivered No. 39 – an understated work of mobilized interior attention . . . His struggle to preserve, and to transmit into a new age, a traditional science was over now. On Friday 14 October in Salle 32, George Ivanovitch Gurdjieff appeared at a Movements class for the last time . . . and there, in front of his appalled pupils, collapsed.

Who can say how the old man fought back in the ensuing week? He did it anyway despite an alphabet of doctor-pupils (Dr Abadie, Dr Conge, Dr Courtenay-Mayers, Dr Egg, Dr Hambaschidze, Dr Vaysse and Dr Walker) who found common ground chiefly in an educated foreboding, and a sense that to 'physic the King' was impossible. Meanwhile on the slender shoulders of young Lise Tracol, who day and night nursed a uniquely incalculable patient, were loaded the disproportionate hopes of hundreds of people. Sometimes Gurdjieff conceded his desperate frailty, sometimes not; he forbad Lise to let him go out and forbad her to keep him in. On Friday Elizabeth Mayall was astonished to find him in a fruit shop buying enormous quantities of bananas 'for the English': 'His appearance gave me a shock. He looked so ill, his face very dark with black rings sunken under his eyes . . . This is the first time I have looked at him and seen an old man.'

That evening of 21 October the proof copy of *Beelzebub* reached Gurdjieff from the publishers. Here at long last, in the author's frail, mottled hands, was his modern *mythos*, his symbolic biography, his mighty 'soldier' who would fight perseveringly for the new world. Gurdjieff was curiously withdrawn, only in real contact with Jeanne de Salzmann. It seemed to some eye-witnesses that, in this unique moment, he had finished his self-imposed task on earth and accepted his dismissal by Higher Powers.

On Saturday the 22nd, Gurdjieff walked out of his flat for the last time. Anxious hours later, Bennett chanced on him alone and stranded in his favourite café without the strength to reach his car. For all of Bennett's days he remembered the ensuing 'promenade' – Gurdjieff's steering transcendent, his pedal-control hindered by sheepskin boots, and his swollen legs too weak to apply the brakes:

> It was the most terrifying car drive of my life. Crossing the Avenue Carnot, a large lorry bore down on us. Gurdjieff could not even slow down. By a miracle we crossed the street, but he could not turn the car. He let it run down and just succeeded in pulling up. I almost had to carry him to the lift.

During the next three days Gurdjieff plummeted in good style – accepting injections for his heart but not for his pain, demanding sheep's brains to eat, and chasing away a dolorous nurse with strict orders: 'No nurses over 20!' The little apartment was by now the focus of an indescribable human concern: 'Mme. de S., Lise, Gabo and all his nearest are doing everything possible. I have a feeling of "us" against "something", as though we were all holding a fort.'

At 11.30 pm on Monday the 24th, Gurdjieff surprisingly called for a dinner table to be set in his bedroom: for the last time the 'Idiots' (how many indeed had passed through his hands) were toasted in Larresingle Armagnac; for the last time in his presence some of his haunting 'Musiks' were given. The pressure on Jeanne de Salzmann was now intense; on Tuesday she phoned Dr Welch in New York, urging him to come immediately and administer a radical liver treatment ... The weather had broken. That night, as Gurdjieff tossed sleeplessly and Dr Welch flew loyally east, an elemental gale shook Paris, tearing off roofs and blowing down trees. Exhausted by his nineteen-hour flight, Dr Welch was hurried straight from the airport to his patient's bedside: 'I was shocked to hear his labored breathing, to see his gray color, and the gaunt wasting of his body, except for his swollen belly and legs. The mark of death was on his face.' 'Bravo, America!' said Gurdjieff. 'Bravo, *docteur*.'

Who can conceive with what terrible gravity Dr Welch's prognosis fell on Jeanne de Salzmann and on Gurdjieff's family by blood or inherency? The patient was sinking. He would never walk again ... But wait!

As I was speaking I looked up and saw him walking toward me, slowly in a kind of caricature of his old vital stride. It was as if he had picked himself up by the scruff of his own neck and was hoisting himself along by a naked will.

At this extraordinary sight, hope revived: let all avenues be exhausted – the full paraphernalia of medical intervention given its slender chance. A tense word or two between Dr Welch and Mme de Salzmann, and an ambulance was summoned. Gurdjieff instructed Lise to pack a suitcase full of bonbons for the nurses, and a tea-spoon in case the hospital had none. He left 6 Rue des Colonels Rénard in bright pyjamas and smoking, against doctor's orders, a Gauloise Bleu.

> He sat upright on the stretcher, and was carried away like a royal prince! All the family was clustered at the street door (the crusty old *concierge* was in tears!) and as they carried him across the pavement he made a little gesture, a sort of wave with his hand and said, '*Au revoir, tout le monde!*'

On the night of Wednesday 26 October, Gurdjieff arrived at the American Hospital at Neuilly and entered the private room on the first floor which he was not destined to leave alive.

The treatment was successful but the patient died: this basically is the sequel. And no one was to blame. (The disbelieving hospital pathologist would later find every interior organ in Gurdjieff's body wasted down to minimal function.) He arrived dropsical. The twelve litres of fluid which bloated his abdomen thrust up against his diaphragm, vexing his breathing; and, since high blood-pressure ruled out albumin, the only medical resource was to tap and drain. Early in the morning of Thursday 27 October, Dr Welch performed the puncture, while his patient – predictably wearing his fez and cloaked by a rich camelhair coat – manœuvred a cup of hot black coffee and a wooden cigarette holder. Even in this dangerous and surreal extremity, Gurdjieff appeared entirely master of the situation: 'Only if you not tired Doctor,' he said to Welch with indulgent irony.

Yet as Thursday dragged on, the old man sank under a welter of intrusive tests and irritating palliatives. By midday he could barely recognize his family. In the afternoon he delivered his final instructions to Jeanne de Salzmann – slowly, painfully:

> The essential thing, the first thing, is to prepare a nucleus of people capable of responding to the demand which will arise ... So long as there is no responsible nucleus, the action of the ideas will not go beyond a certain threshold. That will take time ... a lot of time, even.

These are his last recorded words.

On Friday morning it began to snow. Gurdjieff could no longer speak but, with a huge effort, held out his hand for Jeanne de Salzmann to take. He grew semi-conscious, and, in that cruel, spinning world, became (by Lise's account) *très agité*. So Gurdjieff did not evade this last tribulation – all that was human he drank to the dregs. That evening, sensing death's imminence, Mme de Salzmann phoned the de Hartmanns. Though Gurdjieff himself had banished them twenty long years ago, they seemed indispensable to his life's closing chord. Thomas de Hartmann – now sixty-three and laid low with heart palpitations – jumped from his sick-bed; Olga, within minutes, was driving their old Panhard racing and skidding through the snow from Garches to Neuilly. Too late. By the time they arrived an impenetrable veil of medical prohibition had descended.

By early morning Gurdjieff's agitation had gone. Perhaps his mind had glided into merciful oblivion. Probably so. Yet, perhaps, beneath closed eyelids in the ultimate citadel of consciousness, images floated in slow recessional: Yangi Hissar and the Amu Darya; the 'Vesanelnian Tree' and the 'map of pre-sand Egypt'; 'American canaries' and shiny new bicycles ... There would be movement, incessant movement – across the Arpa Chai, across the Gobi, across the giddy, creaking rope-bridge; movement of the enneagram, movement of the great dancers ... And urgent faces in their thousands emerging and eliding: the woeful, bruised Soloviev, Prince Lubovedsky, and Julia Ostrowska (the night she carried off the beauty prize from Lena Cavalieri)... And Philos, that old flea-bitten dog, converging enthusiastically to his master's side for the last walk together ... The image of the bridge again, over a ravine now deepened to infinity. One step more ...

George Ivanovitch Gurdjieff died in the American Hospital at Neuilly at approximately 10.30 on the morning of Saturday 29 October 1949.

His death, though long foreseen, registered on his pupils like some primordial catastrophe, a monstrous reversal of nature. A death-mask was taken; a hasty post-mortem conducted; and in the candlelit hospital chapel, the embalmed body lay four days on an open bier. On Saturday night the class came straight from the Salle Pleyel to kneel beside the Teacher of Dancing; in their attention, and weight, and terrible simplicity, some have construed the missing 'Movement No. 40'. Day and night vigil was kept, and each afternoon at 3.30 a little black-bearded priest chanted the office.

On Wednesday 2 November, the groups packed the Alexandre Nevski Cathedral in the Rue Daru. Meanwhile at Neuilly a knock-about surrealism was yet again inflecting the storyline: the undertakers had found Gurdjieff too big for his coffin and were frantically telephoning for a replacement. From 4 pm to 6 pm the congregation stood without a cough or rustle, scarcely a breath, until the priests themselves became moved by 'a remarkable quality of silence which is so rare as to be noted as unique.' When Gurdjieff was finally borne in, a deep, rolling salute of unaccompanied Russian voices broke from the choir balcony ... As the service ended and the officiating priest closed the *ikonostasis*, a local power failure occurred and the glimmer of a hundred individual candles prevailed in a darkness otherwise profound; on a hundred faces, taut with suffering yet sober in resolve, was prefigured the decent, awkward continuity of the Work.

On Thursday 3 November, the day of the funeral, high requiem mass was sung in the Cathedral. 'So great was the attentiveness it was as if a mass of flames rose above the coffin.' Though whether it was fully appropriate that the apologist of Beelzebub and Judas Iscariot should be subsumed in the pungent incense and liturgical proprieties of Russian Orthodoxy; and whether the golden-robed priests, sleep-walking their solemn patterns before the catafalque, appreciated the real situation, or were equal to it – these are matters of opinion.

> O Holy God, Holy Firm, Holy Immortal, have mercy upon us. Give rest eternal in blessed falling asleep, O Lord, to the soul of thy servant George, departed this life, and make his memory immortal.

In blessed falling asleep! Here at least institutional religion had forgivably got it upside down. Whoever – whatever – had been 'George Ivanovitch Gurdjieff' was surely struggling to awake. Was he in Purgatory? (He had given the concept an extraordinary, even sublime, new development.) Or was he in Paradise? Certainly not for long: 'Paradise is only good for two or three days. Imagine what it would be if next year, year after, hundred years. Must not be satisfied with Paradise – must find way to *Soleil Absolu*.'

From left to right the long line of pupils, replete with sensation, moved to the foot of the coffin to kiss the little icon of Saint-George-the-Victor – Gurdjieff's 'very expensive' saint whose aid was negotiable only in the coinage of intentional suffering. Idiots! All of them idiots. But idiots of the great myth, unparalleled in our century; idiots who, thanks to Gurdjieff alone, had inhaled a sense of their own idiocy. Each, in their private grief, remembered, promised, wondered:

> They will turn you into a scarecrow, an old fossil, a pope, an ordinary idiot, or perhaps even into a philosopher ... I shall never again know a more brazen seeker after God, nor a heathen more ambitious for his soul ... Who has dared to live your life, and who will fulfil it? In the end you have drawn real tears from me.

Mr Gurdjieff made his last (and accident-free) car trip high on an imposing funeral carriage. Slowly the cortège passed up Rue des Colonels Rénard – where four fat coaches infuriatingly got jammed – and gathered pace out through the suburbs towards the Prieuré. He was buried in the family plot at Avon between his wife and his mother. The massed crowd was silent, though the undertaker wept. As the sun went down and the frost deepened, they left him there.

That night Jeanne de Salzmann convened fifty senior pupils at the apartment. She said: 'When a Teacher like Mr. Gurdjieff goes, he cannot be replaced.'[31] And everyone could follow her.

Chronology

The special difficulties of Gurdjieffian chronology seem likely to prevail over investigative scholarship. The very date of his birth is in dispute, although Gurdjieff himself stipulates 1866. Between then and 1912 we are chasteningly reliant on Gurdjieff's own four impressionistic accounts, which – in the nature of myth – are innocent of consistency, Aristotelian logic and chronological discipline. Notoriously problematical are 'the missing twenty years' from 1887 to 1907; the journals of the epoch's great Central Asian geographers (Sven Hedin, Sir Aurel Stein, Albert von Le Coq, Paul Pelliot and Count Kozui Otani) do not provide the collateral support for Gurdjieff's account which, here and there, might be expected. My chronology for this period is hence offered provisionally and I have not followed it slavishly in my relevant chapter, The Long Search. Nevertheless, punctuating Gurdjieff's narrative and certainly not offending it, are a few objective historical events which I differentiate by italicizing. Where Gurdjieff himself actually stipulates a date, I bracket in the chronology a source reference (using the simple code explained in the References section). Although from 1913 to 1949 our chronology appears to stand on the much firmer ground afforded by primary documents, independent witness, cross-reference, and reasonable inference, the difficulty remains that Gurdjieffian memoirists focus on interior content. For a school which places a premium on relationship, they seem (with the honourable exception of P. D. Ouspensky) strangely oblivious to the correlative value of an honest date.

Date	Event
1866	
?Jan.	G. born in Cappadocian Greek quarter of Alexandropol on Russian side of Russo-Turkish border.
1870–72	
	Birth of G.'s only brother Dmitri Ivanovitch Gurdjieff (?1870) and eldest sister (?1871).
1873	
summer	G.'s father Giorgios Giorgiades, impoverished when

Date   *Event*

                                rinderpest wipes out his large cattle herd, opens a
                                lumber-yard.

1874–76

                                Birth of two further sisters.

1877

                                Giorgiades' lumber-yard fails and he opens a small
                                carpentry shop. G. precociously begins to contribute
                                to family income. *Russia declares war on Turkey (24
                                Apr.) and captures Turkish border citadel town of
                                Kars (18 Nov.).*

1878

                                Giorgiades moves his family to Kars, and re-estab-
                                lishes his carpentry shop in the Greek quarter. Father
                                Dean Borsh of Russian military cathedral assumes
                                responsibility for G.'s private education, co-opting as
                                tutors four graduates of the Theological Seminary. G.
                                reads intensively in library of Kars military hospital.

1879–80

                                G. falls under moral influence of his tutor Dean
                                Bogachevsky.

1881

                                G.'s eldest and favourite sister dies. G. narrowly
                                escapes death in shooting accident on Lake Alageuz.
                                He becomes fascinated by witnessing certain 'para-
                                normal phenomena'.

1882

                                In an adolescent duel of sorts with Piotr Karpenko,
                                G. narrowly escapes death on an artillery range.

1883

                                Leaving home, G. moves to Tiflis but fails to enter the
                                Archdeacon's choir or the Georgian Theological
                                Seminary. During breaks from casual work as a stoker
                                for the Transcaucasian Railway Company, he makes
                                pilgrimage on foot to Echmiadzin and studies for
                                three months at Sanaine Monastery under Father
                                Yevlampios. He develops close friendships with
                                Sarkis Pogossian and Abram Yelov.

1884

                                G. crystallizes his motivational question as to the
                                significance of organic and human life.

Date   *Event*

1885
  summer   G. visits Constantinople (where he meets Ekim Bey) to study the Mevlevi and Bektashi dervishes. He returns to Alexandropol, where his parents now again live, via Hadji Bektash, Konya, and Aksehir.

1886

G. and Pogossian, digging haphazardly in the ruined city of Ani, find reference to the 'Sarmoung Brotherhood', supposedly a wisdom school founded in Babylon c. *2500 BC*.

1887

As a courier of the Armenian protectionist society, the Armenakans, G. sets out with Pogossian for Kurdistan, quixotically resolved to 'find the Sarmoung'. En route however, his chance discovery near Zakho of a 'map of pre-sand Egypt' diverts him circuitously to Alexandria (where Pogossian leaves him). In Cairo, G. makes a strong bond with two elder seekers: Prince Yuri Lubovedsky and Professor Skridlov.

1888–9

G. visits Thebes with Lubovedsky; Abyssinia and the Sudan with Skridlov; and Mecca and Medina alone and in disguise. G. and Skridlov visit remains of Babylon at Nippur, Iraq. Returning to Constantinople, G. meets Vitvitskaia and escorts her to Russia.

1890–93

As a political envoy (probably of the newly constituted Armenian Social Revolutionary Party, the Dashnakzutiun) G. visits Switzerland and subsequently bases himself in Rome.

1894–5

Sultan Abdul Hamid II instigates massacre of Armenians throughout Turkey. Again centred on Alexandropol, G. is prime mover in the foundation (1895) of the 'Seekers of Truth', a heterogeneous and youthful grouping seeking traditional and esoteric knowledge.

1896

G. goes to Crete, seeking traces of the ancient 'Imastun brotherhood', but also as an agent of the Ethniki Hetairia, a Hellenist Spartacist society. *The Greek*

Date   *Event*

population revolts (Feb.) against Turks. While in the
Sfakia region, G. is shot [TS7] and evacuated, unconscious, to Jerusalem. He recuperates at Alexandropol.

1897

Accompanying the Seekers of Truth, G. sets out
(M183) from Nakhichevan (1 Jan.) through Turkestan
to Tabriz and Baghdad (Expedition 1). (Episode of
Ekim Bey and the Persian dervish.) To facilitate wider
travels in Central Asia, G. becomes a Tsarist political
agent and ? establishes some connection with the
Buryat Mongol Agwhan Dordjieff, a high Tibetan
official. With the Seekers G. travels from Orenburg
through Sverdlovsk to Siberia (Expedition 2).

1898

In New Bokhara (Easter) G. befriends Soloviev a
physical and social derelict. Guided blindfold by inter-
mediaries on a twelve-day pony-trek from Bokhara, G.
and Soloviev gain access to the chief Sarmoung Monastery (purported source of G.'s profoundest insights,
symbolism and Sacred Dances). Unexpectedly they find
Lubovedsky already there but in failing health. To G.'s
sorrow, Lubovedsky promptly leaves to end his days
under spiritual supervision elsewhere. Following a
period of monastic study, G. explores the Gobi (?Tak-
lamakan) desert with Skridlov and the Seekers of Truth
(Expedition 3). After Soloviev's accidental death
[M165], G. returns to Keriya Oasis.

1899

G. stays in Merv. In dervish disguise he and Skridlov
travel up the river Amu Darya (Oxus) into Kafiristan.
(Episode of Skridlov and Father Giovanni.) G. returns
to Baku and studies Persian magic. In Ashkhabad he
and Vitvitskaia (only woman member of the Seekers)
earn large sums with his 'Universal Travelling Workshop'.

1900

G. sets out (2 Jan.) from Chardzhou with Seekers
(Expedition 4) through the Pamirs to India [M252].
(Episode of Karpenko and the *ez-ezounavouron.*)
The Seekers then disband and separate.

1901

? G. presented to Tsar Nicholas II (23 July) in Livadia.

Date	Event
	? Disguised as a Transcaspian Buddhist, G. enters Upper Tibet and studies with the 'Red Hat' Lamas. ?He marries a Tibetan.
1902	
	Shot a second time [TS9] during a mountain clan affray, G. recovers in the Yangi Hissar oasis on the edge of the Taklamakan desert. He takes an oath to abjure hypnotism and animal magnetism except for scientific and altruistic purposes.
1903	
	G. returns to Tibet. *Col. Francis Younghusband invades Tibet (5 Jul.) from India.*
1904	
	British massacre Tibetans at Guru (31 Mar.) Younghusband enters Lhasa (3 Aug.). Anguished at the untimely killing of an initiated lama, G. resolves to combat the mass suggestibility and hysteria which occasion wars. Hydropsy obliges him to leave Tibet and return to his parents in Alexandropol. Having recuperated, G. sets out again (winter) for Central Asia but, near the Chiatura railway tunnel, is accidently shot a third time [TS9] in a skirmish between Cossacks and Gourians. With difficulty he goes via Ashkabad to Yangi Hissar where he again recuperates.
1905–7	
	?After two years in an indeterminate Central Asian Sufi community, G. settles in Tashkent, the Uzbek capital of Russian Turkestan. He briefly visits Samara, comforting Vitvitskaia on her deathbed.
1908–10	
	Based in Tashkent as a 'Professor-instructor' in supernatural sciences, G. begins teaching in a deliberately charlatanesque mode, while studying the reaction among his Europeanized Russian 'guinea-pigs'. He amasses considerable wealth by trading in oil, fish, cattle, carpets, cloisonné, etc. Slowly he gravitates west towards metropolitan Russia.
1911	
	G. synthesizes disparate strands of accumulated knowledge into a cohesive system employing a special

Date	*Event*
	and at points quasi-scientific, vocabulary. On 13 Sept. he renews his oath [H11] to abjure hypnotism, etc., binding himself for twenty-one years to lead an 'artificial life'.
1912	
c. New Year	G. arrives in Moscow and attracts his first associates (his cousin Sergei Mercourov, Vladimir Pohl, and Rachmilievitch). ? G. marries Julia Ostrowska in St Petersburg.
mid.	G. reads *Tertium Organum*, identifying its author P. D. Ouspensky as a prospective pupil.
1913	
	In St Petersburg, under the assumed name of 'Prince Ozay', G. cultivates Lev Lvovitch (?and Shamzaran Badmieff).
winter	In St Petersburg G. informally takes his first English pupil, the musical student Paul Dukes.
1914	
spring	In St Petersburg (having abandoned 'Prince Ozay' persona) G. interests Dr Leonid Stjoernval.
Aug. 1	*Germany declares war on Russia. (St Petersburg renamed Petrograd on Sept. 1).*
Nov. 13	G. advertises his ballet, *The Struggle of the Magicians*, in *Golos Moskvi* (attracting Ouspensky's attention).
Dec.	G. supervises his pupils' writing of sketch, *Glimpses of Truth*.
1915	
April	In Moscow G. accepts Ouspensky as pupil. (A week later Ouspensky returns to Petrograd.)
autumn	G. intermittently visits Petrograd where he lectures and meets Ouspensky and his associates.
1916	
Feb.–Aug.	Period of concentrated activity: increasingly centred on Petrograd, G. conveys virtually his entire 'System' of ideas to a group which expands from six (incl. Stjoernval, Ouspensky, and Andrei Zaharoff) to thirty.
Aug.	On a visit to Finland, G. promotes in Ouspensky an intense telepathic experience.
c. Dec. 16	In Petrograd G. accepts as pupil the composer, Thomas de Hartmann (and in Feb. 1917 his wife Olga).

Date	Event
1917	
Feb. 23	Parting from his pupils, a 'transfigured' G. finally leaves Petrograd, setting out via Moscow for Alexandropol with Julia Ostrowska.
Mar. 16	*Revolution: forced abdication of Tsar Nicholas II; formation of Kerensky government.*
Mar.–Jun.	G. lives in retirement with his family in Alexandropol.
Jul. (early)	G. sets out for Petrograd but on reconsideration settles in Essentuki in Caucasus.
Jul.–Aug.	With thirteen pupils summoned from Moscow and Petrograd (incl. Ouspensky and Zaharoff), G. undertakes six weeks' intensive psycho-somatic experimentation at Essentuki.
Aug.(end)	The de Hartmanns join G. at Essentuki. Ouspensky's trust in G. begins to waver. G. moves to Tuapse on Black Sea coast.
Aug.–Dec.	G. and his nucleus (augmented in Oct. by Dr and Mme Stjoernval) wander up and down Black Sea coast to avoid embroilment in Civil War. *7 Nov. (OS 26 Oct.) Bolshevik revolution brings Lenin to power.*
1918	
spring	G. returns to Essentuki (Jan.). Perceiving Alexandropol as under Turkish threat, G. invites his family to join him (all comply except his father and eldest sister); he summons his pupils (12 Feb.) and begins intensive work. Ouspensky separates from G. (Mar.).
Jul.(mid)	G.'s eldest sister and her family reach him in Essentuki as refugees, bringing news that Turks have shot his father in Alexandropol on 15 May.
Jul.(late)	As Essentuki becomes increasingly threatened by Civil War, G. plants a fabricated newspaper story of his forthcoming 'scientific expedition' to Mount Induc.
Aug. 6	Posing as a scientist, G. leaves Essentuki with a following of fourteen (which does not include G.'s family or Ouspensky). They go by train to Maikop where hostilities detain them three weeks.
Aug.–Sept.	Crossing Red and White lines five times, G. leads his party on foot over northern Caucasus range to Black Sea port of Sochi (where many pupils, incl. Zaharoff, leave him).

Date	Event
1919	
Jan.(mid)	G., with his residual nucleus (Mme Ostrowska, the Stjoernvals, and the de Hartmanns), voyages south from Sochi to Poti. They entrain for the Georgian capital Tbilisi, where they settle.
spring	G. meets and accepts as pupils the artist Alexandre Salzmann and his wife Jeanne (Easter). Prompted by the arrival in Tbilisi of his brother Dmitri, G. sends Olga de Hartmann (early May) on a return trip to Essentuki to retrieve possessions and carry messages.
summer	In collaboration with Jeanne Salzmann, G. gives first public demonstration of his Sacred Dances (Movements) in Tbilisi Opera House (22 Jun.). He summers in Borjom (Jul.–Aug.).
autumn	Having returned to Tbilisi, G. constitutes (mid-Sept.) his Institute for the Harmonious Development of Man (founder members: Dr Leonid Stjoernval, Thomas and Olga de Hartmann, Alexandre and Jeanne Salzmann, and ? Julia Ostrowska).
winter	G. continues to teach his 'System' under the auspices of the Georgian Menshevik social democratic republic. After accepting Elizabeta Galumnian and Olga Hinzenberg ('Olgivanna') as pupils, G. begins intensive work on *The Struggle of the Magicians*.
1920	
spring	*Marked deterioration in socio-political conditions in Georgia*, and in viability of G.'s Institute. He accepts as pupil Major Frank Pinder (Mar.).
May(late)	G. leads a party of thirty pupils on foot from Tbilisi to Black Sea port of Batoum, where they embark for Constantinople (Istanbul).
Jun.	G. settles in Constantinople (7 Jun.) and rents an apartment in Koumbaradji Street in Péra. Ouspensky (in Constantinople since Feb.) confides his own group of pupils to G.
Jun.–Aug.	With Ouspensky and Thomas de Hartmann respectively, G. works on the scenario and music of *The Struggle of the Magicians*; they study the ceremony of the Mevlevi dervishes.
Sept.	G. rents substantial accommodation at 13 Abdullatif Yemeneci Sokak near the Galata Tower.

Date	*Event*
Oct.	G. re-animates his Institute, giving public lectures and semi-public rehearsals of the Sacred Dances. (Ouspensky disassociates himself and withdraws to Prinkipo.)
Nov.(mid)	G. learns that his sister Anna Anastasieff and all her children (excepting her son Valentin) have just been massacred by Turks at Baytar.
Dec.	Thanks to Alexandre Salzmann, G. receives a letter from Jacques-Dalcroze in Geneva, inviting him to settle at Hellerau near Dresden. G. accepts and applies for visas.
1921	
Jan.(early)	G. renews contact with the Sultan's nephew, Prince Mehmet Sabaheddin, and briefly meets Capt. J. G. Bennett.
May(mid)	Following several months of declining public interest, G. closes his Institute and retires to the island of Prinkipo.
Aug.	On receipt of visas, G. with his nucleus travels by train from Turkey to Germany; departs Constantinople (13th); arrives Sofia, Bulgaria (15th); arrives Belgrade, Serbia (16th); arrives Budapest, Hungary (17th) and departs (21st); transits Czechoslovakia and arrives Berlin (22nd). (Around this time, Ouspensky leaves Constantinople for London but his wife Sophie chooses to accompany G.)
Sept.	Having settled in the suburb of Schmargendorf, G. adopts Olga de H. as his private secretary.
Nov. 24	In Berlin G. gives his inaugural lecture in Europe.
winter	Accompanied by the Salzmanns, G. visits the Dalcroze Institute at Hellerau, and through Harald Dohrn seeks part possession; a legal case ensues.
1922	
Feb. 13	G. pays his first brief visit to London, capturing the allegiance of Ouspensky's many prominent pupils, notably the editor A. R. Orage.
Mar. 15	On G.'s second and last visit to London, he confirms his ascendancy and clashes with Ouspensky. While influential pupils seek UK residential status for G., he returns to Berlin.
late spring	G. issues his third prospectus in English, German, and French.

Date	Event
Jun.	G. loses civil action to acquire Hellerau possession, and is effectively barred from settling in Britain.
Jul. 14	G. brings his pupils from Germany to Paris, hires facilities at the Dalcroze Institute, and delegates Olga de H. to seek a large property.
Oct. 1	On the basis of generous financial help from England, G. acquires and moves to his most famous seat: the Prieuré des Basses Loges at Fontainebleau-Avon.
Oct.	G. is simultaneously occupied with Prieuré administration and Parisian business ventures. On 17 Oct. he accepts as a permanent Prieuré guest the terminally ill New Zealand authoress Katherine Mansfield.
Nov.	G. begins intense work on the Sacred Dances. At end of Nov. he institutes the building of a large Study House in the Prieuré grounds.
Dec. 16	G. averts a major fire at the Prieuré.

1923

Date	Event
Jan.	G. acquires notoriety after Katherine Mansfield dies (9th) and is buried on the same day (12th) that the Study House is opened.
Feb.	Reporters (notably E. C. Bowyer) and academics (notably Prof. Denis Saurat) interview G. at the Prieuré and produce popular but not unsympathetic accounts.
May	G. learns to drive. At his new Paris apartment, 9 Rue du Commandant-Marchand, he entertains Ezra Pound.
summer	G.'s 'open evenings' of his music, Sacred Dances, etc., given in the Prieuré Study House, are regularly attended by local dignitaries and occasionally by cultural figures, e.g. Diaghilev and Sinclair Lewis.
Dec.	Although fatigued, G. produces his first major public demonstration of Sacred Dances in Europe. Premièred (16th) at the Théâtre des Champs-Elysées, it has a mixed reception. G. extricates his mother and sister from Russia and domiciles them at the Prieuré.

1924

Date	Event
spring	With *c.* thirty-five pupil-dancers, G. sails (4 Jan.) on the s.s. *Paris* for America, where public demonstrations in New York (Jan.–Feb.) and Philadelphia, Boston, and Chicago (Mar.) secure the interest of significant new pupils (notably Margaret Anderson,

Date   *Event*

Muriel Draper, Jane Heap, Gorham Munson, C. S. Nott, and Jean Toomer). G. founds New York branch of his Institute (8 Apr.).

summer   G. returns to France (Jun.). He loses occupancy of Commandant-Marchand and acquires a new apartment at 47 Boulevard Peréire. Driving alone from Paris to Fontainebleau, G. has a near fatal motor-car crash (8 Jul.). Nursed by his wife and mother, he makes a slow and painful recovery – against medical expectation. Still convalescent, G. formally 'disbands' his Institute (26 Aug.) but in fact disperses only his less dedicated pupils.

autumn–winter   G. empowers Orage to supervise the Work in America (Oct.). Having resolved in future to propagate his ideas by writing, G. commences (16 Dec.) his magnum opus: *Beelzebub*.

1925
Mar.   Orage's report that the first instalment of *Beelzebub* is unintelligible, heralds G.'s long stylistic struggle.

summer   G.'s mother dies of chronic liver disease at the Prieuré (end Jun.). G. begins intensive period of musical composition with Thomas de Hartmann (29 Jul.).

winter   G.'s wife Mme Ostrowska contracts cancer. Neither orthodox radiotherapy nor G.'s unorthodox treatment give satisfactory results.

1926
Jan. 8   Mabel Dodge Luhan offers G. substantial property at Taos, New Mexico, but (1 Feb.) he declines.

Feb.–Jun.   G. struggles intensely but unavailingly for Julia Ostrowska's life but she dies (26 Jun.). Ouspensky attends her funeral.

Jul.   Aleister Crowley briefly visits Prieuré and G. emphatically repudiates him.

1927
spring   Short of money, G. is obliged to relinquish his flat in Boulevard Péreire (16 Apr.). G. culminates his musical collaboration with Thomas de Hartmann (1 May).

summer   Many American pupils and voyeurists visit Prieuré. G. meets, but fails to impress, his future secretary Solita Solano. He repudiates the poet Waldo Frank.

autumn   Convinced by a serious decline in health that he has insufficient time to undertake a necessary and radical

Date	Event
	revision of *Beelzebub* he undergoes a crisis (6 Nov.) and contemplates suicide.
1928	
Jan.(mid)	A. R. Orage, accompanied by his young bride Jessie, makes a brief, stormy, and final visit to the Prieuré.
May 5	To stimulate his writing G. vows to 'banish' on various pretexts all those who make his life too comfortable.
summer(early)	G. encourages senior pupils away on extended visits: Mme Ouspensky to England, and the Salzmanns to Frankfurt. He discourages Jane Heap from settling at the Prieuré, but mandates her to start an 'artists' group' in Montmartre.
summer(late)	Alexandre Salzmann defends G. against ideological attacks of French occultist René Guénon.
autumn	Provisionally satisfied with *Beelzebub*, G. commences his second book *Meetings*.
1929	
Jan.	Accompanied only by the de Hartmanns, G. embarks on s.s. *Paris* for his second visit to America. They resist his promptings to make independent lives.
spring	Between arrival in New York (23 Jan.) and departure for France (5 Apr.) G. renews contacts with pupils and amasses funds.
summer(early)	G. again prompts Mme Ouspensky to visit England. He finally prevails on the de Hartmanns to leave the Prieuré and helps them settle in Courbevoie. He appoints Louise Goepfert as his secretary (Jun.).
autumn	G. facilitates the departure of Fritz Peters from the Prieuré (Sept.). On visits to Frankfurt and Berlin with Louise Goepfert and Olga de Hartmann, G. intentionally alienates Olga. *The Wall Street stock market crash (Oct.) affects G.'s American followers.*
1930	
spring	After burning all his personal papers, and engineering a painful and final parting from Olga de Hartmann, G. sails (Feb.) aboard s.s. *Bremen* on his third trip to America. In New York he intentionally creates difficulties, sabotaging negotiations with Alfred Knopf to publish *Beelzebub*. He sails for France (Apr.) leaving Orage disillusioned.
autumn (late)	In Paris Alexandre Salzmann attracts René Daumal (subsequently G.'s first French pupil).

Date	Event
winter	On a fourth trip to America, G. effectively breaks with Orage. Arriving in New York (13 Nov.), he demands (1 Dec.) of Orage's pupils that they repudiate their teacher. Orage himself returns (10 Dec.) from holiday in England and surprisingly endorses G.'s action, repudiating himself. G. leaves for Chicago (29 Dec.).
1931 Jan.	Returning to New York, G. has an inconclusive encounter with certain intellectuals, including John Watson, the behaviourist.
Mar. 13	After a final parting from Orage, G. sails for France, leaving the American groups in disarray.
spring	G. briefly receives Thornton Wilder at the Prieuré.
summer	G. refuses Ouspensky access to the Prieuré, creating a final breach. Mme Ouspensky leaves Asnières and moves permanently to England.
autumn	G. is involved in a theatrical incident with a revolver.
winter	G. sails (Nov.) on fifth, brief visit to the USA, focusing on Jean Toomer's Chicago group. In New York the author-adventurer Nadir Khan ('Achmed Abdullah') mistakes G. for the Lama Agwhan Dordjieff.
1932 Jan. 16	G. sails for Cherbourg on the s.s. *Bremen*.
Feb.	In Paris G. is approached by the American lesbian authoress, Kathryn Hulme, a member of Jane Heap's group; he shows her the Prieuré, now run down.
May 11	G. supervises the enforced closure of the Prieuré and dispersal of its final occupants; he takes a room in the Grand Hôtel, adjoining the Café de la Paix.
Aug.	Orage refuses an opportunity to renew contact with G.
Sept. 13	G. begins drafting his controversial, autobiographical tract *Herald*.
winter	On a disastrous sixth visit to America G. gives an impression of venality, alienating Jean Toomer and his Chicago group.
1933 Mar. 7	G. writes bizarre 'Supplementary Announcement' to *Herald*.
Apr.	Alexandre Salzmann, critically ill, meets G. at the Café Henri IV in Fontainebleau.

Date	Event
May?	G. loses the Prieuré irrevocably after the mortgagees foreclose.
autumn	G. commences his seventh visit to the USA. From his apartment at the Henry Hudson Hotel, he renews contact with New York pupils of Orage.

1934

spring	Death of Alexandre Gustav Salzmann (3 Mar.). G. visits the Chicago groups (May), intentionally alienating Fritz Peters on the train journey.
summer	G. pays an extended visit to Olgivanna at Taliesin, Wisconsin (Jun.–Jul.), deeply impressing her husband Frank Lloyd Wright. Mabel Dodge Luhan refuses G.'s request (18 Aug.). for the ranch she originally volunteered in Jan. 1926. Back in New York (Sept.), G. gives two unfortunate interviews to the popular writer Rom Landau.
autumn–winter	G. repudiates *Herald* and calls in all copies (Oct.). Shocked to learn of Orage's death (5 Nov.), and wishing to avoid a spate of empty condolences, G. travels to Washington, Boston, Chicago and certain Southern States.

1935

Jan.	G. returns to New York.
Apr.–May	Conjectural events attend G.'s completion (9 Apr.) of the Prologue to *Life is Real*. He travels to Washington anticipating, from a Senator Bronson Cutting, generous financial support to repurchase the Prieuré. Profoundly depressed when Cutting dies (6 May) in an air crash, G. applies unsuccessfully to return to Russia. Doubly disappointed, he abandons writing and disappears.
Jun.–Aug.	G. makes putative but unsubstantiated journeys to? Germany, Leningrad and Central Asia.
Sept.	Rom Landau publishes his bestseller *God is My Adventure*, vilifying G. and confusing him with Dordjieff.
Oct.	G. reappears in Paris. Jane Heap moves (18th) from Paris to London. Three of her American women pupils immediately gravitate to G. who constitutes his first Parisian group (21st) in Hôtel Napoleon Bonaparte.
Christmas	G. takes new apartment in Rue Labie near the Salle Pleyel.

Date	Event
1936	
spring	G. constitutes 'The Rope' (early Jan.), an exclusively lesbian group meeting in Rue Labie (initially comprising Elizabeth Gordon, Solita Solano, Kathryn Hulme and 'Wendy'. He makes many tours by car to European locales.
Jun.	G. gives Georgette Leblanc, Margaret Anderson and Monique entrée to his current work, though not to 'The Rope'.
Jul. (end)	Having temporarily suspended group work with his lesbian pupils, G. makes his first token contact with René Daumal and Jeanne de Salzmann's Sèvres group.
Aug.	Unable to afford a château he has located on the Marne, G. moves to a small Paris apartment at 6 Rue des Colonels Rénard.
winter	On reconvening his lesbian group (Oct.), G. finds Georgette Leblanc seriously ill, but he alleviates her condition.
1937	
spring	G. resumes extensive car trips. His brother Dmitri contracts cancer.
Aug.	Dmitri dies, despite G.'s efforts to help him.
autumn	'The Rope' and subsidiary lesbian groupings effectively dissolve (as Kathryn Hulme and Wendy settle in America, and Anderson and Leblanc in Normandy). Solita Solano becomes G.'s secretary.
1938	
	Dr Leonid Stjoernval dies near Reims (Apr.). As Jeanne de Salzmann adds the author Luc Dietrich to her existing circle of pupils (René and Vera Daumal, Philippe Lavastine, Henri and Henriette Tracol, etc.), G. implicitly confirms her as his deputy.
1939	
spring	Accompanied by Solita Solano, G. sails (Mar.) on s.s. *Paris* on his brief penultimate trip to America. *The international crisis steadily worsens.* Having resisted pressure to settle in New Jersey, G. sails (19 May) on s.s. *Normandie* for France.
summer	G. contemplates trip to England to assist Mme Ouspensky medically, but Ouspensky disapproves and the plan is dropped.

Date	*Event*
autumn	*Outbreak (1 Sept.) of the Second World War.* G. remains in Paris (throughout War) at 6 Rue des Colonels Rénard, which he stocks with provisions.
1940	
spring	Jeanne de Salzmann's group, meeting at 54 Rue du Four, grows in size and influence. G. consolidates his contact with Philippe Lavastine and René Daumal.
Jun.	*With Allied resistance collapsing*, G.'s followers attempt (12th) to relocate him in the countryside but he returns to 6 Rue des Colonels Rénard (14th) *just as Germans occupy Paris.*
winter	Food being scarce and the weather exceptionally harsh, G. begins helping an extended family of needy neighbours. Jeanne de Salzmann formally presents her French group to G. (Oct.).
1941	G.'s French group meeting at 6 Rue des Colonels Rénard enlarges. *Hitler's invasion of Russia (22 Jun.) and America's declaration of war on Germany (11 Dec.) predicate the ultimate liberation of Paris.* Georgette Leblanc dies (20 Oct.) of cancer.
1942	
spring	To obtain further credit, G. fabricates story that he has been given a Texas oil-well.
May 29	G. advises his Jewish pupils to 'go underground' when *the Germans oblige them to wear the yellow Star of David*. The are harboured by Christian group members.
Jun.(late)	Jeanne de Salzmann presents Luc Dietrich to G.
Jul. 16–17	G.'s advice is vindicated as *Parisian Jews are deported in 'Operation Spring Wind'*. René and Vera Daumal no longer have access to G.
Nov.	*Germans overrun France's Unoccupied Zone.*
1943	Further influx of French pupils. G. active in teaching enneagram-based Movements at the Salle Pleyel and developing his ritual 'Toasts to the Idiots'.
1944	Death of René Daumal (21 May) and Luc Dietrich (12 Aug.) precedes *liberation of Paris (25 Aug.)*. In

Date	*Event*
	autumn G. is arrested for currency offences but discharged.
1945	*Hitler's suicide (30 Apr.) and VE Day (6 May).* G. receives first visits of American pupils (Kathryn Hulme and Fritz Peters). He attracts unwarranted criticism over the death of Irène-Carole Reweliotty (11 Aug.) *Japan's surrender (14 Aug.) ends war.* Lise Tracol becomes G.'s residential housekeeper.
1946	G.'s relationship with Katherine Mansfield is pilloried in the magazine *l'Illustration* (19 Jan.) First influx of London pupils to Paris from Jane Heap's group.
1947	Ouspensky returns to England (Jan.) from America. G. invites him to Paris but Ouspensky declines. When Ouspensky dies (2 Oct.) Mme Ouspensky, still at Mendham, makes overtures to G.
1948 Jan.	Mme Ouspensky advises her husband's British followers at Lyne to contact G.
summer	G. summons Ouspensky's pupils (Jun.) but they still vacillate. He reintegrates J. G. Bennett in his work (after twenty-five years) and cures his wife Winifred (Aug.). G. recovers astonishingly after serious injury in a car crash (8 Aug.) and promptly issues a general invitation to Paris: pupils of Jane Heap, Ouspensky, Mme Ouspensky, Orage, Bennett (but not Nicoll) commingle with French.
winter	Eager to buy the Château de Voisins and to publish *Beelzebub*, G. sails for New York (arr. 17 Dec.). Here he raises funds and authorizes Mme Ouspensky to publish *Fragments*.
1949 spring	Announcing *Beelzebub*'s imminent publication, G. nominates three literary executors (J. G. Bennett, Lord Pentland, and René Zuber). He sails for France (Feb.) in *Queen Mary* with large entourage (including Iovanna Lloyd Wright).
summer	G. makes car expeditions to Vichy (Jun.); Geneva

Date	*Event*
	(Jul.) to meet Mme Stjoernval; and finally Montignac (Aug.) to see the Lascaux cave paintings. His ideas are favourably mentioned on Italian radio in connection with the Montessori system.
Sept.	G. announces he will sail for New York on 20 Oct.; he buys La Grand Paroisse, ostensibly as a new centre.
Oct.	Under intense pressures G.'s health fails. Having choreographed (No. 39) his last Movement (11th), he collapses at Movements class (14th). Nursed by Lise Tracol and surrounded by doctors, his condition fluctuates. Receipt of *Beelzebub*'s proofs (21st) suggests the apotheosis of his life's work. Seriously ill, he supervises the Toasts to the Idiots for the last time (24th). He is taken by ambulance to the American Hospital at Neuilly (26th), where Dr Welch performs an abdominal puncture. G. gives his final instructions to Jeanne de Salzmann (27th), becomes unconscious (28th), and dies around 10.30am (29th). Religious services are held on successive days.
Nov. 3	G. is buried in the family plot at Fontainebleau-Avon. Under the leadership of Jeanne de Salzmann, his groups re-dedicate themselves to practise and transmit his ideas.

Index to Notes

———— ❖ ————

Miscellaneous

Notes

GURDJIEFF HIMSELF

1. *Gurdjieff's Date of Birth (p. 9)*

Gurdjieff was born in 1866 – towards this provisional conclusion three separate arguments converge.

a. Gurdjieff himself, explicitly and implicitly, indicated 1866. (See Paris group notes for 16 December 1943, where he says, 'I am seventy-eight years old and have had many disillusionments'; also *W* 64 and *I* 70 where, in 1949, G. claims he 'have already eighty-three years'.)

b. The famous Photos Andrieux portraits of him, taken in 1949, are redolent of a man of eighty-three.

c. 1866 provides (as my chronological table elaborates) the only tenable benchmark for calibrating Gurdjieff's account of his early childhood against incontrovertible historical events (e.g. Gurdjieff's assertion (*M* 40f) that, when he was about seven, his father's herds fell victim to 'cattle plague', brings into perfect reconciliation agricultural records and Gurdjieff's putative birth in 1866. It was in 1872–3 that a calamitous outbreak of rinderpest, originating in the steppes of southern Russia, devastated herds throughout Asia Minor, killing 90–95 per cent of those affected.)

The need to urge 1866 arises because, in the absence of a birth certificate, various illogical dates have been canvassed. The Encyclopaedia Britannica (which incidentally gives an erroneous date for Gurdjieff's death) assigns his birth to 1872 without any rationale. James Webb's special pleading for 26 July 1874 (Webb 54) stands or falls with his highly problematical Ushe Narzunoff–Gurdjieff hypothesis – see Note 3.

Most commentators however, evidently copying one from another, cite 1877 and this error seems likely to prove tenacious; it blindly follows J. G. Bennett's report (*NW* 14) that Gurdjieff's passport stipulated 28 December 1877. The point is lost that Gurdjieff conjured with several passports: some he burnt in Feb. 1930 (*OLWG 155*); others he was putatively using in 1931 ('Diogenes', *Time and Tide* 11 May 1957). His important Nansen passport (see Note 27), which Bennett did not sight, bears the hugely discrepant date 1 January 1864. The reasons why Gurdjieff, in applying for passports, presented conflicting birthdates are conjectural but they clearly supervened over a concern for historical accuracy. Unhappily it is also true that Gurdjieff's senior pupil, Jeanne de Salzmann, countenanced 13 January

1877, Gregorian calendar (actually citing 1 January 1877, Julian calendar) – – see editorial note to Gurdjieff's *Recontres avec des hommes remarquables* (Julliard, Paris, 1960)... With due respect, anyone proposing 1877 has not reflected sufficiently.

On the night of 17 November 1877 Gazi Mukhtar Pasha was defeated by the Armenian general, Count Mikhail Tarielovich Loris-Melikov, and Tsarist forces entered the city of Kars. Nothing in Gurdjieff's early years provides a more trustworthy chronological fulcrum than the arrival in Kars, promptly thereafter, of Gurdjieff, his parents, his *younger* brother and three *younger* sisters. Those obdurate for 1877 as Gurdjieff's date of birth must somehow explain why his formal education began in Kars a few months later; how the birth of four siblings, as well as a four-year lapse between two business failures of his father, can be compressed; why Gurdjieff's many pronouncements on war make no mention of his own birth during the Russo-Turkish conflict; and why he appeared to be eighty-three when only seventy-two. Altogether their task is not without difficulties, involving as it does the contradiction of Gurdjieff himself.

Although this note constitutes the first close argument for 1866, one or two pupils with direct access have already asserted it; see for example Popoff 148 and Gorham Munson, 'Black Sheep Philosophers: Gurdjieff – Ouspensky – Orage', *Tomorrow* IX(6), February 1950, New York, p. 20. Significantly Thomas Daly also settles on 1866 in his new definitive edition of *OLWG*.

2. Gurdjieff's Name (p. 9)

Infant nomenclature is a standard biographic hazard. My solution – of calling our hero 'Gurdjieff' *ab initio* – is anomalous but convenient. In childhood he was called 'Tatakh', in early youth 'Darky', later the 'Black Greek', and in his prime the 'Tiger of Turkestan'. In later life names, cover-names, and nicknames continued to accrete around him: 'Prince Ozay', the 'Miracle', 'Monsieur Bonbon', the 'Professor' and the 'Teacher of Dancing'. The standard nomenclature George Ivanovitch Gurdjieff, emerged by transliteration and inconsistent national adaptation from the original Giorgios Giorgiades (or Georgiades): the Greek patronym became first Gurd*jián* in Armenian, then Gurd*jieff* in Russian; the Christian name, Giorgios, took the western form George; Ivanovitch was interpolated following Russian usage.

As to pronunciation, Russian would strictly require a tri-syllabic Guyrd-*zhee*-ev. Current English usage favours Gurd-*jeeff*, though some prefer an unaccented Gur-dji-eff. Evidently here, as elsewhere in the Gurdjieffian canon, there is room for ambiguity.

3. 'Re-identifying' Gurdjieff (p. 243)

Since Gurdjieff's putative decade in Central Asia (1897–1907) finds no corroboration in the journals of contemporary explorers (Sven Hedin, Sir Aurel Stein, Albert von Le Coq, Paul Pelliot and Count Kozui Otani), attempts to re-identify him are unsurprising. In winter 1931 in New York, the author-adventurer Nadir Khan (nom de plume 'Achmed Abdullah') briefly met Gurdjieff and mistook him for the remarkable Buryat Mongol, Agwhan Dordjieff (Ngawang Lobsang), tutor to Thupten Gyatso Pelzangpo (1876–1933), the thirteenth Dalai Lama. Gurdjieff incidentally did not disabuse him. In September 1935 the popular writer Rom Landau gave wide currency to Nadir Khan's error in his best-selling work, *God is My Adventure*. Alexandra David-Néel, an authority on Tibet, demolishes this equation in 'Gurdjieff-Dordjieff', *Nouvelles Littéraires*, Paris, 11 April 1954: Dordjieff (*c.* 1850–1938) was significantly older than Gurdjieff, pre-deceased him, and looked nothing like him.

Altogether more closely argued is James Webb's bold thesis (Webb, Ch. 2) equating Gurdjieff with Dordjieff's associate, Ushe Narzunoff (1874–d.?) (or Norzanoff), a Kalmuk Buddhist and Zaissan whose story is outlined in Alistair Lamb's *Britain and Chinese Central Asia* (Routledge & Kegan Paul, 1960). Although photographs of Narzunoff, which Webb self-defeatingly adduces, look nothing like Gurdjieff, a biographical and historical parallelism (impossible of précis) warns against hasty dismissal of the entire idea. Narzunoff disappeared from historical view in Nov. 1908, not long before Gurdjieff emerged in Moscow and St Petersburg. By 1913 Gurdjieff was teaching Paul Dukes under the assumed name 'Prince Ozay' (cf. Tibetan 'Odzay' meaning a ray of light). Given variants in transliteration, 'Ushe' and 'Ozay' might well be synonymous. Perhaps also worth passing mention is the putative identification of Gurdjieff in 1931, travelling under the name of 'Naar' ('Diogenes', *Time and Tide*, 11 May 1957). Further research in Russian sources seems indicated.

GURDJIEFF'S TEACHING

4. Aphorisms and Script (p. 228)

Gurdjieff's forty aphorisms (thirty-eight of which appear in V 281–4) call to mind the forty Movements of his last series. The sayings range from simplistic homilies (e.g. 'Respect every religion') to penetrative insights (e.g. 'Blessed is he who has a soul; blessed is he who has none; but woe and grief to him that has it in embryo.') Gurdjieff originally codified his aphorisms in 1922 at the Prieuré, where they were inscribed above the walls of the Study House. For this purpose Alexandre Salzmann devised a cursive script of indisputable beauty which reads vertically from top to bottom. The aphorisms were transliterated from phonetic English (French being irrelevant at the Prieuré) in the manner of a simple, invariant, substitution cipher. Unhappily perhaps only 1 per cent of today's Gurdjieffians can read this script, let alone approach its symbolic rationale.

5. Attention (p. 54)

In empiric terms, Gurdjieff's contribution to the modern study of attention is arguably unique. Admittedly in the early days of experimental psychology, attention was a core concept to men like Wilhelm Max Wundt, Edward Bradford Titchener, and William James. The experimentation of such pioneers was not self-referential however, and soon regressed into a sterile academic debate between the Functionalist school which viewed attention as a process, and the Structuralist school which was preoccupied with sensory clarity. Among medical psychologists one should mention the once pre-eminent and now strangely neglected figure of Pierre-Marie-Félix Janet, father of psychological analysis, who argued persuasively that patients deficient in attention encountered difficulty in synthesizing experience, and hence proved susceptible to hysterical dissociation. Also worthy of note for his practical emphasis on relaxation and attention is the obscure figure of Roger Vittoz of Lausanne, the analyst of T. S. Eliot. See *The Discovery of the Unconscious: the History and Evolution of Dynamic Psychiatry* by Henri F. Ellenberger, Allen Lane: The Penguin Press, 1970.

It was William James (1842–1910) who offered the dictum 'my experience is what I agree to attend to', but it was Gurdjieff who extrapolated this insight into a *pratique* for the mobilization and direction of attention, within the context of a persuasive phenomenology of consciousness. By the last decade of the twentieth century the various proponents of gestalt, transactional psychology, S-R learning theory, the Jungians, Kleinians and embattled Freudians, had long since consigned attention to the ideological and methodological periphery, leaving only lay Gurdjieffians working on attention, according to their canon, as the quintessential challenge to understanding. For a succinct evocation of the Gurdjieffian position, see William Segal, 'The Force of Attention', *The Structure of Man*, Green River Press, Stillgate Publishers, Vermont, 1987. For a fuller account, see C. Daly King, *The Psychology of Consciousness*, Kegan, Paul, Trench, Trubner & Co., 1932, especially chapter X, 'The Legitimacy of the Self-observational Technique'.

6. The Way of Blame (p. 189)

The issue of blame clings tenaciously to Gurdjieff. As one pupil cogently expresses it:

He is accused, blamed, for having been present, for having been absent, for helping and for refraining from helping, for talking and for being silent, when a variety of events ranging in people's imagination from rape to taking the veil, from natural death to suicide, from bankruptcy to brilliant success took place in the lives of this one or that one of his followers.

In fact the commonest accusations against Gurdjieff have elicited rebuttals more persuasive than the charges. The implausible allegation (Pauwels 62f) that, as a colleague of the geo-politician Karl Haushofer, Gurdjieff played a formative role in shaping Nazi ideology and even suggested use of the inverted swastika, is refuted by Haushofer's son, Dr Heinz Haushofer (letter of 31 Dec. 1956, *Frankfurter Allgemeine Zeitung*). The aspersion that Gurdjieff abused Katherine Mansfield sexually need not be dignified with comment; the accusation that his Prieuré regime hastened her death gives insufficient weight to her extended pathological history (see Dr Brice Clarke MD, 'Katherine Mansfield's Illness', *Proceedings of the Royal Society of Medicine*, vol. 48, April 1955, pp. 1029–32). (For a detailed exploration of this issue see Moore, *Gurdjieff and Mansfield*.) The allegation that Gurdjieff caused the death of his eminent French pupil René Daumal is at variance not only with the viewpoint of Daumal's widow Vera but with the explicit letter of his brother Jack Daumal (*Le Figaro Litteraire*, 27 March 1954). And finally the charge that Gurdjieff precipitated the 'suicide' of the young Irène-Carole Reweliotty conflicts both with her death certificate and her mother (see '*Une Lettre de Mme Reweliotty*', *L'Aurore*, 11 October 1973): both attribute the death to heart disease following a long history of pulmonary tuberculosis. The latest censorious canard – of Gurdjieff's recklessly 'sending a woman back from the Crimea through the battle lines between the Reds and the Whites, back to Moscow' – is attributed to Robert Aitken, a Roshi of the Soto Zen sect, in Helen Tworkov's *Zen in America*, North Point Press, San Francisco, 1989 ... Until a proper scholastic canon accretes around Gurdjieffian studies, further colourful inventions will be made with impunity.

Beginning with shrill condemnation by the 1920s literati (e.g. D. H. Lawrence and Wyndham Lewis) critiques of Gurdjieff now range from Pauwels' unscholarly, commercial sensationalism to Whitall N. Perry's *Gurdjieff in the Light of Tradition* (Perennial Books, 1978), an acidulous polemic written from the standpoint of the philosophical school of Frithjof Schuon. Gurdjieff, least of all, would have sought immunity from criticism of any stripe. For a scholarly account of the spiritual 'Way of Blame' and a differentiation of *Malamatis* and *Qalandaris*, see J. Spencer Trimingham, *The Sufi Orders in Islam*, Clarendon Press, 1971, Appendix B.

7. Gurdjieff as proto-Ecologist (p. 52)

Gurdjieff's search originated *c*.1884 with his irrepressible striving:

to understand clearly the precise significance, in general, of the life process on earth of all the outward forms of breathing creatures and, in particular, the aim of human life in the light of this interpretation.

Unsurprisingly, the philosophy of ecology (though not its praxis) owes a huge if unrecognized debt to Gurdjieff. As early as 1916 he had contributed fundamental constituents to the ecological paradigm which only gained currency fifty years later. In Gurdjieff's formulation (F 138) beginning, 'Organic life forms something like a sensitive film which covers the whole of the earth's globe . . . ,' is presaged the concept of the 'Biosphere' as a creation of the sun – a model developed a decade later (see *La géochimie*, Paris, 1924; *Biosfera*, Leningrad, 1926), with full regard for the canons of scientific empiricism, by the Russian geo-chemist Vladimir Ivanovich Vernadsky (1863–1945). More recently, and debatably, it has been extrapolated in terms of an autonomous, homeostatic, planetary mechanism by James Lovelock in *Gaia: A New Look at Life on Earth*, Oxford University Press, 1979.

Gurdjieff's 'Diagram of Everything Living' (F 323, Fig. 58) is a ladder of subhuman, human, and supra-human entities, hierarchically disposed on the deceptively simple basis of what they eat and what eats them. From his simplest statement: 'In nature everything is connected and everything is alive', (F 322), to his intellectually challenging exposition of the '*Trogoautoegocratic* process' ('Eating myself I am maintained') (*B passim*) runs the thesis of 'reciprocal maintenance', the unceasing cosmic interaction of energies and substances. Gurdjieff's 'Model of the Universe' is quintessentially symbiotic.

Gurdjieff disdained slogans and tendered to the ecological movement nothing comparable to Albert Schweitzer's 'Reverence for Life' or Ernst Schumacher's 'Small is Beautiful'. He was neither concerned with a pantheistic liberal theology nor a utilitarian aesthetic. His vision was not teleocentric, still less anthropocentric; he envisioned nothing less than a dynamic and sacred universe with all its relationships implacably submitted to the Law of Three and all transformations to the Law of Seven. Nevertheless his intellectual triumph was to reserve within this awesome schema a plausible avenue for a man's evolution in terms of being.

8. The Enneagram (p. 32)

Gurdjieff's most cherished symbol was his enneagram, or nine-sided figure; he extolled it as an universal glyph, a schematic diagram of perpetual motion. The specific application of the enneagram which he demonstrated to the 1916 Moscow and Petrograd groups, was as a dynamic model for synthesizing, at macrocosmic and microcosmic level, his 'Law of Three' and 'Law of Seven'. Later, at Fontainebleau in 1922, he choreographed and taught the first of those many Sacred Dances or 'Movements', whose beautiful but rigorously prescribed evolutions enact the enneagram (through individual and ensemble displacements), as a *moving* symbol.

To construct Gurdjieff's enneagram: describe a circle: divide its circumference into 9 equal parts; successively number the dividing points clockwise from 1 to 9, so that 9 is uppermost; join points 9, 3 and 6 to form an equilateral triangle with 9 at the apex; join the residual points in the successive order 1, 4, 2, 8, 5 and 7 to form an inverted hexagon (symmetrical about an imaginary diameter struck perpendicularly from 9). In relation to the integers 3 and 7 – which in Gurdjieff's model, as in metaphysical systems generally, are crucially significant – the sequence 142857 has noteworthy properties (lost incidentally when transposed to notations other than denary). It deploys all integers except 3 and its multiples. As a recurring decimal, it results from dividing 1 (the Monad) by 7. Its cyclical progression yields every decimalized seventh (thus 2 sevenths = .285714; 3 sevenths = .428571 and so on).

For Gurdjieff's original formulation see *F* 286–95; but for arguably the deepest exposition of the laws which the symbol encapsulates, see *B*, Ch. XXXIX and XL. For commentaries on the enneagram, meditated by P. D. Ouspensky and Maurice Nicoll, see, respectively, *F* 376–8 and *Psychological Commentaries on the Teaching of G. I. Gurdjieff and P. D. Ouspensky* (Vincent Stuart), 1952, vol. 2, 379–438.

No light, incidentally, is shed on Gurdjieff's life or teaching by the pastiche version of the enneagram – a sort of facile psychometric typology – which in the 1980s began to percolate from the 'Human Potential Movement' into universities and Roman Catholic retreat centres. At the root of this free adaptation stands the Instituto de Gnoselogia (founded Arica, Chile, 1968) and the ARICA Institute, Inc. (founded New York, 1971). Those associated with this phenomenon – Claudio Naranjo, Charles T. Tart, and the clever Bolivian ideological opportunist Oscar Ichazo – appear to have borrowed the exterior form of Gurdjieff's symbol without grasp of its interior dynamic. For a critique of this divagation see 'The Enneagram: A Developmental Study' by James Moore, *Religion Today: A Journal of Contemporary Religions*, Vol. 5, No. 3.

9. Gurdjieff and Science (p. 43)

Gurdjieff was not a scientist but a spiritual master. Although fearless of offending modern science, his cast of mind was far from unscientific. Indeed in the psychological domain, his empiricism, his insistence on experimentation and verification by repetition, mirror (more than the psychoanalytic corpus) the hypothetico-deductive methodology of Galileo, Boyle and Lavoisier. Sectors exist in the physical sciences where his concepts anticipated by decades paradigms today verging on orthodoxy, e.g. see Note 7 on ecology. He commanded an impressive practical and theoretical knowledge of vibration.

Two oblique defences of Gurdjieff's spectacularly unscientific assertions are available to his apologists:

a. that he was being deliberately provocative to shock and to attract blame (see Note 6). (For example, Gurdjieff's claim that our sun neither lights nor heats he himself presented as the 'Arch-absurd'.)

b. that essentially he was writing allegorically (for example his 'moon' merely representing the unconscious mind in its *luna*tic mode.)

Pushed to extremes, however, such special pleading could well betray Gurdjieff's projected model of the universe. Certainly his cosmology of 1916 (see *Fragments*) seems propounded not as provocation or allegory but as quasi-scientific fact, deserving the compliment of straightforward evaluation as such in the context of science's rapidly shifting paradigms.

Gurdjieff's universe is sacred; science's secular. Gurdjieff's universe is essentially qualitative; science's quantitative. Gurdjieff's universe has an ontological dependence on the Creator, and a hierarchy of subordinate levels; science's universe is isotropic and value-free. Gurdjieff's universe has a centrum (the 'Holy Sun Absolute'); science's universe is diffuse. Gurdjieff's universe is growing in 'being'; science's growing in 'space-time'. Gurdjieff's universe is living (hylozoistic in Spinoza's sense); science's universe (earth's biosphere inexplicably and somewhat anomalously apart) is inert. Gurdjieff situates man at the periphery; science (notwithstanding the Copernican and neo-Copernican revolutions) clings to a psychological anthropocentrism.

Since Clausius's Second Law of Thermodynamics underpins the exact sciences, and violation is deemed inadmissible, the extent, if any, of Gurdjieff's iconoclasm here, assumes critical importance. Unfortunately, without long and complex excursions both into Gurdjieff's idea and into specialist branches of physics, evaluation proves surprisingly difficult. Gurdjieff's ironic treatment of man's search for a 'perpetual motion machine' (*B* 73ff.) hints at his accordance with Clausius; discrepantly however, Gurdjieff's model of the universe tends, infinitely slowly, towards lower entropy (greater order). His cosmos is waxing in potential, quickening into life; science's waning entropically towards absolute thermal equilibrium, stasis, and the concomitant end of time – the formidable 'heat-death of the universe'.

The very existence of organic life bears eloquent witness that negative entropy i.e., greater order is feasible locally, given enthalpy (energy inputs from extraneous sources). Vis-à-vis the earth's biosphere, Gurdjieff is in harmony with science in identifying the sun as the prime source/channel of such inputs. Statistically, within any 'closed system', the entropic tendency is implacable. However the perfectly closed system in nature is elusive on a small scale; while, *grosso modo*, any reconciliation of 'closure' with science's perpetually expanding universe arguably brings physics to the frontier of metaphysics. In practice the earth, the biosphere, humanity, and the moon operate in an open system, permeated by radiations from the transitions of energy states – not least from the sun (one octave of light radiations, three octaves of thermal radiations, half an octave of ultra-violet radiations). In adducing the 'Absolute' as the primordial source of cascading enthalpic inputs, Gurdjieff entrusts the dynamism of his entire system to a primal *mysterium*: but science has analogous recourse to *mysteria* in denoting the fundamental building blocks of its empiric model.

Scientifically viewed, Gurdjieff's prime heresy is surely his attribution to the moon of an ontological 'meaning', and of unsubstantiated macro-effects on the earth and its fauna and flora. For science the moon is basically a dead satellite to be exhaustively denoted without the smallest philosophical or metaphysical connotation; its effects on earth are mechanical, adventitious, and (excepting its causation of oceanic tides) marginal. For Gurdjieff by complete contrast, certain principles of scale and relativity afford the moon a role of paramount if unsuspected significance. His 'moon' transpires as a nascent body, symbiotically coupled with the biosphere, activating all organic life on earth (just as a clock's pendulum impels its mechanism), and reciprocally 'fed' by certain so-to-say 'wavicles', liberated at the death of all terrestrial life forms. (See F 84ff. and 138ff.)

Interestingly, today's science is conceding considerably more causality to the moon than when Gurdjieff propounded his idea in 1916. Biology is less distanced from Gurdjieff's proposition that man is an evolutionary construct of the moon (and of course the sun). Thus: no land animals without prior amphibeans; no amphibeans without tides; and no tides without the moon. There also now emerges the moon's putative effect on atmospheric ozone levels and wind-field tides; on geomagnetic activity and magnetotropism; and on the incidence of earthquakes, precipitation, and hurricane formation. Certain social scientists seriously debate statistical correlations between the moon's synodic and sidereal phases and official returns for the incidence of murder, suicide, epileptic attacks, hospital admissions, and certifications of insanity... The fact remains that, although neither validation nor conclusive invalidation of Gurdjieff's more startling ideas seem amenable to science's conventional repertoire of forces (gravitational, electro-magnetic, strong and weak atomic), the burden of proof rests squarely on his followers. Until that burden is shouldered – an unlikely contingency – the 'hungry moon' must remain simply a prime and highly contentious article of Gurdjieffian faith.

In *Beelzebub* (1926) Gurdjieff embroidered his abstract cosmology with an elaborate and personalized cosmogony, opening to his apologists the respectable defence that poetic creation myths are, *a priori*, incommensurable with a science which skirts meaning, values, and (in lesser degree) consciousness. Here emerges Gurdjieff's assertion that aeons ago 'the comet Kondoor' struck off from earth materia which became our moon. However allegorically rich, this raises big difficulties if maintained literally. Although catastrophic scenarios for the genesis of the moon from earth materia have been countenanced by a succession of eminent scientists (Clerk Maxwell, Thomas Chamberlin, Forest Moulton, Sir James Jeans, Harold Jeffreys, Henry Russell), Gurdjieff's specific idea has never warranted attention. Science has fairly recently abandoned catastrophism and refurbished the original hypothesis of the Swedish polymath and mystic Emmanuel Swedenborg (1688–1722), condensing from diffuse interstellar matter an independent moon which is then gravitationally captured by the earth. Terrestrial and lunar rocks yield broadly the same carbon dating but paradoxically this offends Gurdjieff's theory; his postulated mega-catastrophe would have melted into plasma the moon materia, effectively resetting its geological clock at zero. At present then, no dynamically tenable scientific model exists to accommodate Gurdjieff's selenology; whether its rehabilitation will ever ensue from the notorious volatility of astronomical theory is an open question. (Gurdjieff's allegorical usage of 'the comet Kondoor' as the onset of puberty, is a separate issue.)

10. Mullah Nassr Eddin (p. 9)

In Gurdjieff's own literary celebration of the Turkic folkloric wise fool, the 'incomparable Mullah Nassr Eddin Hodja', he evidently wished to convey something important. Perhaps it is significant that Nassr Eddin's standpoint in the traditional 'droll stories' (whether displaying Machiavellian cunning or utter stupidity), almost always subverts our ordinary concept of reality. Much like Gurdjieff himself, Nassr Eddin is the personification of paradox – surreal yet without any penumbra of nihilism. In the Gurdjieffian literary pantheon the earthy, humorous Nassr Eddin constitutes a counterpoise to the saintly, idealized Ashiata Shiemash and Prince Lubovedsky.

Gurdjieff's particular Nassr Eddin is less the anti-hero of amusing, traditional anecdotes than the shrewd innovator of pithy sayings, e.g. 'as irritable as a man who has just undergone full treatment by a famous European nerve specialist.' For a consolidated list of these sayings, see *Guide and Index to G. I. Gurdjieff's All and Everything: Beelzebub's Tales to His Grandson*, The Society for Traditional Studies, Toronto, 1971, pp. 171–82. Certain references to modernistic subjects, e.g. to Shakespeare, suggest that Gurdjieff himself largely invented or adapted these sayings.

Around 1885 Gurdjieff visited Akshehir where a purported tomb of Nassr Eddin bears the inscription 386. Because the Mullah did most things back-to-front (even riding his donkey facing the tail), his burial is provisionally dated as AH 683 (AD 1284–5). Other dates from the thirteenth to fifteenth centuries have been canvassed and Nassr Eddin's historicity is a contested scholastic arena.

The first edition of the Turkish chapbook of Nassr Eddin jests appeared

in 1837, a German translation in 1857, and a French in 1876. An early
English translation is Henry D. Barnham, *Tales of Nasr-ed-din Khoja*,
Nisbet & Co., 1923. The most comprehensive compendium of Nassr Eddin
stories remains A. Wesseski's *Der Hodscha Nasreddin*, Weimar, 1911. Of
short dissertations, see Fehim Bajraktarevic's superb entry in the *Encyclopaedia of Islam*, vol. 3, pp. 875–8. Gurdjieff of course did not draw on
books for his sense of Nassr Eddin but on the rich oral tradition still prevailing throughout the Near and Middle East.

11. The Struggle of the Magicians (p. 134).

Gurdjieff's Manichean revue *The Struggle of the Magicians* remained
unperformed. Its biographic importance however can hardly be exaggerated, since it links the Gurdjieff of 1914, who advertises it in *Golos Moskvi*,
with the Gurdjieff of 1948 who rehearses it in New York. In autumn 1919
in Tbilisi Gurdjieff began dictating the scenario to Thomas de Hartmann
(*OLWG* 93); and in Constantinople in summer 1920 Ouspensky (*F* 382)
helped Gurdjieff refine the version posthumously published (G. I. Gurdjieff,
The Struggle of the Magicians, The Stourton Press, Capetown, 1957). A
variant text exists in Paris in the archives of the Institut Gurdjieff. Costumes,
designed and cut by Gurdjieff himself, were worn by ushers at the Movements demonstrations in the Théâtre des Champs-Elysées in December
1923. A photograph of the original backcloth, designed under Gurdjieff's
direction by Alexandre Salzmann, appears in Webb (pp. 288–9). Elements
of Gurdjieff's choreography survive as parts of the Movements. His music is
excerpted in the 1985 Triangle Records album (see Note 12); an early
variant of the score for the third Tableau is recorded by Jeanne de Salzmann
on Side 1A of an undated, unnumbered 78 record (Bartok Recording
Studio, New York); miscellaneous sheet music exists in the Thomas de
Hartmann Collection in the Music Library of Yale University.

  The Struggle of the Magicians contributed to the closing chord of
Gurdjieff's life. At the high requiem mass given in the Alexandre Nevski
Cathedral in Paris on 3 November 1949, the homily ended with this
quotation: 'God and all his angels keep us from doing evil by helping us
always and everywhere to remember our Selves.'

GURDJIEFF'S METHODOLOGY

12. Gurdjieff's Music (p. 145)

Consideration of Gurdjieff's music begins with grateful tribute to his loyal and gifted amanuensis, the classically trained Russian musician Thomas Alexandrovitch de Hartmann (1886–1956). Although de Hartmann generously insisted, 'It is not "my music". It is his. I have only picked up the master's handkerchief,' it was he who arranged, scored, and first played, the compositions which Gurdjieff inspired and indicated in essence. Gurdjieff, although not a proficient instrumentalist, variously attempted the piano, the mouth-organ (*TS* 12f), the guitar (Dukes 105), and the portative organ on which, particularly in old age, he extemporized. He could score sufficiently to indicate the key signature and the fundamental melody (*OLWG* 101). Altogether he commanded sufficient means to superintend a collaboration which Laurence Rosenthal has called 'unique in the history of music'.

Gurdjieff began his musical training as a choirboy in the cathedral of Kars, and was enthusiastic enough to seek (though unsuccessfully) entrée to the Archdeacon's choir in Tiflis. As an adult he acquired an intimate knowledge of Middle Eastern and Central Asian traditional and religious music. For his impressive command of Western speculative musicology see Webb 509–13; and of 'mantric' chanting see Dukes 101ff.

In all, Gurdjieff composed around 300 pieces. Most of the Movements and ballet music were created in the early years of the Gurdjieff/de Hartmann relationship; most of the programme music (short descriptive pieces – tender, witty, elegiac, religious, humorous, etc.) in the period of intensive work between 29 July 1925 and 1 May 1927, when the collaboration ended. A third and scarcely precedented category is identifiable as 'ideological music'; for example, 'Holy Affirming, Holy Denying, Holy Reconciling' correlates musically the Law of Three and the Law of Seven.

None of these compositions is a slavish pastiche of ethnic music. Rather Gurdjieff transmutes and recanalizes the subtle essence of an ancient tradition, delivering it to modern man as a summons to awaken and a support for his effort to be. Gurdjieff's determination to influence the West led him to express an œuvre redolent of Asia on that archetypally European instrument the pianoforte – to introduce the unknown in terms of the known. It is true that de Hartmann's specialization (he studied piano under Annette Essipov, a teacher of Prokoviev and Schnabel) predicated this choice – but it is equally true that Gurdjieff chose de Hartmann, preferring him over Vladimir Pohl.

Emphatic rhythms feature strongly in Gurdjieff's music, especially in the men's Movements. Further musicological analysis must begin by recognizing the constraints inherent in Gurdjieff's choice of instrument. His rich melodies are evoked within predetermined harmonic schemes. Analysts will find strong emphasis on the tonic, and, since the music is largely modal, scant recourse to modulation. Rather we find a prevalence of grace notes which, gliding into the adjacent tone, somehow impart the taste of quartertones (unplayable *per se* on the piano). A characteristic feature is the elision from a semitone to a minor third; a favourite mode is D E F G A B flat C sharp D (sometimes the E is flat). Intriguingly, small recourse is had to the scale adduced in Gurdjieff's Law of Seven. (This is the modern major scale, an inversion of the Greek diatonic Dorian – E D C B A G F E – the mode operated by the Demiurge in Plato's *Timaeus*.)

Although the Gurdjieff/de Hartmann music is – as yet – seldom brought to life outside authentic Gurdjieffian circles, a representative introduction to the œuvre, re-recorded from tapes of de Hartmann's playing, is now available on compact disc and cassette from Triangle Records, Triangle Editions, Inc., P.O. Box 452, Lenox Hill Station, New York, New York 10021. The definitive edition of the piano scores is under publication in Germany by B. Schott's *Söhne* (which produced first editions of Mozart, Beethoven, and Wagner), the last of four volumes being due in 1992. For a substantial if not exhaustive citation of the Gurdjieff/de Hartmann music, see *Gurdjieff: An Annotated Bibliography* by J. Walter Driscoll and the Gurdjieff Foundation of California (Garland Publishing, New York 1985), pp. 8–10. Serious musicologists are referred to the de Hartmann papers in the music library of Yale University.

13. The Sacred Dances (p. 41)

Of Gurdjieff's many roles – ideologue, man of action, author, 'physician-hypnotist', etc. – he arguably most rejoiced in being 'a rather good teacher of temple dances' (*B* 9). Such dances professedly served two vital functions: the harmonious evolution of the dancers themselves and the transmission of esoteric knowledge to remote generations. Today his 100 or so ensemble dances termed 'Movements' (or 'exercises' pre-1928), represent to many Gurdjieffians the Work's immaculate heart – a spiritual legacy of incalculable significance.

With the important caveat that Gurdjieff did not encourage choreographic analysis, seven categories, more or less discrete, emerge: rhythms (harmonic, plastic and occupational); the six preliminary exercises or 'Obligatories'; ritual exercises and medical gymnastics; women's dances; men's ethnic dances – 'dervish' and Tibetan; sacred temple dances and tableaux; and the thirty-nine Movements of Gurdjieff's last, partly enneagrammatic, series. The predominantly Central Asian provenance of Gurdjieff's ethnic, temple, and ritual dances is conveyed in programme notes he sanctioned. Yet these three categories are not simply *Danses trouvés*; no contemporary Central Asian geographer or anthropologist reports such structured dances. As to the evolutions based on the enneagram symbol (see Note 8), they seem, despite some Pythagorean redolence, unprecedented. Evidently then, Gurdjieff's Movements – creations and adaptations alike – bear the stamp of his own genius as a Master of Dance.

Manifestly Gurdjieff is not in debt to classical ballet, nor to any Western schools of dance, eurhythmics or movement. The reverse possibility – of Gurdjieff's (unintentional) influence on modern ballet – cannot be dismissed so easily. Diaghilev pressed Gurdjieff, unavailingly, to include the Sacred Dances as a novelty item in one of his *Ballets Russes* seasons. Lincoln Edward Kirstein, founder (1934) and director (1940) of the prestigious School of American Ballet, was a Prieuré pupil from July 1927, and apropos his work with George Balanchine, outspokenly acknowledged Gurdjieff's sovereign influence (in dedicating his book *Nijinsky Dancing*, Kirstein writes: 'As in everything I do, whatever is valid springs from the person and ideas of G. I. Gurdjieff'; see also his Letter to the Editor, *Times Literary Supplement*, 27 Jun. 1980.)

Gurdjieff's didactic recourse to dance was lifelong. On 13 November 1914 he advertised his 'ballet' *The Struggle of the Magicians*, and in March 1918 in Essentuki actually began teaching (*F* 372). Over an early five-year period he had economical recourse to public demonstrations, notably Tbilisi (June 1919), Paris (December 1923), New York (January–February 1924). Here his chief purpose was evidently to plunge participants into intense and formative experiences, his secondary aims being to 'nourish the times' and attract suitable pupils. During Gurdjieff's decade of authorship (1925–35), his Movements were sustained in different milieux by gifted women pupil-teachers (notably Jeanne de Salzmann, Jessmin Howarth, and Rose Mary Nott). In August 1936, with recourse to the Salle Pleyel studios and Jeanne de Salzmann's Sèvres group, Gurdjieff entered his last richly creative teaching period, sustained and developed throughout the Second World War. He gave his final Movement (No. 39) on 11 October 1949, only eighteen days before his death.

Gurdjieff's dance licenses no 'expressionism', euphemistically ascribable to inspiration or intuition. Each Movement's external form is 'mathematically' predetermined from beginning to end (cf. Japanese *Kata*). Every posture, gesture, rhythm has its appointed place, duration and weight. Reliance on habit, reflex functioning, and symmetry is minimal; the participant's arms, legs and head must often conform to independent contrapuntal rhythms; interior exercises in sensation and counting in canon may be added, and silent or spoken prayer. These diverse demands are reconcilable only by the dancer's mobilized attention equipoised among intellect, feeling, and body.

Gurdjieff held (*B* 476) that millennia ago Sacred Dance was essentially a mode of communication, a universal language with its own grammar, vocabulary, and semantic usage. Each dance was a book, each sequence or rhythm a phrase, each gesture or posture a word. The success of Gurdjieff's heroic attempt to rehabilitate this usage is difficult to gauge. Certainly the enneagrammatic Movements are intellectually penetrable (commensurate with one's grasp of the symbol) to an extent probably unique in dance. Yet no agreed Gurdjieffian vocabulary of gesture (cf. *mudra*) promotes understanding of other categories. Doubtless the individual dancer is more permeable to meaning than are academics, still less voyeurs; and such individualistic gleanings arguably remain reconcilable with claims to universal objectivity whenever they coalesce and the class understands as one.

By 1922 Alphons Paquet, a German Quaker, had published in *Delphische Wanderung* (Drei Masken Verlag, Munich) the first brief adventitious description of Gurdjieff's Sacred Dance. The public demonstrations of 1923–4 generated many journalistic cameos. In general, writers viewed the dances as exotic entertainment, evincing negligible insight into their true function and meaning. Only one philosophic charge of any substance emerged: that Gurdjieff had plucked sacred dance from its proper devotional framework and degraded it to the level of a Nietzschean system of self-development, which recognized no Higher Power. These critics, not having participated in the Movements, must be excused their failure of intuition.

Transmission of the Sacred Dances is direct, from teacher to pupils; no text-book exists, nor could usefully exist. Articles have been sparse, belated, and uneven. A substantial, independent, and inevitably misinformed piece is Mel Gordon's 'Gurdjieff's Movement Demonstrations: The Theatre of the Miraculous', *Drama Review*, XXII(2), June 1978, New York, pp. 32–44. Altogether more illuminating and sensitive, though slight in technical and historical detail, is Pauline de Dampierre's 'Sacred Dance: The Search for Conscious Harmony', interview with Jacques Le Vallois, *American Theosophist*, vol. 73, no. 5, May 1985. James Moore's 'Katherine Mansfield and Gurdjieff's Sacred Dance', *Katherine Mansfield: Centennial Essays* (Louisiana State University Press, 1991) offers a specific historical cameo. The rationale of Gurdjieff's œuvre is finely evoked in 'Movements, Sacred Dances and Ritual Exercises', the programme note to the public demonstration at the Fortune Theatre, Drury Lane, 18 and 19 May 1950. A significant effort of the traditional Gurdjieff groups since his death has been to create, and preserve for the future, a visual record. At a considerable expense of time, effort, and money, nearly ten archival films have been made in Paris by the French, English, and American groups, collaborating together under Jeanne de Salzmann's supervision. The only fragment so far publicly available is the last ten minutes of Peter Brook's film, *Meetings with Remarkable Men* (1979).

See also Notes 11 and 21.

14. Toasts to the Idiots (p. 281)

Gurdjieff's 'Toast to the Idiots', with its 'Science of Idiotism', was perhaps his strangest and most innovative method of teaching. At regular ritualistic meals which he hosted, formulary toasts were drunk to successive categories of 'idiot', sometimes with improvised 'additions' illuminating the specific idiocy and type. The toasts were proposed by 'the Director', generally a man but sometimes a woman, seated on Gurdjieff's left (of these, Bernard Lemaitre was the most notable during Gurdjieff's last years). All guests – excepting of course those in the particular category being saluted – were then obliged to drink the toast in Armagnac or vodka. As well as the Director, other participants assigned specific roles at these meals were *Verseur, Poubelle, Egout, Bouche d'Egout* and *Egout pour Sweet*. (For an evocative seating plan, see Rina Hands *The Diary of Madame Egout Pour Sweet*, Two Rivers Press, 1991, p. 3.)

Gurdjieff introduced his Toast to the Idiots in 1922, and from 1940 gave it increasing emphasis. Although not divesting 'idiot' of its pejorative sense, he re-invested it with the meaning of individuality (from a Greek root meaning 'I make my own'). Though idiocy was universal – God himself being the Unique Idiot (No. 21) – a subsidiary differentiation afforded a human typology at once 'poetic' and profound. Each pupil, relying simply on intuition, was initially required to choose his own idiot from among the first twelve (1 ordinary; 2 super; 3 arch; 4 hopeless; 5 compassionate; 6 squirming; 7 square; 8 round; 9 zigzag; 10 enlightened; 11 doubting; 12 swaggering). Considerable interest – once existential, now purely historical – attaches to certain assignments given by Gurdjieff himself (Orage a super idiot, Dr Stjoernval an arch idiot, Jessie Orage a squirming idiot, J. G. Bennett a round or doubting idiot, etc.). Gurdjieff designated only one person as 'going out of idiocy' namely Jeanne de Salzmann (*McCorkle* 76).

Since Gurdjieff's meals demanded a mobilized attention, and were never remotely orgiastic, toasts beyond twelve were seldom even approached. The subsequent order of idiots (nowhere reliably published) is believed to be: 13 born; 14 patented; 15 psychopathic; 16 polyhedral. Although idiots 1–16 might seem to occupy a plateau of being, only differentiated behaviourally, there are hints of a desirable evolution to the ensuing type (e.g. from hopeless to compassionate). Certainly each type, of itself, offered scope for evolution or involution. The distinction most alluded to in memoirs is that between the *subjectively* hopeless idiot, aware of his nullity and hence a candidate for an honourable death, and the *objectively* hopeless idiot, enmeshed in egoism and hence doomed to perish like a dog (cf. Armenian *merneel*, human death; *satkeel*, animal death). In fact, however, all the idiots were comparably differentiated. Consider the passage:

> Zigzag is high idiot, goes this way, that way. Takes different I's for reminding factor. Struggles against *merde* he knows he is … If he does this, then I admire him with all my presence! But ordinary zigzag idiot with five Fridays in the week is shit of shit.

Idiots 17–21 constituted a spiritual hierarchy, reflecting progressive gradations of 'objective reason'. Idiot 18 represented the highest development which a human being could reach, but in order to attain it, he had first voluntarily to descend again from 17 to category 1, the ordinary idiot. Idiots 19 and 20 were reserved for the sons of God.

For the provenance of ritualistic meals involving an inviolable succession of ceremonious, patriarchal toasts, we need look no further than the still living Georgian tradition, with its presidency by the *tamada* and dispensation by the *tolumbashi*. However the provenance of Gurdjieff's 'Science of Idiotism' is entirely unresolved. J. G. Bennett's suggestion (*NW* 157) that he borrowed the whole procedure from a Sufi community in Turkestan, seems particularly extravagant in view of the Islamic interdiction on alcohol.

The Toast to the Idiots was discontinued immediately on Gurdjieff's death in 1949, it being felt that, without his decisive presence, it stood in danger of becoming a mere form without content.

GURDJIEFF'S SUBSIDIARY PUPILS

15. *J. G. Bennett's Youthful Adventurism (p. 225)*

J. G. Bennett (hereafter JGB) was held on remand in Athens central jail for approximately a month between 7 March and 4 April 1928. His apologia for this episode in *Witness*, Ch. 12, is at variance with anecdotal recollections in Work circles and with the primary documents in Foreign Office 371 (pieces 12919 and 12920), much as his account of prior military service is difficult to reconcile chronologically with War Office records. JGB was arrested on 3 March on the instructions of an examining magistrate in the small Greek seaport of Kavalla, accused of bribing the local Land Registrar to fabricate title deeds relating to Ottoman Imperial property, in which JGB had a concessionary interest: the formal charge was 'moral instigation of other persons to commit forgery of public documents.'

Combined together in an effort to extricate JGB were his second wife Winifred, powerful Work friends in London (including Lady Malcolm), eminent business associates in the Aegean Trust Ltd, and the British Ambassador Sir Percy Lyham Loraine (who deprecated JGB but could not countenance a British national featuring as the protagonist in 'another Tichborne case with an oriental flavour'). On 4 April, having stoically faked appendicitis by drinking iodine, JGB was removed from Athens jail to a municipal nursing home; on 19 April the charge was reduced to defrauding the company he represented; and on 25 April he was released on bail of 1,000,000 drachmas. Public Record Office papers indicate that, under continued Foreign Office pressure, reluctantly applied, all charges against JGB were dropped on 13 August 1928. JGB however claims that a year later, on 27 September 1929 he was tried on the original charge before the Court of Appeal in Salonika and, defending himself in Greek, was acquitted with costs awarded against the government.

PRO files in the FO 371 series present a composite picture of JGB's adventurism between 1921 and 1931 which is positively Buchanesque: in 1921 he was offered (as were others) the vacant throne of Albania; between

1921 and 1924 he was in virtual partnership with John Wesley de Kay (1872–1938), a florid adventurer who, during the First World War rightly or wrongly featured in MI5 files under the code name 'Mordecai' as 'chief of the sabotage and murder section of the German Secret Service' (piece 12179); in 1922 JGB was appointed to represent the interests of the eight widows of Abdul the Damned; in 1926 he was suspected of smuggling hashish from Salonika; in 1927 of plotting a fraud involving a 'salted' gold mine at Avret Hissar near Kilkish; and in 1929 he attempted to compromise Sir Robert Arthur Johnson KBE, Deputy Master and Comptroller of the Royal Mint (piece 13661). JGB was abetted by Lt-Col. George Maitland Edwards (also known in Work circles). Embarrassed at various times by JGB were Ouspensky (*W* 157) and the eminent British diplomat Eric Graham Forbes Adam, who committed suicide in Constantinople on 7 July 1925.

Censorious judgement on JGB would be beside the point. There is room for more than one view of his actions during this time, and in any case they are hardly Gurdjieff's affair, since the two men were only in contact for thirty-three days in 1923. At first sight JGB's lifestyle seems redolent of the younger Gurdjieff himself during the phase when he painted sparrows and sold them as 'American canaries' – although whether, throughout this decade, JGB sustained a comparable current of spiritual search seems unlikely.

16. *Sergei Dmitrievich Mercourov (p. 72)*

My provisional identification of 'M' (the unknown sculptor who introduced P. D. Ouspensky to Gurdjieff – see *F* 6) as Sergei Dmitrievich Mercourov (1881–1952), the eminent Leninist monumental artist, offers an intriguing prospect of deeper investigation into Gurdjieff's family background.

The surname Mercourov, in various transliterations, emerges both in Gurdjieff's reference to his uncle in Alexandropol, 'the esteemed Giorgi Mercourov' (*M* 71), and in Olga de Hartmann's reference to 'the sculptor Merkouroff, whose family lived next door to Mr Gurdjieff's parents in Alexandropol' (*OLWG* ix). (In the definitive edition of *OLWG*, edited by Thomas C. Daly and T. A. G. Daly, the Christian name, Dmitri, is added.) In *Glimpses of Truth* (*V* 33) Gurdjieff confirms his contact in Moscow in 1914 with 'a companion of my early childhood, a famous sculptor'. He leaves a further clue in associating this sculptor with Gogol's death mask ... S. D. Mercourov surely fits this specification beyond the admissability of coincidence: he was born in Alexandropol on 21 October 1881; he achieved fame in Moscow at the relevant time; and, not least, he sustained an unprecedented interest in death masks (taking those of Toumanian, Leo Tolstoy, Gorky, Scriabin, Mayakovsky, Zetkin, Eisenstein and Khrimian Hairik, Catholicos of all Armenians).

Whether S. D. Mercourov was a first or second cousin to Gurdjieff is unclear and caution is needed. As his patronym reflects, Mercourov's father was named Dmitri not Giorgi. Moreover, according to Gurdjieff, Giorgi Mercourov's son had 'nearly finished school' (M 71) in 1888 (M 65), whereas S. D. Mercourov, aged only seven, was then standing on the threshold of an education which took him successively to Alexandropol Town Gymnasium, Tiflis Gymnasium, Kiev Polytechnic, Zurich University, and Munich Academy of Fine Arts.

Whatever the precise relationship, the dramatic irony of this general identification pivots around no less an individual than Lenin (Vladimir Ilyich Ulianov). In the composite figure of 'LENtrohamsanin' (B 390–410) Gurdjieff encapsulates both his acknowledgement of Lenin's stature and his detestation of his character and anti-traditional influence. By contrast S. D. Mercourov in 1918 had amicable conversation with Lenin; in 1937 executed the statue of Lenin on the Moscow Canal; in 1939 was awarded the Order of Lenin; and in 1941 won the state prize for his monument of Lenin now in the Hall of Conferences in the Great Kremlin Palace ... To cap all, when Lenin died on 21 January 1924, Mercourov took his death mask.

Whereas Gurdjieff went largely unrecognized during his lifetime, S. D. Mercourov was showered with honours. From 1945 to 1949 he was Director of the Pushkin State Museum. He released only one book, *Zapiski skul'ptara* (*A Sculptor's Notes*) posthumously published in 1953. Mercourov died in Moscow on 8 July 1952 and lies buried in Novodevichye cemetery beneath the statue of 'Thought', which he created in Moscow *c.* 1913, when – I submit – he was directly under Gurdjieff's influence. Further information: Mercourov Memorial House, Prospekt Haghtanaki 47, Leninakan, Armenia.

17. Miss Ethel Merston (p. 169)

Ethel Merston was one of Ouspensky's London pupils who first met Gurdjieff at his lectures in West Kensington in February–March 1922. She originally went to the Prieuré in the hope that Gurdjieff would cure her chronic spinal ailment. Her protracted stay there from autumn 1922 to summer 1927 surely deserves a more sympathetic memorial than Fritz Peters' devastatingly funny child's-eye vignettes (P1). Unfortunately her own affecting account (Ch. X of her memoirs) is so clumsily written that publication even in the academic press seems a remote possibility.

Miss Merston's father was a German-Jewish émigré and her mother of aristocratic Portuguese-Jewish origins. After an education at the Canon Holland or Baker Street school, Ethel successively joined the Voluntary Aid Detachment (for nursing in the First World War) and the Women's Royal Naval Service. In 1932, five years after leaving the Prieuré, Ethel transferred her spiritual search to India, settling in the ashram of Sri Ramana Maharshi at Tiruvannamalai. (For some of her exchanges there in 1939 see *Talks with Sri Ramana Maharshi*, 3rd edn, Tiruvannamalai, 1963.) Following the deaths of Gurdjieff (1949) and Maharshi (1950), Miss Merston sustained a tentative contact with J. G. Bennett (of who she seems to have formed a mixed opinion.)

18. *Frank Pinder (p. 137)*

Frank Pinder (1882–1962) (full name Francis William Stanley Pinder) is important as Gurdjieff's second English pupil (the first being Paul Dukes). The Gurdjieffian ideal of a 'learned being' seems not disgraced in Pinder, although both his scholarship and his practicality were tinged with idiosyncracy.

Pinder entered the Gurdjieffian scene in July 1919 in Ekaterinodar, capital of the Kuban, when (serving under General Holman as head of the British Economic Mission to the Volunteer Army of General Anton Ivanovitch Denikin) he was induced by letters from A. R. Orage to employ the destitute P. D. Ouspensky to write press summaries. Pinder may also then have known Mme Ouspensky and Andrei Zaharoff who worked in the official propaganda section. Pinder subsequently moved to Rostov-on-Don and his fate when on 8 January 1920 the city fell to the Bolsheviks is clouded: the Gurdjieffian apocrypha which has him captured, condemned to death, and making a spectacular escape by train, cannot be substantiated from Army or Public Record Office records. Nor can J. G. Bennett's assertion (*NW* 123) that Pinder was the British Intelligence officer responsible for security of the Baku-Batoum pipeline.

Pinder's first direct contact with Gurdjieff came in March 1920 when appointed to Tbilisi, the capital of the Georgian Menshevik social democratic state, as cultural attaché under the Chief British Commissioner, Oliver Wardrop. Evidently Gurdjieff contacted Pinder on the commendation of Ouspensky and the two men collaborated in the sale of antique carpets to outlets in Constantinople. Both men soon left Tbilisi for Constantinople, Gurdjieff in late May and Pinder in July (ostensibly en route to Warsaw).

On 15 March 1922, when visiting London for a second time to lecture at 38 Warwick Gardens, Kensington, Gurdjieff brought Pinder as his interpreter; Pinder sided emphatically with Gurdjieff in the breach which then occurred with Ouspensky. In October 1922, when Katherine Mansfield was making overtures to Gurdjieff, it was Pinder whom Gurdjieff chose to interview her in the Select Hôtel and subsequently to interpret. Katherine described Pinder as a 'quite remarkable man . . . rather like the chief mate on a cargo steamer.' On 4 January 1924 when Gurdjieff took most of his pupils to America, he left Pinder in charge of the Prieuré; it was hence Pinder who in February played host to D. H. Lawrence and Aleister Crowley during their brief voyeuristic visits. Crowley diarized Pinder as a 'hell of a fine fellow ... a really wonderful evening with Pindar (sic)'. Certain material which Pinder then came across among Gurdjieff's personal papers (subsequently burnt by Gurdjieff in 1930) offended him, and he suspended his connection for more than a decade, only reappearing in Gurdjieffian circles c. 1937.

Thereafter Pinder maintained contact and was active in the debate of 1948–9 surrounding the publishing of *Beelzebub*. Despite his seniority, Pinder, neither before nor after Gurdjieff's death, aspired to a teaching role. Nevertheless his penetration of *Beelzebub*, informed by his wide-ranging command of languages, was deep. Miscellaneous PRO papers bear on Pinder around the time he first met Gurdjieff. As a pupil of Gurdjieff, Pinder is sketched in *N2* Ch. 10, supported by primary papers in the possession of Adam Nott.

19. *Lady Rothermere (p. 160)*

None of Gurdjieff's patrons was more generous or flamboyant than Mary Lilian, Viscountess Rothermere (1875–1937). Born Mary Lilian Share, the daughter of George Wade Share an unsuccessful City hardware merchant and subsequent bankrupt, her marriage in 1893 at the age of eighteen to the newspaper magnate Harold Sidney Harmsworth, set her on the path to rank and riches. Harmsworth's rise in society kept pace with his business success: in 1910 he was created a baronet; in 1914 a baron; and in 1919 was made first Viscount Rothermere of Hemsted. By the time Lady Rothermere met Gurdjieff on 13 Feb. 1922 at 38 Warwick Gardens, West Kensington, at the age of forty-seven, she had lost her sons, Harold Alfred Vyvyan St George and Vere, in the First World War, and, despite a natural joie de vivre, was open to ideas of commensurate weight.

In fact Lady Rothermere enters the Gurdjieffian scene the previous year. The very planting of Gurdjieff's ideas in England may be dated from her famous telegram to Ouspensky in summer 1921: 'Deeply impressed by your book *Tertium Organum* wish meet you New York or London will pay all expenses.' (*W* 69) When Ouspensky reached London in August 1921, Lady Rothermere bought him a flat at 55a Gwendwr Road, West Kensington; launched him socially at dinner parties in Circus Road, St John's Wood; sent copies of his book to all her friends; and introduced him to T. S. Eliot (see David Garnett, *The Flowers of the Forest*, Chatto & Windus, 1955, p. 225).

After Gurdjieff's two visits to London in Feb.–Mar. 1922, Lady Rothermere transferred her allegiance, generously offering him her studio in

Circus Road for his Institute. She seemed the most powerful member of the lobby which attempted, unsuccessfully, to persuade Edward Shortt the Home Secretary to sanction Gurdjieff's immigration with his Russian entourage; in actuality her influence haemorrhaged with her earlier estrangement from her husband.

When Gurdjieff settled in Paris in July 1922, Lady Rothermere took rooms there in the Hôtel Westminster. Following joint consultation with Gurdjieff and Ouspensky, she matched the generosity of Ralph Philipson in funding the acquisition of the Prieuré. Her brief visits to the Institute at Fontainebleau saw her more in the role of patroness than engaged participant, and Gurdjieff treated her with indulgent but ironic humour. Less charitable were her social acquaintances who condemned her in defamatory terms. Thus Vivienne Eliot to Ezra Pound, 2 Nov. 1922: 'She is unhinged – one of those beastly raving women who are the most dangerous. She is now in that asylum for the insane called La (sic) Prieuré where she does religious dances naked with Katherine Mansfield.'

Although Lady Rothermere's personal contact with Gurdjieff diminished as he embraced writing and she new enthusiasms, her patronage endured. In summer 1929, when Gurdjieff appointed Louise Goepfert his secretary, he tasked her to write to Lady Rothermere requesting the continuance of funds (McCorkle 30). When Lady Rothermere died from cancer in Switzerland in 1937, she had made an unsurpassed material contribution to Gurdjieff's work.

20. Jean Toomer (p. 201)

Although the writer 'Jean' (Nathan Pinchback) Toomer (1894–1967) contributed to the early dissemination of Gurdjieff's ideas in America, his aspiration outran his capacity and he was eclipsed by A. R. Orage. Excited by Ouspensky's *Tertium Organum* and by Gurdjieff's New York demonstrations in spring 1924, Toomer went to the Prieuré late in July. Unfortunately Gurdjieff's prior motor-car accident on 8 July forbad useful contact, and when Gurdjieff 'disbanded' the Institute in October 1924, Toomer returned disappointed to New York.

Here Toomer's inexcusable attempt to teach Gurdjieff's Sacred Dances, without knowing them, ended predictably in fiasco after six weeks. The episode set the tone for his repeated initiatives to advance Gurdjieff's cause – with himself in a precocious and self-bestowed leadership role. Toomer's relationship with Orage, Jessmin Howarth, and Gorham Munson, though fundamentally amicable, came under strain. Of the various groups and workshops which Toomer instituted – Harlem (1925), Chicago (1926), Portage, Wisconsin (1931), and Doylestown, Pennsylvania (1937, 1942, and 1954), only the Chicago group has been capable of resurrection. Given Gurdjieff's heavy concentration on writing and his vow of 5 May 1928 to banish pupils, Toomer's scope for face-to-face contact was limited. He first actually spoke to Gurdjieff in summer 1926 at the Prieuré, and returned for brief summer visits in 1927 and 1929. The two men's trans-Atlantic correspondence and intermittent liaison in New York and Chicago in the early 1930s focused largely on Gurdjieff's pressing financial needs. Toomer's marriages to Margery Latimer (30 Oct. 1931) and Marjorie Content (1 Sep. 1934) respectively weakened and terminated his link with Gurdjieff. They never met again after March 1935.

Toomer features somewhat awkwardly in his two best known Gurdjieffian roles: catalyst in Mable Dodge Luhan's attempt to plant the Work in Taos, New Mexico (winter 1925–6); and protagonist in the dubious 'Portage Potential' intensive (Jun.–Sept. 1931). In the end he did not become the great Gurdjieffian *avatar* he yearned to be ('History will say, Jean Toomer of Chicago. Toomer the Chicagoan'). Indeed from 1934 to 1952 he stood quite outside the movement. His real – and valuable – contribution to the Work in America was to project at least its semblance beyond the New York intelligentsia. Conceivably too, his pioneer links with the Matthias Alexander Technique and with the Quakers have an 'ecumenical' significance of sorts. After a return to Gurdjieffian circles in 1953, and a final decade of invalidism, Jean Toomer died on 30 March 1967 aged seventy-three. For a full account see Kerman and Eldridge (Select Bibliography).

GURDJIEFF'S ACQUAINTANCES

21. *Emile Jacques-Dalcroze (p. 150)*

Emile Jacques-Dalcroze (1865–1950), creator of eurhythmics, was a contemporary of Gurdjieff – born to Swiss parents in Vienna. After studies under Anton Brückner in Vienna, and Délibes and Fauré in Paris, he was appointed professor of harmony and *solfège* at the Geneva Conservatoire in 1892. Here he developed his complex system styled *La Méthode Rythmique* or *Gymnastique Rythmique*, on which he lectured throughout Europe from 1900 to 1912. In 1911 his favourable impression upon two enlightened Polish-German philanthropists, Wolff and Harald Dohrn, led to the building of the ambitious Hellerau Bildungsanstalt to Dalcroze's own design.

Here at Hellerau between 1911 and 1914, in the sunset of *belle époque*, the work of Dalcroze was supported by two future eminences in the Gurdjieffian pantheon: Alexandre Salzmann, a world authority on stage lighting and sets, and his wife Jeanne Salzmann – 'like a flame, a beautiful dancer with a lithe and supple body.' The outbreak of the First World War severed Dalcroze's connection with Hellerau and he returned to Geneva, Jeanne Salzmann's original home. Here in 1915 he founded the Institut

Jacques-Dalcroze in which (excepting two years' teaching in Paris) he worked until his death.

The interface between Dalcroze eurhythmics and Gurdjieff's Sacred Dance dates from the Tbilisi period, when Jeanne Salzmann put her Dalcroze pupils at Gurdjieff's disposition for the demonstration at the Opera House on 22 June 1919. In winter 1921, when Gurdjieff came to Hellerau more or less under the patronage of Dalcroze, he evidently presented a programme of sorts at the Bildungsanstalt before becoming embroiled in litigation. Jessmin Howarth and Rose Mary Nott – Dalcroze students who abandoned eurhythmics and attached themselves to Gurdjieff around this time – later became respected teachers of Gurdjieff's dances. When Gurdjieff first arrived in Paris in July 1922, he established himself in the Institut Jacques-Dalcroze in the Rue de Vaugirard.

The question of direct personal contact between Gurdjieff and Dalcroze is clouded. Mrs Nott and Mrs Nathalie Tingey OBE had, in old age, some vague sense of a tripartite meeting among Gurdjieff, Dalcroze, and Rudolf von Laban (choreographer, movement analyst, and originator of the notation system 'Kinetography Laban'). Although the attenuated influence of Gurdjieff's ideas upon Laban is persuasively alleged by Oscar Bienz, it is far from easy to furnish a chronological niche for this triple convention. General literature bearing on Hellerau (e.g. *The Era of Expressionism*, ed. Paul Raabe, trans. J. M. Ritchie, Calder & Boyars, 1974) is unilluminating, and the issue begs deeper research in primary German-language sources. Jaques-Dalcroze did however attend (and react against) Gurdjieff's Movements demonstration in Paris at the Théâtre des Champs-Elysées in Dec. 1923. Presumably Alexandre Salzmann then introduced them, but no record is extant.

22. *Prince Mehmet Sabaheddin (p. 149)*

Prince Mehmet Sabaheddin (1877–1948) is doubly significant: firstly for introducing J. G. Bennett to Gurdjieff (an option Ouspensky forwent); and more importantly for the shadow his movements cast over Gurdjieff's. Bennett's report (W 63) that Gurdjieff first met the Prince 'when he [Sabaheddin] was returning from Europe to Turkey after the Young Turk revolution of 1908' raises peculiar problems and vistas. Sabaheddin did indeed return to Turkey on 2 September 1908, bringing for interment at Eyup the bones of his father Damat Mahmut Pasha; Gurdjieff however, according to his own account, was then in Tashkent.

Sabaheddin's reported assertion that he and Gurdjieff met three or four times between 1908 and 1912 would also seem to situate Gurdjieff at least intermittently in Constantinople, contrary to the Gurdjieffian canon. Certainly it was in Constantinople that Sabaheddin was politically engrossed from 1908 to April 1913, when – implicated in the dangerous plots of his secretary and agent Satvet Lutfi Bey – he narrowly escaped justice and fled.

Sabaheddin's movements between 1913 and 1921 have presumably little or no relevance to Gurdjieff, since Gurdjieff's independently documented Russian and Georgian epochs allow Sabaheddin no reasonable entry, and because Sabaheddin himself confirms they did not meet between 1912 and 1921. For what it is worth, Sabaheddin, having been tried by court martial *in absentia* and sentenced to death for his part in the assassination on 11 June 1913 of Grand Vizier Mahmut Sevket Pasha, lived abroad in the pay of various European governments. Between 1915 and 1916 he is to be found in Athens (see John Presland, *Deedes Bey: A Study of Sir Wyndham Deedes 1883–1923*, Macmillan & Co, 1942, p. 197); and from 1917–18 in Geneva (see Foreign Office 371, piece 3398). In December 1918 the newly enthroned Sultan Mehmet VI Vahdettin rehabilitated Sabaheddin and instigated his return to Constantinople (see FO 371, piece 349).

Of all the 'Princes' in the Gurdjieffian canon (Prince Lubovedsky, Prince Nijeradze, Prince Mukransky, etc.), Prince Sabaheddin is arguably the only identifiable historical figure, and certainly the best connected. As the son of Damat Mahmut Celaleddin Pasha and Seniha Sultana (sister of Sultan Abdul Hamid II), Sabaheddin was, on his father's side, the grandson of a Grand Vizier, and, on his mother's side, the grandson of Sultan Abdul Mejid; he was the nephew of three successive brother Sultans – Abdul Hamid II (reigned 1876–1909), Mehmet V Reshad (1909–1918), and Mehmet VI Vahdettin (1918–1922) occupant of the throne when Gurdjieff re-encountered Sabaheddin in 1921.

Sabaheddin appears as a modest figure in the voluminous literature describing – either in personal or historical terms – the emergence of modern Turkey (see works by Djemel Pasha, P. Fesch, E. Kuran, B. Lewis, D. von Mikusch, E. E. Ramsaur and S. J. and E. K. Shaw). He shows there not as the spiritual choirboy of J. G. Bennett's memoir but as an unscrupulous, impractical, and failed ideologue of the liberal wing of the Young Turks – and an obsessive schemer for political power. This genre of books is of small use to Gurdjieffian scholars, being devoid of reference to Sabaheddin's undoubted theosophical and anthroposophical aspirations and connections. However it is conceivably worth passing mention (in view of Gurdjieff's putative link in youth) that, in 1907 in Paris, Sabaheddin held joint presidency of the 2nd Congress of Ottoman Liberals with K. Malumian of the Dashnakzutiun.

Evidence of contact between Gurdjieff and Sabaheddin after 1921 is lacking. A Greek secret-service file of 1926 purports to link Sabaheddin, his daughter Fethiye Hanum, and J. G. Bennett with hashish smuggling from Salonika (FO 371, piece 12920). The Prince died in obscurity on 30 June 1948 at Colombier near Neuchatel.

23. Frank Lloyd Wright (p. 252)

Perhaps some contention will always attach to the Gurdjieff-Wright relationship; certainly it involves the jealously guarded reputations of two
remarkable men with independent followings. Effectively it began on 25
August 1928, when Frank Lloyd Wright (hereafter FLW) made his third
marriage, to Olgivanna Hinzenberg one of Gurdjieff's dedicated pupils from
1919 to 1924. Olgivanna's fidelity to Gurdjieff's ideas and her influence
upon FLW can hardly be exaggerated. Hence when young applicants in
summer 1932 responded to FLW's circular letter headed, 'An Extension of
the Work in Architecture at Taliesin to Include Apprentices in Residence',
they and their successors necessarily fell under an occulted Gurdjieffian
influence, which strongly affected both the regime and ideology at Taliesin –
though not of course architectural praxis. The whole argument is developed
with unusual scholarship and intuition by Robert C. Twombly in 'Organic
Living: Frank Lloyd Wright's Taliesin Fellowship and Georgi Gurdjieff's
Institute for the Harmonious Development of Man', *Wisconsin Magazine of
History*, vol. 58, no. 2, winter 1974–5.

The two protagonists first met in June 1934 at Taliesin East, Spring
Green, Wisconsin, when Gurdjieff was sixty-eight and FLW sixty-five. Their
rapport and mutual regard bred several further meetings, with FLW host at
Taliesin, and Gurdjieff host at 6 Rue des Colonels Rénard and in New York.
Among various of Gurdjieff's pupils also given generous hospitality at
Taliesin were Jeanne de Salzmann, C. Stanley Nott, Rose Mary Nott, and
Thomas and Olga de Hartmann. From the fraught months immediately
preceding the Second World War, up to America's declaration of war on
Germany (11 Dec. 1941), Gurdjieff enjoyed an option to settle in Wisconsin.

There should be no suggestion that FLW (any more than Katherine
Mansfield) became Gurdjieff's pupil in the conventional sense; he was a
proud, independent genius whose most creative work was accomplished
before he even met Gurdjieff. Nevertheless these two men, generally parsi-
monious in praise, held each other in a special mutual regard which endured
for fifteen years. When in August 1949 Gurdjieff saw the prehistoric cave
paintings at Lascaux, his first impulse was to convey an impression to FLW.
Only Gurdjieff's death (29 Oct. 1949) prevented his spending Christmas at
FLW's second seat: Taliesin West, Paradise Valley, Phoenix, Arizona (see
Harry Adaskin, *A Fiddler's Choice: Memoirs 1938 to 1980*, November
House, Vancouver, 1982, p. 99). Whether Gurdjieff's influence on FLW's
latter years was as formative as Louis Sullivan's on his early ones is a matter
of conjecture, but that FLW's esteem for Gurdjieff was sincere and totally
lacking condescension is evidenced by his tribute in the *Wisconsin State
Journal*, 3 Nov. 1951.

A relationship so rare would be profaned by cheap debate as to ascendancy.
When (shortly after Gurdjieff's death) FLW was presented with a medal at
Cooper Union in New York, he sought the chairman's permission to make

an announcement. He said: 'The greatest man in the world has recently died. His name was Gurdjieff.' (See Gorham Munson, 'Black Sheep Philosophers: Gurdjieff – Ouspensky – Orage', *Tomorrow* IX(6), New York, Feb. 1950). Predictably FLW's unstinting support of Gurdjieff earned him the due amount of lies and slanders; in a secret memorandum of 1954, FBI director J. Edgar Hoover reported that Gurdjieff (who had been five years in his grave) was brainwashing FLW.

MISCELLANEOUS

24. *The Bell Song (p. 121)*

The famous Bell Song, '*Où va la jeune Hindoue?*', by Léo (Clement Philibert) Délibes (1836–91), is from Act 2 of *Lakmé*, premièred at the Opéra-Comique, Paris, on 14 April 1883. Twice, at least, Gurdjieff urged Olga de Hartmann to sing it: on having successfully crossed the mountains from Essentuki in September 1918; and immediately preceding the Movement's demonstration aboard the s.s. *Paris* in January 1924. His commendation is significant as one of his exceptionally rare nods towards mainstream European culture.

In scoring *Lakmé* and *The Struggle of the Magicians*, Délibes and Thomas de Hartmann respectively confronted the identical problem: of evoking, rather than imitating, traditional oriental music. Délibes, although gravitating for his effects to such unusual keys as F sharp major, D flat major, and G flat major, frequently modulates to unrelated keys and exploits 'false relations' to create a rich harmonic palette; his string section has recourse to harmonics, *sur le chevalet* bowing, and multiple *divisi*; the percussion section to *crotales*, *Glockenspiel* and *petites timbales*. (One must wonder incidentally whether Olga actually commanded the interpolated high E's, which mark the Bell Song, or 'The Legend of the Pariah's Daughter', as a test piece for a coloratura soprano.)

Without querying the fundamental disparity of level between *Lakmé* and *The Struggle of the Magicians*, we may safely acknowledge structural parallels. As originally produced, *Lakmé* had four sections of dialogue and two *mélodrames* (text by the librettists Gondinet and Gille, spoken over orchestral accompaniment); and the extant series of temple dances by priestesses, in Act 2, reminds us that Délibes was a teacher of Jaques-Dalcroze. Thus, although *Lakmé* is formally conceived as an opera and *The Struggle of the Magicians* as a ballet, both might be thought of as multi-media revues with an exotic eastern setting. Délibes' heroine Lakmé and Gurdjieff's heroine Zeinab are equally precipitated into moral and spiritual jeopardy through misconceived love, at play in a charged religious context; both are virgin priestesses. It may or may not be relevant that in 1914 Gurdjieff advertised his ballet as 'the property of a certain Hindu'. Not of course that he actually commended Indian religiosity, whether of the Mimamsa and Vedanta, Sankhya and Yoga, or Nyaya and Vaisesika schools; indeed his voice was consistently against it, from 1915 when he told Ouspensky (*F* 15) that it constituted (in the pejorative sense) mere 'philosophy', to 1949 when he stigmatized India as only a '*bordel* for Truth' (*I* 68). (See also Note 11 on *The Struggle of the Magicians*.)

25. The Conference of the Birds (p. 160)

The Hoopoe is the resourceful hero of the elaborately discursive allegorical classic *Mantiq al-Tayr* (*The Conference of the Birds*) by the Persian mystical poet Farid ud-Din Abu Hamid Muhammad ben Ibrahim (*c*.1180–*c*.1220), generally called 'Attar the perfumer'. The 'Simurgh' is first advanced as the divine king of all birds, in effect the Godhead. Most of the birds persuaded by the Hoopoe to seek the Simurgh perish on the pilgrimage; the surviving thirty realize that they themselves are the Simurgh (Persian *si murgh* meaning thirty birds).

In Attar's subtle speciation of character, and in the birds' varying responses to the quest for the Simurgh, some readers have seen striking parallels with patterns of Gurdjieffian aspiration, even with Gurdjieff's typology of the 'Idiots'. Of various translations (see E. FitzGerald, Boston, 1899; and R. P. Masani, 1924) the most accessible in English is that by the Gurdjieffian C. S. Nott, from the French of Garcin de Tassy, 1863 (The Janus Press, London, 1954).

26. Prince Mukransky (p. 66)

Gurdjieff made repeated reference to the legendary Georgian Prince Mukransky, jokingly claiming to be his nephew (*B* 50), though denying that Mukransky supported him financially (*M* 248). The stereotype of the rich and prodigally hospitable Mukransky has its prototype in sixteenth-century Georgia, when Bagrat, son of Constantine King of Karthly, received from his brother King George IX a forested apanage in the district of Mukran (so named from *mukra*, the oak). In 1649, upon the extinction of the royal line, the Mukran family was elevated to the throne.

27. Gurdjieff's Nansen Passport (p. 167)

By decrees of the Supreme Soviet of November and December 1921, Gurdjieff (as an anti-Bolshevik émigré) was officially rendered stateless (*apatrides*). In summer 1922, Dr Fridtjof Nansen, the League of Nations High Commissioner for Russian Refugees, introduced his restricted passport. This document (renewable annually at a cost of 25 francs) conferred on Gurdjieff an internationally recognized identity, and latitude to cross national borders, subject to visa requirements. Nevertheless, over Gurdjieff's entire stay in France there brooded the threat of expulsion (*refoulement*), and over his nine trips to America the concern that he would not be granted a re-entry visa to France.

28. Poincaré (p. 167)

Louis Pauwels' assertion (Pauwels 31) that Gurdjieff's admission to France was personally facilitated by Poincaré seems both extravagant and superfluous. When on 15 January 1922 Raymond Nicolas Landry Poincaré became Prime Minister (replacing Aristide Briand), he and his resolutely anti-Bolshevik *Bloc national* fostered an immigration policy notable for its wide liberality. No one can dogmatize concerning the number of Russian refugees domiciled in France in 1922, since estimates by the League of Nations, the American Red Cross, and the French Census Board range from 70,000 to 400,000; there is however a firmer basis for assessing the number in Paris at *c*.45,000. Gurdjieff then, notwithstanding his biographic singularity, must be viewed historically as one of thousands of displaced persons who made Paris the effective 'Capital of Russia-in-Exile'. For background see: Poincaré's obituary in the Russian émigré newspaper, *Vozrozhdenie (Resurrection)*, 16 October 1934, Paris; and *New Mecca, New Babylon: Paris and the Russian Exiles, 1920–1945* by Robert H. Johnston, McGill-Queen's Univ. Press, Kingston & Montreal, 1988.

29. The Particule Nobiliare (p. 258)

The *particule nobiliare* (a prefixed *de, von,* or *zu*) signalled, in various European countries, derivation from the landed aristocracy. Its usage – notwithstanding Gurdjieff's own humble origins – touches all five founder members of his Institute for the Harmonious Development of Man.

The case of the de Hartmanns is most clearcut: they used the *particule nobiliare* consistently, and were plainly entitled to it. Thomas de Hartmann was not only an officer in the Imperial Guards but a personal protégé of Tsar Nicholas II, and the grand-nephew of Eduard von Hartmann, author *inter alia* of *The Philosophy of the Unconscious*; Olga was the sister-in-law of Baron Peter von Nettlehorst and Baron Klüge von Klügenau, and, by a morganatic line, a great-grand-daughter of Kaiser Wilhelm I . . . The case of the Stjoernvals is also consistent, if less well known: by Russian usage, they too were entitled to the *particule nobiliare* but simply chose not to use it.

The case of the Salzmanns or de Salzmanns invites further elucidation.

Although Thomas de Hartmann makes an early and isolated reference to Alexandre von Salzmann, it is simply as 'Salzmann' that Alexandre features in the copious literature related to the school of Jaques-Dalcroze at Hellerau from 1911–14; he reappears, indelibly, as Salzmann in Katherine Mansfield's correspondence of 1922; and Beryl de Zoete meets him as Salzmann at the Théâtre des Champs-Elysées in 1932. However after Alexandre's death at Leysin near Geneva on 3 March 1934, his widow convenes the seminal Sèvres group as Mme Jeanne de Salzmann. Various theories, none remotely convincing, purport to explain this change, e.g. that the 'de' may have served to distance Jeanne from growing anti-German feeling in France as war impended (though in fact she was born in Switzerland). Jessie Orage has gone so far as to suggest (v.v.) that the family enjoyed no right to the *particule nobiliare*, and that Jeanne co-opted it in emulation of Olga de Hartmann; but this seems wholly out of character with Jeanne de Salzmann and her scale of values.

30. Possible Gurdjieff–Stalin Connection (p. 256)

Gurdjieff's claim (NW 99) that he had been with Stalin (Joseph Vissarionovich Djugashvili) at the Theological Seminary in Tiflis seems implausible; indeed we lack evidence that Gurdjieff was ever a seminarian. Stalin was born in 1879, Gurdjieff in 1866 (see Note 1); Stalin attended the seminary from 1 September 1894 until his expulsion on 28 May 1899, a period when Gurdjieff was purportedly engaged in expeditions in Central Asia with the Seekers of Truth. Equally unconvincing is the variation (Webb 45) which has the seminarian Stalin lodging with the Gurdjieff family in Tiflis, and absconding owing a substantial sum. Only Dmitri Gurdjieff was then living in Tiflis, and in any case the strictly regimented seminary had no extramural students.

Although the characters and beliefs of Gurdjieff and Stalin are at polar opposition, Gurdjieff strangely does not inveigh against Stalin as he does, in coded language, against Lenin and Trotsky. There remains just sufficient circumstantial evidence to keep alive the faint possibility of some youthful Gurdjieff–Stalin liaison. Stalin, in an early revolutionary phase, assumed the cover-name and identity of 'Nizheradze' (a deceased carpet dealer in Baku). Gurdjieff (M 191) refers to a certain 'Nijeradze' as one of his companions – indeed he evidently suppressed an entire and poignant chapter relating to 'Prince Nijeradze' (NW 178). In May 1935 Gurdjieff unaccountably explored the option of going to live in Stalinist Russia (but could not accept the proffered terms of admission).

In 1940 Gurdjieff's cousin and former pupil S. D. Mercourov (see Note 16) won the State Prize for his granite statue of Stalin at the All-Union Agricultural Exhibition in Moscow. In 1967 Stalin's only daughter Svetlana

Iosifovna Alliluyeva defected to America. In 1970 (abandoning plans to holiday with Elizabeth Shoumatoff, sister-in-law of Olga de Hartmann) Svetlana went to Taliesin West where she married the widower of Olgivanna Lloyd Wright's first daughter. Olga de Hartmann and Olgivanna were the two most senior of Gurdjieff's former pupils then living, independently, in the USA. The proximity of Stalin's daughter to both of them may have been pure coincidence; this is the sense of Svetlana's acidulously anti-Gurdjieffian account. See Svetlana Alliluyeva, *The Faraway Music*, Lancer International, New Delhi, 1984, p. 87.

31. Gurdjieff's Posterity (p. 318)

The question of Gurdjieff's posterity – affecting existentially thousands of lives – is necessarily emotive. He himself was determined to perpetuate his ideas in a pure form, and, on the other hand, was convinced that the trajectory of any teaching is inescapably deflected under the Law of Seven. Commercial distribution of Gurdjieff's writing and music aside, how then has his posthumous influence been exerted – by whom, how authentically, and subject to what exigencies? This vast, contentious subject may ultimately find its calmest and most thorough exploration in studies by disinterested non-Gurdjieffian historians. All they will lack is experiential knowledge of the subject they address. At least they can hardly fail to improve on pertinent offerings by peripheral Gurdjieffian figures, e.g. J. H. Reyner and Kathleen Riordan Speeth. For scholars capable of intelligent analysis and synthesis, the lineaments of Gurdjieff's posterity already begin to emerge in *Gurdjieff: An Annotated Bibliography* by J. Walter Driscoll and the Gurdjieff Foundation of California, Garland Publishing, New York, 1985. Mapped out there are the avenues, byways, and blind-alleys of a movement with considerable and ever-increasing traffic.

By the time of her death on 25 May 1990 aged 101, Jeanne de Salzmann had created the nucleus which Gurdjieff tasked her to build, and consolidated (generally under the name of Gurdjieff Foundations or Societies) substantial and enlarging foci of study in London, Paris, New York, California, Caracas, Sydney, and elsewhere – their strictly hierarchical or 'apostolic' character ensuring, as far as institutional format can, a recognizable line of transmission from Gurdjieff himself. It is eloquent that the vast majority of Gurdjieff's surviving pupils acknowledged the primacy of Jeanne de Salzmann, and aligned themselves with this family of societies.

A factor objectively affecting the currents of any movement is the order in which its proponents die. Listed below therefore is the successive mortality of some significant figures who studied under Gurdjieff and survived him: James Young 1950, Dr Maurice Nicoll 1953, Thomas de Hartmann 1956, Roland Kenney 1961, Frank Pinder 1962, Mme Grigrorievna Ouspensky

1963, Jane Heap 1964, Kenneth Walker 1966, Sir Paul Dukes 1967, Jean Toomer 1967, Gorham Munson 1969, Elizabeta Stjoernval 1972, Margaret Anderson 1973, J. G. Bennett 1974, Jean Vaysse 1975, Solita Solano 1975, C. S. Nott 1978, Anna Butkovsky-Hewitt 1978, Fritz Peters 1979, René Zuber 1979, Olga de Hartmann 1979, Rose Mary Nott 1979, Henriette Lannes 1980, Kathryn Hulme 1981, Lord Pentland 1984, Olgivanna Lloyd Wright 1985, Jessie Orage 1985, Louise March 1987, Basil Tilley 1988, Jeanne de Salzmann 1990.

Albeit two Gurdjieffian usages (The Toasts to the Idiots and the production of 'tricks, half-tricks and real phenomena') have not been pursued, the Gurdjieff Foundations and Societies still offer a virile and integrated programme embracing group work, Sacred Dancing, music, drama, special studies and research projects, craft work, etc. It is these societies which supported Mme de Salzmann in her major creation of archival films of Gurdjieff's Sacred Dance; and precisely this sector which I commend both to future historians and to present-day enquirers in quest of the genuinely Gurdjieffian.

Altogether more clamant and problematical are the movements and literatures adhering firstly to pupils whose spiritual itineraries diverged (notably J. G. Bennett who, after Gurdjieff's death, successively embraced Subud, Pseudo-Sufism, and various other teachings), and secondly to implicit and explicit pretenders to Gurdjieff's mantle (Idries Shah, E. J. Gold, Robert Burton, Gary Chicoine, etc.) who in fact never met him. It is just here that organizations created in opposition, imitation, and even derision – the protean 'centres', 'fellowships', 'academies', etc. – regularly appear in a blaze of self-advertisement and disappear in the murk of disillusion. History can safely be trusted to judge these entities on their merits.

Gurdjieff's more authentic posterity has not entirely escaped an intriguing national inflexion: in the USA the semblance of his ideas has been facilely appropriated by a broad spectrum of 'New Age' and 'Human Potential' movements; Latin America has seen some unavoidable conciliation of the Roman Catholic Church; Britain, after extrication by Henriette Lannes from the cold climate of Ouspensky's intellectuality, must today accommodate a welcome but disproportionate interest from teachers of the Matthias Alexander Technique; and France evinces sympathy to a doctrine of quietism and grace (interestingly contrasted with Gurdjieff's 'Obligolnian strivings'), supported by practices redolent of Kundalini Yoga. Such inevitable and perhaps ephemeral variations may find synthesis in the newly emergent spirit of internationalism. Meanwhile they provide (to adapt a striking sentence of Jeanne de Salzmann) 'an opportunity to measure the force of a thought which, passing through a great diversity of echoes, keeps its own resonance and its power of action'.

Key to References

Abbreviated Sources

A1	*The Fiery Fountains* (Margaret Anderson)
A2	*The Unknowable Gurdjieff* (Margaret Anderson)
B	*Beelzebub's Tales to His Grandson* (Gurdjieff)
F	*In Search of the Miraculous* (P. D. Ouspensky)
I	*Idiots in Paris* (J. G. & E. Bennett)
M	*Meetings with Remarkable Men* (Gurdjieff)
N1	*Teaching of Gurdjieff* (C. S. Nott)
N2	*Journey through This World* (C. S. Nott)
NW	*Gurdjieff: Making a New World* (J. G. Bennett)
OLWG	*Our Life with Mr Gurdjieff* (Thomas de Hartmann)
P1	*Boyhood with Gurdjieff* (Fritz Peters)
P2	*Gurdjieff Remembered* (Fritz Peters)
PP	*With Gurdjieff in St Petersburg and Paris* (Butkovsky-Hewitt)
TS	*Life is Real Only Then: When 'I Am'* (Gurdjieff)
V	*Views from the Real World* (Gurdjieff)
W	*Witness* (J. G. Bennett)

How Quotation Sources are Indicated

Each quotation is identified by a 'tag-phrase' based on the quotation proper. The provenance of quotations from the abbreviated sources shown above is self-evident, e.g.

M37   means G. I. Gurdjieff, *Meetings with Remarkable Men*, page 37.

Quotations identified simply by an author's name and relevant page number are from the *one and only* book by that author cited in the Select Bibliography (pp. 403–5). The provenance of quotations from sources not cited in the Select Bibliography is specified in full.

Standard Abbreviations

f.	and on the following page
ibid.	in the same work (book or article) as that cited *immediately above*
idem	in the same work (book or article) *and on the same page* as that cited immediately above
op. cit.	in the book by this author, cited *previously* in this chapter's references
oral	an accepted part of the oral tradition attaching to Gurdjieff
q.	quoted in the ensuing reference
v.v.	in conversation with the author
passim	here and there throughout

References

———— ❖ ————

Part I Chapter 1

THE AROUSING OF THOUGHT

'If you are first' (10)	M 47
'Eldest of my grandsons' (11)	B 27
'This strange tooth had seven shoots' (11)	ibid. 33
'Such people *see*, can *see*' (14)	NW 21
'not a single book on neuropathology' (14)	M 70
'hysteria is hysteria' (17)	idem
'a whole sensation of myself' (17)	ibid. 205
'an unconquerable living terror' (18)	idem
'Boil down nine Jews' (19)	ibid. 114
'an "irrepressible striving"' (20)	H 13
'between Urmia and Kurdistan' (23)	M 91
'decided to go there' (23)	idem

Chapter 2

THE LONG SEARCH

'I was not alone' (25)	F 15f.
'seekers of pearls in manure' (25)	TS 7
'I also am businessman' (27)	Hulme 63
'all sorts of terrors' (27)	TS 27
'conversations with revolutionaries' (27)	idem
'for a certain political aim' (27)	M 211
'access to the "holy-of-holies"' (27)	H 17
'arm-in-arm with the priest Vlakov' (28)	M 93
'sharp energetic events' (28)	TS 27
'the island of Haninn' (28)	M 37
'elder comrade and closest friend' (29)	M 118
'My God! What I experienced' (29)	M 99
'The prince was a very rich man' (29)	M 119
'spoiled and depraved to the core' (30)	TS 25

'self-love, vanity, pride, jealousy' (30)   *TS* 21
'sew up their mouths' (30)   *M* 197
'Help me, O Lord' (30)   *M* 143
'I take an oath' (30)   *TS* 25
'symbol, technique, dance' (31)   *NW* 105
'the golden road to Sarmakand' (31)   James Elroy Flecker
'ebony brought from Africa' (32)   *NW* 64
'The details I shall recount' (32)   *M*161
'priestly mixture of Sivaite mysticism'   L. A. Waddell, *The Buddhism of*
(33)   *Tibet* 30
'blaze of "orders" and "regimentals"'   *B* 613
(33)
'punctured by a second stray bullet' (33)   *TS* 9
'He is God and I am God' (34)   ibid. 23
'tenseness and psychic contrivance' (34)   *TS* 9
'smash these filthy lecherous lamas'   Peter Fleming, *Bayonets to Lhasa: The*
(34)   *First Full Account of the British*
                                              Invasion of Tibet in 1904, Rupert
                                              Hart-Davis, 1961, 132

'the "Terror of the Situation"' (35)   *B passim*
'the influence of "mass hypnosis"' (35)   *TS* 27
'being-impulse called "love-of-kind"'   *B* 579
(35)
'two-headed worm of inquisitiveness'   *TS* 28
(35)
'exteriorization of sensitivity' (35)   *M* 43
'taking-away-of-responsibility' (35)   *H* 19
'third bullet plunked into me' (35)   *TS* 9
'workshops-for-psychopathism' (37)   *H* 22
'rendering conscientious aid to   ibid. 20
sufferers' (37)
'freely moving "Guinea-Pigs"' (37)   ibid. 22
'Great Solomon, King of Judah' (37)   ibid. 12
'absolutely unnatural life' (38)   *H* 12
                                              Wyndham Lewis, 'Letter to Violet
                                              Schiff' (20 Sept. 1922), British Library
'moving like a being apart' (38)   Margaret Anderson, *The Strange*
                                              Necessity: The Autobiography
                                              resolutions and reminiscences to
                                              1969, Horizon Press, New York, 221

Part II

THE REVELATION IN QUESTION

'In order to study this movement' (40)   J. B. Priestley, *Man and Time,* Aldus
                                              Books, 1964, 264

'No system of gnostic philosophy' (41) — Philip Mairet, *A. R. Orage: A Memoir*, Reintroduction XXIV, University Books, New York, 1966

'exacting benevolence of his gaze' (41) — Henri Tracol, *Man's Awakening and the Practice of Remembering Oneself*, Guild Press, 1968, 2

'how to secrete God-stuff' (41) — Richard Rees, 'Monsieur Gurdjieff', *Twentieth Century*, vol. 164, no. 981, Nov. 1958, 439

'today's "a-religious" man' (42) — Michel de Salzmann, 'Footnote to the Gurdjieff Literature', *Parabola*, V(3), New York, Aug. 1980

'exactly as an "Old Jew" (42) — B 777

'The higher blends with the lower' (44) — ibid. 751

'This apparatus is *organic life*' (45) — F 85

'the precise significance of life' (46) — H 13

'a source of "offensive-shame"' (46) — B 136

'the Omni Most Holy Sun Absolute' (46) — ibid. *passim*

'the erroneous calculations' (46) — ibid. 82

'asphyxiating stink' (46) — ibid. 81

'slavery to foreign circumstances' (47) — ibid. 88

'Everything in *Beelzebub* historical' (48) — NW 65

'poor bored fishermen' (49) — B 418

'an honest and humble Austro-Hungarian' (49) — ibid. 561

'the devoted and favourite Apostle' (49) — ibid. 739

'mother-in-law, John Thomas, and cash' (51) — ibid. 343

'burning question of the day' (51) — ibid. *passim*

'infuriated offensive abuse' (51) — ibid. 341

'There is no progress whatever' (51) — F 51

'most terrible of all horrors' (52) — B 1056

'We always make a profit' (52) — F 326

'a photographically exact snapshot' (54) — B 1207

'eats impressions excretes behaviour' (54) — A. R. Orage, *On Love: With Some Aphorisms & Other Essays*, The Janus Press, 1957, 48

'way of the sly man' (57) — F 50

'Is the saint the man?' (57) — Peter Brook, q. James Moore, *The Guardian*, 20 July 1976, 10

'in the depths too deep' (57) — Philip Mairet, *A. R. Orage: A Memoir* J. M. Dent, 1936, 81

'the road to Philadelphia' (57) — V 191

'the being of a mineral' (58) — F 65

'A man may be born' (60)	F 217
'The first striving' (60)	B 386
'the consequences of the properties' (61)	ibid. *passim*
'Only understanding can lead to being' (61)	M 242
'Blessed is he who has a soul' (61)	V 283
'I have good leather to sell' (61)	Kenneth Walker, *A Study of Gurdjieff's Teaching*, Jonathan Cape, 1957, 16
'One man can do nothing' (61)	F 30
'Gurdjieff was a master' (62)	M, Translator's Note X

Part III Chapter 1

PRINCE OZAY

'Begin in Russia, finish in Russia' (64)	NW 108
'If I am acting' (66)	V 178
'the nephew of Prince Mukransky' (66)	B 50
'in accordance with a rhythm' (66)	V 8
'astonished by its special atmosphere' (66)	F 271
'uniquely and sincerely beloved wife' (67)	TS 36
'John Jones and Mary Smith' (67)	M 9
'utterly different from all the others' (67)	Gurdjieff, *Magicians*, 23f.
'an aura of gentle firmness' (67)	P1 75
'on the verge of moral ruin' (67)	M 127
'men in quotation marks' (68)	B *passim*
'Nature of woman is different' (68)	P1 114
'most powerful and hated man in Russia' (68)	Colin Wilson, *Rasputin*, Arthur Barker, 1964, 113
'Death is after him!' (69)	Edmond Taylor, *The Fall of the Dynasties*, Doubleday & Co., New York, 1963, 172
'an opera glass on someone's head' (69)	Wilson, op. cit., 142
'one cannot shed blood' (69)	James Webb, *The Occult Establishment*, Richard Drew Publishing, 1981, 196
'He was extraordinary' (70)	Robert de Ropp, *Warrior's Way*, George Allen & Unwin, 1980, 103
'pouring from the empty into the void' (70)	B 95f.'
'"French champagne" could not be taken' (70)	ibid. 403

'Turk, Tartar, Teuton, or Tibetan' (71)   Dukes 106
'rocky wastes and inaccessible hills'   ibid. 105
(71)
'great agitation of minds in Russia'   M 225
(72)
'only one book to *study*' (72)   Dukes 120
'twice two makes seven and a half'   M 210
(73)
'And only in that search' (73)   P. D. Ouspensky, *Tertium Organum: The Third Canon of Thought; a Key to the Enigmas of the World*, Knopf, New York, 1922, 306
'cat-like strength and subtlety' (74)   Harold C. Schoenberg, *The Great Pianists*, Gollancz, 1969, 332
'intellectual dabblers in the occult' (74)   Dukes 120
'You believe in ventilation!' (74)   ibid. 100
'about G2 below middle C' (74)   idem
'like a mild electric current' (75)   ibid. 103
'in a desert place' (75)   ibid. 102
'no two persons' breath exactly alike'   idem
(75)
'the World's tonic note' (75)   ibid. 107
'every octave is a replica' (75)   idem
'much better than whisky' (75)   ibid. 104
'triumphant, exultant, majestic' (75)   ibid. 111
'gospel became intensely personal' (76)   ibid. 109
'inclined to stoutness' (77)   PP 66
'Wearing a trance-like expression' (77)   ibid. 67
'His Majesty the Emperor' (77)   Taylor, op. cit., 226
'Solemnly I swear' (78)   ibid. 242
'everything finished between Wilhelm'   ibid. 227
(78)
'What is war?' (78)   F 24

Chapter 2

HOLY AFFIRMING

'My first meeting with him' (81)   F 7
'an Indian raja or Arab sheikh' (81)   idem
'to meet him was always a test' (82)   M, Translator's Note ix
'simple, courteous, approachable' (82)   OLWG 5
'Take neither purse nor scrip!' (82)   F 165
'when you went to India' (82)   ibid. 16
'the assurance of a specialist' (82)   ibid. 12
'truth *in the form of a lie*' (83)   ibid. 314
'a kind of feline grace' (83)   ibid. 10

'I have found the Miracle' (83) — *PP* 35

'Exterminate all the Armenians' (84) — David Marshall Lang, *The Armenians: A People in Exile*, George Allen & Unwin, 1981, 27

'splashed about in the bloody mud' (84) — L. D. Trotsky, *History of the Russian Revolution*, vol. 1, Gollancz, 1932, 84

'diamond-studded morsels' (85) — Carl Zigrosser, *My Own Shall Come to Me: A Personal Memoir and Pictures Chronicle*, Casa Laura, Philadelphia, 1971, 158

'a grasp of fundamental points' (86) — *F* 53

'Why not have a meeting tonight' (86) — ibid. 31

'this "acting" in G. was strong' (87) — ibid. 33

'a bird with ruffled feathers' (87) — *PP* 70

'looked forward to meeting with joy' (87) — ibid. 36

'an abstract eternal quest' (88) — ibid. 74

'*Only super-efforts count*' (88) — *F* 232

'everyone must strip himself' (89) — ibid. 247

'*I should like some raspberry jam*' (89) — ibid. 253

'Mystics indeed!' (89) — *PP* 81

'God preserve us from such people' (89) — ibid. 79

'And with this the miracle began' (90) — *F* 262

'Why did he say that?' (90) — idem

'I went into the forest' (90) — idem

'*I replied mentally*' (90) — ibid. 263

'neither red, green, nor yellow magic' (90) — ibid. 226

'struggle with mechanicalness' (91) — ibid. 268

'How can I resign?' (91) — Colin Wilson, *Rasputin and the Fall of the Romanovs*, Arthur Barker, 1964, 198

'*legs which were not yet torn off*' (91) — *F* 51

'taken his trousers off him' (92) — ibid. 273

'Go – not knowing where' (93) — *OLWG* 2

'There are usually more whores here' (93) — ibid. 4

'the eyes of Mr Gurdjieff' (93) — ibid. 3

'The bullet which killed him' (93) — Edmund Taylor, *The Fall of the Dynasties*, Doubleday & Co., New York, 1963, 255

'like a black panther' (94) — *OLWG* 6

'husband and wife are both interested' (94) — ibid. 7

'look, you can push us' (94)   ibid. 8
'He was different!' (95)   F 324

Chapter 3

MIRAGES OF SAFETY

'looking at the stars' (97)   M 48
'occasionally laughing a little' (98)   F 342
'a lonely and forgotten grave' (98)   M 57
'If you want to rest' (98)   F 340
'first man shot for theft' (98)   idem
'I hardly saw G. alone' (98)   ibid. 342
'good to go to Persia' (99)   ibid. 341
'hawkers selling sunflower seeds' (99)   idem
'an almost pedantically regular life'   M 45
(99)
'the Caspian sea was glittering' (99)   F 342
'wait five years' (99)   idem
'tell them in Moscow and Petersburg'   ibid. 343f.
(100)
'difficult even in six years' (100)   ibid. 346
'Tibetan, Persian and other dishes'   idem
(100)
'This is astrology' (101)   ibid. 367
'Silence reigned all around' (101)   M 245
'my confidence in G. began to waver'   F 368
(102)
'invariably smart and elegant Zaharoff'   OLWG 11
(102)
'a ruling prince or statesman'   F 325
(102)
'Zaharoff's feet will smell' (103)   OLWG 13
'The night is so wonderful' (103)   ibid. 15
'The Caucasus, wolves, jackals   ibid. 17
howling' (103)
'not even a thermometer' (104)   ibid. 22
'Realize everything you can' (104)   Webb 156
'darkness, snow, rain, wind' (105)   F 178
'What is there to think about?' (105)   idem
'He bought sunflower seeds' (106)   OLWG 28
'Evreinoff came up to Gurdjieff' (106)   PP 105
'Will you invite us for supper?' (106)   OLWG 30
'I remember the oranges he ordered'   idem
(106)
'infuriated offensive abuse' (107)   B 341
'something like Sodroojestvo' (107)   F 373

Chapter 4

THE CAUCASIAN PIMPERNEL

'If one thing could be different' (122)   *F* 21f.
'language of the smile' (123)   *Hulme* 121
'centre of hell to its edge' (123)   *M* 276

Chapter 5

AMONG THE MENSHEVIKS

'to run about the city' (125)   *M* 279
'a great deal left over' (126)   *M* 280
'I will be there' (126)   *OLWG* 83
'practically no trace of infection' (127)   idem
'former dervish, former Benedictine'   René Daumal, *Mount Analogue: An*
(127)   *Authentic Narrative*, Vincent Stuart,
                                             1959, 6
'something wild and savage in him'   Carl Zigrosser, *My Own Shall Come*
(127)   *to Me: A Personal Memoir and Picture*
                                             Chronicle, Casa Laura, Philadelphia,
                                             1971, 165
'He is a very fine man' (127)   *OLWG* 80
'you must learn how to turn' (128)   idem
'feet made strong rapid movements'   *OLWG* 81
(128)
'rightness of Mr Gurdjieff's Work'   idem
(128)
'I was filled with terror' (128)   ibid. 85
'only if the ship went down' (129)   ibid. 87
'things said only for disciples' (129)   *F* 14
'to speak of Komitas Vardapet' (130)   Thomas de Hartmann, 'The Folk Song
                                             and Its Collectors', *Anahit*, Paris,
                                             1935; original lecture given Tbilisi,
                                             1919
'magic circle of kerosene' (130)   *OLWG* 90
'people sitting like corpses' (130)   idem
'Ararat in a shroud of mist' (130)   *OLWG* 91
'carved living chunks of experience'   Kenneth Walker, *A Study of*
(131)   *Gurdjieff's Teaching*, Jonathan Cape,
                                             1957, 18
'centre of the world's culture" (132)   Bechhofer-Roberts 64
'What name would you give?' (132)   *OLWG* 92
'squeezing a tube of toothpaste' (132)   idem
'true international fraternities' (132)   *F* 381
'such an important establishment'   *M* 280
(133)
'Anyone can play a good one' (133)   *OLWG* 93
'there were also waiting-lists' (133)   *M* 281
'I wish for immortality' (134)   *N1* 84

'She could paint, or sculp' (134)   Frank Lloyd Wright, *An
                                                 Autobiography*, Longman, Green,
                                                 1932, 444

'schools of a Black Magician' (134)   *F* 17
'Why are you so astonished?' (135)   *OLWG* 96
'the public will never understand' (135)   *F* 17
'They have finally moved' (135)   *OLWG* 94
'curious individual named Gourjiev'   Bechhofer-Roberts 65
(136)
'extraordinary all-round intelligence'   ibid. 66
(136)
'every second man had a bandage'   ibid. 250
(136)
'muddy waters of the Kura river' (136)   ibid. 66
'my friend Mr Ouspiensky' (136)   ibid. 81
'mysterious monasteries in Thibet' (137)   ibid. 68
'it seemed like a joke' (137)   *OLWG* 96
'circumstances of horror' (137)   Bechhofer-Roberts, 'The Forest
                                                 Philosophers', *Century Magazine*,
                                                 CVIII (1), New York, May 1924, 67

'Johnnie Walker's spiritual consoler'   Nott papers
(137)
'a real Sauchiehall Street haggis' (138)   idem
'Begin in Russia: end in Russia' (138)   *NW* 108
'I decided to liquidate everything' (138)   *M* 281
'The hall had many slender columns'   *OLWG* 97
(138)

Chapter 6

THE STRUGGLE OF THE MAGICIANS

'some obscure Nestorian sect' (140)   J. G. Bennett, *The Crisis in Human
                                                 Affairs*, Prologue, Hodder and
                                                 Stoughton, 1948
'The *corpus vile* of Constantinople'   *The Times*, Special Correspondent, 31
(140)   March 1919
'all kinds of dervish nonsense' (141)   *M* 178
'onanism, monkism, Athenianism' (142)   *B* 382
'a famous European nerve specialist'   *B* 972
(142)
'there was no *way back*' (143)   P. D. Ouspensky, *A New Model of the
                                                 Universe: Principles of the
                                                 Psychological Method in Its
                                                 Application to Problems of Science,
                                                 Religion, and Art*, RKP, 1931, 388
'very glad to see G.' (143)   *F* 382

'exacting benevolence of his gaze' (143)   Henri Tracol, *Man's Awakening and the Practice of Remembering Oneself*, Guild Press, 1968, 2

'meetings sounded like pandemonium' (144)   W61

'G. the artist and G. the poet' (144)   F 383

'I never feel, I *know*' (145)   PP 21

'the "talent" of the New Testament' (145)   OLWG 1

'upper voice as an embellishment' (145)   ibid. 101

'wholly-manifested-intonation' (146)   B 3

'ever more violent and terrible' (146)   Gurdjieff, *Magicians* 37

'language made even Lenin blush' (147)   Denis Saurat, 'A Visit to Gourdjiev', *Living Age* CCCXLV, Jan. 1934

'Mr Gurdjieff very extraordinary man' (147)   W 134

'Lord Creator and all His assistants' (147)   Gurdjieff, *Magicians* 47

'most terrible of all horrors' (148)   B 1056

'her husband had beaten her' (148)   M 217

'to distinguish mama from papa!' (149)   B 1066

'too delicate for this earth' (149)   W 111

'the contemplation of Jesus Christ' (149)   ibid. 52

'all the King's horses' (150)   Arnold J. Toynbee, *The Western Question in Greece and Turkey: A Study in the Contact of Civilisations*, Constable, 1922, 185

'The Holy Virgin a living reality' (150)   W 53

'very dangerous Russian agent' (150)   NW 90

'better than I understood myself' (150)   W 65

'Salzmann's tall, thin, ironic figure' (151)   Beryl de Zoete, *The Thunder and the Freshness*, Neville Spearman, 1963, 23

'Deeply impressed by your book' (152)   W 69

'a lubricant to living' (152)   Claude Bragdon, *The Secret Springs*, Andrew Dakers, 1939, 267

'Gurdjieff's lightly tinted whiteness' (152)   Lizelle Reymond, *To Live Within*, George Allen & Unwin, 213

'to organize work in Germany' (152)   F 384

'For me he is X' (153)   W 166

'run on Homburg hats was over' (153)   Harold Armstrong, *Turkey in Travail: The Birth of a New Nation*, John Lane The Bodley Head, 1925, 105

'wiseacring of the Young Turks' (153)   M 283

'owing to you I could buy this meat' (153)   OLWG 103

Chapter 7

MR GURDJIEFF CHANGES TRAINS

'Russian, go away' (154) — OLWG 104

'sense of complete assurance' (154) — NW 132

'Jericho-trumpet-in-crescendo' (155) — B 89

'the pervert balls in Berlin' (155) — Stefan Zweig, q. Edmond Taylor, *The Fall of the Dynasties: The Collapse of the Old Order 1905–1922*, Doubleday & Co., 1963, 396

'comprehensible element proscribed' (155) — ibid. 395

'to act the part of a countess' (156) — V 167

'Why are these idiots behind me?' (156) — OLWG 105

'behaved as if born at court' (156) — idem

'Mr Gurdjieff did not know' (157) — OLWG 106

'their famous Bismarck's "pet cat"' (157) — B 429

'my work of infinitely more importance' (158) — A. S. Neill, '*Neill! Neill! Orange Peel*', Weidenfeld, 1973, 120

'Herr Neill, ich liebe Sie' (158) — ibid. 117

'full of prophecies of disaster' (158) — P1 56

'they appeared even before he arrived' (159) — F 384

'with gold knives and forks' (159) — David Garnett, *The Flowers of the Forest*, Chatto & Windus, 1955, 225

'in a depressing purplish-grey" (160) — Loran Hurnscott, *A Prison, A Paradise* 185

'His shaved Tartar's skull' (160) — Roland Merlin, '*Le drame de Katherine Mansfield*', L'Illustration 16, 19 Jan. 1946

'the topic of Australian frozen meat' (161) — B 10

'You are a machine' (161) — V 76

'in London I am irritable' (161) — ibid. 79

'you must find a teacher' (161) — ibid. 81

'I *knew* Gurdjieff was the teacher' (161) — N1 27

'His eyes were hazel' (162) — idem

'Brighter than the sun' (162) — Edwin Muir, *An Autobiography*, Hogarth Press, 1940, 173

'lock-hospitals and ugly accidents' (162) — A. R. Orage, *New Age* X, 24, 11 Apr. 1912, 564

'secret knowledge behind knowledge' (162) — Edwin Muir, op. cit., 173

'referring to someone's parentage'   *B* 10
(163)
'Normal human beings the exception'   *NW* 135
(164)
'Pinder is interpreting for me' (164)   *N2* 91
'Gurdjieff's attacking him' (164)   idem
'Everything more vivid' (164)   Pogson 72
'will *have* to choose a teacher' (164)   *N2* 99
'an interview with the Home Secretary'   Kenneth Walker, *A Study of*
(164)   *Gurdjieff's Teaching*, Jonathan Cape,
       1957, 13

'the welfare of British medicine (165)   idem
'chemico-analytic cabinets' (165)   Bechhofer-Roberts, 'The Forest
       Philosophers', *Century Magazine*
       CVIII (1), New York, May 1924, 78

'Permission was refused to the colony'   ibid. 69
(166)
'Blödsinn, Blödsinn, Du mein   *B* 661
Vergnügen' (166)
'cross-roads of all races' (166)   *M* 284
'the protection of Poincaré' (167)   Pauwels 31
'Is there a gas stove?' (167)   *OLWG* 109
'Gurdjieff cut out the materials' (168)   Young 34
'ex-officer of Czar's bodyguard"   ibid. 35
(168)
'thick, red-cord piping and tassels'   *PP* 127
(168)
'All of you are deformed' (168)   *V* 82
'outstanding event for a psychologist'   Young 37
(169)
'untidy nest of reddish hair' (169)   *P1* 36
'bench on the Boulevard de la   Merston (Ch. X) 1
Madeleine' (169)
'either snow or rain or something'   *M* 285
(170)
'the gardener has to leave' (170)   *OLWG* 110
'The foxes have holes' (171)   Matthew 8: 20
'the maddest periods of my life' (171)   *M* 285

Chapter 8

HAIDA YOGA

'greeted by Mrs Serious Problem' (172)   *M* 285f
'need to know European languages'   ibid. 286
(172)

'no retirement into the desert' (173) — *F* 48

'Skorry! Queeker! queeker!' (173) — Bechhofer-Roberts, The Forest Philosophers', *Century Magazine* CVIII (1), New York, May 1924, 73

'avoid identifying and muscle tension' (173) — Pogson 84

'leapt about a hundred yards' (173) — idem

'Must be done in half time' (173) — ibid. 83

'no belief in medical treatment' (174) — Katherine Mansfield, *The Letters of Katherine Mansfield*, Constable, 1928, 256

'life which death will not destroy' (174) — Olgivanna 8

'special trout caught in our pond' (174) — Merston (Ch. X) 2

'working for the cinematograph' (174) — Bechhofer-Roberts, op. cit., 70

'incredible tension of my forces' (175) — *M* 289

'my opportunities for gay revels' (175) — idem

'floor of the New York Stock Exchange' (175) — ibid. 286

'patience is the Mother of Will' (176) — *W* 121

'an ingenuity almost diabolical' (176) — Clifford Sharpe, 'The Forest Philosophers', *The New Statesman* part 1, XX (516), 3 Mar. 1923, 627

'Some people went mad' (176) — *W* 121

'something sinister in this house' (176) — Denis Saurat, '*Visite à Gourdjieff*', *La Nouvelle Revue Française*, XLI, 242, Paris, Nov. 1933

'trained to clean the cows' (176) — Mansfield 695

'full of life and humour and ease' (176) — ibid. 680

'speed and tension, and high hopes' (177) — *NW* 140

'ingredients that boiled and simmered' (177) — idem

'even by those odours' (177) — *B* 651

'small whitey pinky pebbles' (177) — Mansfield 680

'down magical rabbit holes' (177) — Webb 260

'literally cry with fatigue' (177) — *N1* 28

'prolonged spell in winter trenches' (178) — Sharpe, op. cit., 627

'what happens to Jung's disciples' (178) — Bechhofer-Roberts, op. cit., 77

'an abundance of untried strength' (178) — Adèle Kafian, 'The Last Days of Katherine Mansfield', *Adelphi*, XXIII, Oct.–Dec. 1946, 36

'help her all you can' (178) — Olgivanna 6

'pick the flowers and rest *much*' (178) — Mansfield 677

'Live in your body again' (178) — idem 695

'ancient Assyrian group Dance' (179) — Mansfield 684
'a fanatical Muslim polygamist' (179) — W 266
'room for Flaubert's *Cœur Simple*' (179) — Mansfield 685
'interesting and animated work' (179) — F 385
'yellow dance stockings to dry' (180) — Mansfield 695
'to take in the paranoiac' (180) — Merston (Ch. X) 4
'it had to fall to pieces' (180) — F 389
'very motley company' (180) — ibid. 385
'like mystical Micawbers' (180) — Bechhofer-Roberts, op. cit., 76
'stupid, lazy, dense, riff-raff' (180) — V 109
'more like Bokhara than Avon' (181) — Mansfield 690
'mother-in-law, John Thomas and cash' (181) — B 343

'that of a solemn goat' (181) — Young 34
'surly, angry, even fierce workman' (181) — Mansfield 694
'all the requisite number of limbs' (181) — Fritz Peters, *Balanced Man: A Look at Gurdjieff Fifty Years Later*, Wildwood House, 1979, 44

'hairless as a new-born babe' (181) — ibid. 68
'*real art* – a little masterpiece' (181) — Mansfield 692
'We old men, Nicole, we have coffee' (182) — Pogson 86
'Thomas, go and burn some leaves' (182) — OLWG 113

'go to café and drink coffee' (182) — N1 28
'so much emphasis on physical work' (182) — OLWG 116
'a violent kick on the shins' (182) — Merston (Ch. X) 11
'we worked with our bare hands' (183) — OLWG 120
'went for him like a fishwife' (183) — NW 147
'You get black coffee' (183) — Merston (Ch. X) 11
'no bigger than half a crown' (183) — ibid. 5
'neither Russians nor English' (183) — V 284
'Mr Gurdjieff with a hammer' (184) — Mansfield 696
'House will either stand or collapse' (184) — OLWG 120

'Throw everyone into the work' (184) — ibid. 112
'*Fêter le Noel* in tremendous style' (184) — Ida Baker, *Katherine Mansfield: The Memories of LM*, Michael Joseph, 1971, 224

'absolutely secure in love' (185) — Mansfield 700
'last nail finally driven in' (185) — OLWG 121
'without quotation marks' (185) — B *passim*
'How grateful I could be for it' (185) — Olgivanna 12
'it is my body which is the shell' (186) — William Orton, *The Last Romantic*, Cassell, 1937, 274

'never eaten food so delicious' (186)   *N1* 56
'the little rugs of Beluchistan' (186)   Baker, op. cit., 226
'play the Essentuki Prayer' (186)   *OLWG* 121

Chapter 9

RIDING THE TIGER

'slobbering boy reporters' (188)   M 23
'an almost awesome quiet' (188)   M 153
'the Levantine psychic shark' (188)   Wyndham Lewis to Violet Schiff, 20
                                            September 1922, British Library.
'naked with Katherine Mansfield' (188)   Vivienne Eliot, letter to Ezra Pound, 2
                                            Nov. 1922
'a child withouten stain' (188)   John Middleton Murry, 'In Memory of
                                            Katherine Mansfield', *Adelphi* 1, Jan.
                                            1924, 664–5
'the spiritual quackery of Gurdjieff'   John Middleton Murry, letter to
(189)   Beatrice Campbell, 1955.
'a dark purple taffeta dress' (189)   Adèle Kafian, 'The Last Days of
                                            Katherine Mansfield', *Adelphi* XXIII
                                            1, Oct.–Dec. 1946, 37
'a fool called me a fool' (189)   V 267
'arenas of tranquillity of the heart'   J. Spencer Trimmingham, *The Sufi*
(189)   *Orders in Islam*, Clarendon Press,
                                            1971, 267
'in his arms a large lamb' (189)   Denis Saurat, *Nouvelle Revue française*
                                            XLI, 1 Nov. 1933
'long, virulent tongues of flames' (189)   ibid.
'all these people were mad' (190)   ibid.
'ferocity changed into strength' (190)   ibid.
'very motley company' (190)   F 385
'Rackmielevitch need not fast' (190)   W 118
'able to drive by inspiration' (190)   Young 38
'tearing of gear-wheel cogs' (190)   idem
'drove like a wild man' (191)   Hulme 66
'sit on the bumper' (191)   W 119
'Gurdjieff made Persian soup' (191)   Noel Stock, *The Life of Ezra Pound*,
                                            RKP, 1970, 253
'everything will be different' (192)   Pogson 83
'It was gruelling task' (192)   NW 146
'fitful dancing of glow worms' (192)   ibid. 147
'simply a *maison de fous*" (192)   Bechhofer-Roberts, 'The Forest
                                            Philosophers', *Century Magazine*,
                                            CVIII (1), New York, May 1924, 69
'a cabaret and a harem' (192)   Mark Schorer, *Sinclair Lewis: An*
                                            American Life, New York, 1961, 378

'the woman fidgetted' (193) — Merston (ch. X) 4

'feeling of supreme satisfaction' (193) — Young 40

'their stay has become useless' (193) — V 107

'my cerebral cavity' (193) — TS 30

'up the chimney forever' (193) — idem

'I looked at my watch' (193) — M 290

'tapping with his whip' (193) — idem

'tricks, half-tricks' (194) — 'Ce que L'Institut Gurdjieff a voulu nous présenter', L'Echo des Champs-Elysées, 1(37), Dec. 1923

'Professor Gurdjieff is celebrated' (194) — 'L'Institut Gurdjieff', Le Figaro, 13 Dec. 1923

'fountains filled with champagne' (194) — OLWG 123

'a moment of grief and grandeur' (195) — 'Théâtre des Champs-Elysées', Le Temps, 15 Dec. 1923

'Mr Gurdjieff scolded her strongly' (195) — OLWG 124

'How did everything go?' (196) — ibid. 123

'demonstration caused an uproar' (196) — Ian E. Black, A Friend of France, Jonathan Cape, 1941, 19

'a super-unique tragi-comic situation' (196) — M 293

'Please relieve me of this thing' (196) — idem

'almost jumped for joy' (196) — idem

'stories of Mullah Nassr Eddin' (197) — M 292

'the piano slowly slid' (197) — OLWG 126

'"dollar-foxtrotting" followers' (197) — B 1051

'Gurdjieff is coming!' (197) — Munson 208

'a clearing house for ideas' (198) — Webb 280

'my first American friend' (198) — Lincoln Kirstein, letter to James Moore, 19 Mar. 1981

'pealed gold-leaf salon' (198) — W. J. Welch 101

'not umpiring parlour games' (198) — Seabrook 169

'no "erotic" dances were shown' (198) — N1 8

'Remember yourself, you idiot!' (198) — Louise Welch 8

'a monk in a tuxedo' (198) — Webb 282

'the soldiers of Christophe' (199) — Seabrook 166

'the original frozen position' (199) — ibid. 166

'Dr Gurdjieff and his magical secret' (199) — Webb 268

'Dance as your souls dictate' (199) — idem

'The Forest Lovers' (199) — N1 19

'jobless, alcoholic and homosexual' (200) — Munson 214

'full-blown Lesbian case' (200) — Webb 279

'this man in motion' (201) — Webb 282

'sleepless for hours afterwards' (201) — Munson 208

'Pythagoras or a charlatan' (201)   ibid. 256
'a large baked potato' (201)   N1 22
'you are a booby' (201)   ibid. 21
'Arack, Doosico, Scotch whisky' (202)   B 923
'How can you judge?' (202)   OLWG 130
'this "dollar-growing country"' (202)   M 248
'only cooks were in demand' (203)   OLWG 128
'all must get to "Philadelphia"' (203)   V 191
'Coomaraswamy was fast asleep' (203)   Louise Welch 9
'"Mister Bellybutton"' (203)   B 935
'a "flea" on my neck' (203)   ibid. 936
'mad about breathing exercises' (203)   V 164
'His eyes rested on us' (204)   M 297
'beans mixed with thumbtacks' (204)   TS 90
'ableness to do it brilliantly' (204)   ibid. 92
'a very special time' (204)   Louise Welch 10
'a rotten, self-conscious place' (204)   Mabel Dodge Luhan, *Lorenzo in Taos*, Secker, 1933, 128
'a tip-top man' (204)   John Symonds, *The Great Beast*, Mayflower Books, 1973, 303
'acted like a small boy' (205)   A1 94
'are they not Asklay slaves?' (205)   B 675

Chapter 10

DEATH AND THE AUTHOR

'charge-and-crash"' (206)   B 1185
'bit of live meat in a clean bed' (206)   ibid. 1186
'If today is like yesterday' (207)   F 100
'I tell you, I'm terribly afraid' (207)   Webb 294f.
'Strange events, incomprehensible' (207)   V 3
'If God exists, Mr Gurdjieff lives' (207)   OLWG 135
'Many people, many people' (208)   N1 80
'Russians were on their knees' (208)   Louise Welch 41
'mainspring of machine had broken' (208)   N1 81f.
'my totally mutilated body' (208)   TS 31
'sucked me out like vampires' (208)   TS 45
'one cigarette after another' (209)   OLWG 138
'cut down half the forest' (209)   N1 82
'the Institute will be nothing' (209)   OLWG 139f.
'no one could recall the sequence' (209)   N1 82
'"Schachermacher-workshop-booths"' (210)   B 1188

'when in full strength and health' (210)   *TS* 4

'drove his car as if possessed' (210)   *P1* 128

'not an ordinary experience' (211)   idem

'on account of his smart appearance' (211)   *TS* 92

'write what I will dictate' (211)   *OLWG* 145

'become today a professional writer' (211)   *B* 9

'It was in the year 223' (212)   *B* 51

'fear-of-drowning-in-my-own-thoughts' (212)   *B* 4

'write furiously in his notebooks' (212)   *P1* 130

'"not-to-be-trifled-with-enthusiasm"' (212)   *H* 42

'the *bon ton* literary language' (213)   *B passim*

'two peacocks, a cat and a dog' (213)   *TS* 37

'Ici Repose La Mère de Celui' (213)   Landau 258

'respected dollar-holders!' (214)   *M* 249

'generations of Connecticut clergymen' (214)   Louise Welch 2

'"Prossy's complaint"' (214)   Holbrook Jackson, 'A. R. Orage: Personal Recollections', *Windmill* 3:1, 1948

'pampered out of all proportion' (214)   *TS* 95f.

'completely uncontrolled fury' (214)   *P1* 31

'fallen in love with a native' (215)   Louise Welch 49

'not even their "astral smell"' (215)   *TS* 61

'in regard to her constancy' (216)   Webb 340

'heart pounded like a baulking horse' (216)   *TS* 38

'the terrible disease flowed in her' (216)   *B* 913

'She is very old soul' (216)   *P1* 78

'gazing triumphantly off into space' (217)   ibid. 91

'Madame Ostrowsky is dead' (217)   ibid. 102

'The question of death' (218)   *TS* 154

'large number of muslin breech-cloths' (218)   *P1* 106

'well-mannered hard drinker' (218)   ibid. 107

'an unusual heaviness about him' (218)   ibid. 104

'the frontal region and the occiput' (218)   Walker 147

'silent and withdrawn' (218)   *P1* 107

'his unreliability and evil nature' (219)   ibid. 109

'a chocolate bar in torn box' (219)   ibid. 110

'the boy took no notice of Crowley' (220)   N1 122

'patient, tenacious, modest, ashamed' (220)   John Symonds, *The Great Beast*, Mayflower Books, 1973, 402

'sweet slightly nauseous smell' (220)   ibid. 412

'You filthy, you dirty inside!' (220)   Webb 315

'sorry I cannot give him a million' (220)   ibid. 360

'the size and power of his eyes' (221)   A2 28

'I decided I rather disliked him' (221)   ibid. 29

'Go back to hell, you devil' (221)   Webb 346

'What angry man say?' (221)   idem

'organism had gradually degenerated' (221)   TS 7

'three years more of life' (221)   TS 6

'to write for donkeys – very hard' (222)   Munson 270

'Bury the dog deeper' (222)   NW 274

'its splendour and full majesty' (222)   TS 5

'exhaustion from "black" thoughts' (222)   TS 2f.

'to destroy myself also' (222)   TS 34

'I wish . . . and will be!' (222)   TS 2

'the day of Saint-George-the-Victor' (223)   H 85

'you burn in boiling oil' (223)   Jessie Orage v.v.

'wise advice from my oldest friends' (223)   TS 43

'to remove from my eyesight' (224)   ibid. 45

'endure your lofty solitude' (224)   Webb 321

Chapter 11

SCATTERING ACORNS

'great agitation of minds in Russia' (225)   M 225

'model for a lyric saint' (226)   A1 13

'elaborate old-fangled euphoria' (226)   Janet Flanner, 'A Life on a Cloud: Margaret Anderson', *Janet Flanner's World: Uncollected Writings 1932–1975*, Secker & Warburg, 1980, 328

'conscious, developed human being' (227)   Solita Solano, q. *Little Review*, May 1929, 81

'dark chestnut hair and flashing eyes' (227)   W 115

'This man, of Greek extraction' (229)   Jean-Pierre Laurant, *Le Sens Caché selon René Guénon*, Lausanne, 1975

'*Il n'y a pas de René Guénon*' (229)   Webb 467

'a whole other book to write' (229)   *OLWG* 151

'super-most-super-heavenly-nectar'   B 1237
(229)

'You are not dead' (230)   Katherine Mansfield, *The Letters of Katherine Mansfield*, Constable, 1928, 134

'long ago Shubert theatrical disaster'   Wolfe 7
(231)

'New York needed a shaking up' (231)   Webb 364

'on the brink of leaving everything'   *OLWG* 153
(231)

'Thank God I'm free again!' (231)   Webb 365

'bring the *Little Review* to an end'   *Little Review*, May 1929, 5f.
(231)

'to work with Mr G.'s method' (232)   ibid. 66

'the edge of a nervous breakdown'   *OLWG* 153f.
(232)

'a coffin will be in this room' (233)   ibid. 154

'Mr Gurdjieff asked me to do   idem
something' (233)

'Not only did Jane capitulate' (234)   P1 173

'So you decide to go?' (234)   idem

'in life anything can happen' (234)   idem

'Shops were empty of customers' (234)   N2 24

'that awful quality of curiosity' (235)   *OLWG* 155

'you will never see me again' (235)   ibid. 156

'UNIQUE PHENOMENAL
GRANDMOTHER' (235)   Webb 366

'AMBASSADOR FROM HELL' (235)   idem

'They special from Persia' (236)   Louise Welch 82

'without a new initiation' (236)   ibid. 108

'press the most sensitive corn' (236)   TS 51

'First clean house, your house' (236)   N2 19

'Gurdjieff a great stumbling block'   ibid. 20
(236)

'his frame shaking with laughter' (236)   Webb 322

'the title of Father Sogol' (236)   René Daumal, *Mount Analogue: An Authentic Narrative*, Vincent Stuart, 1959, 32

'This monkey-cage agitation' (237)   ibid. 33

'restores my hope and purpose' (237)   Claude Mauriac, '*Daumal à la recherche de l'absolu*', *Le Figaro*, Paris, 2 Feb. 1970

'Green roses, Purple mimosas' (237)   M 26

'"candidate for the madhouse"' (238)   TS 70

'"yellow malaria of Kushka"' (238)   ibid. 65

'any relations with Mr Orage' (238)   ibid. 100

'you also Mr. Orage, will sign' (239)   ibid. 121
'began to sob with bitter tears' (239)   ibid. 124f.
'the nine-minute egg category' (239)   Seabrook 187
'But who here can read?' (239)   Wolfe 15
'Intelligentsia they are called' (239)   ibid. 18
'scattered and hostile group' (240)   N2 14
'I needed rats for my experiments'   ibid. 38
(240)
' "I the *unique* idiot" ' (240)   Thornton Wilder, *The Journals of Thornton Wilder*, ed. Donald Gallup, 143
'Yes, I smell him' (240)   ibid. 144
'I sing song to you' (240)   ibid. 146
'by showing him money' (240)   ibid. 147
'nice man to drink vodka with' (241)   N2 107
'an air of intolerable melancholy' (241)   Monk Gibbon, *The Masterpiece and the Man: Yeats as I Knew Him*, Rupert Hart-Davis, 1959, 91
'the loneliest man in the world' (241)   Hulme 70

Chapter 12

HOLY DENYING

'He had grown fat' (242)   Claude Bragdon, *The Secret Springs*, Andrew Dakers, 1939, 327
'every son-of-a-bitching thing' (242)   Webb 423
'I give you exercise' (242)   ibid. 327
'You will want to shoot yourself' (243)   ibid. 328
'We spoke in Tadjik' (243)   Landau 264
'I am a fairly wise man' (243)   idem
'grim, humourless devotion' (243)   P2 21
'transported by Joshua Gurdjieff!'   Louise Welch 117
(243)
'climbing trees like squirrels' (244)   Webb 415
' "free" meaning "licentious" ' (244)   P2 18
'the sepia taste of Trans-Siberia' (244)   Thomas Mona, '*Petits déjeuners en ville*', *Le Matin de Paris*, 11 Jan. 1980
'a broad-shouldered Buddha' (244)   Hulme 64
'Geep? Mees Geep?' (244)   ibid. 62
'we listen to *grenouilles*' (244)   ibid. 66
'trespass through a haunted house'   ibid. 69
(244)
'damaged by rats and mice' (244)   N2 69
'a shoddy ready-made brown suit'   ibid. 70
(245)
'*Impossible, pas possible!*' (245)   ibid. 71

'*last* Saturday, *last* Armagnac' (245)   McCorkle 59

'with lawsuits and bodily harm' (245)   ibid. 60

'Do quiet yourself' (246)   ibid. 58

'Can I do anything for you?' (246)   ibid. 65

'Now only money, money' (246)   idem

'I would not even cross the Channel' (246)   Webb 371

'the work of a man no longer sane' (247)   Landau 254

'finished and given to the printer' (247)   H 45

'Every person you see is shit' (247)   P2 24

'money, money and more money' (247)   Webb 420

'struck through my sexual centre' (248)   Landau 244

'a changed man, changed for the worse' (248)   Webb 421

'rapidly increased circulation' (248)   H 84

'His life was a blight' (248)   Webb 422

'extremely emaciated and ghastly pale' (248)   Beryl de Zoete, *The Thunder and the Freshness: The Collected Essays of Beryl de Zoete*, Neville Spearman, 1963, 22

'Achieved printed on 26th August' (249)   H 88

'almost set one's teeth on edge' (249)   Landau 253

'a strong "wish to fuck"' (250)   P2 34

'in loud stentorian tones' (250)   ibid. 35

'Was I a mere tool?' (250)   Webb 422

'his extraordinary faculties' (251)   ibid. 423

'descriptions of his digestive process' (251)   P2 40

'varieties of strong-smelling cheeses' (251)   idem

'we are going to special place' (252)   N2 80

'the oldest and toughest fowls' (252)   ibid. 152

'how to prepare sauerkraut' (252)   Edgar Tafel, *Apprentice to Genius: Years with Frank Lloyd Wright*, Dover Publications, New York, 1979, 139

'genuine prophets have been made' (252)   Frank Lloyd Wright, 'At Taliesin', *The Capital Times*, 26 Aug. 1934

'distinguished from all others' (253)   Frank Lloyd Wright, *Wisconsin State Journal*, 3 Nov. 1951, section 2, p. 3.

'yellow wildcat sparkle' (253)   Svetlana Allilueva, *The Faraway Music*, Lancer International, New Delhi, 1984, 57

'no hypnotist has succeeded' (254)   Landau 248

'I give you non-smoking cigarette' (254)   ibid. 246

'a distinct weakness in my body' (254)   ibid. 248

'thank the circumstances' (254)	*TS* 50
'like a "mettlesome horse"' (254)	ibid. 150
'a whirlpool of oppressive thoughts" (254)	ibid. 152
'I am sorry about Mr Orage's death' (254)	ibid. 154
'learned from the list of "sympathies"' (255)	ibid. 156
'their world famous "sympathy"' (255)	ibid. 155
'deep-rooted minutiae' (255)	ibid. 44
'Begin in Russia, finish in Russia' (255)	*NW* 108
'Death is in hurry to reach man' (255)	*TS* 166
'naive, stupid, but still real' (256)	*P2* 27
'enemies multiplying in great numbers' (256)	*TS* (revised edition) 174
'remove from my eyesight' (256)	ibid. 45
'He never knew what hit him' (257)	*Washington Post*, 7 May 1935
'the untimely death of my old friend' (257)	idem
'he must not teach anything' (257)	*NW* 182

Chapter 13

MODALITIES OF HEALING

'conquer the phantoms of sleep' (259)	Landau 232
'failed utterly to convince me' (259)	ibid. 263
'strange tastes must be destroyed' (259)	*F* 257
'a fanatic about homosexuality' (259)	Fritz Peters, *Balanced Man: A Look at Gurdjieff Fifty Years Later*, Wildwood House, 1978, 43
'burn up all the oxygen' (260)	Hulme 76
'Gurdjieff cried "Oie, oie!"' (260)	ibid. 78
'a featherweight of brittle bone' (260)	Solita Solano, 'The Hotel Napoleon Bonaparte', *Quarterly Journal of the Library of Congress* 34, Oct. 1977, 311
'a Buddha on a pedestal' (260)	Hulme 85
'three quick warning rings' (261)	ibid. 87
'Crocodile meat I do not like' (261)	ibid. 82
'habitueés of the incalculable' (261)	ibid. 98
'I eat with whole attention' (261)	ibid. 91
'flushes and small livid angers' (261)	ibid. 89
'freely moving "Guinea-Pigs"' (262)	*H* 22
'roped together for safety' (262)	Hulme 92
'a very *expensive* saint' (262)	ibid. 96

'a fairy-tale nurse' (262) — *A1* 14

'my struggle with death' (262) — *A2* 143f.

'I feel charged like a dynamo' (263) — ibid. 148

'my head fainting with fury' (263) — *A1* 119

'the *other* kind of food' (263) — Hulme 106

'a work at each moment' (263) — Vera Daumal, 'Notes: La littérature à propos de Gurdjieff et de René Daumal', *La Nouvelle Revue Française* II(22), 1 Oct. 1954, Paris 720f.

'Our Reverence, Miss Gordon' (264) — Hulme 123

'must have more *solid* place' (264) — ibid. 130

'"God helps me"' (264) — *A2* 149

'So this is the higher life!' (265) — *A1* 119

'Turk, Greek, Arab, Armenian' (265) — Hulme 114

'Ikons, underwear, toys and perfume' (265) — ibid. 123

'perenially flat pocket-book' (265) — ibid. 129

'Another *swallach* year' (266) — idem

'throw them in the sea' (266) — ibid. 138

'"Je suis mort!"' (266) — ibid. 144

'Your brother is our brother' (266) — ibid. 158

'walking about under parasols' (267) — *A1* 123

'life rises in me like the sea' (267) — *A2* 155

'A blessing was upon me' (267) — *A1* 124f

'*guardian* of the thesaurus' (268) — Solita Solano, letter to John C. Broderick, 20 Jul. 1966

'You give your excrement' (268) — Random 174

'horrors on an enormous scale' (268) — *N2* 123

'that good life. For dog' (269) — Wolfe 23

'triple-distilled alcohol' (269) — Hulme 169

'never can his "I" be drunk' (269) — ibid. 173

'she also must make effort' (269) — *N2* 123

'I have given you enough for years' (270) — *A1* 143

Chapter 14

C'EST LA GUERRE

'the predictions of Nostradamus' (271) — Giles Perrault, *Paris under the Occupation*, André Deutsch, 1989, 20.

'*Messieurs, je suis chez moi*' (272) — *A1* 136

'Now I have lost Gurdjieff' (272) — ibid. 171

'By what grocer's miracle?' (272) — Pierre Schaeffer, q. Pauwels 410

'establishment will re-open at three' (273) — Perrault, op. cit. 9

'I am over sixty' (274)	*A1* 162
'an odour would be diffused' (274)	M 15
'rented babies in their arms' (274)	Janet Flanner, *Janet Flanner's World: Uncollected Writings 1932–1975*, Secker & Warburg, 1980, 51
'on pain of death' (275)	Zuber 1
'purest white, colour of virtue' (275)	Perrault, op. cit. 15
'My family very big' (276)	P2 92f.
'5 kilos of sweets every day' (276)	Gurdjieff (Group exchange 1943)
'the worst collection in Paris' (276)	P2 108
'Many bombs have fallen' (277)	A1 174
'It does not refer to us' (277)	F 326
'We always make a profit' (277)	idem
'Il vient, je le sais' (278)	A1 180
' *"beaucoup de courage"* ' (278)	idem
' *"nous allons mourir sans mourir?"* ' (278)	idem
'line between resistance and treason' (278)	Paul Webster & Nicholas Powell, *Saint-Germain-des-Pres: French post-war culture from Sartre to Bardot*, Constable
'letter brings such good news' (278)	Hulme 216
'Death to the Jew!' (279)	*Au Pilori*, 14 Mary 1941, q. Perrault, op. cit. 174
'Remember the man who came' (279)	Pierre Matauschek & Jacques Revignes, 'René Daumal: Soldat du Je', Presse de la Manche, 5 Apr. 1974
'this mountain of orange peel' (279)	Random 221
'a shin-bone, a knee and two thighs' (280)	Pierre Schaeffer, q. Pauwels 405
'That, special Georgian dish' (281)	Zuber 26
'the role of *"Directeur"* ' (281)	Gurdjieff (Group exchange 1943)
'half-denuded roasted calf's-head' (281)	W. J. Welch 123
'like stabs of a knife' (281)	Pierre Schaeffer, q. Pauwels 443
'Have you anything to offer me?' (281)	ibid. 412
'astronaut ... state of weightlessness' (282)	Zuber 10
'All your life has been a preparation' (282)	Random 243
'They can never find anything' (283)	W 256
'Old boy, how many times?' (283)	idem
'a poor old man' (283)	ibid. 257
'Good place? Hein?' (283)	idem
'the old familiar out-of-order sign' (284)	Hulme 211
'You have lost too much' (284)	idem
'Not expect ... not expect' (284)	ibid. 212
'Vrai café!' (284)	idem

'I saw the wrath of God' (285)   ibid. 214
'The houri on the label' (285)   ibid. 216
'I stood up, rigid' (285)   P2 81
'a violent, electric blue light' (285) ibid. 82

Chapter 15

HOLY RECONCILING

'rich pantry of foods and thoughts'   Hulme 257
(288)
'the lawful infirmities of old age' (288) B 364
'leonine, alert, watching' (288)   W. J. Welch 134
'then is possible die' (288)   P2 112
'an insidious intoxication' (288)   Roland Merlin, '*Le drame de
                                        Katherine Mansfield*', *L'Illustration*
                                        16, 19 Jan 1946

'Gurdjieff has cast a spell on me' (289) Pauwels 355
'a kind of phlegmy rattle' (289)   Hulme 259
'*il est très fatigué*' (289)   ibid. 260
'*Petite Sœur de —* ' (289)   idem
'very, *very*, good relations' (289)   ibid. 258
'He is a multitude' (289)   Staveley 51
'I am your new father' (289)   ibid. 6
'I invite *you* to my next marriage'   ibid. 31
(290)
'from now three hours' (290)   I 70
'Oh, is scandal!' (290)   Staveley 12
'precisely like any clown' (290)   ibid. 13
'if a Higher Teacher came?' (291)   W 243
'You out of mouse make elephant'   Webb 462
(291)
'Get in touch with Mr. Gurdjieff' (292) Walker 134f.
'You are sheep without a shepherd'   Webb 461
(292)
'an old man, grey with weariness'   Dorothy Caruso, *A Personal History
(292)   by Dorothy Caruso*, Hermitage House,
                                        New York, 1952, 172
'Haven't I a soul?' (292)   ibid. 177
'You are your father' (292)   idem
'something rich and strange' (292)   ibid. 178
'some angel or even greater Being'   W 226
(293)
'what will you do?' (293)   ibid. 240
'He has never been mad' (293)   idem
'as dangerous as Everest' (294)   Pierre Schaeffer, q. Pauwels 409
'No, I not remember' (294)   W 246

'"You are in pain?"' (294)   idem
'"Where is your pain now?"' (294)   ibid. 247
'It was a dead man, a corpse' (295)   ibid. 249
'You like? Then take!' (295)   Caruso, op. cit. 180
'To the health of all Hopeless Idiots'   Oral
(295)
'Addition: by the way' (296)   Oral
'*Veut-il donc mourir?*' (296)   W 250
'It hurts: great suffering I have' (296)   Caruso, op. cit. 180
'how to live with pain' (296)   W 250
'Let all come' (296)   ibid. 251
'he looked younger than before' (296)   Caruso, op. cit. 181
'Strait is the gate' (296)   Matthew 7:15
'chapel faces of Plymouth Brethren'   Walker 154
(297)
'You must feel, you must feel' (297)   N2 239
'All must have enema each day' (298)   Staveley 57
'"*Le patron* is demanding attention"'   Walker 145
(298)
'the vibrant tones of a Jeremiah' (298)   W 253
'right in the mill – so God help us'   Tilley 41, 10 Sept. 1948
(298)
'Walker was rejuvenated' (298)   W 253
'You will not easily find me' (299)   Oral
'Every page has grammatical errors'   N2 242
(299)
'It is a rough diamond' (299)   idem
'We French are the stingiest people'   Pierre Schaeffer, q. Pauwels 429
(300)
'How you situated? You are English?'   Tilley 40, 10 Sept. 1948
(300)
'You first cousin to elephant' (300)   ibid. 43, 16 Sept. 1948
'a fervent young Frenchman' (300)   Robert S. de Ropp, *Warrior's Way*,
                                            George Allen & Unwin, 1980, 199
'a swelling sense of harmony' (301)   Caruso, op. cit. 182
'pure *comme bébé*' (301)   W 257

Chapter 16

AU REVOIR, TOUT LE MONDE

'I am Gurdjieff. I *not* will die!' (302)   I 107
'You move like worms in shit!' (302)   Robert de Ropp, *Warrior's Way*,
                                            George Allen & Unwin, 1980, 199
'playing no favourites' (302)   Popoff 123
'whirling with satanic fury' (303)   ibid. 125
'His abdominal girth was heroic' (303)   W. J. Welch 133

'Who have idea for night?' (303)	Wolfe 29
'I, seven-times doctor' (303)	W. J. Welch 127
'monastery where Jesus Christ' (304)	Ropp, op. cit., 198
'red carnation prostitute wears' (304)	W. J. Welch 126
'candidate for perishing like a dog' (304)	W 260
'he tell what I say' (305)	idem
'esteemed representative for England' (306)	W 260
'You now write letter' (306)	ibid. 261
'all my present and former adepts' (306)	idem
'reap the harvest which I have sown' (306)	ibid. 262
'Read, read – is for everybody' (306)	Hulme 280
'Only Mr. Gurdjieff could have written' (306)	W 262
'many sons away in monasteries' (307)	Popoff 152
'when my smell became intolerable' (308)	Tilley 56
'a fantastic cake in violent colours' (308)	ibid. 61
'I would like to go to Chamonix' (308)	Dorothy Caruso, *A Personal History by Dorothy Caruso*, Hermitage House, New York, 1952, 184
'This man is going to die' (308)	Pierre Schaefer, q. Pauwels 425
'All the musicians were masturbators' (309)	I 3
'Tibet, Monsieur? Or Dieppe?' (309)	ibid. 17
'Either way very expensive' (309)	idem
'All this very valuable thing is' (309)	ibid.
'I only a poor old dancing teacher' (310)	ibid. 25
'a monster of *modesty*' (310)	Zuber 16
'Many men on earth more than me' (310)	Wolfe 25
'I can write cheque with 7 "*zéros*"' (310)	I 35
'Perhaps Pope Rome heard' (310)	W 271
'think about the Last Supper' (311)	Pierre Schaeffer, q. Pauwels 443
'*All* English must become followers' (311)	I 30
'Because of Judas' (311)	ibid. 46
'Tell him that such place exist' (312)	W 272
'"I must take habit of pain"' (312)	Caruso, op. cit. 187
'rather good teacher of temple dances' (313)	B 9
'You are nothing but hieroglyphs' (313)	Pierre Schaeffer, q. Pauwels 436

'black rings sunken under his eyes'   *I* 93
(313)
'most terrifying car drive of my life'   W 278
(314)
'No nurses over 20!' (314)   Tilley 73
'we were all holding a fort' (314)   *I* 96
'The mark of death was on his face'   W. J. Welch 139
(314)
'hoisting himself along by naked will'   ibid. 138
(315)
' "Au revoir, tout le monde" ' (315)   *I* 100
'Only if you not tired Doctor' (315)   W. J. Welch 139
'essential thing to prepare a nucleus'   V Foreword viii
(315)
'a mass of flames above the coffin'   Zuber 41
(317)
'must find way to *Soleil Absolu*' (317)   W 272
'They will turn you into a scarecrow'   Pierre Schaeffer, q. Pauwels 448
(318)
'Mr. Gurdjieff cannot be replaced'   W 282
(318)

Select Bibliography

This compact bibliography relates particularly to *Gurdjieff: The Anatomy of a Myth*. Excluded in principle is a complementary œuvre of books expounding Gurdjieff's teaching but without biographic relevance. All books cited are first editions and, unless otherwise indicated, British hardbacks. Academics seeking a comprehensive source are referred to *Gurdjieff: An Annotated Bibliography* by J. Walter Driscoll and the Gurdjieff Foundation of California, ISBN 0-8240-8972-3, published in New York by Garland Publishing, 1985. This work contains 1743 entries; a second and substantially augmented edition is in preparation.

GURDJIEFF, GEORGE IVANOVITCH

Gurdjieff's material is listed below in the order that he produced it (which the sequence of publication does not reflect).
The Struggle of the Magicians, The Stourton Press, Capetown, 1957.
Views from the Real World, Routledge & Kegan Paul, 1973.
Beelzebub's Tales to His Grandson, Routledge & Kegan Paul, 1950.
Meetings with Remarkable Men, Routledge & Kegan Paul, 1963.
Life is Real Only Then, When 'I Am', Triangle Editions, New York, 1975.
Herald of Coming Good, La Société Anonyme des Editions de L'Ouest, Angers (France), 1933.

Note: Gurdjieff himself repudiated *Herald of Coming Good* and withdrew it from circulation. By contrast P. D. Ouspensky's important work *In Search of the Miraculous: Fragments of an Unknown Teaching* (cited overleaf), substantially comprises Gurdjieff's direct speech, the accuracy of which he gratefully confirmed.

LETTERS AND DIARIES

Bennett, John G. & Elizabeth *Idiots in Paris: Diaries of J. G. Bennett and Elizabeth Bennett, 1949*, Coombe Springs Press, 1980.
Mansfield, Katherine *Katherine Mansfield's Letters to John Middleton Murry 1913–1922*, ed. John Middleton Murry, Constable, 1951.
Tilley, Basil *Letters from Paris and England 1947–1949*, privately printed at the Phene Press, 1981.

MEMOIRS

Anderson, Margaret *The Fiery Fountains*, Rider & Co., 1953.

Bechhofer-Roberts, C. E. *In Denikin's Russia and the Caucasus, 1919–1920: Being the Record of a Journey to South Russia, the Crimea, Armenia, Georgia and Baku in 1919 and 1920*, Collins, 1921.

Bennett, J. G. *Witness*, Hodder & Stoughton, 1962.

Butkovsky-Hewitt, Anna *With Gurdjieff in St. Petersburg and Paris*, Routledge & Kegan Paul, 1978.

Dukes, Sir Paul *The Unending Quest*, Cassell, 1950.

de Hartmann, Thomas *Our Life with Mr. Gurdjieff*, Cooper Square Publishers, New York, 1964.

Hulme, Kathryn *Undiscovered Country*, Little, Brown & Co., Boston, 1966.

Kenney, Rowland *Westering*, Dent, 1939.

Landau, Rom *God is My Adventure*, Ivor Nicholson & Watson, 1935.

Leblanc, Georgette *La Machine à Courage: Souvenirs*, Janin, Paris, 1947.

McCorkle, Beth *The Gurdjieff Years 1929–1949: Recollections of Louise March*, The Work Study Association, New York, 1990 (paperback).

Merston, Ethel *Memoirs* (unpublished).

Nott, C. S. *Teachings of Gurdjieff: The Journal of a Pupil. An Account of Some Years with G. I. Gurdjieff and A. R. Orage in New York and at Fontainebleau-Avon*, Routledge & Kegan Paul, 1961.
Journey Through This World: The Second Journal of a Pupil. Including an Account of Meetings with G. I. Gurdjieff, A. R. Orage and P. D. Ouspensky, Routledge & Kegan Paul, 1969.

Olgivanna (Mrs Frank Lloyd Wright) 'The Last Days of Katherine Mansfield', *The Bookman* LXXIII(1) March 1931, New York, pp. 6–13.

Ouspensky, P. D. *In Search of the Miraculous: Fragments of an Unknown Teaching*, Routledge & Kegan Paul, 1950.

Peters, Fritz *Boyhood with Gurdjieff*, Gollancz, 1964.
Gurdjieff Remembered, Gollancz, 1965.

Pogson, Beryl *Maurice Nicoll: A Portrait*, Vincent Stuart, 1961.

Popoff, Irmis B. *Gurdjieff: His Work on Myself . . . with Others . . for the Work*, Vantage, New York, 1969.

Saurat, Denis 'A Visit to Gourdyev', *Living Age* CCCXLV(4408), January 1934, pp. 427–33.

Seabrook, William *Witchcraft: Its Power in the World Today*, Harrap, 1940.

Staveley, A. L. *Memories of Gurdjieff*, Two Rivers Press, Aurora (Oregon), 1978.

Walker, Kenneth *Venture with Ideas*, Jonathan Cape, 1951.

Welch, William J. *What Happened in Between: A Doctor's Story*, George Braziller, New York, 1972.

Wolfe, Edwin *Episodes with Gurdjieff*, Far West Press, San Francisco, 1974 (paperback).

Young, James Carruthers 'An Experiment at Fontainebleau: A Personal Reminiscence', *New Adelphi* I(1), Sept. 1927, pp. 26–40.

Zuber, René *Who are You, Monsieur Gurdjieff?*, Routledge & Kegan Paul, 1980 (paperback).

Note:

a. A definitive and substantially enlarged edition of *Our Life with Mr Gurdjieff* by Thomas and Olga de Hartmann, edited by Thomas C. Daly and T. A. G. Daly, is forthcoming from Penguin Books Ltd in 1992.

b. The Rochester Folk Art Guild and the March family have represented that they are unassociated with *The Gurdjieff Years 1929–1949: Recollections of Louise March*, edited by Beth McCorkle.

COMPENDIA OF MEMOIRS

Anderson, Margaret *The Unknowable Gurdjieff*, Routledge & Kegan Paul, 1962.
Pauwels, Louis *Gurdjieff*, Times Press, Douglas (Isle of Man), 1964 (paperback).

HISTORICAL AND LITERARY STUDIES

Bennett, J. G. *Gurdjieff: Making a New World*, Turnstone Books, 1973.
Kerman, Cynthia Earl & Eldridge, Richard *The Lives of Jean Toomer: A Hunger for Wholeness*, Louisiana State Univ. Press, USA, 1987.
Moore, James *Gurdjieff and Mansfield*, Routledge & Kegan Paul, 1980.
Munson, Gorham *The Awakening Twenties: A Memoir History of a Literary Period*, Louisiana State Univ. Press, USA, 1985.
Random, Michel *Les puissances du dedans: Luc Dietrich, Lanza del Vasto, René Daumal, Gurdjieff*, Denöel, Paris, 1966.
Webb, James *The Harmonious Circle: The Lives and Work of G. I. Gurdjieff, P. D. Ouspensky, and Their Followers*, Thames & Hudson, 1980.
Welch, Louise *Orage with Gurdjieff in America*, Routledge & Kegan Paul, London & Boston, 1982, (paperback).

PRIMARY PAPERS

Important Gurdjieffian primary papers and photographs are increasingly gravitating to bibliographic collections under the supervision of Michel de Salzmann in Paris and of the Gurdjieff Foundation of California. A significant secondary element remains in private family holdings. Certain special collections in the public domain in the USA, although in general not Gurdjieffian *per se*, include relevant material relating to specific pupils. Some of these are itemised below:

Archive of the Library of Congress, Washington, DC: Margaret Anderson, Jane Heap and Solita Solano. Fisk University Library, Nashville, Tennessee: Jean Toomer. Maryland University, McKelvin Library (Porter Room): Djuna Barnes and Jane Heap. Princeton University Library: Zona Gale. Wesleyan University, Olin Library: Gorham Munson. Wisconsin State Historical Society: Zona Gale. Wisconsin University, Milwaukee, Golda Meir Library: Margaret Anderson. Yale University, Beinecke Rare Book and Manuscript Library, New Haven, Conn.: Muriel Draper, Kathryn Hulme, Mabel Dodge Luhan, Piotr Demianovich Ouspensky and Jean Toomer. Yale University, Music Library, New Haven, Conn.: Thomas de Hartmann.

Index

--- ❖ ---